The Ultimate Pirate Collection: Blackbeard, Francis Drake, Captain Kidd, Captain Morgan, Grace O'Malley, Black Bart, Calico Jack, Anne Bonny, Mary Read, Henry Every and Howell Davis

By Charles River Editors

Early 18th century depiction of Blackbeard

About Charles River Editors

Charles River Editors was founded by Harvard and MIT alumni to provide superior editing and original writing services, with the expertise to create digital content for publishers across a vast range of subject matter. In addition to providing original digital content for third party publishers, Charles River Editors republishes civilization's greatest literary works, bringing them to a new generation via ebooks.

Introduction

Grace O'Malley (circa 1530- circa 1603)

"When analyzed within the historical context of the traumatic epoch in which she lived, she emerges as a fearless leader, by land and by sea, a political pragmatist and tactician, a ruthless plunderer, a mercenary, a rebel, a shrewd and able negotiator, the protective matriarch of her family and tribe, a genuine inheritor of the Mother Goddess and Warrior Queen attributes of her remote ancestors. Above all else, she emerges as a woman who broke the mould and thereby played a unique role in history. It is thirty years since my biography first helped write Granuaile back into history—she had more than created her own legend." - Anne Chambers, *Granuaile: Grace O'Malley - Ireland's Pirate Queen*

In the 400 years since her death, Grace O'Malley has represented many things to many people, including queen, legend, pirate, and folk hero. Her nickname, Granuaile, was given to her by the Irish peasants whose cause she supported, and that name had its origins in the fact that she chopped off her hair when she took to the sea as a young girl. Though she spent plenty of time on land with a family and estates, her life and legacy have been defined by the time she spent sailing.

Like many figures of the Elizabethan Era, it's often hard to separate fact from fiction when discussing the life and career of Granuaile, whose native Ireland was undergoing a dramatic transformation as England's Tudor rulers began trying to seize control of it. Granuaile became a powerful ruler in her own right, which led to conflict with England, during which she proved a more than able opponent. She is best remembered for her piracy against the English, but that eventually led to negotiations between the famous folk hero and Queen Elizabeth I, and by the end of the Nine Years War, she was leading raids against England's enemies.

Given her background, heritage, and life, Granuaile was a natural candidate to become an Irish folk hero, a powerful symbol of courage, defiance, and independence. *The Ultimate Pirate Collection* looks at the life and legends of the famous female pirate, attempting to separate fact from fiction while analyzing her lasting legacy. Along with pictures depicting Granuaile and important people, places, and events in her life, you will learn about the famous pirate like you never have before.

Sir Francis Drake (1540-1596)

"There must be a beginning of any great matter, but the continuing unto the end until it be thoroughly finished yields the true glory." – Sir Francis Drake

The life of Sir Francis Drake, or, more precisely, the tale of it, is one of those prime examples that history is written by the winners. Drake was the most famous sailor of the Elizabethan Era, and he has long been considered a hero by the English. His successes against the Spanish as a captain and a privateer were legendary, and Drake was celebrated for fighting the Queen's enemies, sinking their ships, and capturing the treasure that would otherwise be used to finance attacks on England. Drake vigorously pursued every mission given to him by Elizabeth I, and brought all his skill, experience and training to bear against her enemies. He was recognized at court for his valor, praised in story and song, and remembered for the kind of personality and esprit de corps that the English have long desired and celebrated in their military heroes.

While that might have summarized Sir Francis Drake's life from an English perspective, that's not at all how the Spanish remember "El Draque" ("The Dragon"), the 16th century's most notorious pirate. Referred to as "the main cause of wars" in one 1592 letter to the Spanish King Phillip II, Drake harassed Spanish ships in several oceans and was so despised by the Spanish that Phillip II placed the equivalent of a 7 million dollar bounty on his head. This should come as no surprise, given that Spanish accounts tell of a captain who attacked and boarded Spanish merchant ships to steal their treasure and made off with it in the kind of haughty and dramatic ways that have become standard fare in pirate lore. El Draque also had no qualms about killing those who refused his requests. At the same time, Spain was hardly above using privateers and piracy themselves, as one English writer would later put it, "The Spaniards had carried barbarism to such a pitch in seizing our ships and condemning their crews to the galleys, that Queen Elizabeth was never averse to meeting murder and plunder by more than the equivalent in retaliation."

Which version of Drake's life is more accurate? As usual, the reality falls somewhere inbetween. For most of his career, Drake was unquestionably a privateer and not a member of any organized Navy, thus answering to nobody except the Queen, and had he failed, he might have been shackled in irons and imprisoned. It was due to the fact he was successful that he was instead given a seat of honor at Elizabeth's own table in her own court. While privateers were used by all European powers during times of war, Drake also happened to target enemy ships when no state of war existed, thus clearly veering into the realm of piracy. Naturally, Elizabeth's enemies claimed that he was engaging in piracy with her blessing, which was probably true at times and untrue at others.

While contemporary accounts reveal two very different sides of the same man, Drake's legacy has since been shrouded in legend, with tales concerning buried treasure, encounters with Native Americans, and his famous circumnavigation of the globe. *The Ultimate Pirate Collection* looks at the life, career, legends, and controversies of the Elizabethan Era's most famous captain. Along with pictures of important people, places, and events in his life, you will learn about Sir Francis Drake like you never have before.

Henry Morgan (circa 1635-1688)

Although Captain Morgan has become somewhat synonymous with spiced rum in the 21st century, Henry Morgan has been one of the best known pirates and privateers for centuries, long before an alcohol was named after him. The swashbuckling captain, who fought nearly as hard as he drank, has long been a favorite among authors looking to write exciting novels about pirates, beginning with *Captain Blood*, written by Rafael Savtinin during the late 1800s. John Steinbeck wrote about him in *Cup of Gold* in 1929, and Berton Braley composed a poem about him, aptly titled This is the ballad of Henry Morgan, a few years later. James Michner devoted a chapter to Morgan in his 1989 hit Caribbean, and he inspired Michael Crichton's character in Pirate Latitudes, Charles Hunter.

Of course, few young people reach adulthood without drinking too much Captain Morgan spiced rum at least once in their lives, and most people are instantly familiar with a "Captain and Coke", but Morgan's name is all over the Western hemisphere too. Those who have partied and vacationed in the Caribbean Islands are also familiar with Morgan, and many have stayed at the Hotel Henry Morgan in Honduras or at the Port Morgan resort in Haiti. Some of the wealthiest may have stayed at Captain Morgan's Retreat and Vacation Club in Belize. Even gamers have met Morgan in Sid Meier's Pirates and the Age of Pirates 2.

In addition to being one of the most famous pirates, there is more of a historical record about Morgan than most, in no small part due to the fact that Morgan had certain advantages many subsequent pirates did not enjoy. Morgan was a Welshman born into aristocracy, subsequently served in the Royal Navy, and viewed piracy as more of a way to serve his country than it was to line his own pockets (though he did plenty of that too.) As a result, Morgan acted with the approval and support of the Crown, which was only too happy to have Morgan and others sail to the Americas and steal from archenemies like Spain. Morgan would go on to have a daring and lucrative career, engaging in adventurous attacks that were legendary in their own time for their success.

The Ultimate Pirate Collection looks at the life and legacy of the famous pirate, attempting to separate fact from fiction. Along with pictures depicting Captain Morgan and important people, places, and events in his life, you will learn about the captain like you never have before.

Captain William Kidd (circa 1645-1701)

"My name is Captain Kidd, who has sailed, who has sailed,

My name is Captain Kidd, who has sailed.

My name is Captain Kidd;

What the laws did still forbid

Unluckily I did while I sailed, while I sailed." - A verse from *Captain Kidd's Farewell to the Seas*

There are a number of famous pirates in history, but one of them may not have been a pirate at all. Captain William Kidd has been remembered for over 300 years as a pirate and his name is synonymous with piracy today, but he was far from the most bloodthirsty or most prosperous because he insisted he wasn't one at all. In fact, Kidd's entire reputation is based on the most notorious trial in the history of piracy.

Like many pirates, Kidd got his start by being an English privateer assigned to fight the French, and later he was ironically asked to attack pirates around the English colonies of New Hampshire and New York. Kidd established some connections with powerful people in the New World, affording him the luxury of a large ship with which to capture pirates, but he would become notorious and controversial for killing one of his own crew members in 1697. When Kidd found himself at odds with the Royal Navy over the impressments of his crew, charges of piracy were lobbed at him, and by 1698 he was a wanted man.

Aware of what would happen if he was caught, Kidd was tricked into coming to Boston by an investor in his expedition who betrayed him and had him arrested. In addition to being personally questioned by Parliament, Kidd's trial became a political football between the Whigs and Tories, and ultimately it produced a controversial conviction and execution of the notorious captain in 1701. Historians and scholars have been debating whether Kidd was a pirate or murderer ever since.

The Ultimate Pirate Collection looks at the controversial life and career of the infamous captain, attempting to separate fact from fiction while analyzing his lasting legacy. Along with pictures depicting important people, places, and events in his life, you will learn about Kidd like you never have before.

18th century woodcut of an enslaved man and Henry Every

Henry Every (1659-??)

"NONE of these bold Adventurers were ever so much talked of, for a while, as Avery; he made as great a Noise in the World as Meriveis does now, and was looked upon to be a Person of as great Consequence." - Captain Charles Johnson, *A General History of the Robberies and Murders of the most notorious Pyrates*

The Golden Age of Piracy generally refers to the era when history's most famous pirates roamed the seas of the West Indies from 1670-1720, engaging in colorfully daring and oftentimes murderous attacks on any ship they felt emboldened enough to take on. And it is no coincidence that while the end of the Golden Age was marked by the death of Blackbeard, the beginning of it was marked by the rise of Henry Every.

Though Every is no longer as well-remembered as the likes of Blackbeard or Black Bart, in his day he was the "King of Pirates", and he is recognized as blazing the trail and setting the gold standard for the pirates that followed him. In addition to popularizing the famous skull and crossbones logo that would become the most famous pirate flag, Every conducted what is considered the most profitable pirate raid in history, leading to what is considered the first worldwide manhunt in history when the English put a large bounty on his head.

As amazing as Every's pirate career was, the most incredible part about it was that he survived it. In fact, Every's one of the few famous pirates to ever actually retire, or at least so it's believed. A year after conducting the raid that netted him over half a million pounds, Every dropped off the historical record, and while speculation swirls as to what actually became of him, what is known is that he never met his fate at the hands of English authorities or any of the other sworn enemies he had made during his piracy.

The Ultimate Pirate Collection looks at the life and legends of the famous pirate, attempting to separate fact from fiction while analyzing his lasting legacy. Along with pictures depicting Every and important people, places, and events in his life, you will learn about the famous pirate like you never have before.

1736 engraving depicting Blackbeard

Blackbeard (circa 1680-1718)

"So our Heroe, Captain Teach, assumed the Cognomen of Black-beard, from that large Quantity of Hair, which, like a frightful Meteor, covered his whole Face, and frightened America more than any Comet that has appeared there a long Time. This Beard was black, which he suffered to grow of an extravagant Length; as to Breadth, it came up to his Eyes; he was accustomed to twist it with Ribbons, in small Tails, after the Manner of our Ramilies Wiggs, and turn them about his Ears." - Charles Johnson, *A General History of the Robberies and Murders of the most notorious Pyrates*

It would be an understatement to say that pop culture's perception of piracy and pirates has been primarily influenced by Captain Edward Teach, known to the world as Blackbeard, the most famous pirate of all time. An English pirate who terrorized the high seas near the Carolinas in the early 18th century, a period often referred to as the Golden Age of Piracy, Blackbeard was the gold standard, and in the 300 years since his death he has inspired legends that have spanned books like *Treasure Island*, movies, and even theme park rides.

Of course, like any legendary figure, Blackbeard is remembered today based more on myths than reality. People continue to let their imaginations go when it comes to Blackbeard, picturing a pirate who captured more booty than any other pirate, hid buried treasure, and lit his hair on fire before battle. People have long claimed that his ghost still haunts the Atlantic Ocean, and his contemporaries were so scared of him that they claimed to have seen his headless body swim around his pirate boat three times.

The myths and legends surrounding Blackbeard tend to obscure the life he really lived, but his piracy was also notorious enough to capture headlines during his time. The British Crown put a higher price on his head than any other pirate of the era, and when an author writing under the pseudonym Charles Johnson wrote about Blackbeard in *A General History of the Robberies and Murders of the most notorious Pyrates*, a legend was born.

The Ultimate Pirate Collection looks at the mysterious life and death of Blackbeard, separating fact from fiction while analyzing his lasting legacy. Along with pictures depicting Blackbeard and important people, places, and events in his life, you will learn about the famous pirate like you never have before.

18th century depiction of Black Bart

Black Bart Roberts (1682-1722)

"Roberts was a tall black Man, near forty Years of Age…of good natural Parts, and personal Bravery, tho' he applied them to such wicked Purposes, as made them of no Commendation, frequently drinking *Damn to him who ever lived to wear a Halter*…Roberts himself made a gallant Figure, at the Time of the Engagement, being dressed in a rich crimson Damask Wastcoat and Breeches, a red Feather in his Hat, a Gold Chain round his Neck, with a Diamond Cross hanging to it, a Sword in his Hand, and two Pair of Pistols hanging at the End of a Silk Sling, flung over his Shoulders (according to the Fashion of the Pyrates;)…" - Captain Charles Johnson, *A General History of the Robberies and Murders of the most notorious Pyrates*

The Golden Age of Piracy generally refers to the era when history's most famous pirates roamed the seas of the West Indies from 1670-1720, engaging in colorfully daring and oftentimes murderous attacks on any ship they felt emboldened enough to take on. And it is no coincidence that the end of the Golden Age was marked by the deaths of Blackbeard and Bartholomew Roberts, best known as Black Bart.

Black Bart may not be as well known today as other pirates of the era, but he was truly the gold standard during the Golden Age of Piracy. Despite the fact he was initially reluctant to become a pirate and had to be talked into it, Roberts and his crew captured nearly 500 ships in just a few years, making him the most successful pirate in history. As tales of his exploits made their way around Europe and the Americas, Black Bart became a legend in his own time, with Captain Charles Johnson noting at the beginning of his famous pirate history, "It will be observed, that the Account of the Actions of Roberts runs into a greater Length, than that of any other Pyrate, for which we can assign two Reasons, first, because he ravaged the Seas longer than the rest, and of Consequence there must be a greater Scene of Business in his Life: Secondly, being resolved not to weary the Reader, with tiresome Repetitions: When we found the Circumstances in Roberts's Live, and other Pyrates, either as to pyratical Articles, or any Thing else, to be the same, we thought it best to give them but once, and chose Roberts's Life for that Purpose, he having made more Noise in the World, than some others.

Although he was the most successful pirate of his time, he suffered a fate typical of the era's legendary pirates. In a battle with a Royal Navy ship in February 1722, Black Bart was killed by artillery on deck and his ships were captured, but not before his crew had tossed his body overboard, never to be seen again. Black Bart's death in battle was so important that pirate historian Marcus Rediker would later write, "The defeat of Roberts and the subsequent eradication of piracy off the coast of Africa represented a turning point in the slave trade and even in the larger history of capitalism."

While Black Bart's success and infamous demise were both important parts of his story, the main reason he has endured is that he gave rise to some of the best known pirate stereotypes. In addition to making his crew swear to and uphold a pirate code, Roberts was known as a colorfully courageous commander who looked the part with extravagant costumes. It is thus no surprise that Roberts has been depicted as one of the foremost pirates of the age in literature and film, including in Robert Louis Stevenson's *Treasure Island*.

The Ultimate Pirate Collection looks at the life and legends of the famous pirate, attempting to separate fact from fiction while analyzing his lasting legacy. Along with pictures depicting Roberts and important people, places, and events in his life, you will learn about the famous pirate like you never have before.

Howell Davis (circa 1690-1719)

"[Davis] (allowing for the Course of Life he had been unhappily engaged in) was a most generous humane Person." – Captain William Snelgrave

Despite having one of the shortest careers of history's most famous pirates, Captain Howell Davis had one of the most colorful and important years during the Golden Age of Piracy. Though little is known about his life before July 1718, when he joined a pirate crew after they captured the slaver ship he was working on, it's a testament to his abilities that he became the captain of one of the pirates' ships very quickly after they had commandeered his ship. It also didn't take him long to earn a reputation for being devious and cunning, and more than once he was able to lie and bluff his way to taking a ship that probably could have defended itself against him.

It was during one of his most daring escapades that one of his ruses was undone on the island of Principe, a Portuguese holding at the time. Though Davis didn't know it, one of his deceptions was unmasked, and the island's governor put his own plot in motion, setting Davis up for an ambush that left him and some of his men dead. But even in death, Davis remained influential; he had taken a pirate named Bartholomew Roberts under his wing, and Black Bart would succeed Davis as captain upon his death.

Black Bart and Howell Davis looks at the life and legacy of the famous pirate, attempting to separate fact from fiction. Along with pictures depicting Captain Davis and important people, places, and events in his life, you will learn about the pirate like you never have before.

Calico Jack Rackham (1682-1720)

"The Day that Rackam was executed, by special Favour, he was admitted to see [Anne Bonny]; but all the Comfort she gave him, was, that she was sorry to see him there, but if he had fought like a Man, he need not have been hang'd like a Dog." - Captain Charles Johnson, *A General History of the Robberies and Murders of the most notorious Pyrates*

One of the most famous pirates of all time is Calico Jack, and though he would accomplish many things in his career that would earn him notoriety among the pirates of his age, the simple truth is that he is remembered mostly for his association with Anne Bonny and Mary Read, two of history's most famous women pirates. In fact, had it not been for his involvement with them, his name might have disappeared from the history books entirely. And fittingly, even his nickname, "Calico," came from the type of fabric he preferred for his shirts, the same fabric typically used for women's everyday clothing. Rackham preferred attractive print fabrics produced for trade with natives in the New World, a flamboyant taste worthy of the common pirate stereotype.

Before Rackham had even met Anne Bonny, who would become his lover, he had managed to make a name for himself as part of Charles Vane's pirate crew, and it was after a mutiny that he became the captain of a pirate ship. This would allow Calico Jack to make yet another contribution to pirate history and legend: the "Jolly Roger" pirate flag. Flying the simple yet frightening flag that featured a white skull and crossed swords against a black banner, Calico Jack ensured his targets knew they were in trouble as soon as they could spot the flag. To this day, the flag remains synonymous with piracy.

Still, it seems Calico Jack will never escape the shadow of his famous female shipmates, despite the fact he was their captain. For his part, Jack never seems to have minded the women who stood beside and behind him through most of his short career, and if anything it seems he enjoyed having the fairer sex aboard, in more ways than one. Their most adventurous and notorious year, 1720, would also be Rackham's last, after they were eventually caught by authorities and tried. In one of the Golden Age of Piracy's most famous anecdotes, one of Calico Jack's last wishes was to see Anne Bonny one more time, and she "consoled" him by telling him that if he fought like a man he wouldn't have been hanged like a dog.

The Ultimate Pirate Collection looks at the mysterious life and legends of the famous pirate, attempting to separate fact from fiction while analyzing his lasting legacy. Along with pictures depicting Calico Jack and important people, places, and events in his life, you will learn about the pirate captain like you never have before.

18th century depiction of Anne Bonny and Mary Read

Anne Bonny (1702-??) and Mary Read (??-1721)

"NOW we are to begin a History full of surprizing Turns and Adventures; I mean, that of Mary Read and Anne Bonny, alias Bonn, which were the true Names of these two Pyrates; the odd Incidents of their rambling Lives are such, that some may be tempted to think the whole Story no better than a Novel or Romance; but since it is supported by many thousand Witnesses, I mean the People of Jamaica, who were present at their Tryals, and heard the Story of their Lives, upon the first discovery of their Sex; the Truth of it can be no more contested, than that there were such Men in the World, as Roberts and Black-beard..." - Captain Charles Johnson, *A General History of the Robberies and Murders of the most notorious Pyrates*

One of the most famous pirates of all time, and possibly the most famous woman to ever become one, was Anne Bonny. The Irish-born girl moved with her family to the Bahamas at a young age in the early 18th century, which at that time was a hotbed for piracy by the likes of Blackbeard, but the redhead with a fiery temper would go on to forge her own reputation. After marrying a poor sailor who accepted clemency to give up piracy, Anne began a legendary affair with Calico Jack Rackam and became pregnant with his child, but that did not stop them from plundering the high seas aboard his pirate ship *Revenge*, at least until they were captured by British authorities. Anne avoided execution by "pleading her belly", getting a temporary stay of execution due to her pregnancy.

It is at that point that Anne Bonny drops off the historical record and becomes the stuff of legends. It's unclear whether she was eventually executed or pardoned or even ransomed, and it's unclear what became of her child. Her relationship with Mary Read aboard the Revenge is also the stuff of legends, and people have been filling in the gaps ever since.

Among all the pirates of the "Golden Age of Piracy", none were as unique as Mary Read, who was one of just two known women to be tried as a pirate during the Golden Age, alongside her own crewmate (and possible lover) Anne Bonny. Like Anne, Mary Read was an illegitimate child who spent some of her childhood dressed up as and disguised as a little boy through incredibly strange circumstances. But unlike her future shipmate, Mary ultimately took a liking to it, and she continued to disguise her gender to take on roles reserved for men, including in the British army. During that time, she fell in love with a Flemish soldier and eventually married him.

Mary Read might have been content to live out her life with her husband in Holland, but after his death, she headed for the West Indies, only to have her ship commandeered by pirates. But Read, who had worked on a ship before, was only too happy to join the pirate crew and play the role of privateer. And in 1720, that crew was captured by Calico Jack, who already had his lover Anne Bonny as part of his crew and now unwittingly added a second female when Mary opted to join.

Together the three played a legendary role as shipmates and possible lovers while continuing their piracy around the Bahamas, only to eventually be captured by authorities in October 1720. Most of the crew was executed, but Mary was able to successfully "plead the belly" and thereby receiving a stay of execution. This spared her the noose, but Mary would die of illness while still imprisoned in 1721.

The Ultimate Pirate Collection looks at the mysterious lives and legends of the two famous female pirates, attempting to separate fact from fiction while analyzing their lasting legacies. Along with pictures depicting Anne Bonny, Mary Read, and other important people, you will learn about the famous pirates like you never have before.

Grace O'Malley

Chapter 1: Early Years

Grace O'Malley was born around 1530 in Ireland, with both of her parents, father Eoghan Dubhdara O'Maille and mother Margaret, being from Clew Bay in Country Mayo. As a clan chieftain, Eoghan was very powerful and one of only a handful of Irish chiefs who had not yet knuckled under to English domination and King Henry VIII. Margaret was just as independent; unlike most women of her age, she had personal wealth in the form of land in Umhall, Ireland. She had inherited this property from her own mother and would in turn pass it on to her daughter.

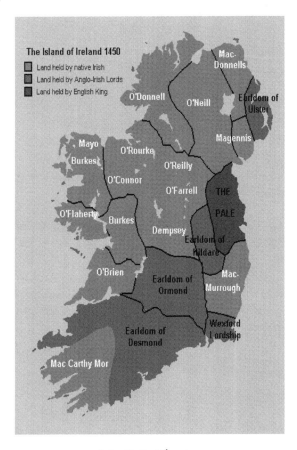

Ireland in the 15th century

Unlike most of their neighbors, the O'Malleys made their living from the sea, sailing up and down the western coast of Ireland trading merchandise within their own country, as well as Scotland and even far away Spain. They were also known to practice a little piracy on the side, attacking and plundering ships that made their way into their territory. Because the ocean was both their home and their livelihood, they built several castles along the coast, helping them come to dominate most of what is now South-West County Mayo in Ireland. They were even able to tax anyone who fished along the shores of their territory, including fishermen from as far away as England.

According to English law at that time, Henry VIII was King of England, but only Lord of Ireland. Because of the nature of travel and communication, there was much less direct supervision of the Irish people by the English crown, so the Irish people were primarily under the supervision of their own countrymen, princes and lords who had rule the land for generations.

Henry VIII

According to Irish tradition, Grace was a bit of a renegade from birth. One story claims that while she was still very young, she wanted to go on a trading trip to Spain with her father. When trying to explain to her why she could not accompany him, Eoghan made the mistake of saying that it was because her long hair would tangle up in the ship's ropes. Seeing this situation as easily solvable, Grace cut her hair short, like the style worn by the sailors themselves. Her father, though embarrassed by her appearance, still knew when he was beaten and allowed her to go with him. For her own part, Grace earned the nickname "Grainne Mhaol", which meant "Bald Grace." The name stuck and over time evolved into Granuaile, as she was often known.

While Granuaile spent most of her early years at her family's castle in Belclare, she was probably sent to live with another family by the time she was 12 years old. Fosterage, as this was known, was a common practice among Anglo-Saxon nobility at that time, in the belief that exposure to the skills and culture of other families made a girl more well-rounded and marriageable. There was also a greater chance for her to come into contact with young men from similarly placed families. As a result of the fosterage, Granuaile received the high level of education typically given to the daughters of nobility at that time. While mathematics and the sciences were not considered necessary for young women, they were taught at least some foreign languages, and when Granuaile met with Elizabeth I later in her life, she was able to converse with the queen in fluent Latin. She also appears to have known a smattering of English, Scottish, Spanish and French, possibly picking up these other languages during her travels around the English Isles.

Henry VIII is remembered primarily for his several wives and the various fates they suffered, but his treatment of his subjects, especially those in Ireland, was even worse. Around the time Granuaile turned 13, Henry instituted a new policy concerning the Irish. Called "surrender and re-grant," it was based on idea that all the lands of the English Isles were dependent on the English monarch for government and protection. Those chieftains who gave up their lands to the Henry and recognized him as King of Ireland instead of the previously titled Lord of Ireland retained control of their property and clans. However, they would also be required to live by English law and show up for all called parliament meetings.

According to Granuaile's chief biographer, Anne Chambers:

"Thus started the Tudor conquest of Ireland by means of a policy of subtle effectiveness. As the chieftains and lords accepted the terms and titles of the English king, so they became obligated to abandon the Irish laws and customs that had endowed them with their positions of power in the first place. Their acceptance of the English terms ran contrary to the Gaelic principles of election and land tenure. Some chieftains felt coerced into acceptance, others did so out of greed or disillusionment with the impermanence of the Gaelic system, which allowed for little continuity, but most accepted only for as long as it suited their own purpose."

By the time he died in 1547, Henry had managed to take control of much of Ireland, as one chieftain after another agreed to his terms, but the O'Malleys felt no such need for English rule. The fishing along the coast provided them with enough income to maintain their former glory and power.

Chapter 2: A Wife and a Pirate

In 1546, Granuaile married Donal an Chogaidh O Flaithbheartaigh ("Donal of the Battle"), the heir of the O'Flaherty clan and thus an excellent match for the only child of the great O'Malley chieftain. The two newlyweds soon settled into Donal's castle near Slyne Nead on the coast of

Bunowen, a beautiful setting for the two to begin their life together. Looking across the Killary fiord, Granuaile could see the lands at Umhall that would one day be hers. There was also a deep harbor from which Donal could sail his boats.

Though Granuaile may have often looked out her window with longing when these boats sailed away, she was at this point in her life content with the role of wife and mother. During the first years of her marriage she bore Donal three children in rapid succession. The first, Owen, was easygoing and not aggressive at all, very unlike either of his parents. The second child, daughter Margaret, was strong-willed and determined like her mother. Their last child, Murrough, was considered to be the child most like his father; he was aggressive and always seemed to be looking for a fight.

Unfortunately, Donal's own aggressive nature soon caught up with him, and sometime in the early 1550s he was killed in a battle with a nearby clan, the Joyces. Following his death, Granuaile immediately seized hold of the leadership of her local clansmen. She started by extracting revenge against those who had killed her husband, sailing her ships up the coast to recapture the castle he had died defending. According to Irish law and tradition, Granuaile was entitled to one-third of Donal's estate as well as her own dowry upon his death, but Donal's clan claimed that they could not afford to return the dowry, or even to give Granuaile here share of the estate. This appears to have been true, since Granuaile took no measures to force the payment due to her. It is likely both the dowry and the estate had already been spent on Donal's many battles.

Of course, by this time Granuaile must have realized that piracy rendered the need for Donal's money moot. She then triumphantly returned to her family home on Clare Island, and though she did not inherit from the estate, many of her husband's people remained loyal to her and her sons and happily followed her back to her father's home.

Clare Island

As it turns out, Bunowen castle proved to be an excellent port from which Granuaile could begin her new life as a pirate. It provided an excellent view of Clew Bay, allowing those in its tower to see any ship that passed, and the castle itself was so situated that most of those passing never even noticed it until it was too late and the pirates were upon them.

Before long, Granuaile and her men were regularly attacking ships sailing in and out of the nearby port at Galway., and their deeds became so notorious that at one time the citizens had ascribed above the town gate, "From the ferocious O'Flahertys, Good Lord deliver Us." Just as her father had before her, Granuaile determined to extract a toll from any ship that passed through her waters. Using swift and maneuverable galleys, she and her men would seem to appear out of nowhere, forcefully board a merchant vessel, and demand a portion of the cargo as a sort of "protection money." Their intimate knowledge of every cove and bay along their native shores made them nearly impossible to catch.

Eventually, the local merchants and fishermen were complaining to the English Council in the capital city of Dublin. One such complaint read, "The continuing roads used by the O'Malleys and O'Flaherties with their galleys along our coasts, where there have been taken sundry ships and barks bound for this poor town, which they have not only rifled to the utter overthrow of the owners and merchants, but also have most wickedly murdered divers of young men to the great terror of such as would willingly traffic."

It is only fair to note that not all of Granuaile's business activities were illegal. She also hired her ships out to transport "gallowglass" fighters, who were Scotsmen hired each summer by Irish chieftains to help fight battles over land and property. Granuaile would use her fleet of galleys to bring them to Ireland in May and then return them to Scotland the following September.

As time went on, Granuaile added to her own crew, recruiting men from many different Irish clans. The fact that they were willing to leave their own families and lands to follow this woman is a testament to two factors. First, the political situation in Scotland at that time saw laws being enacted by the Tudors that had weakened family ties and left many clan members feeling adrift in a new type of society. Then there was Granuaile herself, who apparently possessed an ability to lead and motivate people who previously had no affiliation or loyalty to her.

In 1566, Granuaile married Risdeard an Iarainn Bourke, known as "Iron Richard" due to his reputation for wearing an ancient coat of mail that he had inherited from his ancestors. He was a chieftain of his clan and one of the most powerful men in Connacht at the time, and from all appearances it seems Granuaile married Bourke for his money and/or his castle. Rockfleet Castle, the traditional home of the Bourke family, was located near Newport, a well-situated port that would provide an excellent harbor for her ships. Bourke also owned property along the coast that included a number of hidden harbors from which pirates could attack their prey.

Rockfleet Castle

Granuaile took an interesting path in marrying Risdeard. Instead of vowing to remain wed "until death do us part," she married according to Brehon law, an Irish tradition that allowed them to commit to each other for only a year. After that year, they were supposed to make a more permanent commitment to each other, but Granuaile had other plans; she and her crew took possession of the castle at Rockfleet and refused to come out. Instead, she simply stood at a high window and yelled out to her husband below, "Richard Burke, I dismiss you." This was sufficient to divorce him, and since she had possession of the castle at that time, she was able to retain it as her personal property. From that day forward, Rockfleet Castle remained in the possession of the O'Malleys.

Though they were no longer married according to Irish law, the English continued to consider them husband and wife. It also appears that they continued to operate as allies throughout the rest of Risdeard's life. Later, after his death, Granuaile referred to herself as his widow. Another reason why the English continued to recognize Granuaile and Risdeard's marriage is that they had a child, Theobald, together. According to legend, he was actually born on Granuaile's ship during a battle against the Algerians. Chambers writes:

> "As the battle raged, her captain came below where she lay with her new-born son and begged her to come up on deck so that her presence might rally her men. With the words 'may you be seven times worse off this day twelve months, who cannot do without me for one day', she wrapped a blanket around herself and joined her men. Uttering a ferocious oath she roared them into action, while at the same time emptied a musket at the Algerians, crying, 'Take this from un-consecrated hands.' The fact that attacks by North African pirates on outlying areas along the south and west coasts of Ireland were recorded frequently during this period lends credence to this traditional account of Tibbott-ne-Long's birth."

Chapter 3: A Tale of Vengeance

Another instance of Granuaile's defiance in the face of anyone who would dare cross her is the matter of Doona Castle. As the story goes, Granuaile decided to make a pilgrimage for St. Brigid's Day to a certain holy well located on Clare Island, but she soon lost interest in making her peace with God when word reached her that a foreign ship had landed on the rocks near Achill Head. She ordered her crew to turn the ship around and return immediately to the other boat. According to legend, a huge storm blew up just as she was leaving, perhaps giving the lady pirate cause to wonder if she had made the right decision, but her lust for treasure kept her going, and she soon arrived at the ship. When she did, she was disappointed to find that much of it had already washed away, but she was able to rescue a 15 year old boy who had managed to survive the accident by clinging to a large outcropping of rock. She ordered that he be taken below and given something to eat while she oversaw the loading of the remaining salvage.

When she finally got around to interviewing him, she discovered that his name was Hugh de Lacy and that he was from a wealthy family in Wexford. She also discovered that he was very attractive and, though he was no older than her own oldest son, she soon took him as a lover. This was just one of several such incidents that led to Granuaile's reputation for promiscuity.

For a short while, all appeared to be well. Hugh de Lacy sailed with her around the islands near her home and enjoyed his life as a "kept man" of an older woman. However, he made the mistake one day of going deer hunting near Doona Castle, the home of the infamous MacMahon clan, and when they discovered him on their property they shot him dead for poaching. It is unclear how exactly Granuaile heard of what happened, whether it was via a messenger or even perhaps having the boy's dead body brought to her, but she flew into a rage when she found out and immediately plotted to avenge his death.

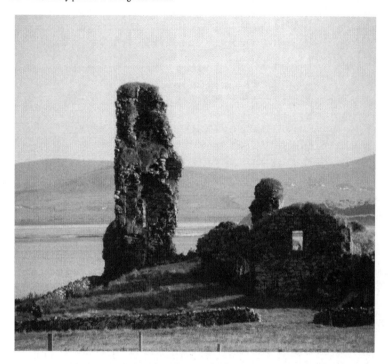

The remains of Doona Castle

Though she was furious and bloodthirsty, Granuaile was also shrewd. She patiently bided her time until the MacMahons began their usual family pilgrimage to Caher, a holy island near Clare Island. Standing at the top window of her castle there, Granuaile watched quietly as the families left their boats and walked toward the ancient church to worship. As soon as they were out of sight, she and her men attacked, first taking possession of the boats so that no one could escape. Next, she attacked the men themselves, killing everyone who might have had anything to do with the boy's death. While that might have satisfied some people, it was not enough for Granuaile, who next sailed for Doona and attacked the local garrison stationed at the castle. She quickly defeated them and took the castle for her own.

Not surprisingly, this was not the only incident when Granuaile went out for revenge. On another occasion, one of her fellow chieftains tried to steal some of her property. When she came after him, he went into hiding in a nearby church, begging the holy hermit who lived there to give him sanctuary. Long-held church tradition mandated that no one take action against anyone living in a house of worship, but this tradition was not enough to stop Granuaile. She surrounded the church with her men and ordered that no food or any other sort of supply be allowed in. Trapped, the chieftain persuaded the hermit to help him dig a tunnel through the church floor to the edge of the nearby cliff. From there he lowered himself by rope into a boat he had hired and escaped. Fearing reprisals, the hermit informed Granuaile of what had happened, but he also gave her a good scolding for bringing violence into a holy place.

Like many older women, Granuaile was committed to teaching those around them good manners. However, her means were a bit unorthodox, as can be seen in the case of Howth Castle. Howth is located at one of the principal ports of Dublin, and during one of her voyages Granuaile anchored there to take on water and supplies. Custom dictated that the Lord of the Castle should also provide her with food and lodging while she was there, but when she arrived at the castle gates, she found them locked and was told that Lawrence, the Earl of Howth, was at dinner and unavailable to receive her.

Howth Castle today

Seeing this as yet another example of the breakdown of traditional values, Granuaile returned to her ship to consider how best to teach the Earl some manners. At about this time, she ran into his grandson and saw a chance to make her point. She kidnapped the boy and left for home. Lawrence gave chase and offered her any sum of money for the return of his only heir, but rather than accept his money, Granuaile offered to return the boy on one condition: the castle at Howth must always welcome anyone looking for a meal or night's lodging. They must even set an extra place at every meal, just in case some unexpected guest should show up. The Earl happily agreed to these demands and joyfully returned home with the boy, after which he implemented the promised policy. It remains the rule at Howth Castle to this day.

While Granuaile was able to keep pretty good control over her immediate sphere of influence, there were forces at play in the world around her that she, and many others, would find more difficult to manage. By 1577 war was brewing between England and Spain. The two had only barely been at peace since Queen Elizabeth I succeeded to the throne after her sister Bloody Mary's death in 1558, because the Spanish King Philip II was determined to return England to the Catholic faith.

Elizabeth I

On a more local scale, war broke out between two of Ireland's more prominent clans during the late 1560s, destabilizing the local political system. With most of her time and money committed to fending off the Spanish, Elizabeth had little capital to invest in stabilizing the region. Instead, she decided to influence the local culture by recommending that the younger sons of her nobility migrate to the area, beginning a long-term project of English colonization of the neighboring country.

By this time, Granuaile had become something of a legend in the English Isles. In 1577, Scottish poet Sir Henry Sidney accompanied his father to visit the notorious woman. After meeting her, he reported the following back to the English court:

> "There came to me also a most famous feminine sea captain called Grany Imallye, and offered her service unto me, wheresoever I would command her, with three galleys and two hundred fighting men, either in Ireland or Scotland. She brought with her her husband, for she was as well by sea as by land well more than Mrs. Mate with him. He was of the Nether Burkes and now, as I hear, Mackwilliam Euter, and called by nickname Richard in Iron. This was a notorious woman in all the coasts of Ireland."

This account provides yet another example of Granuaile's ability to appear to cooperate without actually intending to. While she gave lip service to obeying English law and putting aside her pirating pursuits, she had no intention of doing so. Within weeks she was back at work again, this time attacking the property of the English Earl of Desmond in Munster. Unfortunately for Granuaile, she finally overreached on this occasion and was captured by the Earl's men, who in turn brought her to stand trial before him at Askeaton Castle. He declared her guilty of her crimes and confined her in the jail at Limerick, keeping her there for about two years and only periodically hauling her out to display to various English lords as a sign of his loyalty and support of Elizabeth's laws and policies.

Though Granuaile was released in 1579, her troubles were by no means at an end. The city of Galway was immediately concerned about the effect her return to the pirating life would have on their business, and they were so unimpressed by English security that they hired a band of mercenaries to attack her in Rockfleet Castle and prevent her from leaving. Though she beat them back and escaped, there was more trouble soon to come.

Chapter 4: The Good Wife

In July of 1579, Spain finally made her move against England. Rallying as many Catholic countries as possible around them, the Spanish sailed toward Ireland with the express purpose of rallying the Irish clans into a war against their English oppressors. While Granuaile remained dubious about participating, her husband Richard went all in and became one of the leaders of the fight. He allied with Granuaile's former jailor, the Earl of Desmond, to attack numerous villages up and down the coast that remained loyal to the Queen. However, he was soon defeated by Sir Nicholas Malby, one of the queen's supporters, and forced to surrender.

At this point, it appears that Granuaile may have intervened on her husband's behalf and helped him to negotiate an agreement that saved both his skin and his property:

"The Humble Petition of Richard Bourke to His Worship, Sir Nicholas Malby, Knight, governor in Thomond, 22 April 1580

He most humbly beseeches the same in respect he has fallen from his duty towards God and her Majesty. And he and all his according therein to defect been attempted and plagued by your worship and her Majesty's force under your charge. And driven to fly into remote places with their goods and cattle whereby these his lands lie and are become waste. This it will please your worship to your great goodness as you have received him into grace without distress so likewise it will please you to grant commission to deponent not only to call back his followers with their goods to inhabit the country whereby her Majesty may be assured of her rents and duties and the deponent and followers there without any assurances of their pay; but also that the said deponent may have commission to restore your petitioners to such demands and challenge as he has against any person or persons in that, the county of Mayo. And that, moreover, your petitioner may have your worship's commission to take up such duties and demands from time to time as is due upon his followers of the baronies of Carra Owles and Erries as all by sea as land. The same to continue during such time as he shall remain dutiful towards her Majesty. And that no deponent may have to deal with him or his saving; only such a one as your worship shall make choice of. And according his most bounden he shall pray."

The nature and wording of the petition allowed Richard to not only retain his personal property but also his command over his followers. By this time, the English army and navy was stretched to its limits, so they were more than willing to take a chance that he would make good on his promise to use his leadership and troops to support Elizabeth.

Not long after this incident, both Richard and Granuaile teamed up to take on a new problem: establishing Richard's right to become the MacWilliam (head) of his clan. He had been in line for the position for years, but when the previous MacWilliam died, he was supplanted by the man's brother. This was unacceptable to both Richard and his wife, who had married him at least in part for his future troops. Together they put together an army of more than 2,000 men and 200 horses, only to have word win out over swords. Wanting to keep her newly vowed ally in power, Elizabeth issued the following patent declaring Richard the sole head of his clan.

"Know you that of our special grace, certain knowledge and free will, together with the advice and consent of our beloved and faithful counselor Arther Grey of Wylton, knight of our order of the Garter and our deputy general in our Kingdom of Ireland, and with the advice and consent of our Council in that kingdom we grant, give, authorize and confer upon our believe subject, Richard Bourke, alias Richard Inyeran Bourke, alias Mac William Eoghter Bourke, that he be chief of his clan and seneschal of the feudal tenants and followers of our people and nation and of his own clans and their lands and tenements in our province of Connaght and of the border castles with their manors, lands, tents and hereditaments with their revenues and privileges with which he now lawfully possesses in the said province. And that, for the protection of the said castles, lands ,tents and hereditaments and of the rest entrusted to him as well as for the protection of our subjects therein dwelling against enemies or rebels, invaders or plunderers, or violators or disturbers of our peace he may call of arms our subjects therein dwelling and lead them in pursuit as often as and whenever it shall be necessary for our service and the defense of these same our subjects and his own people and that he protect and advance our peace and good government and a similar life among our good subjects within the boundaries of his jurisdiction and that he be minister of our justice and laws within the same boundaries for as long as he occupies the office of our seneschal. Finally, that he may ax, exact and levy within the limits of the said office (except for free church lands and waste lands) his reasonable expenses whenever he shall be ordered to appear at Dublin, Athlone or Galway. By the chief of our ministers in the government of our said kingdom or by our lord president or agreement, article and clause specified and contained in the indenture annexed to this our letter, patent and which are to be observed and fulfilled by the same Richard."

This agreement is highly significant for a number of reasons. First, the Crown actually rewarded someone who was only recently in rebellion against it. Second, it recognized the title "MacWilliam," one of many Gaelic titles that England at that time was trying to eliminate. Finally, Elizabeth herself formed an agreement with two avowed pirates who had only recently terrorized her people. While these factors make this agreement something of a triumph of Granuaile and Richard's own power and prestige, it is also a testament to just how desperate Elizabeth was to keep her kingdom under control. She was even willing to make a compact with pirates to see her ends achieved.

For Granuaile, piracy was a family affair. As soon as her son Tibbott was old enough to hold a gun, she insisted that he join forces with her and his father to attack nearby castles. However, Tibbott appears to have not had his parents' taste for battle. During one of his first fights, against nearby Kinturk Castle, he became afraid that the battle might be going against them and sought shelter behind his mother. This led her to scream at him in front of all the men, "Are you trying to hide behind my backside, the place you came from?" Her words served their purpose, and Tibbott came out from behind her and continued to fight. A few years later, Kintuck Castle became his permanent home.

As time went by, it became more and more difficult for Richard and Granuaile to tolerate the rule of Englishmen that they believed had less social and political standing than themselves. Though they are largely remembered as pirates (outside of Ireland), it's important to remember that both of them were descended from Irish royalty. Granuaile's father was the equivalent of an English Earl, while Richard, as a MacWilliam, had a rank at least as high as that of a English lord. For them, the administrators sent to govern Ireland were more suited to serve in their own retinues than to rule over them. Unfortunately for Richard, his problems would not last much longer, because he would die in 1583 of natural causes. In describing Richard, Chambers observes:

> "Despite their personal and at times political difference, Richard-an-Iarainn was a worthy and suitable consort for Granuaile. While often forced to play a supporting role to her more prudent and politic ways, they seem to have been a well-matched couple who together, as well as individually, made an impact on political events. Richard-an-Iarainn was content and even encouraged his wife's unusual role, and his standing in the male-dominated society of Gaelic Ireland does not appear to have been diminished by his wife's unorthodox ways. In an age that was more male-oriented than most, Richard-an-Iarainn emerges as a man sufficiently liberated from the shackles of misplaced male pride to have acknowledged, encouraged and capitalized on his wife's ability and success."

No doubt forgetting that she had once before had to fight to inherit one-third of her first dead husband's property, Granuaile wasted no time in establishing a legal claim to her share. She also took possession of several of his castles and kept them for the rest of her life for her own use. Thus, at the time of Richard's death, Granuaile was about 53 years old and perhaps the most powerful woman in Ireland. She had her own army, a large castle to live in and several other smaller castles to use when she wanted to, a large fleet of ships, and plenty of livestock.

Unfortunately for Granuaile, her power also bred problems. The English were stepping up their efforts to stamp out the Irish aristocracy, and one of their new policies involved ending the office of the MacWilliam. This was especially offensive to Granuaile, who had assumed that her son would one day inherit that office for himself. She began to show her displeasure by attacking English merchant ships, often stealing their cargoes.

Given the fact that her power and her piracy were so notorious, the English officials in Ireland soon decided to make a special example of her. Their reasoning may very well have been that if they could stop her, they would have more time to spend chasing other pirates. They may have also reasoned that defeating her would give them a tougher reputation with the pirates and any other rebellious Irishmen they were trying to control.

Whatever their reasons, their campaign against Granuaile began with capturing her son Tibbott. But the English had no intention of ransoming him back to his powerful mother; by this time, the policy among the English lords was to hold the heirs to Irish clans and indoctrinate them in English ways. The assumption was that they could then later be released and return to their clans ready to cooperate with their new "lords." That is how Tibbott came to learn to read and write English, as well as speak it like a proper gentleman.

Though the English controlled much of Tibbott's life, he was by no means a normal prisoner. During this time he met and married Maeve O'Coonor Sligo. Meanwhile, Granuaile's oldest son Owen also married, but he would not live long enough to establish a home of his own. Instead, he was killed by the brother of Sir Richard Bingham after he was caught trying to hide his cattle from the English lord in order to avoid paying taxes.

Sir Richard Bingham

Naturally, Granuaile was enraged by her son's execution. She became one of the leaders of the Irish rebellion, setting sail for Scotland to recruit soldiers to help her. However, before she could get there, Bingham captured her and several of her kinsmen, killing some of them and imprisoning her. Though Bingham threatened her with execution, she was eventually released thanks to the negotiations of her daughter Margaret's husband, known as the Devil's Hook.

Though Granuaile was released, she was by no means reformed. As soon as she obtained her freedom, she once more set out for Scotland, but once again she did not reach her destination. This time a storm damaged her ships and forced her to put in to Ulster for three months of repairs. She used this time wisely, meeting with clan chieftains to bolster support for the rebellion, but before she had her forces in place, the rebellion ended with Bingham being replaced by Sir John Perrot.

John Perrot

As soon as she learned that there was a new English lord in Ireland, Granuaile set sail to meet him, figuring that since Perrot had long been highly critical of Bingham, he might hear her out. Her gamble paid off, and she quickly received a full pardon from Perrot not only for herself but also her children.

Chapter 5: A Pirate to the End

A close brush with execution might have reformed some women, but it had no effect on Granuaile, who immediately acquired more ships and men and went back to business as usual. But unfortunately, business as usual did not last for long. On July 12, 1588, the legendary Spanish Armada started for the English channel. The Spanish plan was to take this invasion, led by the Duke of Parma, to the coast of southeast England, where they would be released to conquer Elizabethan England for the Spanish monarch and Catholic Christendom. The Armada included over 150 ships, 8,000 sailors and 18,000 soldiers, and it boasted a firepower of 1,500 brass guns and 1,000 iron guns. Just leaving port itself took the entire Armada two days.

16th century depiction of the Spanish Armada

The English navy was strong and well-prepared, but they were understandably concerned about what might happen if Spanish ships landed or even just washed ashore, in Ireland. As a result, Perrot was again replaced by Bingham, leading to tensions rising with Granuaile. For her part, Granuaile had done business with the Spanish for years and was neither charmed nor frightened by them. If she had a chance, she would board and plunder their ships, but if they cooperated she would have no issue with them. In fact, Granuaile so thoroughly despised the English that she would even help them hide from their English enemies.

As everyone who has been taught history now knows, the Armada was one of the most famous military debacles in history. Whether it was simple mathematical miscalculation or plain bad luck, coupled with English fire ships assailing the Spanish Armada, the Aramada was defeated – decisively so. By the time the Armada found its reluctant way home in awful conditions, it had permanently lost over one third of the ships. On the Irish coast, the Armada had suffered further losses.

Suspecting that Granuaile was up to no good, Bingham sent his sheriff to her castle in February 1589 to look for hiding Spanish sailors. While it appears that Granuaile may not have been there when he arrived with 250 men, her grandson Richard Bourke resisted the invasion of their home. When the sheriff continued his assault and marched onto the castle grounds, Bourke and his men responded by attacking the group, killing the sheriff and about 25 of his soldiers.

Not surprisingly, this incident intensified the disdain between the Irish and the English, especially Bingham. Looking on from London, Elizabeth became concerned that perhaps part of the problem lay with the governor himself, so she sent investigators to Dublin to determine what, if any, fault was his. When the committee acquitted him of any wrongdoing, they returned him to his office with strict orders that he was to get control of his territory and end the rebellion. Bingham thus set about eliminating the problem by trying to eliminate the people involved. This was particularly hard on Granuaile's family, which lost a lot of kinsmen and lands. She in turn sought sanctuary in the only place she felt safe, living on board her ships and sailing up and down the coast plying the only trade she knew: piracy.

It was at about this time that she heard that her second son, Murrough, had committed the ultimate treason against his family by joining the English. Apparently he agreed to cooperate with Bingham if he would send troops to help Murrough in his own battle against a nearby neighbor. According to Bingham's later report, Granuaile determined to discipline her son for his errant way by attacking his castle at Ballinehencie, burning the surrounding town and stealing most of his livestock and property. She also killed several of the men who tried to stop her. It seems her actions worked, since there is no record of Murrough working with the English following those reprisals. And though Granuaile had no problem attacking her offspring to teach them a lesson, she did not want anyone else harming them. When Scottish mercenaries attacked her clan near Erris, she chased them all the way back to Scotland and made sure that they knew better than to come after her family again.

In spite of her fighting spirit, Granuaile still knew that she could not hold back the encroaching English forever. By early 1592, she and her son were the only two leaders among the Irish who continued to resist English rule, and eventually Bingham had anchored so many warships in the harbors around her castle that she could no longer find a sheltered cove to harbor in overnight. He was also able to capture most of her ships, leaving her unable to continue to make a living. When Tibbott approached her about making peace with their triumphant adversaries, she realized that there was nothing else left to do and gave him her blessing.

Though she was down, Granuaile was not yet done. In this, her most desperate hour, she hatched her most desperate plan; she would lay her case directly before Elizabeth. In her first letter to the queen, dated July 1593, Granuaile gave her side of a story that she knew Elizabeth has already heard from Bingham. She began by portraying herself not as a powerful pirate leader but as a little old lady just trying to do the best she can to survive in a war torn country:

> "In most humbler wise shows unto your most excellent Majestie your loyal and
> faithful subject Grany ny Mally of Conaught in your highness' realm of Ireland: that

whereas by means of the continual discord, strifes and dissention that heretofore long time remained among the Irish, especially in West Conaught by the seaside, every chieftain, for his safeguard and maintenance and your gracious means the said province is reduced to that civil course that the chieftains, freeholders or gentlemen have compounded and is assigned what and how much he is to have; in which composition no order was taken for your fond subject what maintenance she ought to have of her former husband's lands and by the same is restrained to use her former course to her utter decay and ruin; in tender consideration whereof and in regard to her great age, she most humbly beseeches your Majesty, in your princely bounty and liberality, to grant her some reasonable maintenance for the little time she has to live."

She then proceeded on to ask for help for her family, who she once again portrayed as the helpless victims of circumstance:

"And whereas your said subject's two sons are the lawful heirs of the lands of their said fathers whereof they now stand seized and possessed, that it would please you Royal Majesty to direct your gracious letters to your Lieutenant Deputy of your said realm willing him to accept a surrender at the hands of her said sons, yielding to Your Majesty, your heirs and successors such yearly rents as conveniently such lands may yield and they to hold the same, by letters patents to them and their heirs forever and to grant the like for the lands of Walter Burgh Fitz Theobald Reogh and Shane Burke Mac William Mac Moiler, cousin germain to her said son."

Finally, Granuaile asked Elizabeth for the one thing neither of them had ever enjoyed for long: peace.

"And lastly that it would please your Majestie to grant unto your said subject under your most gracious hand of signet free liberty during her life to invade with sword and fire all your highness' enemy's wheresoever they are or shall be without any interruption of any person or person whatsoever. Thus shall you said subject, according to her bounden duty, ever remain in all obedient allegiance to resist all remnants of rebellious enemies and pray continually for your Majesty's long life and prosperous reign."

The tenor of this letter is so humble and conciliatory that it does not seem that it could have been written by the fearless pirate herself, but piracy was by its very nature deceptive and Granuaile was a master of diplomacy. The problem was that the ships carrying mail to England sailed very slowly, while events in Ireland moved at a much quicker pace. Before the letter could reach the queen, Bingham, who famously referred to Granuaile as the "nurse to all rebellions in the province for forty years", arrested Tibbott and accused him of burning his home and killing his men. Granuaile knew that her son was unlikely to receive a fair trial and even less likely to survive a conviction, so she decided to go to London herself and talk to the Queen in person.

The meeting between the two queens was quite an enlightening experience for each. Making sure Elizabeth realized she considered herself an equal, Granuaile refused to bow to the English Queen, symbolic of the fact that Elizabeth was not Queen of Ireland and thus not her queen. One colorful account claims Granuaile even walked into the meeting with a dagger on her. According to Chambers:

> "As a meeting of two queens of equal standing, when the two women were introduced Elizabeth held out her hand, but Granuaile being the taller of the two, the English queen was forced to raise her hand to the Irish 'queen.' It was perceived there during the course of their meeting Granuile required a handkerchief and Elizabeth took from her pocket a lace-edged one of fine cambric. Upon using it, Granuaile threw it into the nearby fire, bringing the surprised retort from Elizabeth that it was meant to be put in her pocket. Equally surprised, Granuaile told the queen that in Ireland they had a higher standard of cleanliness. When Elizabeth offered to confer her with the title of countess, Granuaile is said to have declined the offer on the basis that a title could not be conferred on one of equal status. When Elizabeth bemoaned the cares of royalty, looking around her sumptuous surroundings, Granuaile witheringly told her 'that the poor women in Mayo had greater cares and greater industry to their credit' than the queen of England."

By the time Granuaile was finished speaking with the queen, she had received Elizabeth's personal promise that her son's case would be looked into. In the meanwhile, Bingham had heard of the meeting and was regularly sending letters to Elizabeth trying to persuade her to see matters his way. He failed, however, and in September 1593 Elizabeth instructed him to free Tibbott and his men and to return their lands. She further ordered that money should be deducted from their taxes and given to Granuaile for her upkeep.

These orders enraged Bingham who, though he had to follow them in the letter of the law, had no intention of giving Granuaile one ounce more of support than he was required to. He continued to harass her and her kinsmen at every opportunity, forcing her to make another visit to London the following year to seek relief once again. Elizabeth granted her the relief she sought again, but this time there were requirements made of Granuaile too. Over the remaining years of her life, Granuaile and her family would become increasingly supportive of the English representatives in Ireland.

Though Granuaile herself was still practicing some limited plundering as late at 1601, she was no longer involved in Ireland's fight against England. While the date of her death is uncertain, it definitely represented the end of an era when the last surviving Gaelic chieftain was buried quietly on some green Irish hill.

Since her death, Granuaile has long been remembered as a pirate, but she lived over a century before the "Golden Age of Piracy" made men like Blackbeard famous and created the stereotypes that modern societies remember pirates by. Pirates continue to be romanticized as people who have lived outside the boundaries of normal societies and refused to play by the rules, and nowhere is this more evident than the continuing interest in the pirates of centuries past. As the subjects of books, movies, and even theme park rides, people continue to let their imaginations go when it comes to pirates, with buried treasure, parrots, and walking the plank all ingrained in pop culture's perception of them.

While that explains some of the reasons Granuaile's life and legacy continue to resonate, she was clearly a different kind of woman altogether. Far from being a member of an unprivileged class seeking to steal booty from any ship she could, Granuaile was both a queen and a rebel who defiantly fought to protect her home and way of life against the English. Naturally, while foreigners might remember her as a pirate and one of many famous rebels opposing the English over the centuries, Ireland has remembered her as a folk hero, and she has become the subject of all the poetry, songs, plays, and movies that come along with such a standing. 19th century writer James Hardiman may have summed up Granuaile's legacy the best when he wrote, "Her name has been frequently used by our Bards, to designate Ireland. Hence our Countrymen have been often called 'Sons of old Grana Weal.'"

Bibliography

Chambers, Anne (2012) *Granuaile: Grace O'Malley - Ireland's Pirate Queen*

Cook, Judith (2004) *Pirate Queen: The Life Of Grace O'Malley*

Druett, Joan (2000). *She Captains: Heroines and Hellions of the Sea*

Gerstl, Hugo (2011) *Amazing Grace: The Story of Grace O'Malley the Notorious Pirate Woman*

Heyman, Richard (2012) *The Cock and the Hen The Story of Grace O'Malley*
Russell, Jesse and Ronald Cohn (2012) *Grace O'Malley*

Sjoholm, Barbara (2004) *The Pirate Queen: In Search of Grace O'Malley and Other Legendary Women of the Sea*

Sir Francis Drake

Chapter 1: Drake's Early Years

The future courtier, captain, privateer and pirate Sir Francis Drake was born during the early 1540s in the small village of Tavistock in Devon, England, the oldest of twelve sons born to Edmund and Mary Mylwaye Drake. Edmund was a farmer and one of the earliest members of the Protestant Reformation, and he named his first son after Francis Russell, Earl of Bedford. Bedford also stood as the boy's godfather.

Drakes godfather

Ironically, the boy who would grow up to become one of the national heroes of his day was subjected to such religious persecution by fellow countrymen that he and his family were forced to leave their home in Devon because of disagreements over the new English Prayer Book. They sided with the Crown's version of the new Book of Common Prayer and thus settled in Kent, where most of the Protestants agreed with their views. Edmund was so erstwhile about his religion that he was ordained a deacon in the local church and given the pastorate of Upnor Church. In recognition of his loyalty to the Protestant Crown, the senior Drake was later made a chaplain in the Royal Navy. As biographer William Wood would colorfully describe it, "[Edmund's] friends at court then made him a sort of naval chaplain to the men who took care of His Majesty's ships laid up in Gillingham Reach on the River Medway, just below where

Chatham Dockyard stands to-day. Here, in a vessel too old for service, most of Drake's eleven brothers were born to a life as nearly amphibious as the life of any boy could be. The tide runs in with a rush from the sea at Sheerness, only ten miles away; and so, among the creeks and marshes, points and bends, through tortuous channels and hurrying waters lashed by the keen east wind of England, Drake reveled in the kind of playground that a sea-dog's son should have."

Given a childhood that included so much time spent at sea, it was only natural that Edmund eventually sent young Francis to apprentice with the captain of a small type of boat called a barque. Used primarily to traverse the English Channel, these boats were popular with both French and English merchants. Despite being just 10 years old, Francis proved up to the physical challenges, and contemporary accounts claim that the boy "so pleased the old man by his industry that, being a bachelor, at his death he bequeathed his bark unto him by will and testament."

In 1563, when he was still in his early 20s, Drake left the safety of the English Channel and sailed with his cousin, Sir John Hawkins, to the newly founded English colonies in America. This voyage remains a stain on Drake's record to this day, as it was one of the first slave-trading expeditions to North America. Though two other ships had previously brought slaves to America, Hawkins is considered to be the first captain to take the business of trafficking in human beings seriously and establishing the triangular route from Africa to Europe to the New World.

Sir John Hawkins

The first trip that Drake made with Hawkins was to what was then known as the Spanish Main. They were carrying a load of people that the Spanish were willing to "buy" to work on their plantations. According to Hawkins's own records, they obtained some of the slaves from African warlords who were only too willing to sell their captured rivals in order to get rid of them. Not having enough to make a full load, they also captured a human cargo from Portuguese traders who were on their way to the New World from Africa. Once they had their ships full, Hawkins and Drake sailed to South America, where they exchanged the newly enslaved peoples for barrels of tobacco and other goods from the New World.

Pleased with their success, the two returned to the New World again the following year, but things did not go nearly as well the second time around. While resupplying at the port of San Juan de Ulúa in 1568, Drake and Hawkins were attacked by a fleet of Spanish warships, losing all but two of their ships and almost all of their crew. Drake and Hawkins personally escaped by swimming away during the chaos and making their way back to England. At the time, several European nations were on the brink of war, including England, France, and Spain, and news of what happened at Ulúa caused Queen Elizabeth I some serious consternation. William Wood explained:

> "Just as the winter night was closing in, on the 20th of January, 1569, the *Judith* sailed into Plymouth. Drake landed. William Hawkins, John's brother, wrote a petition to the Queen-in-Council for letters-of-marque in reprisal for Ulua, and Drake dashed off for London with the missive almost before the ink was dry. Now it happened that a Spanish treasure fleet, carrying money from Italy and bound for Antwerp, had been driven into Plymouth and neighboring ports by Huguenot privateers. This money was urgently needed by Alva, the very capable but ruthless governor of the Spanish Netherlands, who, having just drowned the rebellious Dutch in blood, was now erecting a colossal statue to himself for having 'extinguished sedition, chastised rebellion, restored religion, secured justice, and established peace.' The Spanish ambassador therefore obtained leave to bring it overland to Dover.
>
> But no sooner had Elizabeth signed the order of safe conduct than in came Drake with the news of San Juan de Ulua. Elizabeth at once saw that all the English sea-dogs would be flaming for revenge. Everyone saw that the treasure would be safer now in England than aboard any Spanish vessel in the Channel. So, on the ground that the gold, though payable to Philip's representative in Antwerp, was still the property of the Italian bankers who advanced it, Elizabeth sent orders down post-haste to commandeer it. The enraged ambassador advised Alva to seize everything English in the Netherlands. Elizabeth in turn seized everything Spanish in England. Elizabeth now held the diplomatic trumps; for existing treaties provided that there should be no reprisals without a reasonable delay; and Alva had seized English property before giving Elizabeth the customary time to explain."

Queen Elizabeth I

As Elizabeth was mulling over what to do next concerning the hostilities, it turned out that Drake's career as a slaver was already finished. These initial three trips as a slaver proved to be the only such trips that Drake would participate in, and while it is possible that he had some sort of attack of conscience, it is more likely that he came to believe that there was more money to be made elsewhere. At the time, the slave trade was technically illegal in England, though it was not typically seriously enforced. Also, it is only fair to note that Drake's involvement in the slave trade was not necessarily out of any sense of racism so much as it was simply a profitable proposition. He would later recruit African slaves (known as Maroons) who escaped from Spanish owners and add them to his crew, depending on them during battles and praising their efforts.

While Drake was done with the slave trade, he was far from done with the Spanish. He and Hawkins began plotting their revenge against the Spanish, who they hated not only for what they perceived to be personal slights but because they were Catholic. Raised by a devout Protestant, Edmund's influence clearly rubbed off on Francis, who had been taught from an early age that Papists were at best ignorant and superstitious and at worst heretics. Not long after his marriage to Mary Newman in 1569, Drake returned to the West Indies in search of his former captors.

Chapter 2: The Captain

Though it is unclear whether or not Drake found the revenge he was seeking, his trips to America did solidify his reputation as skilled seaman. This led, in 1572, to his first trip as an independent captain of his own ship. Never one to shy away from a challenge, Drake chose to attack England's most serious enemy at that time, Spain, near the infamous Spanish Main.

In the mid-16th century, Spain had colonized much of present-day Central America, South America and parts of North America, giving them control over the Gulf of Mexico and the Caribbean Sea. At the center of it was the Isthmus of Panama, which provided the center of the gold and silver trade from Peru. Ships coming from South America landed on the western coast of this narrow strip of land and unloaded their cargo, which then had to be carried overland to the eastern shore of the isthmus and loaded into other ships that would take it on to Spain. Several hundred years later, this process would be eliminated by the construction of the Panama Canal, but at the time this allowed he Spanish to avoid having to sail their ships south and around South America. It also happened to provide an excellent opportunity for theft and piracy.

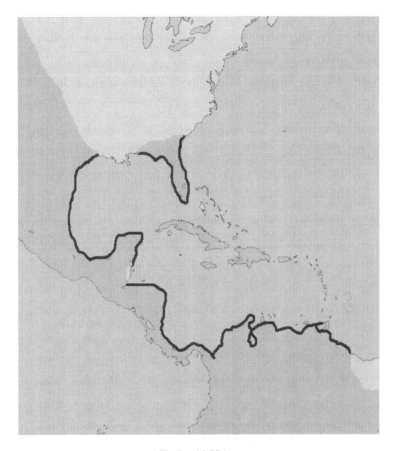

The Spanish Main

Drake sailed from Plymouth, England, on May 24, 1572, headed for Nombre de Dios, where he planned to capture the town and as much Spanish gold as he could get his hands on. With him he took 73 men and the *Pascha* and the *Swan*, two small ships built for speed and maneuverability rather than fighting. He began his attack on the town in late July of that year, and soon took possession of it and its treasure, but he was gravely wounded in battle and forced to withdraw to a safer location where he and his crew could fully recover. Wood described the audacious and chaotic attack:

> "Springing eagerly ashore the Englishmen tumbled the Spanish guns off their platforms while the astonished sentry ran for dear life. In five minutes the church bells were pealing out their wild alarms, trumpet calls were sounding, drums were beating

round the general parade, and the civilians of the place, expecting massacre at the hands of the Maroons, were rushing about in agonized confusion. Drake's men fell in—they were all well-drilled—and were quickly told off into three detachments. The largest under Drake, the next under Oxenham—the hero of Kingsley's Westward Ho!—and the third, of twelve men only, to guard the pinnaces. Having found that the new fort on the hill commanding the town was not yet occupied, Drake and Oxenham marched against the town at the head of their sixty men, Oxenham by a flank, Drake straight up the main street, each with a trumpet sounding, a drum rolling, fire-pikes blazing, swords flashing, and all ranks yelling like fiends. Drake was only of medium stature. But he had the strength of a giant, the pluck of a bulldog, the spring of a tiger, and the cut of a man that is born to command. Broad-browed, with steel-blue eyes and close-cropped auburn hair and beard, he was all kindliness of countenance to friends, but a very 'Dragon' to his Spanish foes.

As Drake's men reached the Plaza, his trumpeter blew one blast of defiance and then fell dead. Drake returned the Spanish volley and charged immediately, the drummer beating furiously, pikes levelled, and swords brandished. The Spaniards did not wait for him to close; for Oxenham's party, fire-pikes blazing, were taking them in flank. Out went the Spaniards through the Panama gate, with screaming townsfolk scurrying before them. Bang went the gate, now under English guard, as Drake made for the Governor's house. There lay a pile of silver bars such as his men had never dreamt of: in all, about four hundred tons of silver ready for the homeward fleet—enough not only to fill but sink the Pascha, Swan, and pinnaces. But silver was then no more to Drake than it was once to Solomon. What he wanted were the diamonds and pearls and gold, which were stored, he learned, in the King's Treasure House beside the bay.

A terrific storm now burst. The fire-pikes and arquebuses had to be taken under cover. The wall of the King's Treasure House defied all efforts to breach it. And the Spaniards who had been shut into the town, discovering how few the English were, reformed for attack. Some of Drake's men began to lose heart. But in a moment he stepped to the front and ordered Oxenham to go round and smash in the Treasure House gate while he held the Plaza himself. Just as the men stepped off, however, he reeled aside and fell. He had fainted from loss of blood caused by a wound he had managed to conceal. There was no holding the men now. They gave him a cordial, after which he bound up his leg, for he was a first-rate surgeon, and repeated his orders as before. But there were a good many wounded; and, with Drake no longer able to lead, the rest all begged to go back. So back to their boats they went, and over to the Bastimentos or Victualling Islands, which contained the gardens and poultry runs of the Nombre de Dios citizens."

Drake and his men stayed in and around the Isthmus for the next year, attacking Spanish galleons periodically and continuing to gather any booty they could. After a year of acting on his own, Drake teamed up with French privateer Guillaume Le Testu (who may have been working for Italy) to go after a load of gold being transported overland on the isthmus. They sailed into a port near Darien in modern day Panama and followed the famous Spanish Silver Train to Nombre de Dios. There they attacked the mule train in March of 1573 and captured more than 20 tons of gold and silver, a prize so rich that it proved to be more than they could carry away with them. Instead, they took the more valuable gold and buried buried the silver in a secret site known only to them, one of the first known incidents involving pirates and buried treasure.

Prior to leaving the site of his victory, Drake, in typically dramatic style, climbed a tall palm tree and looked to the west, and from that high vantage point he became the first Englishman to see the Pacific Ocean. He also began to make plans in the back of his mind to someday sail it. However, at that moment he had more pressing concerns.

During the attack on the mule train, Le Testu was wounded and subsequently captured by their Spanish victims, and he was later tried and convicted of piracy and beheaded. This left Drake completely in charge of the expedition, so he ordered his men to drag and carry as much of the treasure as they could back to the cove where their boats were anchored. The grueling trip across 18 miles of mountainous jungle took several days and left the men exhausted, but the worst was yet to come. This exhaustion turned to rage when they arrived at the cove to find that their boats had been taken by the Spanish.

Knowing that his men were starving and that the Spanish would no doubt soon return, Drake instructed his crew to bury the rest of the treasure right there on the beach. He then sent two of his best sailors aboard a makeshift raft ten miles up the coast to where he had left his flagship. Thankfully for Drake and his crew, the two sailors made it there and soon returned for the rest of the men.

When the flagship arrived, the crew that had been left behind was shocked by Drake's worn out appearance. They immediately assumed that the raid had been a failure and were reluctant to ask how the others had fared. In a moment more suited to a Hollywood movie than real life, Drake allowed them to worry for a few minutes before pulling out a solid gold necklace from under his shirt and crying, "Our voyage is made, lads!" He then had them dig up the gold buried on the beach and set sail back to England. A crewman later recounted the journey home:

"'Within 23 days we passed from the Cape of Florida to the Isles of Scilly, and so arrived at Plymouth on Sunday about sermon time, August 9, 1573, at what time the news of our Captain's return, brought unto his friends, did so speedily pass over all the church, and surpass their minds with desire to see him, that very few or none remained with the preacher, all hastening to see the evidence of God's love and blessing towards our Gracious Queen and country, by the fruit of our Captain's labour and success. Soli Deo Gloria."

They arrived in Plymouth to a hero's welcome in August of 1573, though the Queen was not at that time able to publicly acknowledge his success, since a treaty recently signed with Philip II of Spain technically made Drake's activities illegal.

Perhaps because of this change in the political atmosphere, Elizabeth assigned Drake to a handle a more domestic crisis upon his return. In 1575, he sailed with a group of English soldiers to Rathlin Island in Ulster, Ireland, where they were ordered to put down a rebellion of the Irish against the English plantation owners. While Drake remained at sea safeguarding the English contingent, the soldiers brutally put down the rebellion. More than 600 men, women and children surrendered to the English, and while it was traditional at that time to execute the leaders of such an incident, the English instead killed everyone they had captured, including the women and children. It is unclear how involved Drake actually was in this incident. Records show that he was in charge of the ships transporting the British troops, under the command of John Norreys, to the Island. At the time of the actual massacre, he may very well have been patrolling the coast, searching for Scottish troops who had threatened to reinforce the Irish.

Chapter 3: The Pirate

While pirates are traditionally considered to be outlaws, such was not the case with Francis Drake. While the Spanish considered him a thief and a criminal, the English considered him a hero, and he was a very public presence when he was home. In fact, his exploits made him a favorite courtier of Elizabeth I of England, and the Queen met with him regularly to congratulate him of his attacks on the Spanish. She also made sure that he was present at every major court event, where he could very conspicuously entertain the lords and ladies with his tails of sailing, fighting and treasure hunting.

Though he was popular at home, Drake was much too valuable an asset to the crown to keep on land for very long. Despite having signed a treaty earlier in the 1570s, Spain and England were back at each other's throats just a few years later, and in 1577 Elizabeth sent him to the Pacific coast of North America to hunt and harass Spanish vessels plying those waters. Drake later described being summoned and given orders to hunt Spanish ships: "Secretary Walsingham declared that Her Majesty had received divers[e] injuries of the King of Spain, for which she desired revenge. He showed me a plot [map] willing me to note down where he might be most annoyed. But I refused to set my hand to anything, affirming that Her Majesty was mortal, and that if it should please God to take Her Majesty away that some prince might reign that might be in league with the King of Spain, and then would my own hand be a witness against myself." It was Drake who suggested that he be allowed to raid the Pacific Ocean, which was incredibly daring because the waters around the southern tip of South America were so treacherous that the Spanish had long avoided them whenever possible.

In a mistake unusual for such a skilled seaman, Drake departed during the early winter in November of 1577. Because of the cold and rough seas, he did not get very far before having to dock at the port of Falmouth, in Cornwall. There they rested for a few days before returning to Plymouth to make repairs to the battered ships.

Still determined to leave as soon as possible, Drake sailed again on December 13th. This time he took the *Pelican* and the *Christopher,* as well as the *Swan,* the *Pascha* and one other ship with him. With about 165 crewmen, the 5 boats were so crowded that they were forced to add a sixth ship, the *Mary*, which Drake purchased cheaply from a captain who had previously captured it off the coast of the Cape Verde Islands in Africa. With the additional ship came another captain, the Italian Nuno da Silva, whose knowledge of South American seas would prove to be an invaluable asset to Drake.

As it turned out, Drake would not have a problem with overcrowding for long. He lost many of his crew in the Atlantic crossing. By the time he reach San Julian, located in modern day Argentina, he no longer had enough men to continue to man all his ships. As a result, he was forced to leave behind both the *Christopher* and the *Swan* on the coast. They also burned the *Mary* after they discovered that her hull was beginning to rot and would no longer be seaworthy.

Upon arriving in San Julian, the remaining crew were met with a grim reminder of the task before them. There, on the sandy shore, were the weathered skeletons of the crew members of Ferdinand Magellan. A mere 50 years before, these men had made the ill-fated decision to mutiny against their captain while he himself was looking for treasure and glory. He had had them killed there on the beach and left the unburied bodies hanging on display as a gruesome reminder to any other sailors that might think they knew better than their leader how to run an expedition

Ironically, Drake found himself facing an issue related to mutiny at this same juncture. He heard rumors that Thomas Doughty, his own co-commander on the expedition, was practicing witchcraft. Like most people of that era, and especially those with a devoutly Protestant background, Drake both abhorred and feared anything related to the occult. He charged Doughty with both treason and mutiny, though there was little evidence of either. Doughty replied by asking to review Drake's commission from the Queen to see if he was authorized to act on such charges. Drake refused his request to see the documents, and also his request to be transported to England for trial. Instead, he proceeded to try the case himself, there on the shores of South America.

What most of the men present that day did not know was that Drake had long been concerned about Doughty's role in the expedition. While the public story was that Drake was simply going exploring, the back story was that Elizabeth herself had instructed him to attack and plunder as many Spanish ships as possible. This could not be made public because England and Spain were not technically at war with each other. However, prior to leaving, Drake had confided their secret orders to Doughty.

Doughty had made it clear both initially and later that he was not comfortable with attacking ships without some sort of provocation. He even went as far as to approach a member of Parliament with his concerns. When he was encouraged to go along with the plan anyway, he did so, but not without often voicing his concerns about both Drake's commission and his methods in carrying it out.

During the trial, evidence came to light from several sources, all of whom accused Doughty of speaking badly about both the ships and their captain. He also appears to have been very critical of the men aboard and made many enemies. However, there appears to have been little evidence of behavior that would rise to the level of mutiny. Still, within the context of an unknown land and a still rather young captain, there was little room for error. Those hearing the charges, nudged along no doubt by Drake himself, found Doughty guilty and agreed to his execution.

What follow is perhaps one of the strangest scenes in the history of the seas. Doughty asked to receive Holy Communion prior to his execution. Not only did Drake agree to his request, but he also joined him in the sacred rite. According to the ship's chaplain, Francis Fletcher:

"The general himself communicated at this Sacred ordinance, with this condemned penitent gentleman, who showed great tokens of a contrite and repentant heart, as who was more deeply displeased with his own act than any man else. And after this holy repast, they dined also at the same table together, as cheerfully, in sobriety, as ever in their lives they had done aforetime, each cheering up the other, and taking their leave, by drinking each to other, as if some journey only had been in hand.

After dinner, all things being brought in a readiness, by him that supplied the room of the provost-marshal; without any dallying, or delaying the time, he came forth and knelt down, preparing at once his neck for the ax, and his spirit for heaven; which having done without long ceremony, as who had before digest this whole tragedy, he desired all the rest to pray for him, and willed the executioner to do his office, not to fear nor spare."

Biographer William Wood described the Doughty affair in a similar manner:

"[W]itchcraft was not Thomas Doughty's real offence. Even before leaving England, and after betraying Elizabeth and Drake to Burleigh, who wished to curry favor with the Spanish traders rather than provoke the Spanish power, Doughty was busy tampering with the men. A storekeeper had to be sent back for peculation designed to curtail Drake's range of action. Then Doughty tempted officers and men: talked up the terrors of Magellan's Strait, ran down his friend's authority, and finally tried to encourage downright desertion by underhand means. This was too much for Drake. Doughty was arrested, tied to the mast, and threatened with dire punishment if he did not mend his ways. But he would not mend his ways. He had a brother on board and a friend, a 'very craftie lawyer'; so stern measures were soon required. Drake held a sort of court-martial which condemned Doughty to death. Then Doughty, having played his last card and lost, determined to die 'like an officer and gentleman.'

Drake solemnly 'pronounced him the child of Death and persuaded him that he would by these means make him the servant of God.' Doughty fell in with the idea and the former friends took the Sacrament together, 'for which Master Doughty gave him hearty thanks, never otherwise terming him than "My good Captaine."' Chaplain Fletcher having ended with the absolution, Drake and Doughty sat down together 'as cheerfully as ever in their lives, each cheering up the other and taking their leave by drinking to each other, as if some journey had been in hand.' Then Drake and Doughty went aside for a private conversation of which no record has remained. After this Doughty walked to the place of execution, where, like King Charles I,

> 'He nothing common did or mean
> Upon that memorable scene.'

'Lo! this is the end of traitors!' said Drake as the executioner raised the head aloft."

With the Doughty affair behind him, Drake decided to weather the rest of the winter in San Julian before moving one in his expedition. Prior to leaving for the next phase of his mission, he made a rousing speech before his men, saying in part:

"For by the life of God, it doth even take my wits from me to think on it. Here is such controversy between the sailors and gentlemen, and such stomaching between the gentlemen and sailors, it doth make me mad to hear it. But, my masters, I must have it left. For I must have the gentleman to haul and draw with the mariner, and the mariner with the gentleman. What! let us show ourselves to be of a company and let us not give occasion to the enemy to rejoice at our decay and overthrow. I would know him that would refuse to set his hand to a rope, but I know there is not any such here…"

With that, Drake took his remaining crew and three remaining ships around the Magellan Strait off the southern tip of South America during the summer of 1578 and arrived in the Pacific Ocean that September. However, the Straits took their toll, and Drake lost two more ships, with one sinking and the other returning to England. This left him only his flagship in which to continue his journey. Wood described the harrowing ordeal:

"Drake sailed for the much dreaded Straits, before entering which he changed Pelican's name to the Golden Hind, which was the crest of Sir Christopher Hatton, one of the chief promoters of the enterprise and also one of Doughty's patrons. Then every vessel struck her topsail to the bunt in honor of the Queen as well as to show that all discoveries and captures were to be made in her sole name. Seventeen days of appalling dangers saw them through the Straits, where icy squalls came rushing down from every quarter of the baffling channels. But the Pacific was still worse. For no less than fifty-two consecutive days a furious gale kept driving them about like so many bits of driftwood. 'The like of it no traveller hath felt, neither hath there ever been such a tempest since Noah's flood.' The little English vessels fought for their very lives in that devouring hell of waters, the loneliest and most stupendous in the world. The Marigold went down with all hands, and Parson Fletcher, who heard their dying call, thought it was a judgment. At last the gale abated near Cape Horn, where Drake landed with a compass, while Parson Fletcher set up a stone engraved with the Queen's name and the date of the discovery."

A modern replica of Drake's *Golden Hind*

Like other explorers before him, Drake had continued to sail south, reaching a previously undiscovered island that he named Elizabeth Island in honor of his Queen and patroness. He remained close to the South American coast while turning north in his only remaining ship, the *Golden Hind*. From this sturdy craft he engaged in one attack after another of Spanish sea towns and coastal villages, while also capturing Spanish ships and stealing their more accurate nautical charts. He also pressed those that he could into service within his own fleet. Just as importantly, Drake moved onto the next target before word of his whereabouts could spread widely.

While on his way to Peru, Drake stopped in at the port at Mocha Island, which proved to be a mistake because the local natives had already developed a distrust of European visitors. According to the records of the voyage:

"When Frances Drake had passed the Straits of Magellan, the first land he fell with was an island named Mocha, where he came to an anchor, and hoisting out his boat, he, with ten of his company, went on shore, thinking there to have taken in fresh water. Two of the company, going far into the island were intercepted and cut of by the Indians that inhabit the island, who, as some as then saw our men come to anchor, thought they would come on land (as they did indeed), and laid an ambush of about 100 Indians; and where our boat was fast on ground and all the men gone on land, the ambush broke out and set upon them, and before they could recover their boat and get her on float, they hurt all our men very sore with their arrows.

More died of their wounds, the rest escaped their wounds and were cured. They stayed here but one day, but set sail toward the coast of Chile, where arriving they met with an Indian in a canoe near the shore, who thinking them to have been Spaniards, told them that behind there, at a place called St. Yago, there was a Spanish ship, for which good news they gave him diverse trifles. The Indian being joyful thereof went on shore and brought them ... sheep and a small quantity of fish, and so they returned back again to St. Yago to seek the Spanish ship (for they had overshot the place before they were where); and when they came thither, they found the same ship."

Once he was situated off the coast of Lima, Drake and his men captured 25,000 pesos worth of Peruvian gold, the equivalent of about $10 million today. He also heard rumors that another ship, the *Nuestra Señora de la Concepción*, had recently departed, full of treasure and headed for Manila. Drake decided to go after the ship and managed to capture it. Its hold proved to be the most valuable one to date and included eighty pounds of gold, as well as a large, solid gold crucifix and twenty-six tons of silver. The chests also contained a wide variety of jewels and 13 chests of royal plate.

One Spanish letter described Drake's passage through the Straits and their attempts to capture him:

"A ship belonging to English raiders passed through the Strait of Magellan into the Pacific Ocean and reached the port of Santiago in the province of Chile on 6th December last year, 1578. This ship plundered one laden with a large quantity of gold that was in port there, and also other ships in ports along this coast, and did other damage. On the 13th February it arrived off the port of this city [i.e., Callao, port of Lima] and we were taken entirely unawares by so surprising an event, for, although there had been so much time for me to be warned from Chile of the presence of this ship, nothing was done. The excuse for this was that the Governor was away at the front in the region of the Araucanians, and neither the royal officials nor the city council were willing to take responsibility for chartering a ship to bring me the news, which, if it had arrived, would have saved so much loss and avoided the expense to His Majesty and to private citizens.

This has grown considerable because of the loss of a ship that the raider plundered which was carrying a large sum in silver dispatched from this country to the kingdom of Tierra Firme. We have taken a great deal of trouble to capture this raider and have sent two armed ships in search of him."

In the summer of 1579, Drake made landfall somewhere north of Spain's colonial borders, where he found a safe harbor and anchored his ships for long term repairs. While some of his men devoted themselves to making repairs to the ships' hulls and rigging, Drake sent others into the surrounding jungle to obtain fresh food and water. Having learned his lesson from his earlier encounter on Mocha Island, he worked hard to make sure that there was no trouble with the local peoples. Scholar Robert F. Heizer, who wrote a short book discussing the debates over where Drake landed in present-day California, noted what was written by Drake's chaplain in a diary that summer:

'June 21.—On this day the ship was brought near shore and anchored. Goods were landed, and some sort of stone fortification was erected for defense. The Indians made their appearance in increasing numbers until there was a 'great number both of men and women.' It is clearly apparent that the natives were not simply curious, but acted, as Fletcher points out, 'as men rauished in their mindes' and 'their errand being rather with submission and feare to worship vs as Gods, then to haue any warre with vs as with mortall men.' It would seem that the natives demonstrated clearly their fear and wonderment at the English, and it is certain that they behaved as no other natives had done in the experience of the chronicler. The English gave their visitors shirts and linen cloth, in return for which (as Fletcher thought) the Indians presented to Drake and some of the English such things as feathers, net caps, quivers for arrows, and animal skins which the women wore. Then, having visited for a time, the natives left for their homes about three-quarters of a mile away. As soon as they were home, the Indians began to lament, 'extending their voices, in a most miserable and dolefull manner of shreeking.' Inserted between the passages dealing with the departure of the Indians to their homes and their lamenting is a description of their houses and dress. The houses are described as 'digged round within the earth, and haue from the uppermost brimmes of the circle, clefts of wood set up, and joyned close together at the top, like our spires on the steeple of a church: which being couered with earth, suffer no water to enter, and are very warme, the doore in the most part of them, performes the office of a chimney, to let out the smoake: its made in bignesse and fashion, like to an ordinary scuttle in a ship, and standing slopewise: their beds are the hard ground, onely with rushes strewed vpon it, and lying round about the house, haue their fire in the middest....' The men for the most part were naked, and the women wore a shredded bulrush (tule? Scirpus sp.) skirt which hung around the hips. Women also wore a shoulder cape of deerskin with the hair upon it."

Drake's cousin John would later discuss some of their interactions with the Native Americans after being captured by the Spanish and forced to give a deposition:

"There he [Francis Drake] landed and built huts and remained a month and a half, caulking his vessel. The victuals they found were mussels and sea-lions. During that time many Indians came there and when they saw the Englishmen they wept and scratched their faces with their nails until they drew blood, as though this were an act of homage or adoration. By signs Captain Francis told them not to do that, for the Englishmen were not God. These people were peaceful and did no harm to the English, but gave them no food. They are of the colour of the Indians here [Peru] and are comely. They carry bows and arrows and go naked. The climate is temperate, more cold than hot. To all appearance it is a very good country. Here he caulked his large ship and left the ship he had taken in Nicaragua. He departed, leaving the Indians, to all appearances, sad."

Prior to leaving, Drake claimed the land on behalf of England and in honor of the Holy Trinity. He gave it the name Nova Albion, meaning "New Britain." He also appears to have left behind some of hims own men to try to establish a colony there, though this remains unclear due to the secret nature of the voyage and the colony itself. Drake is believed to have altered his own records in order to keep the Spanish from discovering the exact location of the colony.

Controversy had long surrounded the exact location of Nova Albion. Drake's own records of its establishment, as well as those of his men, were destroyed in a fire in the late 17th century. A bronze plaque that was found in Marin County, California, was for years believed to have been the marker of the village's original location. However, it was later proven to be a hoax. Today, historians believe that the most likely location of Nova Albion was actually as far north as present day Drakes Bay on the coast of California. One scholar who has advocated that site noted an old Native American legend from the region that was supposed to have been about Drake:

> "First of all comes an old Indian legend which comes down through the Nicasios to the effect that Drake did land at this place [Drake's Bay]. Although they have been an interior tribe ever since the occupation by the Spaniards and doubtless were at that time, it still stands to reason that they would know all about the matter. If the ship remained in the bay thirty-six days it is reasonable to suppose that a knowledge of its presence reached every tribe within an area of one hundred miles and that the major portion of them paid a visit to the bay to see the 'envoys of the Great Spirit,' as they regarded the white seamen. One of these Indians named Theognis who is reputed to have been one hundred and thirty years old when he made the statement, says that Drake presented the Indians with a dog, some young pigs, and seeds of several species of grain.... The Indians also state that some of Drake's men deserted him here, and, making their way into the country, became amalgamated with the aboriginals to such an extent that all traces of them were lost, except possibly a few names [Nicasio, Novato] which are to be found among the Indians."

Given that the Spanish were now all too aware that Drake was in the area, sailing back south along South America would have been suicidal. Thus, upon leaving the western coast of North America, Drake sailed across the Pacific to what is now the eastern coast of Indonesia. There he experienced another bit of bad luck when the Golden Hind was trapped for three days on a coral reef. At first, Drake was concerned that he might not be able to save his favorite ship, but his crew worked non-stop for three days to remove all the cargo and lighten its load. When the next tide came in, they were able to shift it off the reef and get it sailing again.

While in Indonesia, Drake became friends with the leader of the local people, the sultan of the Moluccas, and by the time he made his way from there to Africa, he had acquired significant knowledge related to the ways and means of Portuguese trade. Wood explained:

> "From California Drake sailed to the Philippines; and then to the Moluccas, where the Portuguese had, if such a thing were possible, outdone even the Spaniards in their fiendish dealings with the natives. Lopez de Mosquito—viler than his pestilential name—had murdered the Sultan, who was then his guest, chopped up the body, and thrown it into the sea. Baber, the Sultan's son, had driven out the Portuguese from the island of Ternate and was preparing to do likewise from the island of Tidore, when Drake arrived. Baber then offered Drake, for Queen Elizabeth, the complete monopoly of the trade in spices if only Drake would use the Golden Hind as the flagship against the Portuguese. Drake's reception was full of Oriental state; and Sultan Baber was so entranced by Drake's musicians that he sat all afternoon among them in a boat towed by the Golden Hind. But it was too great a risk to take a hand in this new war with only

fifty-six men left. So Drake traded for all the spices he could stow away and concluded a sort of understanding which formed the sheet anchor of English diplomacy in Eastern seas for another century to come. Elizabeth was so delighted with this result that she gave Drake a cup (still at the family seat of Nutwell Court in Devonshire) engraved with a picture of his reception by the Sultan Baber of Ternate."

Drake's trip around the African coast was less eventful, with him rounding the Cape of Good Hope safely and with little trouble. He reached Sierra Leone in late July 1580 before turning his ship north toward Plymouth and home. When he arrived back home on September 26, 1580, Drake had only about one third of his original crew still with him, but he also had a large cargo of spices and Spanish treasure with him. The Queen's 50% share of his fortune comprised more than half of her entire income for that year.

Chapter 4: The Knight

Though Spain still considered him a pirate, the English people considered him a hero. He was hailed upon his homecoming as the first Englishman to circumnavigate the globe, and his crew had completed the second circumnavigation after Magellan's crew. Elizabeth herself insisted that she and her most trusted ministers alone should review the records of his journey, and any member of the crew who shared any information about the specifics of their trip risked execution. She was determined that nothing Drake learned on his voyage should fall into Spanish hands.

With his substantial share of the fortune he had acquired, Drake purchase a large manor called Buckland Abbey in Devon, near Yelverton, where he would live for most of the rest of his life when not at sea, and he was only too happy to bask in the fame of being a sea hero. He presented Elizabeth with a special jewel that he chose just for her from his treasure, a jewel pendant made from gold he captured off the coast of Mexico and set with a diamond mined in Africa. At the bottom was a tiny ship carved out of ebony.

Not to be outdone, Elizabeth gave Drake her own miniature portrait, set in a jeweled frame. Unlike most pins of this nature this one was reversible. On the back was a cameo of twin busts. One was of an obviously royal woman, perhaps meant to be Elizabeth herself. The other was of an African man. Known throughout the court as the "Drake Jewel," it became one of Drake's most prized possessions.

The "Drake Jewel" given to Drake by the Queen

While it was a common practice for a sovereign to give elaborate gifts to the nobility, it was practically unheard of for a monarch to bestow such a gift on a commoner. Naturally, Drake wore the pin regularly at court. Elizabeth did not stop with just a gift of jewelry, however. On April 4, 1581, she made a very special visit to the *Golden Hind*. There, on decks embedded with everything from gold dust to their captain's blood, she knighted Drake, creating him Sir Francis Drake. Always the shrewd politician, Elizabeth did not do the dubbing herself but instead handed the job off to the French ambassador, who was only to happy to oblige since he wanted to please the Queen and persuade her to marry his own king's brother. However, by participating in the knighting, the diplomat was also giving tacit approval of the French crown to

Drake's exploits against the Spaniards.

A plaque depicting Drake's knighthood

With the knighthood came a coat of arms. At first, he claimed the right to the arms of the well-known sailor, Sir Bernard Drake, who Sir Francis claimed was a distant relative Sir Bernard, however, took issue with this claim. Though his family, the Drakes of Ash, had also lived in Devon for generations, he assured both the queen and her council that they knew nothing of the Drakes that had moved to Kent. He also confronted Sir Francis about the matter while the two were at court and is said to have boxed the younger man's ears.

In order to smooth out matters between her two courtiers, the queen authorized a new coat of arms for Sir Francis Drake himself. Drake chose a simple pattern the represented his professional exploits and accomplishments. It is an ocean wave with a star above, representing the Arctic Pole, and another below, representing Antarctica. This simple design is surrounded by heraldic feathers and a banner with the motto "*Sic Parvis Magna*" ("Thus great things from small things come"). To the upper left a hand reaches to heaven, holding another banner that reads "With Divine Help."

While Drake was nearing the apex of his career, he suffered a setback in his personal life. His wife of twelve years died in 1581, possibly as the result of pregnancy complications. She was never able to successfully bear a child. Busy with his new life at court, Drake showed little interest in remarrying and instead turned his sight to politics. That September, he was made Mayor of Plymouth, and he also won a seat in parliament, possibly from Camelford. He was reelected a few years later, this time to Bossiney, in 1584.

The following year, Drake made a politically and financially advantageous marriage to Elizabeth Sydenham. 12 years his junior, she was the only living child of Sir George Sydenham, the High Sheriff of Somerset. The two would remain married until Drake's death, but they also never had any children together.

Chapter 5: The Armada

Shortly after Drake's marriage to Sydenham, war finally broke out between England and Spain. Elizabeth immediately dispatched Drake and his fleet to the New World to attack the Spanish ports at Santo Domingo and Cartagena. On his way home in June of 1586, he attacked the Spanish fort at Saint Augustine in Florida. His actions, along with those of other British sailors, provoked Philip II of Spain to begin planning to invade England.

Philip II of Spain

Upon hearing of Philip's plan, Drake decided strike first. Planning to "singe the beard of the King of Spain," he sailed a fleet of British ships into Spanish ports at Cadiz and Corunna. He quickly defeated the naval vessels that were supposed to be defending the ports and completely occupied the harbors. In the process, he sunk more than 35 military and merchant ships, a daring and decisive victory that forced Spain's timeline for attack by a full year.

To make sure that the Spanish navy remained off-kilter, Drake continued to sail up and down the coasts of Iberia between Cape St. Vincent and Lisbon. Over the next month, he destroyed dozens of Spanish ships and thoroughly tangled up his enemy's supply lines, capturing enough barrel-making supplies to prevent the Spaniards from making more than 25,000 barrels. In recognition of these efforts, Drake was made vice admiral of the British fleet, serving directly under Lord Howard of Effingham. This would put him at the forefront of the naval battle against the Spanish Armada during their attempted invasion of England in 1588.

16th century depiction of the Spanish Armada

On July 12, 1588, the legendary Armada started for the English channel. The Spanish plan was to take this invasion, led by the Duke of Parma, to the coast of southeast England, where they would be released to conquer Elizabethan England for the Spanish monarch and Catholic Christendom. The Armada included over 150 ships, 8,000 sailors and 18,000 soldiers, and it boasted a firepower of 1,500 brass guns and 1,000 iron guns. Just leaving port itself took the entire Armada two days.

Always the rogue, Drake broke off from the English fleet as they chased the Armada into the English Channel. As darkness fell around him, he captured the galleon *Rosario*, taking the ship's captain, Admiral Pedro de Valdes, and his entire crew prisoner. In addition to the ship and its personnel, Drake also found a hull full of gold and silver designated for paying the Spanish forces opposing the English.

The actual capture of the *Rosario* was not exactly Drake's finest hour. The fleet was sailing at night, using lamplight to designate where each ship was. When Drake spotted the Spanish ships, he ordered the lamps put out so that they would not give away their positions. While this kept the Spanish from seeing them, it also prevented the English ships from seeing each other. While there were no actual collisions, there were enough near misses to thoroughly aggravate the captains of the other vessels. It took them most of the rest of the night to regain their proper positions.

In spite of this minor glitch, Drake remained firm in his belief that the British Navy would ultimately triumph over Spain. It appears that he spent much of the war on land, resting and waiting for the best time to attack. There is a legend that he was one day lawn bowling in Plymouth when a rider came with the urgent news that the Spanish were approaching. Rather than panic and rush to his ship, Drake merely laughed and assured those around him that he had time to defeat both his bowling opponent and the Spanish fleet. While this story is likely apocryphal, it is also true that the weather kept the English fleet from launching as early as some thought it should. Drake may well have been merely waiting for the most opportune time to take his ships to sea.

A plaque depicting Drake bowling while receiving news about the Armada

As always, Drake was alert to any chance to try a new technique to attack the enemy. During a night time battle fought on July 29, 1588, Drake set fire to a number of captured Spanish ships and sent them floating into the massed Spanish ships along the shores of Calais. Terrified, most of the ships broke formation and sailed for the open seas, which led to a major English victory the next day at the Battle of Gravelines. Writing from his position aboard the Revenge a few days later, Drake described their fight against the Spanish fleet:

"Coming up unto them, there has passed some cannon shot between some of our fleet and some of them, and so far as we perceive they are determined to sell their lives with blows. ... This letter honorable good Lord, is sent in haste. The fleet of Spaniards is somewhat above a hundred sails, many great ships; but truly, I think not half of them men-of-war. Haste.

As everyone who has been taught history now knows, the Armada was one of the most famous military debacles in history. Whether it was simple mathematical miscalculation or plain bad luck, coupled with English fire ships assailing the Spanish Armada, the Aramada was defeated – decisively so. By the time the Armada found its reluctant way home in awful conditions, it had permanently lost over one third of the ships. On the Irish coast, the Armada had suffered further losses. Drake's biographer Wood would summarize the debacle: "In those ten days the gallant Armada had lost all chance of winning the overlordship of the sea and shaking the sea-dog grip off both Americas. A rising gale now forced it to choose between getting pounded to death on the shoals of Dunkirk or running north, through that North Sea in which the British Grand Fleet of the twentieth century fought against the fourth attempt in modern times to win a world-dominion."

Chapter 6: The Final Voyages

Following the defeat of the Spanish Armada in 1588, Elizabeth gave Drake a new assignment. This time she asked him to team up with Sir John Norreys and take on a lengthy mission to tie up the loose ends of the war. They were to patrol the shores of England and Spain and destroy any remaining Spanish ships.

Unfortunately, this final mission of the war did not go very well. While the English fleet was able to destroy a few ships in the Spanish harbor at La Coruna, they did so at a high cost in both life and property. Drake and Norreys lost more than 12,000 men, as well as 20 of the ships that had thus far survived the war. The high losses slowed down the seeking and destroying process to the point that Drake finally abandoned the mission altogether.

Elizabeth then wanted Drake and Norreys to provide nautical support for the rebels in Lisbon who were fighting for their independence from Spain. Elizabeth rightly believed that so long as Portugal was separate from Spain, both countries would be weaker. Also, by backing Portugal in the revolution, she could win a new ally for England against the Spaniards. Elizabeth also instructed Drake and Norreys to try to capture the Azores, a group of islands off the coast of Portugal, which would strengthen England's position against Spain while at the same time obtaining a useful pawn against the Spanish.

Once again, Drake met with failure:

"Lisbon was a failure. The troops landed and marched over the ground north of

Lisbon where Wellington in a later day made works whose fame has caused their memory to become an allusion in English literature for any impregnable base—the Lines of Torres Vedras. The fleet and the army now lost touch with each other; and that was the ruin of them all. Norreys was persuaded by Don Antonio, pretender to the throne of Portugal which Philip had seized, to march farther inland, where Portuguese patriots were said to be ready to rise en masse. This Antonio was a great talker and a first-rate fighter with his tongue. But his Portuguese followers, also great talkers, wanted to see a victory won by arms before they rose.

Before leaving Lisbon Drake had one stroke of good luck. A Spanish convoy brought in a Hanseatic Dutch and German fleet of merchantmen loaded down with contraband of war destined for Philip's new Armada. Drake swooped on it immediately and took sixty well-found ships. Then he went west to the Azores, looking for what he called 'some comfortable little dew of Heaven,' that is, of course, more prizes of a richer kind. But sickness broke out. The men died off like flies. Storms completed the discomfiture. And the expedition got home with a great deal less than half its strength in men and not enough in value to pay for its expenses. It was held to have failed; and Drake lost favor."

Following mixed success with these last two assignments, Drake attacked the Spanish port of Las Palmas on Grand Canary Island in 1595, which did not go well. They had originally hoped to make it to Puerto Rico but then decided to attack Las Palmas because they believed it would be an easy target. Instead, it proved to be a well established fort with excellent arms and men. The English were soundly beaten and forced to leave the area.

Following that defeat, Drake returned to the Americas, perhaps in the hopes a regaining some of his former glory. This also proved to be a mistake, as he suffered one defeat after another. In a final push for success, he attacked San Juan, Puerto Rico. On November 22, 1595, he and John Hawkins tried to land in San Juan with 2,500 men in 27 canoes. They first tried to land at the eastern end of the island, at Ensenada del Escambron, but when that failed they returned to their ships and attempted to sail into San Juan bay. This plan also failed, and Hawkins was killed. A Spanish account reported:

"Everybody was surprised and overjoyed at this happy outcome, when two sail came in sight. We gave them chase until three in the afternoon, when our vice-admiral brought one of them by the lee, grappled with her and took her, leaving the Santa Isabel to keep her company. The flagship and the remaining vessels of the squadron continued in chase of the other ship. About then--that is to say, around four o'clock in the afternoon--the vice-admiral shot off three guns, as a warning to the flagship. Ordered to search the sea, the lookouts sighted nine sail coasting along the island of Guadeloupe. We thereupon abandoned the chase: the flagship returned to the convoy to pick up the frigates and spoke with [Vice-]Admiral Gonzalo Méndez, who transmitted the report he had extracted from the prisoners he had taken, as follows:

First, that they had departed from Plymouth on 8th September in the year aforesaid, in company with a fleet commanded by the generals Francis Drake and [Sir] John Hawkins. The prize and her companion had lost company with the fleet in rough weather, four days earlier. Ships that might lose company had been ordered to rendezvous with the main body either at Bayona [in Galicia, on the north coast of Spain] or at Puerto Santo [in the Canary Islands] or off Guadeloupe [as might be requisite according to the stage of the voyage reached]. If they did not fall in with the fleet at those roadsteads they were to proceed to Puerto Rico where they were told the expedition would spend ten days. They had fallen with the island on the previous afternoon, and had sighted and counted nineteen sail, but had not succeeded in fetching them to speak with them; then they had taken our frigates for ships of their own squadron, and that was why they had fallen in with our flotilla.

Asked how strong their fleet was, they said that it consisted of 26 sail. Of these six were Queen's ships: five of them ranged from 800 down to 500 tons, and the other was of 300. Among the remaining 20 vessels, which were adventured by private persons, some were comparable to them in strength and burthen. All of them were under orders from the Queen.

Asked what effect the fleet was intended to accomplish when it left England, witness said that he knew no more than that it was to proceed to Puerto Rico and there take the silver; but that it was so well victualled and stored that the men believed that they were expected to spend a long time in the Indies."

Drake then left for Potobello, Panama, and his final battle. During the battle for El Morro Castle in December of 1595, the Spanish shot a cannon ball through the hull of his flagship and into his own cabin. The blast should have killed him but he survived and lived through Christmas.

Wood summed up the sentiments of Drake and his crew after that defeat:

"'Since our return from Panama he never carried mirth nor joy in his face,' wrote one of Baskerville's officers who was constantly near Drake. A council of war was called and Drake, making the best of it, asked which they would have, Truxillo, the port of Honduras, or the 'golden towns' round about Lake Nicaragua. 'Both,' answered Baskerville, 'one after the other.' So the course was laid for San Juan on the Nicaragua coast. A head wind forced Drake to anchor under the island of Veragua, a hundred and twenty-five miles west of Nombre de Dios Bay and right in the deadliest part of that fever-stricken coast. The men began to sicken and die off. Drake complained at table that the place had changed for the worse. His earlier memories of New Spain were of a land like a 'pleasant and delicious arbour' very different from the 'vast and desert wilderness' he felt all round him now. The wind held foul. More and more men lay dead or dying. At last Drake himself, the man of iron constitution and steel nerves, fell ill and had to keep his cabin. Then reports were handed in to say the stores were running low and that there would soon be too few hands to man the ships. On this he gave the order to weigh and 'take the wind as God had sent it.'"

In the end, Drake did not even have the dignity of a hero's death. During the first part of January he met a foe he could not defeat: dysentery. As the illness took its toll, Drake sensed that he was dying and asked to be dressed in his best set of armor. One of his crewmen kept a diary of the events of January 28, 1596:

"The 28 at 4 of the clocke in the morning our Generall sir Francis Drake departed this life, having bene extremely sicke of a fluxe, which began the night before to stop on him. He used some speeches at or a little before his death, rising and apparelling himselfe, but being brought to bed againe within one houre died. He made his brother Thomas Drake and captaine Jonas Bodenham executors, and M. Thomas Drakes sonne [the later Sir Francis Drake, first baronet] his heire to all his lands except one manor which he gave to captain Bodenham.

The same day we ankered at Puerto Bello, being the best harbour we found along the maine both for great ships and small...After our comming hither to anker, and the solemne buriall of our Generall sir Francis in the sea"

The 55 year old Drake was entombed in a lead coffin and lowered into the sea off the coast of Portobelo, Panama. To this day, people still search for the coffin.

A plaque depicting Drake's burial at sea

At the time of his death, Drake's fleet was anchored off the coast of Panama hoping to capture some Spanish ships that were rumored to be carrying treasure. However, without Drake's leadership, the other captains lost interest in the expedition and returned to England.

Because Drake died without children, his title and fortune passed to his nephew and namesake. His real legacy, however, belongs to the world. The state of California has honored him with a bay, a Boulevard, a hotel and even a high school named after him. On the other side of the Atlantic, there are also a number of streets and squares that bear his name across Britain. Finally, there is the Sir Francis Drake Channel in the British Virgin Islands. Even 400 years after his death, there are contemporary video games like *Drake's Fortune*, which follows the adventures of Nathan Drake, a treasure hunter who claims to be descended from Drake himself.

Drake continues to be a well known figure in the West today, often viewed as a cross between pirates like Blackbeard and adventurers like Sir Walter Raleigh. While he was an important figure of the Elizabethan Era, scholarly debate focuses on the various aspects of his historic circumnavigation of the globe, which was an inadvertent byproduct of his piracy more than anything else. It was also due in part to Drake's travels and naval career that England was positioned to establish colonies in North America by the early 17th century. In that sense, it's somewhat fitting that his career as a privateer and pirate are also obscured by his other accomplishments.

Sir Francis Drake's Famous Voyage Round the World

After Drake's famous circumnavigation of the world, one of his crewmen, Francis Pretty, wrote a brief account of the historic voyage that was subsequently published in 1910. The following is Pretty's account of the trip:

"The 15th day of November, in the year of our Lord 1577, Master Francis Drake, with a fleet of five ships and barks, and to the number of 164 men, gentlemen and sailors, departed from Plymouth, giving out his pretended voyage for Alexandria. But the wind falling contrary, he was forced the next morning to put into Falmouth Haven, in Cornwall, where such and so terrible a tempest took us, as few men have seen the like, and was indeed so vehement that all our ships were like to have gone to wrack. But it pleased God to preserve us from that extremity and to afflict us only for that present with these two particulars: the mast of our Admiral, which was the Pelican, was cut overboard for the safeguard of the ship, and the Marigold was driven ashore, and somewhat bruised. For the repairing of which damages we returned again to Plymouth; and having recovered those harms, and brought the ships again to good state, we set forth the second time from Plymouth, and set sail the 13th day of December following.

The 25th day of the same month we fell with the Cape Cantin, upon the coast of Barbary; and coasting along, the 27th day we found an island called Mogador, lying one mile distant from the main. Between which island and the main we found a very good and safe harbour for our ships to ride in, as also very good entrance, and void of any danger. On this island our General erected a pinnace, whereof he brought out of England with him four already framed. While these things were in doing, there came to the water's side some of the inhabitants of the country, shewing forth their flags of truce; which being seen of our General, he sent his ship's boat to the shore to know what they would. They being willing to come aboard, our men left there one man of our company for a pledge, and brought two of theirs aboard our ship; which by signs shewed our General that the next day they would bring some provision, as sheep, capons, and hens, and such like. Whereupon our General bestowed amongst them some linen cloth and shoes, and a javelin, which they very joyfully received, and departed for that time. The next morning they failed not to come again to the water's side. And our General again setting out our boat, one of our men leaping over-rashly ashore, and offering friendly to embrace them, they set violent hands on him, offering a dagger to his throat if he had made any resistance; and so laying him on a horse carried him away. So that a man cannot be too circumspect and wary of himself among such miscreants. Our pinnace being finished, we departed from this place the 30th and last day of December, and coasting along the shore we did descry, not contrary to our expectation, certain canters, which were Spanish fishermen; to whom we gave chase and took three of them. And proceeding further we met with three carvels, and took them also.

The 17th day of January we arrived at Cape Blanco, where we found a ship riding at anchor, within the Cape, and but two simple mariners in her. Which ship we took and carried her further into the harbour, where we remained four days; and in that space our General mustered and trained his men on land in warlike manner, to make them fit for all occasions. In this place we took of the fishermen such necessaries as we wanted, and they could yield us; and leaving here one of our little barks, called the Benedict, we took with us one of theirs which they called canters, being of the burden of 40 tons or thereabouts. All these things being finished we departed this harbour the 22nd of January, carrying along with us one of the Portugal carvels, which was bound to the islands of Cape Verde for salt, whereof good store is made in one of those islands. The master or pilot of that carvel did advertise our General that upon one of those islands, called Mayo, there was great store of dried cabritos (goats), which a few inhabitants there dwelling did yearly make ready for such of the king's ships as did there touch, being bound for his country of Brazil or elsewhere. We fell with this island the 27th of January, but the inhabitants would in no case traffic with us, being thereof forbidden by the king's edict. Yet the next day our General sent to view the island, and the likelihoods that might be there of the provision of victuals, about threescore and two men under the conduct and government of Master Winter and Master Doughty. And marching towards the chief place of habitation in this island (as by the Portugal we were informed), having travelled to the mountains the space of three miles, and arriving there somewhat before the daybreak, we arrested ourselves, to see day before us. Which appearing, we found the inhabitants to be fled; but the place, by reason that it was manured, we found to be more fruitful than the other part, especially the valleys among the hills.

Here we gave ourselves a little refreshing, as by very ripe and sweet grapes, which the fruitfulness of the earth at that season of winter, it may seems strange that those fruits were then there growing. But the reason thereof is this, because they being between the tropic and the equinoctial, the sun passeth twice in the year through their zenith over their heads, by means whereof they have two summers; and being so near the heat of the line they never lose the heat of the sun so much, but the fruits have their increase and continuance in the midst of winter. The island is wonderfully stored with goats and wild hens; and it hath salt also, without labour, save only that the people gather it into heaps; which continually in greater quantity is increased upon the sands by the flowing of the sea, and the receiving heat of the sun kerning the same. So that of the increase thereof they keep a continual traffic with their neighbours.

Amongst other things we found here a kind of fruit called cocos, which because it is not commonly known with us in England, I thought good to make some description of it. The tree beareth no leaves nor branches, but at the very top the fruit groweth in clusters, hard at the top of the stem of the tree, as big every several fruit as a man's head; but having taken off the uttermost bark, which you shall find to be very full of strings or sinews, as I may term them, you shall come to a hard shell, which may hold a quantity of liquor a pint commonly, or some a quart, and some less. Within that shell, of the thickness of half-an-inch good, you shall have a kind of hard substance and very white, no less good and sweet than almonds; within that again, a certain clear liquor which being drunk, you shall not only find it very delicate and sweet, but most comfortable and cordial.

After we had satisfied ourselves with some of these fruits, we marched further into the island, and saw great store of cabritos alive, which were so chased by the inhabitants that we could do no good towards our provision; but they had laid out, as it were to stop our mouths withal, certain old dried cabritos, which being but ill, and small and few, we made no account of. Being returned to our ships, our General departed hence the 31st of this month, and sailed by the island of Santiago, but far enough from the danger of the inhabitants, who shot and discharged at us three pieces; but they all fell short of us, and did us no harm. The island is fair and large, and, as it seemeth, rich and fruitful, and inhabited by the Portugals; but the mountains and high places of the island are said to be possessed by the Moors, who having been slaves to the Portugals, to ease themselves, made escape to the desert places of the island, where they abide with great strength. Being before this island, we espied two ships under sail, to the one of which we gave chase, and in the end boarded her with a ship-boat without resistance; which we found to be a good prize, and she yielded unto us good store of wine. Which prize our General committed to the custody of Master Doughty; and retaining the pilot, sent the rest away with his pinnace, giving them a butt of wine and some victuals, and their wearing clothes, and so they departed. The same night we came with the island called by the Portugals Ilha do Fogo, that is, the burning island; in the north side whereof is a consuming fire. The matter is said to be of sulphur, but, notwithstanding, it is like to be a commodious island, because the Portugals have built, and do inhabit there. Upon the south side thereof lieth a most pleasant and sweet island, the trees whereof are always green and fair to look upon; in respect whereof they call it Ilha Brava, that is, the brave island. From the banks thereof into the sea do run in many places reasonable streams of fresh water easy to come by, but there was no convenient road for our ships; for such was the depth that no ground could be had for anchoring. And it is reported that ground was never found in that place; so that the tops of Fogo burn not so high in the air, but the roots of Brava are quenched as low in the sea.

Being departed from these islands, we drew towards the line, where we were becalmed the space of three weeks, but yet subject to divers great storms, terrible lightnings and much thunder. But with this misery we had the commodity of great store of fish, as dolphins, bonitos, and flying-fishes, whereof some fell into our ships; wherehence they could not rise again for want of moisture, for when their wings are dry they cannot fly.

From the first day of our departure from the islands of Cape Verde, we sailed 54 days without sight of land. And the first land that we fell with was the coast of Brazil, which we saw the fifth of April, in the height of 33 degrees towards the pole Antarctic. And being discovered at sea by the inhabitants of the country, they made upon the coast great fires for a sacrifice (as we learned) to the devils; about which they use conjurations, making heaps of sand, and other ceremonies, that when any ship shall go about to stay upon their coast, not only sands may be gathered together in shoals in every place, but also that storms and tempests may arise, to the casting away of ships and men, whereof, as it is reported, there have been divers experiments.

The 7th day in a mighty great storm, both of lightning, rain, and thunder, we lost the canter, which we called the Christopher. But the eleventh day after, by our General's great care in dispersing his ships, we found her again, and the place where we met our General called the Cape of Joy, where every ship took in some water. Here we found a good temperature and sweet air, a very fair and pleasant country with an exceeding fruitful soil, where were great store of large and mighty deer, but we came not to the sight of any people; but travelling further into the country we perceived the footing of people in the clay ground, shewing that they were men of great stature. Being returned to our ships we weighed anchor, and ran somewhat further, and harboured ourselves between the rock and the main; where by means of the rock that brake the force of the sea, we rid very safe. And upon this rock we killed for our provision certain sea-wolves, commonly called with us seals. From hence we went our course to 36 degrees, and entered the great river of Plate, and ran into 54 and 53 1/2 fathoms of fresh water, where we filled our water by the ship's side; but our General finding here no good harborough, as he thought he should, bare out again to sea the 27th of April, and in bearing out we lost sight of our fly-boat wherein Master Doughty was. But we, sailing along, found a fair and reasonable good bay, wherein were many and the same profitable islands; one whereof had so many seals as would at the least have laden all our ships, and the rest of the islands are, as it were, laden with fowls, which is wonderful to see, and they of divers sorts. It is a place very plentiful of victuals, and hath in it no want of fresh water. Our General, after certain days of his abode in this place, being on shore in an island, the people of the country shewed themselves unto him, leaping and dancing, and entered into traffic with him, but they would not receive anything at any man's hands, but the same must be cast upon the ground. They are of clean, comely, and strong bodies, swift on foot, and seem to be very active.

The 18th of May, our General thought it needful to have a care of such ships as were absent; and therefore endeavouring to seek the fly-boat wherein Master Doughty was, we espied her again the next day. And whereas certain of our ships were sent to discover the coast and to search an harbour, the Marigold and the canter being employed in that business, came unto us and gave us understanding of a safe harbour that they had found. Wherewith all our ships bare, and entered it; where we watered and made new provision of victuals, as by seals, whereof we slew to the number of 200 or 300 in the space of an hour. Here our General in the Admiral rid close aboard the fly-boat, and took out of her all the provision of victuals and what else was in her, and hauling her to the land, set fire to her, and so burnt her to save the iron work. Which being a-doing, there came down of the country certain of the people naked, saving only about their waist the skin of some beast, with the fur or hair on, and something also wreathed on their heads. Their faces were painted with divers colours, and some of them had on their heads the similitude of horns, every man his bow, which was an ell in length, and a couple of arrows. They were very agile people and quick to deliver, and seemed not to be ignorant in the feats of wars, as by their order of ranging a few men might appear. These people would not of a long time receive anything at our hands; yet at length our General being ashore, and they dancing after their accustomed manner about him, and he once turning his back towards them, one leaped suddenly to him, and took his cap with his gold band off his head, and ran a little distance from him, and shared it with his fellow, the cap to one and the band to the other. Having despatched all our business in this place, we departed and set sail. And immediately upon our setting forth we lost our canter, which was absent three or four days; but when our General had her again, he took out the necessaries, and so gave her over, near to the Cape of Good Hope. The next day after, being the 20th of June, we harboured ourselves again in a very good harborough, called by Magellan, Port St. Julian, where we found a gibbet standing upon the main; which we supposed to be the place where Magellan did execution upon some of his disobedient and rebellious company.

The two and twentieth day our General went ashore to the main, and in his company John Thomas, and Robert Winterhie, Oliver the master-gunner, John Brewer, Thomas Hood, and Thomas Drake. And entering on land, they presently met with two or three of the country people. And Robert Winterhie having in his hands a bow and arrows, went about to make a shoot of pleasure, and, in his draught, his bowstring brake; which the rude savages taking as a token of war, began to bend the force of their bows against our company, and drove them to their shifts very narrowly.

In this port our General began to enquire diligently of the actions of Master Thomas Doughty, and found them not to be such as he looked for, but tending rather of contention or mutiny, or some other disorder, whereby, without redress, the success of the voyage might greatly have been hazarded. Whereupon the company was called together and made acquainted with the particulars of the cause, which were found, partly by Master Doughty's own confession, and partly by the evidence of the fact, to be true. Which when our General saw, although his private affection to Master Doughty, as he then in the presence of us all sacredly protested, was great, yet the care he had of the state of the voyage, of the expectation of her Majesty, and of the honour of his country did more touch him, as indeed it ought, than the private respect of one man. So that the cause being thoroughly heard, and all things done in good order as near as might be to the course of our laws in England, it was concluded that Master Doughty should receive punishment according to the quality of the offence. And he, seeing no remedy but patience for himself, desired before his death to receive the communion, which he did at the hands of Master Fletcher, our minister, and our General himself accompanied him in that holy action. Which being done, and the place of execution made ready, he having embraced our General, and taken his leave of all the company, with prayers for the Queen's Majesty and our realm, in quiet sort laid his head to the block, where he ended his life. This being done, our General made divers speeches to the whole company, persuading us to unity, obedience, love, and regard of our voyage; and for the better confirmation thereof, willed every many in the next Sunday following to prepare himself to the communion, as Christian brethren and friends ought to do. Which was done in very reverent sort; and so with good contentment every man went about his business.

The 17th of August we departed the port of St. Julian, and the 20th day we fell with the Strait of Magellan, going into the South Sea; at the cape or headland whereof we found the body of a dead man, whose flesh was clean consumed. The 21st day we entered the Strait, which we found to have many turnings, and as it were shuttings-up, as if there were no passage at all. By means whereof we had the wind often against us; so that some of the fleet recovering a cape or point of land, others should be forced to turn back again, and to come to an anchor where they could. In this Strait there be many fair harbours, with store of fresh water. But yet they lack their best commodity, for the water there is of such depth, that no man shall find ground to anchor in except it be in some narrow river or corner, or between some rocks; so that if any extreme blasts or contrary winds do come, whereunto the place is much subject, it carrieth with it no small danger. The land on both sides is very huge and mountainous; the lower mountains whereof, although they be monstrous and wonderful to look upon for their height, yet there are others which in height exceed them in a strange manner, reaching themselves above their fellows so high, that between them did appear three regions of clouds. These mountains are covered with snow. At both the southerly and easterly parts of the Strait there are islands, among which the sea hath his indraught into the Straits, even as it hath in the main entrance of the frete. This Strait is extreme cold, with frost and snow continually; the trees seem to stoop with the burden of the weather, and yet are green continually, and many good and sweet herbs do very plentifully grow and increase under them. The breadth of the Strait is in some places a league, in some other places two leagues and three leagues, and in some other four leagues; but the narrowest place hath a league over.

The 24th of August we arrived at an island in the Straits, where we found great store of fowl which could not fly, of the bigness of geese; whereof we killed in less than one day 3,000, and victualled ourselves thoroughly therewith. The 6th day of September we entered the South Sea at the cape or head shore. The 7th day we were driven by a great storm from the entering into the South Sea, 200 leagues and odd in longitude, and one degree to the southward of the Strait; in which height, and so many leagues to the westward, the 15th day of September, fell out the eclipse of the moon at the hour of six of the clock at night. But neither did the ecliptical conflict of the moon impair our state, nor her clearing again amend us a whit; but the accustomed eclipse of the sea continued in his force, we being darkened more than the moon sevenfold.[*]

[*] In this storm the Marigold went down with all hands.

From the bay which we called the Bay of Severing of Friends, we were driven back to the southward of the Straits in 57 degrees and a tierce; in which height we came to an anchor among the islands, having there fresh and very good water, with herbs of singular virtue. Not far from hence we entered another bay, where we found people, both men and women, in their canoes naked, and ranging from one island to another to seek their meat; who entered traffic with us for such things as they had. We returning hence northward again, found the third of October three islands, in one of which was such plenty of birds as is scant credible to report. The 8th day of October we lost sight of one of our consorts,[*] wherein Master Winter was; who, as then we supposed, was put by a storm into the Straits again. Which at our return home we found to be true, and he not perished, as some of our company feared. Thus being come into the height of the Straits again, we ran, supposing the coast of Chili to lie as the general maps have described it, namely north-west; which we found to lie and trend to the north-east and eastwards. Whereby it appeareth that this part of Chili hath not been truly hitherto discovered, or at the least not truly reported, for the space of twelve degrees at the least; being set down either of purpose to deceive, or of ignorant conjecture.

[*] The Elizabeth. Winter, having slight of the Admiral,
sailed home. The Golden Hind was thus left to pursue her
voyage alone.

We continuing our course, fell the 29th of November with an island called La Mocha, where we cast anchor; and our General, hoisting out our boat, went with ten of our company to shore. Where we found people whom the cruel and extreme dealings of the Spaniards have forced, for their own safety and liberty, to flee from the main, and to fortify themselves in this island. We being on land, the people came down to us to the water side with show of great courtesy, bringing to us potatoes, roots, and two very fat sheep; which our General received, and gave them other things for them, and had promised to have water there. But the next day repairing again to the shore, and sending two men a-land with barrels to fill water, the people taking them for Spaniards (to whom they use to show no favour if they take them) laid violent hands on them, and, as we think, slew them. Our General seeing this, stayed there no longer, but weighed anchor, and set sail towards the coast of Chili. And drawing towards it, we met near the shore an Indian in a canoa, who thinking us to have been Spaniards, came to us and told us, that at a place called Santiago, there was a great Spanish ship laden from the kingdom of Peru; for which good news our General gave him divers trifles. Whereof he was glad, and went along with us and brought us to the place, which is called the port of Valparaiso. When we came thither we found, indeed, the ship riding at anchor, having in her eight Spaniards and three negroes; who, thinking us to have been Spaniards, and their friends, welcomed us with a drum, and made ready a botija of wine of Chili to drink to us. But as soon as we were entered, one of our company called

Thomas Moon began to lay about him, and struck one of the Spaniards, and said unto him, Abaxo perro! that is in English, 'Go down, dog!' One of these Spaniards, seeing persons of that quality in those seas, crossed and blessed himself. But, to be short, we stowed them under hatches, all save one Spaniard, who suddenly and desperately leapt overboard into the sea, and swam ashore to the town of Santiago, to give them warning of our arrival.

They of the town, being not above nine households, presently fled away and abandoned the town. Our General manned his boat and the Spanish ship's boat, and went to the town; and, being come to it, we rifled it, and came to a small chapel, which we entered, and found therein a silver chalice, two cruets, and one altar-cloth, the spoil whereof our General gave to Master Fletcher, his minister. We found also in this town a warehouse stored with wine of Chili and many boards of cedar-wood; all which wine we brought away with us, and certain of the boards to burn for firewood. And so, being come aboard, we departed the haven, having first set all the Spaniards on land, saving one John Griego, a Greek born, whom our General carried with him as pilot to bring him into the haven of Lima.

When we were at sea our General rifled the ship, and found in her good store of the wine of Chili, and 25,000 pesos of very pure and fine gold of Valdivia, amounting in value to 37,000 ducats of Spanish money, and above. So, going on our course, we arrived next at a place called Coquimbo, where our General sent fourteen of his men on land to fetch water. But they were espied by the Spaniards, who came with 300 horsemen and 200 footmen, and slew one of our men with a piece. The rest came aboard in safety, and the Spaniards departed. We went on shore again and buried our man, and the Spaniards came down again with a flag of truce; but we set sail, and would not trust them. From hence we went to a certain port called Tarapaca; where, being landed, we found by the sea side a Spaniard lying asleep, who had lying by him thirteen bars of silver, which weighed 4,000 ducats Spanish. We took the silver and left the man. Not far from hence, going on land for fresh water, we met with a Spaniard and an Indian boy driving eight llamas or sheep of Peru, which are as big as asses; every of which sheep had on his back two bags of leather, each bag containing 50 lb. weight of fine silver. So that, bringing both the sheep and their burthen to the ships, we found in all the bags eight hundred weight of silver.

Herehence we sailed to a place called Arica; and, being entered the port, we found there three small barks, which we rifled, and found in one of them fifty-seven wedges of silver, each of them weighing about 20 lb. weight, and every of these wedges were of the fashion and bigness of a brickbat. In all these three barks, we found not one person. For they, mistrusting no strangers, were all gone a-land to the town, which consisteth of about twenty houses; which we would have ransacked if our company had been better and more in number. But our General, contented with the spoil of the ships, left the town and put off again to sea, and set sail for Lima, and, by the way, met with a small bark, which he boarded, and found in her good store of linen cloth. Whereof taking some quantity, he let her go.

To Lima we came the 13th of February; and, being entered the haven, we found there about twelve sail of ships lying fast moored at an anchor, having all their sails carried on shore; for the masters and merchants were here most secure, having never been assaulted by enemies, and at this time feared the approach of none such as we were. Our General rifled these ships, and found in one of them a chest full of reals of plate, and good store of silks and linen cloth; and took the chest into his own ship, and good store of the silks and linen. In which ship he had news of another ship called the Cacafuego, which was gone towards Payta, and that the same ship was laden with treasure. Whereupon we stayed no longer here, but, cutting all the cables of the ships in the haven, we let them drive wither they would, either to sea or to the shore; and with all speed we followed the Cacafuego toward Payta, thinking there to have found her. But before we arrived there she was gone from thence towards Panama; whom our General still pursued, and by the way met with a bark laden with ropes and tackle for ships, which he boarded and searched, and found in her 80 lb. weight of gold, and a crucifix of gold with goodly great emeralds set in it, which he took, and some of the cordage also for his own ship. From hence we departed, still following the Cacafuego; and our General promised our company that whosoever should first descry her should have his chain of gold for his good news. It fortuned that John Drake, going up into the top, descried her about three of the clock. And about six of the clock we came to her and boarded her, and shot at her three pieces of ordnance, and strake down her mizen; and, being entered, we found in her great riches, as jewels and precious stones, thirteen chests full of reals of plate, fourscore pound weight of gold, and six-and-twenty ton of silver. The place where we took this prize was called Cape de San Francisco, about 150 leagues [south] from Panama. The pilot's name of this ship was Francisco; and amongst other plate that our General found in this ship he found two very fair gilt bowls of silver, which were the pilot's. To whom our General said, Senor Pilot, you have here two silver cups, but I must needs have one of them; which the pilot, because he could not otherwise choose, yielded unto, and gave the other to the steward of our General's ship. When this pilot departed from us, his boy said thus unto our General: Captain, our ship shall be called no more the Cacafuego, but the Cacaplata, and your ship shall be called the Cacafuego. Which pretty speech of the pilot's boy ministered matter of laughter to us, both then and long after. When our General had done what he would with this Cacafuego, he cast her off, and we went on our course still towards the west; and not long after met with a ship laden with linen cloth and fine China dishes of white earth, and great store of China silks, of all which things we took as we listed. The owner himself of this ship was in her, who was a Spanish gentleman, from whom our General took a falcon of gold, with a great emerald in the breast thereof; and the pilot of the ship he took also with him, and so cast the ship off.

This pilot brought us to the haven of Guatulco, the town whereof, as he told us, had but 17 Spaniards in it. As soon as we were entered this haven, we landed, and went presently to the town and to the town-house; where we found a judge sitting in judgment, being associated with three other officers, upon three negroes that had conspired the burning of the town. Both which judges and prisoners we took, and brought them a-shipboard, and caused the chief judge to write his letter to the town to command all the townsmen to avoid, that we might safely water there. Which being done, and they departed, we ransacked the town; and in one house we found a pot, of the quantity of a bushel, full of reals of plate, which we brought to our ship. And here one Thomas Moon, one of our company, took a Spanish gentleman as he was flying out of the town; and, searching him, he found a chain of gold about him, and other jewels, which he took, and so let him go. At this place our General, among other Spaniards, set ashore his Portugal pilot which he took at the islands of Cape Verde out of a ship of St. Mary port, of Portugal. And having set them ashore we departed hence, and sailed to the island of Canno; where our General landed, and brought to shore his own ship, and discharged her, mended and graved her, and furnished our ship with water and wood sufficiently.

And while we were here we espied a ship and set sail after her, and took her, and found in her two pilots and a Spanish governor, going for the islands of the Philippinas. We searched the ship, and took some of her merchandises, and so let her go. Our General at this place and time, thinking himself, both in respect of his private injuries received from the Spaniards, as also of their contempts and indignities offered to our country and prince in general, sufficiently satisfied and revenged; and supposing that her Majesty at his return would rest contented with this service, purposed to continue no longer upon the Spanish coast, but began to consider and to consult of the best way for his country.

He thought it not good to return by the Straits, for two special causes; the one, lest the Spaniards should there wait and attend for him in great number and strength, whose hands, he, being left but one ship, could not possibly escape. The other cause was the dangerous situation of the mouth of the Straits in the South Sea; where continual storms reigning and blustering, as he found by experience, besides the shoals and sands upon the coast, he thought it not a good course to adventure that way. He resolved, therefore, to avoid these hazards, to go forward to the Islands of the Malucos, and therehence to sail the course of the Portugals by the Cape of Buena Esperanza. Upon this resolution he began to think of his best way to the Malucos, and finding himself, where he now was, becalmed, he saw that of necessity he must be forced to take a Spanish course; namely, to sail somewhat northerly to get a good wind. We therefore set sail, and sailed 600 leagues at the least for a good wind; and thus much we sailed from the 16th of April till the third of June.

The fifth of June, being in 43 degrees towards the pole Arctic, we found the air so cold, that our men being grievously pinched with the same, complained of the extremity thereof; and the further we went, the more the cold increased upon us. Whereupon we thought it best for that time to seek the land, and did so; finding it not mountainous but low plain land, till we came within 38 degrees towards the line. In which height it pleased God to send us into a fair and good bay, with a good wind to enter the same. In this bay we anchored; and the people of the country, having

their houses close by the water's side, shewed themselves unto us, and sent a prese[nt to our]
General. When they came unto us, they greatly wondered at the things that we bro[ught. Our]
General, according to his natural and accustomed humanity, courteously intreated [them, and]
liberally bestowed on them necessary things to cover their nakedness; whereupon t[hey supposed]
us to be gods, and would not be persuaded to the contrary. The presents which they sent to our
General, were feathers, and cauls of network. Their houses are digged round about with earth,
and have from the uttermost brims of the circle, clifts of wood set upon them, joining close
together at the top like a spire steeple, which by reason of that closeness are very warm. Their
bed is the ground with rushes strowed on it; and lying about the house, [they] have the fire in the
midst. The men go naked; the women take bulrushes, and kemb them after the manner of hemp,
and thereof make their loose garments, which being knit about their middles, hang down about
their hips, having also about their shoulders a skin of deer, with the hair upon it. These women
are very obedient and serviceable to their husbands.

After they were departed from us, they came and visited us the second time, and brought with them feathers and bags of tabacco for presents. And when they came to the top of the hill, at the bottom whereof we had pitched our tents, they stayed themselves; where one appointed for speaker wearied himself with making a long oration; which done, they left their bows upon the hill, and came down with their presents. In the meantime the women, remaining upon the hill, tormented themselves lamentably, tearing their flesh from their cheeks, whereby we perceived that they were about a sacrifice. In the meantime our General with his company went to prayer, and to reading of the Scriptures, at which exercise they were attentive, and seemed greatly to be affected with it; but when they were come unto us, they restored again unto us those things which before we bestowed upon them. The news of our being there being spread through the country, the people that inhabited round about came down, and amongst them the king himself, a man of a goodly stature, and comely personage, and with many other tall and warlike men; before whose coming were sent two ambassadors to our General, to signify that their king was coming, in doing of which message, their speech was continued about half an hour. This ended, they by signs requested our General to send something by their hand to their king, as a token that his coming might be in peace. Wherein our General having satisfied them, they returned with glad tidings to their king, who marched to us with a princely majesty, the people crying continually after their manner; and as they drew near unto us, so did they strive to behave themselves in their actions with comeliness. In the fore-front was a man of goodly personage, who bare the sceptre or mace before the king; whereupon hanged two crowns, a less and a bigger, with three chains of a marvellous length. The crowns were made of knit work, wrought artificially with feathers of divers colours. The chains were made of a bony substance, and few be the persons among them that are admitted to wear them; and of that number also the persons are stinted, as some ten, some twelve, etc. Next unto him which bare the sceptre, was the king himself, with his guard about his person, clad with coney skins, and other skins. After them followed the naked common sort of people, every one having his face painted, some with white, some with black, and other colours, and having in their hands one thing or another for a present. Not so much as their children, but they also brought their presents.

In the meantime our General gathered his men together, and marched within his fenced place, making, against their approaching, a very warlike show. They being trooped together in their order, and a general salutation being made, there was presently a general silence. Then he that bare the sceptre before the king, being informed by another, whom they assigned to that office, with a manly and lofty voice proclaimed that which the other spake to him in secret, continuing half an hour. Which ended, and a general Amen, as it were, given, the king with the whole number of men and women, the children excepted, came down without any weapon; who, descending to the foot of the hill, set themselves in order. In coming towards our bulwarks and tents, the sceptre-bearer began a song, observing his measures in a dance, and that with a stately countenance; whom the king with his guard, and every degree of persons, following, did in like manner sing and dance, saving only the women, which danced and kept silence. The General permitted them to enter within our bulwark, where they continued their song and dance a reasonable time. When they had satisfied themselves, they made signs to our General to sit down; to whom the king and divers others made several orations, or rather supplications, that he would take their province and kingdom into his hand, and become their king, making signs that they would resign unto him their right and title of the whole land, and become his subjects. In which, to persuade us the better, the king and the rest, with one consent, and with great reverence, joyfully singing a song, did set the crown upon his head, enriched his neck with all their chains, and offered him many other things, honouring him by the name of Hioh, adding thereunto, as it seemed, a sign of triumph; which thing our General thought not meet to reject, because he knew not what honour and profit it might be to our country. Wherefore in the name, and to the use of her Majesty, he took the sceptre, crown, and dignity of the said country into his hands, wishing that the riches and treasure thereof might so conveniently be transported to the enriching of her kingdom at home, as it aboundeth in the same.

The common sort of people, leaving the king and his guard with our General, scattered themselves together with their sacrifices among our people, taking a diligent view of every person: and such as pleased their fancy (which were the youngest), they enclosing them about offered their sacrifices unto them with lamentable weeping, scratching and tearing their flesh from their faces with their nails, whereof issued abundance of blood. But we used signs to them of disliking this, and stayed their hands from force, and directed them upwards to the living God, whom only they ought to worship. They shewed unto us their wounds, and craved help of them at our hands; whereupon we gave them lotions, plaisters, and ointments agreeing to the state of their griefs, beseeching God to cure their diseases. Every third day they brought their sacrifices unto us, until they understood our meaning, that we had no pleasure in them; yet they could not be long absent from us, but daily frequented our company to the hour of our departure, which departure seemed so grievous unto them, that their joy was turned into sorrow. They entreated us, that being absent we would remember them, and by stealth provided a sacrifice, which we misliked.

Our necessary business being ended, our General with his company travelled up into the country to their villages, where we found herds of deer by a thousand in a company, being most large, and fat of body. We found the whole country to be a warren of a strange kind of coneys; their bodies in bigness as be the Barbary coneys, their heads as the heads of ours, the feet of a want [mole], and the tail of a rat, being of great length. Under her chin is on either side a bag, into the which she gathereth her meat, when she hath filled her belly abroad. The people eat their bodies, and make great account of their skins, for their king's coat was made of them. Our General called this country Nova Albion, and that for two causes; the one in respect of the white banks and cliffs, which lie towards the sea, and the other, because it might have some affinity with our country in name, which sometime was so called. There is no part of earth here to be taken up, wherein there is not some probable show of gold or silver.

At our departure hence our General set up a monument of our being there, as also of her Majesty's right and title to the same; namely a plate, nailed upon a fair great post, whereupon was engraved her Majesty's name, the day and year of our arrival there, with the free giving up of the province and people into her Majesty's hands, together with her Highness' picture and arms, in a piece of six pence of current English money, under the plate, whereunder was also written the name of our General.

It seemeth that the Spaniards hitherto had never been in this part of the country, neither did ever discover the land by many degrees to the southwards of this place.

After we had set sail from hence, we continued without sight of land till the 13th day of October following, which day in the morning we fell with certain islands eight degrees to the northward of the line, from which islands came in a great number of canoas, having in some of them four, in some six, and in some also fourteen men, bringing with them cocos and other fruits. Their canoas were hollow within and cut with great art and cunning, being very smooth within and without, and bearing a gloss as if it were a horn daintily burnished, having a prow and a stern of one sort, yielding inward circle-wise, being of a great height, and full of certain white shells for a bravery; and on each side of them lie out two pieces of timber about a yard and a half long, more or less, according to the smallness or bigness of the boat. These people have the nether part of their ears cut into a round circle, hanging down very low upon their cheeks, whereon they hang things of a reasonable weight. The nails of their hands are an inch long, their teeth are as black as pitch, and they renew them often, by eating of an herb with a kind of powder, which they always carry about them in a cane for the same purpose.

Leaving this island the night after we fell with it, the 18th of October we lighted upon divers others, some whereof made a great show of inhabitants. We continued our course by the islands of Tagulanda, Zelon, and Zewarra, being friends to the Portugals, the first whereof hath growing in it great store of cinnamon. The 14th of November we fell in with the islands of Maluco. Which day at night (having directed our course to run with Tidore) in coasting along the island of Mutyr, belonging to the king of Ternate, his deputy or vice-king seeing us at sea, come with his canoa to us without all fear, and came aboard; and after some conference with our General, willed him in any wise to run in with Ternate, and not with Tidore, assuring him that the king would be glad of his coming, and would be ready to do what he would require, for which purpose he himself would that night be with the king, and tell him the news. With whom if he once dealt, we should find that if he went to Tidore before he came to Ternate, the king would have nothing to do with us, because he held the Portugal as his enemy. Whereupon our General resolved to run with Ternate. Where the next morning early we came to anchor; at which time our General sent a messenger to the king, with a velvet cloak for a present and token of his coming to lie in peace, and that he required nothing but traffic and exchange of merchandise, whereof he had good store, in such things as he wanted.

In the meantime the vice-king had been with the king according to his promise, signifying unto him what good things he might receive from us by traffic. Whereby the king was moved with great liking towards us, and sent to our General, with special message, that he should have what things he needed and would require, with peace and friendship; and moreover that he would yield himself and the right of his island to be at the pleasure and commandment of so famous a prince as we served. In token whereof he sent to our General a signet; and within short time after came in his own person, with boats and canoas, to our ship, to bring her into a better and safer road than she was in at that present. In the meantime, our General's messenger, being come to the Court, was met by certain noble personages with great solemnity, and brought to the king, at whose hands he was most friendly and graciously entertained.

The king, purposing to come to our ship, sent before four great and large canoas, in every one whereof were certain of his greatest states (men of property or estate) that were about him, attired in white lawn of cloth of Calicut, having over their heads, from the one end of the canoa to the other, a covering of thin perfumed mats, borne up with a frame made of reeds for the same use; under which every one did sit in his order according to his dignity, to keep him from the heat of the sun; divers of whom being of good age and gravity, did make an ancient and fatherly show. There were also divers young and comely men attired in white, as were the others; the rest were soldiers, which stood in comely order round about on both sides. Without whom sat the rowers in certain galleries; which being three on a side all along the canoas, did lie off from the side thereof three or four yards, one being orderly built lower than another, in every of which galleries were the number of fourscore rowers. These canoas were furnished with warlike munition, every man for the most part having his sword and target, with his dagger, beside other weapons, as lances, calivers, darts, bows and arrows; also every canoa had a small cast base mounted at the least one full yard upon a stock set upright. Thus coming near our ship, in order, they rowed about us one after another, and passing by, did their homage with great solemnity; the great personages beginning with great gravity and fatherly countenances, signifying that the king had sent them to conduct our ship into a better road. Soon after the king himself repaired, accompanied with six grave and ancient persons, who did their obeisance with marvellous humility. The king was a man of tall stature, and seemed to be much delighted with the sound of our music; to whom, as also to his nobility, our General gave presents, wherewith they were passing well contented.

At length the king craved leave of our General to depart, promising the next day to come aboard, and in the meantime to send us such victuals as were necessary for our provision. So that the same night we received of them meal, which they call sagu, made of the tops of certain trees, tasting in the mouth like sour curds, but melteth like sugar, whereof they make certain cakes, which may be kept the space of ten years, and yet then good to be eaten. We had of them store of rice, hens, unperfect and liquid sugar, sugar-canes, and a fruit which they call figo (plantains), with store of cloves.

The king having promised to come aboard, brake his promise, but sent his brother to make his excuse, and to entreat our General to come on shore, offering himself pawn aboard for his safe return. Whereunto our General consented not, upon mislike conceived of the breach of his promise; the whole company also utterly refusing it. But to satisfy him, our General sent certain of his gentlemen to the Court, to accompany the king's brother, reserving the vice-king for their safe return. They were received of another brother of the king's, and other states, and were conducted with great honour to the castle. The place that they were brought unto was a large and fair house, where were at the least a thousand persons assembled.

The king being yet absent, there sat in their places 60 grave personages, all which were said to be of the king's council. There were besides four grave persons, apparelled all in red, down to the ground, and attired on their heads like the Turks; and these were said to be Romans [probably Greeks] and ligiers [resident agents] there to keep continual traffic with the people of Ternate. There were also two Turks ligiers in this place, and one Italian. The king at last came in guarded with twelve lances, covered over with a rich canopy with embossed gold. Our men, accompanied with one of their captains called Moro, rising to meet him, he graciously did welcome and entertain them. He was attired after the manner of the country, but more sumptuously than the rest. From his waist down to the ground was all cloth of gold, and the same very rich; his legs were bare, but on his feet were a pair of shoes, made of Cordovan skin. In the attire of his head were finely wreathed hooped rings of gold, and about his neck he had a chain of perfect gold, the links whereof were great, and one fold double. On his fingers he had six very fair jewels; and sitting in his chair of state, at his right hand stood a page with a fan in his hand, breathing and gathering the air to the king. The same was in length two foot, and in breadth one foot, set with eight sapphires richly embroidered, and knit to a staff three foot in length, by the which the page did hold and move it. Our gentlemen having delivered their message and received order accordingly, were licensed to depart, being safely conducted back again by one of the king's council. This island is the chief of all the islands of Maluco, and the king hereof is king of 70 islands besides. The king with his people are Moors in religion, observing certain new moons, with fastings; during which fasts they neither eat nor drink in the day, but in the night.

After that our gentlemen were returned, and that we had here by the favour of the king received all necessary things that the place could yield us; our General considering the great distance, and how far he was yet off from his country, thought it not best here to linger the time any longer, but weighing his anchors, set out of the island, and sailed to a certain little island to the southwards of Celebes, where we graved our ship, and continued there, in that and other businesses, 26 days. This island is thoroughly grown with wood of a large and high growth, very straight, and without boughs, save only in the head or top, whose leaves are not much differing from our broom in England. Amongst these trees night by night, through the whole land, did shew themselves an infinite swarm of fiery worms flying in the air, whose bodies being no bigger than our common English flies, make such a show and light as if every twig or tree had been a burning candle. In this place breedeth also wonderful store of bats, as big as large hens. Of crayfishes also here wanted no plenty, and they of exceeding bigness, one whereof was sufficient for four hungry stomachs at a dinner, being also very good and restoring meat, whereof we had experience: and they dig themselves holes in the earth like coneys.

When we had ended our business here we weighed, and set sail to run for the Malucos. But having at that time a bad wind, and being amongst the islands, with much difficulty we recovered to the northward of the island of Celebes; where by reason of contrary winds, not able to continue our course to run westwards, we were enforced to alter the same to the southward again, finding that course also to be very hard and dangerous for us, by reason of infinite shoals which lie off and among the islands; whereof we had too much trial, to the hazard and danger of our ship and lives. For, of all other days, upon the 9th of January, in the year 1579 [1580], we ran suddenly upon a rock, where we stuck fast from eight of the clock at night till four of the clock in the afternoon the next day, being indeed out of all hope to escape the danger. But our General, as he had always hitherto shewed himself courageous, and of a good confidence in the mercy and protection of God, so now he continued in the same. And lest he should seem to perish wilfully, both he and we did our best endeavour to save ourselves; which it pleased God so to bless, that in the end we cleared ourselves most happily of the danger.

We lighted our ship upon the rocks of three tons of cloves, eight pieces of ordnance, and certain meal and beans; and then the wind, as it were in a moment by the special grace of God, changing from the starboard to the larboard of the ship, we hoisted our sails, and the happy gale drove our ship off the rock into the sea again, to the no little comfort of all our hearts, for which we gave God such praise and thanks, as so great a benefit required.

The 8th of February following, we fell with the fruitful island of Barateve, having in the mean time suffered many dangers by winds and shoals. The people of this island are comely in body and stature, and of a civil behaviour, just in dealing, and courteous to strangers; whereof we had the experience sundry ways, they being most glad of our presence, and very ready to relieve our wants in those things which their country did yield. The men go naked, saving their heads and loins, every man having something or other hanging at their ears. Their women are covered from the middle down to the foot, wearing a great number of bracelets upon their arms; for some had eight upon each arm, being made some of bone, some of horn, and some of brass, the lightest whereof, by our estimation, weighed two ounces apiece. With this people linen-cloth is good merchandise, and of good request; whereof they make rolls for their heads, and girdles to wear about them. Their island is both rich and fruitful; rich in gold, silver, copper, and sulphur, wherein they seem skilful and expert, not only to try the same, but in working it also artificially into any form and fashion that pleaseth them. Their fruits be divers and plentiful; as nutmegs, ginger, long pepper, lemons, cucumbers, cocos, figu, sagu, with divers other sorts. And among all the rest we had one fruit, in bigness, form and husk, like a bay berry, hard of substance and pleasant of taste, which being sudden becometh soft, and is a most good and wholesome victual; whereof we took reasonable store, as we did also of the other fruits and spices. So that to confess a truth, since the time that we first set out of our country of England, we happened upon no place, Ternate only excepted, wherein we found more comforts and better means of refreshing.

At our departure from Barateve, we set our course for Java Major; where arriving, we found great courtesy, and honourable entertainment. This island is governed by five kings, whom they call Rajah; as Rajah Donaw, and Rajah Mang Bange, and Rajah Cabuccapollo, which live as having one spirit and one mind. Of these five we had four a-shipboard at once, and two or three often. They are wonderfully delighted in coloured clothes, as red and green; the upper part of their bodies are naked, save their heads, whereupon they wear a Turkish roll as do the Maluccians. From the middle downward they wear a pintado of silk, trailing upon the ground, in colour as they best like. The Maluccians hate that their women should be seen of strangers; but these offer them of high courtesy, yea, the kings themselves. The people are of goodly stature and warlike, well provided of swords and targets, with daggers, all being of their own work, and most artificially done, both in tempering their metal, as also in the form; whereof we bought reasonable store. They have an house in every village for their common assembly; every day they meet twice, men, women, and children, bringing with them such victuals as they think good, some fruits, some rice boiled, some hens roasted, some sagu, having a table made three foot from the ground, whereon they set their meat, that every person sitting at the table may eat, one rejoicing in the company of another. They boil their rice in an earthen pot, made in form of a sugar loaf, being full of holes, as our pots which we water our gardens withal, and it is open at the great end, wherein they get their rice dry, without any moisture. In the mean time they have ready another great earthen pot, as set fast in a furnace, boiling full of water, whereinto they put their pot with rice, by such measure, that they swelling become soft at the first, and by their swelling stopping the holes of the pot, admit no more water to enter, but the more they are boiled, the harder and more firm substance they become. So that in the end they are a firm and good bread, of the which with oil, butter, sugar, and other spices, they make divers sorts of meats very pleasant of taste, and nourishing to nature.

Not long before our departure, they told us that not far off there were such great ships as ours, wishing us to beware; upon this our captain would stay no longer. From Java Major we sailed for the Cape of Good Hope, which was the first land we fell withal; neither did we touch with it, or any other land, until we came to Sierra Leona, upon the coast of Guinea; notwithstanding we ran hard aboard the cape, finding the report of the Portugals to be most false who affirm that it is the most dangerous cape of the world, never without intolerable storms and present danger to travellers which come near the same. This cape is a most stately thing, and the fairest cape we saw in the whole circumference of the earth, and we passed by it the 18th of June. From thence we continued our course to Sierra Leona, on the coast of Guinea, where we arrived the 22nd of July, and found necessary provisions, great store of elephants, oysters upon trees of one kind [mangrove], spawning and increasing infinitely, the oyster suffering no bud to grow. We departed thence the four and twentieth day.

We arrived in England the third of November, 1580, being the third year of our departure."

Bibliography

Bawlf, Samuel (2003) *The Secret Voyage of Sir Francis Drake, 1577–1580* Walker & Company

Hughes-Hallett, Lucy (2004) *Heroes: A History of Hero Worship* Alfred A. Knopf, New York.

Kelsey, Harry (1998) *Sir Francis Drake, the Queen's Pirate.*

Konstam, Angus and Peter Dennis (2011) *The Great Expedition – Sir Francis Drake on the Spanish Main 1585-86.*

Nichols, Philip (2010) *Sir Francis Drake.*

Pretty, Francis (2012) *Sir Francis Drake's Famous Voyage Round the World.*

Rodger, N. A. M. (1997) *The Safeguard of the Sea; A Naval History of Britain 660-1649.*

Stafford, Sir Julian (2012) Sir Francis Drake.

Sugden, John. (2012) *Sir Francis Drake.*

Wilson, Derek (1977) *The World Encompassed: Drake's Great Voyage, 1577–80*.

Captain Henry Morgan

Chapter 1: Young Morgan

Henry Morgan was born near Cardiff, Wales, in about 1635, the first son of Robert Morgan and his wife. The elder Morgan was a country squire and had lived at the family home, Llanrumney Hall, since his birth in 1615. He was also a distant cousin of the king, having descended from a younger son of a previous monarch.

Little is known about Henry Morgan's early years. It is known that he had a sister named Catherine, but no other siblings that lived to adulthood, and based on his own words it seems he wasn't terribly interested in education. Years later, when the King appointed him to a post, Morgan would say, "The office of Judge Admiral was not given to me for my understanding of the business better than others, nor for the profitableness thereof, for I left the schools too young to be a great proficient in that or other laws, and have been more used to the pike than the book."

While the particulars of Morgan's early years will probably never be fully known, the era he grew up in was significant in shaping him. Henry grew up during a period marked by civil war, with the King and Parliament setting many houses in England against each other, including the Morgans. Henry's father Robert and uncle Edward supported the King, but their younger brother Thomas fought on the side of Parliament. By the time Henry was old enough to form his own opinion, Parliamentarians had won and Edward had fled for Germany, while Thomas would go on to become Governor of Gloucester in 1645. Edward would later resurface as the Lieutenant Governor of Jamaica in 1665.

Portrait of Thomas Morgan

There is no record of what Robert Morgan did, but his son decided to throw his lot in with the winners, which led to Robert disowning Henry. With a self-avowed education in arms over books, Henry decided farming was not for him anyway and sailed off for the Barbados around 1655.

Henry was still a young adult when he made his way to the Barbados, and without the help of his family, he apparently started his new life as an indentured servant. Though Morgan would actually win a libel suit against his surgeon, Alexandre Exquemelin, who made that claim in his seminal pirate history *The Pirates of Panama*, documents indicate that as of February 1655, one indentured servant in the area was "Henry Morgan of Abergavenny, Labourer, Bound to Timothy

Tounsend of Bristol, Cutler, for three years, to serve in Barbados on the like Condiciouns."

After his time as an indentured servant was up, Exquemelin claimed that Morgan "betook himself to Jamaica, there to seek new fortunes: here he found two vessels of pirates ready to go to sea; and being destitute of employment, he went with them, with intent to follow the exercises of that sort of people: he soon learned their manner of living, so exactly, that having performed three or four voyages with profit and success, he agreed with some of his comrades, who had got by the same voyages a little money, to join stocks, and buy a ship. The vessel being bought, they unanimously chose him captain and commander." However, modern scholars now believe that Exquemelin's chain of events was wrong, and that as soon as he had finished his indentured servitude, Morgan joined Oliver Cromwell's forces planning to invade Hispaniola. Instead, it's now believed that his unit fought in the battle of Santo Domingo, which failed to secure the island, but then subsequently sailed for Jamaica and successfully took that island for England and the Lord Protectorate. Cromwell's forces were soon disbanded, however, when Charles II was restored to the English throne in 1660. This would allow Henry's uncle Edward to return with his family from Germany and be appointed Lieutenant-Governor of Jamaica by the King.

Fortunately, the King's restoration also helped smooth relations between Henry and the rest of his family. He married Edward's daughter, Mary, and the two lived near her father's home on the island. Meanwhile, Edward soon rose to the rank of captain and fought with Christopher Myngs during the early 1660s, becoming captain of his own ship in 1661. He later sailed with John Morris to conquer Honduras and Granada, and in early 1665, he sailed with a fleet of ships sent by the Jamaican governor, Lord Windsor, to plunder the coast of Mexico.

Edward's nephew Henry would follow in his footsteps soon enough, but shortly after 1665, England shifted against piracy and Lord Windsor was ordered to stop the men he had been sending out to plunder Spanish ships. When he refused, he was recalled to England, and Sir Thomas Modyford was appointed in his place. Though Modyford initially gave lip service to stopping piracy in the Caribbean, his actions were inconsistent with his promises. In the fall of 1665, he sent a group of privateers, including Henry Morgan, to attack and secure Santa Catalina and Providence for the English. When the privateer leading this expedition, Edward Mansfield, was captured and killed, Morgan was chose by the men to take his place as admiral of the fleet. He was still only about 30 years old.

Chapter 2: Captain Morgan

Modyford was warned again and again by the Crown that England and Spain were now at peace, and that any English ship attacking a Spanish one was to be seized and the men prosecuted. However, he continued to ignore the instructions coming to him from across the Atlantic, and he kept issuing letters of marque to any English sea captain interested in defending Jamaica by attacking and plundering Spanish ships. Among those happy to receive such letters was Captain Henry Morgan.

In addition to his continued insubordination, Modyford eventually came to believe that the Dutch were also a threat to Jamaica's safety. Instead of stopping the privateers, he issued a letter of marque to Captain Edward Mansvelt, authorizing him to take 15 ships and 600 men to attack and destroy Curacao, a Dutch settlement on the South American coast. For his part, Mansvelt appointed Morgan as his vice-admiral, and the two set off with their fleet of ships, bound to eliminate the Dutch threat in that part of the New World.

A funny thing happened along the way, however. When the ships were out to sea, the admiral and his captains began discussing their orders and came to the conclusion that there was more money to be made by attacking one of the Spanish settlements. They put the question to a vote, and the majority of the crew agreed that they should abandon their plans against Curacao and instead attack the Spanish on Providence Island. Those captains and men who did not agree to this plan were allowed to leave and return to Jamaica, where they wasted no time telling the governor what had become of his expedition.

Since they were now at peace with the British, the Spanish living on Providence Island were woefully unprepared for the coming attack by Morgan and Mansvelt, forcing them to immediately surrender all their forts and withdraw into the countryside. At this point, Morgan began to earn his reputation as one of the most ruthless pirates of his day. He and Mansvelt destroyed all the forts on the island, save one, where they housed their own buccaneers. They then left a group of their pirates behind to hold the island and gather together all the treasure they could find, while they sailed on to Coast Rica looking for their next victim. When they saw a Spanish man-of-war anchored nearby, they decided to fight to claim Providence as their own island, completely run by pirates.

Exquemelin described how the pirates ransacked Providence and a nearby island:

"This fleet arrived, not long after, at the isle of St. Catherine, near the continent of Costa Rica, latitude 12 deg. 30 min. and distant thirty-five leagues from the river Chagre. Here they made their first descent, landing most of their men, who soon forced the garrison that kept the island to surrender all the forts and castles thereof; which they instantly demolished, except one, wherein they placed a hundred men of their own party, and all the slaves they had taken from the Spaniards: with the rest of their men they marched to another small island, so near St. Catherine's, that with a bridge they made in a few days, they passed thither, taking with them all the ordnance they had taken on the great island. Having ruined with fire and sword both the islands, leaving necessary orders at the said castle, they put to sea again, with their Spanish prisoners; yet these they set ashore not long after, on the firm land, near Puerto Velo: then they cruised on Costa Rica, till they came to the river Colla, designing to pillage all the towns in those parts, thence to pass to the village of Nata, to do the same."

In order to hold onto their gains, they would need more ships and men to defend the island, so they returned to Jamaica to recruit reinforcements. Rather than try to stop Morgan and his men, Governor Modyford decided to help them establish an English outpost in Spanish territory, figuring that a settlement on Providence Island, right in the middle of Spanish shipping lanes, could harass Spanish trade. He appointed his own brother, Sir James Modyford, governor of Providence, thereby giving a stamp of respectability and legality to Mansvelt and Morgan's plan.

However, there was still one major problem with the plan: Morgan and his men were pirates, not soldiers. When the Spanish returned to retake their island, most of the pirates grabbed all the plunder they could carry and left. They were only interested in lining their own pockets, not in defending an island for their King. But unfortunately for Mansvelt and some of the pirate garrison, the arriving Spanish heavily outnumbered them. Exquemelin quoted one Spaniard in describing the scene:

> "On Friday the 13th, three negroes, from the enemy, came swimming aboard our admiral; these brought intelligence that all the pirates upon the island were only seventy-two in number, and that they were under a great consternation, seeing such considerable forces come against them. With this intelligence, the Spaniards resolved to land, and advance towards the fortresses, which ceased not to fire as many great guns against them as they possibly could; which were answered in the same manner on our side, till dark night. On Sunday, the 15th, the day of the Assumption of our Lady, the weather being very calm and clear, the Spaniards began to advance thus: The ship St. Vincent, riding admiral, discharged two whole broadsides on the battery called the Conception; the ship St. Peter, that was vice-admiral, discharged likewise her guns against the other battery named St. James: meanwhile, our people landed in small boats, directing their course towards the point of the battery last mentioned, and thence they marched towards the gate called Cortadura. Lieutenant Francis de Cazeres, being desirous to view the strength of the enemy, with only fifteen men, was compelled to retreat in haste, by reason of the great guns, which played so furiously on the place where he stood; they shooting, not only pieces of iron, and small bullets, but also the organs of the church, discharging in every shot threescore pipes at a time.
>
> Notwithstanding this heat of the enemy, Captain Don Joseph Ramirez de Leyva, with sixty men, made a strong attack, wherein they fought on both sides very desperately, till at last he overcame, and forced the pirates to surrender the fort.
>
> On the other side, Captain John Galeno, with ninety men, passed over the hills, to advance that way towards the castle of St. Teresa. Meanwhile Major Don Joseph Sanchez Ximenes, as commander-in-chief, with the rest of his men, set forth from the battery of St. James, passing the port with four boats, and landing, in despite of the enemy. About this same time, Captain John Galeno began to advance with the men he led to the forementioned fortress; so that our men made three attacks on three several

sides, at one and the same time, with great courage; till the pirates seeing many of their men already killed, and that they could in no manner subsist any longer, retreated towards Cortadura, where they surrendered, themselves and the whole island, into our hands. Our people possessed themselves of all, and set up the Spanish colours, as soon as they had rendered thanks to God Almighty for the victory obtained on such a signalized day. The number of dead were six men of the enemies, with many wounded, and seventy prisoners: on our side was only one man killed, and four wounded.

There were found on the island eight hundred pounds of powder, two hundred and fifty pounds of small bullets, with many other military provisions. Among the prisoners were taken also, two Spaniards, who had bore arms under the English against his Catholic Majesty: these were shot to death the next day, by order of the major. The 10th day of September arrived at the isle an English vessel, which being seen at a great distance by the major, he ordered Le Sieur Simon, who was a Frenchman, to go and visit the said ship, and tell them that were on board, that the island belonged still to the English. He performed the command, and found in the said ship only fourteen men, one woman and her daughter, who were all instantly made prisoners."

Among the dead was Mansvelt, and when word reached London of this latest debacle, the Crown again reprimanded Modyford and ordered him to reel in his pirates. Again, Modyford ignored those orders.

Given the presence of Captain Morgan at Providence, there have long been rumors that he buried treasure on the island, the classic pirate stereotype. Of course, there's no reason to assume that he would bury treasure on an island inhabited by his enemies. But Morgan's attack on Providence and his temporary transformation of the island into a pirates' nest would have a long enough legacy that when privateer-turned-pirate Henry Jennings helped turn an uninhabited island into a lawless trading town consisting mostly of pirates and other traders, it was called New Providence. Like Morgan's Old Providence, New Providence was the perfect spot for pirates because it was close to the commercial shipping lanes near the Florida Straits, it was big enough for dozens of ships to dock, and it was shallow enough that the various imperial navies of the European empires had to avoid giving chase too far. Author George Woodbury noted New Providence was "a place of temporary sojourn and refreshment for a literally floating population," and that its residents "were the piratical camp followers, the traders, and the hangers-on…"

While it was obviously treason to ignore the instructions of the King of England, Modyford soon had good reason to be thankful for his close ties to the pirates in his part of the world. Word soon reached his ears that Spain was sending a fleet of ships to attack and take Jamaica, in retaliation for his privateers' actions against Providence. When Modyford heard this, he acted quickly, commissioning Morgan to assemble a fleet to sail around the local island and capture as many Spanish citizens as possible. While Modyford claimed that these actions were necessary to protect British interests in the New World, he was also undoubtedly pleased with what would be his share of the booty that Morgan and his men stole while capturing the citizens. He was also hoping that preserving the King's interests in the Caribbean would return him to the Crown's good graces.

In putting together the crews for the ten ships he would be sailing against the Spanish, Morgan showed the genius that would make him one of the most legendary pirates in the world. Traditionally, a captain in his position would post flyers around a town, inviting anyone interested in adventure and plunder to join his fleet. However, Morgan reasoned that this would likely only attract those pirates with nothing better to do. Instead, Morgan sailed his flagship into ports famous for housing the most daring and bloodthirsty pirates in the Americas. He would then dress in his best clothes and finest jewels and go ashore, attracting much attention and distinguishing himself as an obviously successful man. Before long, men were approaching him, sharing their own credentials, and asking that they might join him. With his pick of all the best pirates in each port, Morgan soon assembled a crew of 500 of the best and brightest buccaneers in the New World.

Instead of trying to retake Providence Island, Morgan set his sights on a much larger target. Once that crew was assembled, Morgan sailed for Cuba, initially hoping to take Havana. However, as he made his way along the coast, attacking every small sea town he came across, he soon became convinced that he lacked the manpower to actually take Havana. Exquemelin described the size of Havana, which at the time was the settlement's biggest city:

"The city and port De la Havanna lies between the north and west side of the island: this is one of the strongest places of the West Indies; its jurisdiction extends over the other half of the island; the chief places under it being Santa Cruz on the north side, and La Trinidad on the south. Hence is transported huge quantities of tobacco, which is sent to New Spain and Costa Rica, even as far as the South Sea, besides many ships laden with this commodity, that are consigned to Spain and other parts of Europe, not only in the leaf, but in rolls. This city is defended by three castles, very great and strong, two of which lie towards the port, and the other is seated on a hill that commands the town. It is esteemed to contain about ten thousand families."

Instead of attacking Havana, Morgan turned his sights on Puerto Principe, but on his way there, his fleet was stymied by heavy storms that blew them off course. They eventually landed on the south side of the island, far from their planned destination, and by this time, the men were out of food and water and were forced to go ashore in search of provisions. While they were searching the island, they came across a group of Frenchmen who had also been forced ashore by the weather. The two groups shared a mutual need for food and water and thus decided to combine their forces. After a few days of working together, the English pirates shared their plans to attack Puerto Principe, and the Frenchmen agreed to help them.

Their plans were somewhat thwarted, however, when a Spanish prisoner Morgan had been holding escaped and made his way to Puerto Principe ahead of them. He warned the inhabitants of Morgan's plans and encouraged them to hide in the hills where the pirates would not be able to find them. As a result, by the time Morgan and his men arrived, there were neither people nor significant treasure left in the city. This enraged Morgan and his crew so much that they resorted to horrendous measures upon taking the town:

"Captain Morgan, with his men, now on the march, found the avenues to the town unpassable; hereupon they took their way through the wood, traversing it with great difficulty, whereby they escaped divers ambuscades; at last they came to the plain, from its figure called by the Spaniards La Savanna, or the Sheet. The governor seeing them come, detached a troop of horse to charge them in the front, thinking to disperse them, and to pursue them with his main body: but this design succeeded not, for the pirates marched in very good order, at the sound of their drums, and with flying colours; coming near the horse they drew into a semicircle, and so advanced towards the Spaniards, who charged them valiantly for a while; but the pirates being very dextrous at their arms, and their governor, with many of their companions, being killed, they retreated towards the wood, to save themselves with more advantage; but before they could reach it, most of them were unfortunately killed by the pirates. Thus they left the victory to these new-come enemies, who had no considerable loss of men in the battle, and but very few wounded. The skirmish lasted four hours: they entered the town not without great resistance of such as were within, who defended themselves as long as possible, and many seeing the enemy in the town, shut themselves up in their own houses, and thence made several shots upon the pirates; who thereupon threatened them, saying, 'If you surrender not voluntarily, you shall soon see the town in a flame, and your wives and children torn to pieces before your faces.' Upon these menaces the Spaniards submitted to the discretion of the pirates, believing they could not continue there long.

As soon as the pirates had possessed themselves of the town, they enclosed all the Spaniards, men, women, children, and slaves, in several churches, and pillaged all the goods they could find; then they searched the country round about, bringing in daily many goods and prisoners, with much provision. With this they fell to making great cheer, after their old custom, without remembering the poor prisoners, whom they let starve in the churches, though they tormented them daily and inhumanly to make them confess where they had hid their goods, money, &c., though little or nothing was left them, not sparing the women and little children, giving them nothing to eat, whereby the greatest part perished."

A depiction of Morgan's attack on Puerto Principe

Even after torturing the population, Morgan was only able to gather together 50,000 gold pieces, not nearly enough to pay the debts accrued in planning their expedition. As a result, they knew they would have to find more treasure before they could return to Jamaica.

Chapter 3: Porto Bello

Desperate to come up with enough wealth to both pay off their debts and make some sort of profit, Morgan and his crew decided to go after the biggest prize in the Americas, the Spanish-held city of Porto Bello. This famous city, located on the coast of Panama, was famous among sailors for its deep port and huge treasure, as it was the central port for shipping Peruvian silver back to Spain. It was also rumored to be the final resting place of England's most famous privateer, Sir Francis Drake, who was said to lie in the bottom of the harbor in a lead coffin.

Drake had once targeted the same region nearly a century earlier. In the mid-16th century, Spain had colonized much of present-day Central America, South America and parts of North America, giving them control over the Gulf of Mexico and the Caribbean Sea. At the center of it was the Isthmus of Panama, which provided the center of the gold and silver trade from Peru. Ships coming from South America landed on the western coast of this narrow strip of land and unloaded their cargo, which then had to be carried overland to the eastern shore of the isthmus and loaded into other ships that would take it on to Spain. Several hundred years later, this process would be eliminated by the construction of the Panama Canal, but at the time this allowed he Spanish to avoid having to sail their ships south and around South America. It also happened to provide an excellent opportunity for theft and piracy.

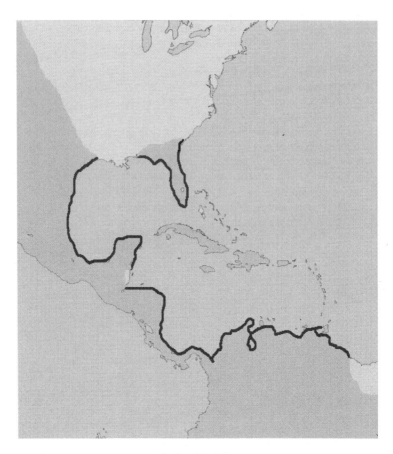

The Spanish Main

Of course, the Spanish also realized how tempting Porto Bello was as a target too, and because of the treasure that it typically held, Porto Bello was well-fortified with three large, well manned forts. However, this did not deter Morgan. The stories of the silver and jewels that its many warehouses held was enough to push aside any doubts or fears that he had about attacking the town.

Unfortunately for Morgan's plan, the Frenchmen who had previously joined his crew were not so certain, and they refused to participate in the expedition. After all, they did not like their fellow crew members, often felt that they received less than their fair share of the treasure, and had borrowed no money in Jamaica, so why should they risk their lives? There was also the matter of a notorious incident between an Englishman and Frenchman at Puerto Principe, when a member of the French crew and one of the Englishmen had fallen into an argument over some treasure. When their feud escalated, they decided to end it with a duel. Before this could happen, however, the Englishman attacked the Frenchman from behind, stabbing him to death. This led the Frenchmen to rise up and swear revenge against the English sailor. In order to keep a full fledged war from breaking out on his ship, Morgan arrested the Englishman and held him in irons pending their return to Jamaica, where he promised to see him hanged.

Though he no longer had his French crew, Morgan nonetheless proceeded against Porto Bello, but when the 10 ships in his fleet reached site of the settlement, many of his men were reluctant to go through with the attack, intimidated by the three forts staring out to sea. Not to be deterred by a few fearful sailors, Morgan gave them a motivating speech, assuring them that though their numbers may have been small, they had the heart to succeed and would receive a larger share of the spoils. He then took a few minutes to remind them what these spoils would likely include: gold, silver, fine gems, even art work and silks.

With his crew finally in the mood to fight, Morgan led his fleet toward Puerto do Naos, where there was a river that would lead them to Porto Bello. Traveling under the cover of darkness, the men positioned themselves outside the first fort. Counting on the element of surprise, Morgan first sent ashore men armed with knives and swords. Moving silently through the underbrush, they were able to attack the fort and kill many of its sleeping inhabitants before anyone could sound the alarm. Exquemelin also explained how they took a prisoner:

"…they had in their company an Englishman, formerly a prisoner in those parts, who now served them for a guide: to him and three or four more they gave commission to take the sentinel, if possible, or kill him on the place: but they seized him so cunningly, as he had no time to give warning with his musket, or make any noise, and brought him, with his hands bound, to Captain Morgan, who asked him how things went in the city, and what forces they had; with other circumstances he desired to know. After every question they made him a thousand menaces to kill him, if he declared not the truth. Then they advanced to the city, carrying the said sentinel bound before them: having marched about a quarter of a league, they came to the castle near the city, which presently they closely surrounded, so that no person could get either in or out.

Being posted under the walls of the castle, Captain Morgan commanded the sentinel, whom they had taken prisoner, to speak to those within, charging them to surrender to his discretion; otherwise they should all be cut in pieces, without quarter. But they regarding none of these threats, began instantly to fire, which alarmed the city; yet notwithstanding, though the governor and soldiers of the said castle made as great resistance as could be, they were forced to surrender. Having taken the castle, they resolved to be as good as their words, putting the Spaniards to the sword, thereby to strike a terror into the rest of the city. Whereupon, having shut up all the soldiers and officers as prisoners into one room, they set fire to the powder (whereof they found great quantity) and blew up the castle into the air, with all the Spaniards that were within. This done, they pursued the course of their victory, falling upon the city, which, as yet, was not ready to receive them. Many of the inhabitants cast their precious jewels and money into wells and cisterns, or hid them in places underground, to avoid, as much as possible, being totally robbed. One of the party of pirates, assigned to this purpose, ran immediately to the cloisters, and took as many religious men and women as they could find. The governor of the city, not being able to rally the citizens, through their great confusion, retired to one of the castles remaining, and thence fired incessantly at the pirates: but these were not in the least negligent either to assault him, or defend themselves, so that amidst the horror of the assault, they made very few shots in vain; for aiming with great dexterity at the mouths of the guns, the Spaniards were certain to lose one or two men every time they charged each gun anew.

This continued very furious from break of day till noon; yea, about this time of the day the case was very dubious which party should conquer, or be conquered. At last, the pirates perceiving they had lost many men, and yet advanced but little towards gaining either this, or the other castles, made use of fire-balls, which they threw with their hands, designing to burn the doors of the castles; but the Spaniards from the walls let fall great quantities of stones, and earthen pots full of powder, and other combustible matter, which forced them to desist. Captain Morgan seeing this generous defence made by the Spaniards, began to despair of success. Hereupon, many faint and calm meditations came into his mind; neither could he determine which way to turn himself in that strait. Being thus puzzled, he was suddenly animated to continue the assault, by seeing English colours put forth at one of the lesser castles, then entered by his men; of whom he presently after spied a troop coming to meet him, proclaiming victory with loud shouts of joy. This instantly put him on new resolutions of taking the rest of the castles, especially seeing the chiefest citizens were fled to them, and had conveyed thither great part of their riches, with all the plate belonging to the churches and divine service."

Morgan and his men had destroyed one of the castles, but things did not go quite so smoothly when they arrived at the second one, because the soldiers manning it had heard the ruckus and were ready to defend themselves. They quickly manned their guns and fired on the attacking pirates, which induced Morgan to take some of the civilian prisoners he had captured and use them to march up to the castle wall and hold ladders in place for his pirates. Exquemelin described how the defenders reacted to the use of human shields:

"To this effect, he ordered ten or twelve ladders to be made in all haste, so broad, that three or four men at once might ascend them: these being finished, he commanded all the religious men and women, whom he had taken prisoners, to fix them against the walls of the castle. This he had before threatened the governor to do, if he delivered not the castle: but his answer was, "he would never surrender himself alive." Captain Morgan was persuaded the governor would not employ his utmost force, seeing the religious women, and ecclesiastical persons, exposed in the front of the soldiers to the greatest danger. Thus the ladders, as I have said, were put into the hands of religious persons of both sexes, and these were forced, at the head of the companies, to raise and apply them to the walls: but Captain Morgan was fully deceived in his judgment of this design; for the governor, who acted like a brave soldier in performance of his duty, used his utmost endeavour to destroy whosoever came near the walls. The religious men and women ceased not to cry to him, and beg of him, by all the saints of heaven, to deliver the castle, and spare both his and their own lives; but nothing could prevail with his obstinacy and fierceness. Thus many of the religious men and nuns were killed before they could fix the ladders; which at last being done, though with great loss of the said religious people, the pirates mounted them in great numbers, and with not less valour, having fire-balls in their hands, and earthen pots full of powder; all which things, being now at the top of the walls, they kindled and cast in among the Spaniards.

This effort of the pirates was very great, insomuch that the Spaniards could no longer resist nor defend the castle, which was now entered. Hereupon they all threw down their arms, and craved quarter for their lives; only the governor of the city would crave no mercy, but killed many of the pirates with his own hands, and not a few of his own soldiers; because they did not stand to their arms. And though the pirates asked him if he would have quarter; yet he constantly answered, 'By no means, I had rather die as a valiant soldier, than be hanged as a coward.' They endeavoured as much as they could to take him prisoner, but he defended himself so obstinately, that they were forced to kill him, notwithstanding all the cries and tears of his own wife and daughter, who begged him, on their knees, to demand quarter, and save his life. When the pirates had possessed themselves of the castle, which was about night, they enclosed therein all the prisoners, placing the women and men by themselves, with some guards: the wounded were put in an apartment by itself, that their own complaints might be the cure of their diseases; for no other was afforded them."

An illustration depicting the civilians carrying ladders to the castle walls

When word reached the third castle that the other two had already fallen, the general in charge chose to surrender rather than fight. This was based more on his perception of how many men Morgan had left than he actually did. The second fight had cost him many lives, and his numbers were severely diminished. Had the Spanish at the third castle put up a fight, they likely could have successfully defended themselves, but with that Morgan's men stormed the city.

When word reach the rest of Spanish forces in the area that Porto Bello had fallen into English pirating hands, they were dismayed and immediately began to organize a counter attack to retake the crucial town. Morgan anticipated that they would respond in this way and was ready for them. He had his men prepare to ambush the Spanish ships as soon as they sailed into the narrow river leading to Porto Bello.

Once the Spanish fleet was driven back, Morgan and his crew settled into a long rest in Porto Bello. Over the next two months they scoured the city, stealing every valuable item that they could carry off. They also captured and held many of the city's most prominent members, offering to ransom them to their relatives for large prices. These ransoms, totaling more than

100,000 pieces of eight, brought the monetary haul alone to more than 12,500 pounds of gold.

Upon hearing what Morgan had done to Porto Bello, the Spanish Governor of Panama sent him an emerald ring and asked how the pirate captain had managed to defeat such well-trained forces with only a few boats and a small army. He also asked that he not attack Panama. With the audacity that made him famous, Morgan sent the governor a pistol with a note attached. In this note, he said that this was the type of weapon that he had used against the Spanish fleet. He also said that he would be coming to Panama someday to reclaim his firearm.

Upon returning to Jamaica, Morgan filed an official report with Modyford.

"We were driven to the south keys of Cuba, where, being like to starve, and finding French in like condition, we put our men ashore, and finding all the cattle driven up country and the inhabitants fled, we marched 20 leagues to Porto Principe on the north of the island, and with little resistance possessed ourselves of the same. There we found that 70 men had been pressed to go against Jamaica; that the like levy had been made in all the island, and considerable forces were expected from Vera Cruz and Campeachy to rendezvous at the Havannah and from Porto Bello and Cartagena to rendezvous at St. Jago of Cuba, of which I immediately gave notice to Governor Modyford. On the Spaniards' entreaty we forbore to fire the town, or bring away prisoners, but on delivery of 1,000 beeves, released them all."

Morgan filed a similar (but more extensive) report with the crown:

"Setting sail in May last, we fell in with the coast of Porto Bello, and being informed of levies made there also against Jamaica, and also by some 89 prisoners who had made their escape from Providence that Prince Maurice and divers Englishmen were kept in irons in the dungeon of the castle of the town, we thought it our duty to attempt that place. The French wholly refused to join in an action so full of danger; so leaving our ships on June 26, forty leagues to leeward at Bogota, we took to our canoes, twenty-three in number, and rowing along the coast, landed at three o'clock in the morning and made our way into the town, and seeing that we could not refresh ourselves in quiet we were enforced to assault the castle, which we took by storm, and found well supplied with ammunition and provisions, only undermanned, being about 130 men, whereof seventy-four were killed, among whom the Castillano was one. In the dungeon were found eleven English in chains who had been there two years; and we were informed that a great man had been carried thence six months before to Lima of Peru, who was formerly brought from Porto Rico, and also that the Prince of Monte Circa had been there with orders from the King of Spain to raise 2,200 men against us out of the Province of Panama, which Porto Bello stands in, the certainty whereof was confirmed by all the Grandees. The Governor of the second castle refusing to permit our ships free entrance into the port, we were forced to attempt the taking of it, which ended in the delivering up the castle and marching out with colours flying, and the third castle immediately surrendered to five or six Englishmen. And now having possession of the town and three castles, in the former were 900 men that bare arms, the fifth day arrived the President of Panama, with about 3,000 men; whom we beat off with considerable damage, in so much that next day he proffered 100,000 pieces of eight for delivery of the town and castles in as good condition as we found them. In the first castle there were 30 brass guns besides iron, in the second 13, all brass, and in the third 14 guns. On the 2d August, making the best of our way homewards, we arrived at Jamaica about the middle of that month; only Captain Edward Collier put on shore in the Bay of Cordivant, within four leagues of Santa Marta, for provisions, and had the good luck to take the Governor's kinsman prisoner, from whom he had again information of the strong intention of the Spaniard against Jamaica as also of the revolt of the Indians, their taking of Monposse and putting to the sword men, women, and children, and intending to surprise Santa Fe, and further that there was found the richest gold mine in the King of Spain's dominions, for keeping which they were fortifying strongly at Santa Marta.

We further declare to the world that in all this service of Porto Bello, we lost but eighteen men killed and thirty-two wounded, and kept possession of the place thirty-one days; and for the better vindication of ourselves against the usual scandals of that enemy, we aver that having several ladies of great quality and other prisoners, they were proffered their liberty to go to the President's camp, but they refused, saying they were now prisoners to a person of quality, who was more tender of their honours than they doubted to find in the President's camp among his rude Panama soldiers, and so voluntarily continued with us till the surrender of the town and castles, when with many thanks and good wishes they repaired to their former homes."

Chapter 4: Provoking a Fight

By this time, Modyford had become desperate for some way to cover his own support for local piracy. He had first tried to convince the Crown that he had never authorized Morgan to attack the city but only the ships in its port. When that failed to convince his accusers, he reminded the Crown that there were rumors that the Spanish had planned to attack Jamaica. However, he feared that the mere rumors of an attack would not be sufficient to get him out of trouble. Therefore, he concocted a far more audacious plan; he would actually try to provoke an attack by the Spanish against Jamaica.

A few months later, the King of England sent the *HMS Oxford* to Port Royal to help protect Jamaica, but rather than keep it under his own command, Governor Modyford gave the ship to Morgan to add to his own personal fleet. He then commissioned Morgan to go and stir up as much trouble as possible with the Spanish, in the hopes that his audacity might provoke an attack on Jamaica.

Along with this new ship, Morgan sailed from Jamaica with a much larger crew. He had replaced those he had lost in Porto Bello and added more sailors, bringing his pirate crew up to 900. They sailed their 11 ships to Isla Vaca and anchored there long enough to decide how to proceed next. In spite of his reputation as a scourge against his enemies, Morgan was a fairly democratic and fair captain when it came to his own men, and he often sought their opinions on plans.

After much debate, the men agreed to attack Cartagena, one of the wealthiest and most important cities in Spanish America. Among its other virtues, it was the storage site for gold waiting to be shipped from Peru back to Spain, and the men were sure that attacking it would certainly provoke the Spanish to retaliate by attacking Jamaica. They also knew that if they were successful, they would capture a major haul of Spanish treasure.

Thus, Morgan sailed on toward Cartagena in March 1669, planning to pick up a French ship that he'd had his eye on along the way. Knowing from experience that French crews did not function well on English ships, Morgan made a plan to trick the French into surrendering their vessel. He learned from one of his many sources that this particular ship had been loaned desperately needed supplies by an English merchant ship, so he approached the ship and invited the captain and his highest ranking officers on board for dinner. When they arrived, he promptly arrested them for piracy, accusing them of taking the supplies without permission.

That evening, fate intervened. While celebrating their success with a rum fueled party, some of the pirates decided that they needed some fireworks. In trying to decide what to shoot off, they accidentally lit some explosives stored on board Morgan's brand new flagship, the *Oxford*. The resulting explosion destroyed the ship and killed several hundred pirates in the crew. Morgan used that setback as a way to add to his charges against the French ship by blaming her men for causing the explosion, supposedly to punish him for capturing their officers.

Once Morgan captured the French ship, he ordered it searched, and he found a document signed by the Governor of Baracoa commissioning the French ship to trade in any Spanish port in the New World. However, it also included permission for them to attack English pirate ships that they perceived to be threatening Spanish territory. Morgan was able to use this letter to show that the French ship was indeed a threat to him and his men. Since the French captain was unable to offer any clear defense against these charges, Morgan took the ship and arrested the rest of the crew, sending them to Jamaica to stand trial.

Seeing their fellow sailors blown up had a very detrimental effect of morale, and some of Morgan's men deserted, but by the time they were ready to sail again, Morgan had 11 ships and 800 men to man them. The French ship was a large and significant asset with its 36 cannons. Thus, when their issues with the French were finally resolved, Morgan and his men set out again for Cartagena.

Unfortunately, Morgan's journey hit another snag with the weather. They were forced to sail into the wind the entire way, an exhausting and stressful experience, and by the time they arrived, Morgan's force had been reduced by nearly a third, with only 500 men well enough to fight. Even the supremely self-confident Morgan knew he had far too few men with which to attack the well-fortified Cartagena.

Instead, one of his captains, a Frenchman, suggested that they instead attack Maracibo, noting that he had been there three years earlier and that it would make a valuable and easily obtainable prize. What the Frenchman could not have predicted was how difficult it would prove for Morgan and his men to reach Maracaiblo. Unlike the cities they had previously attacked, Maracaibo was not located on the ocean but on a large lake by the same name. The lake was connected to the sea by a shallow, narrow channel that in some places was only twelve feet deep. When Morgan first saw the winding river with its scattered islands and sandbars, he was inclined to turn back, but the Frenchman convinced him that he remembered a way to navigate through the dangerous waters and safely reach the city.

What the Frenchman did not know was that the Spanish had recently completed work on a new fort named San Carlos located at the narrowest spot in the channel. By the time they saw the fort, the men keeping watch had spotted them and opened fire. With no way to go further, Morgan was forced to put his men ashore, where many were picked off by Spanish snipers. When darkness fell that night, Morgan once again tried to attack the fort, this time traveling on land up to the gates. However, when they entered it they found that there were no Spanish left manning it. Instead, they discovered a lit explosive left burning in such a way as to blow them to kingdom come. Morgan managed to remove the line before the fire reached the powder kegs, so no one was injured.

Knowing that the Spanish were not expecting the English pirates to arrive at the city via the channel, Morgan ordered a group of men to steal all the supplies they could from the fort and then carry them on board. He sent another detail to bury the ships' cannons on the beach, where they would not be discovered. Finally, he gathered his toughest fighters together and formulated a plan to arrive at the city with some lingering element of surprise. He ordered his men into as many small landing ships and canoes as they could find, and they sailed silently into the city, only to find that their delay had given the residents time to escape along with as many of their possessions as they could carry. The furious pirates searched the city, hoping to find some sort of leftover valuables, but when they found none, they captured and tortured as many of the citizens as they could, hoping to learn where more items were hidden. Exquemelin described the scene:

> "As soon as they had entered the town, the pirates searched every corner, to see if they could find any people that were hid, who might offend them unawares; not finding

anybody, every party, as they came out of their several ships, chose what houses they pleased. The church was deputed for the common corps du guard, where they lived after their military manner, very insolently. Next day after they sent a troop of a hundred men to seek for the inhabitants and their goods; these returned next day, bringing with them thirty persons, men, women, and children, and fifty mules laden with good merchandise. All these miserable people were put to the rack, to make them confess where the rest of the inhabitants were, and their goods. Among other tortures, one was to stretch their limbs with cords, and then to beat them with sticks and other instruments. Others had burning matches placed betwixt their fingers, which were thus burnt alive. Others had slender cords or matches twisted about their heads, till their eyes burst out. Thus all inhuman cruelties were executed on those innocent people. Those who would not confess, or who had nothing to declare, died under the hands of those villains. These tortures and racks continued for three whole weeks, in which time they sent out daily parties to seek for more people to torment and rob, they never returning without booty and new riches.

Captain Morgan having now gotten into his hands about a hundred of the chief families, with all their goods, at last resolved for Gibraltar, as Lolonois had done before: with this design he equipped his fleet, providing it sufficiently with all necessaries. He put likewise on board all the prisoners, and weighing anchor, set sail with resolution to hazard a battle. They had sent before some prisoners to Gibraltar, to require the inhabitants to surrender, otherwise Captain Morgan would certainly put them all to the sword, without any quarter. Arriving before Gibraltar, the inhabitants received him with continual shooting of great cannon bullets; but the pirates, instead of fainting hereat, ceased not to encourage one another, saying, 'We must make one meal upon bitter things, before we come to taste the sweetness of the sugar this place affords.'"

Upon reaching Gibraltar, the pirates learned the Spanish had rebuilt and reinforced San Carlos, and they also discovered three Spanish ships blocking the channel. Their captain, Don Alonso del Campo y Espinosa, Admiral of the Spanish Fleet, sent the following letter to Morgan:

"Having understood by all our friends and neighbours, the unexpected news that you have dared to attempt and commit hostilities in the countries, cities, towns, and villages belonging to the dominions of his Catholic Majesty, my sovereign lord and master; I let you understand by these lines, that I am come to this place, according to my obligation, near that castle which you took out of the hands of a parcel of cowards; where I have put things into a very good posture of defence, and mounted again the artillery which you had nailed and dismounted. My intent is, to dispute with you your passage out of the lake, and follow and pursue you everywhere, to the end you may see the performance of my duty. Notwithstanding, if you be contented to surrender with humility all that you have taken, together with the slaves and all other prisoners, I will let you freely pass, without trouble or molestation; on condition that you retire home presently to your own country. But if you make any resistance or opposition to what I offer you, I assure you I will command boats to come from Caraccas, wherein I will put my troops, and coming to Maracaibo, will put you every man to the sword. This is my last and absolute resolution. Be prudent, therefore, and do not abuse my bounty with ingratitude. I have with me very good soldiers, who desire nothing more ardently than to revenge on you, and your people, all the cruelties, and base infamous actions, you have committed upon the Spanish nation in America.

Dated on board the royal ship named the Magdalen, lying at anchor at the entry of the lake of Maracaibo, this 24th of April, 1669.

"Don Alonso del Campo y Espinosa."

Not surprisingly, Morgan and his men didn't care to either surrender or be arrested, and Morgan replied to the letter, "If Don Alonso will not let me pass, I will find means how to do it without him." Between the fort and the ships, Morgan's crew was completely outgunned, but Morgan had a trick up his sleeve. First, he ordered most of the men manning the *Satisfaction*, his largest ship, to prepare the ship to be burned. According to his own report:

"They gathered all the Pitch, Tar, and Brimstone they could find in the whole Town, wherewith to prepare the Fire-ship abovementioned. Likewise they made several inventions of Powder and Brimstone, with great quantity of Palm-leaves very well ointed with Tar. They covered very well their counterfeit Cannon, laying under every piece thereof many pounds of Powder. Besides which they cut down many outworks belonging to the Ship, to the end that the Powder might exert its strength the better. Thus they broke open also new Port-holes; where, instead of Guns they placed little Drums of which the Negroes make use. Finally the Deck was handsomely beset with many pieces of Wood dressed up in the shape of men with Hats and Monteras, and likewise armed with Swords, Muskets, and Bandaleers."

Those left set it on fire and, when it was well ablaze, steered it toward the *Magdalena*, the Spanish flagship. In the meantime, other pirates pulled alongside and threw grappling hooks into the rigging, securing the boat so that it could not sail out of harm's way. Just as the *Satisfaction* plowed into the enemy ship, splitting her nearly in two and setting her on fire, the men who had been board the *Satisfaction* jumped into the water and were picked up by their pirate comrades.

With the *Magdalena* out of the way, Morgan turned his attention to the *San Luis*. He ran it ashore and quickly boarded and conquered it. Likewise, the pirates took the *La Marquesa* without firing a single shot, boarding her after her rigging tangled and she was unable to maneuver.

Illustration of the burning ships

In spite of his success against the ships, Morgan was still unable to maneuver around the wreckage cluttering the narrow channel and escape. After much thought, he cleverly worked out a plan that would prove successful. He sent many of his men across land to fire on the fort. While they drew the soldiers' attention and fire, he drifted past the fort, using only the tide to silently carry him along. After that, he picked up his men and set off for Jamaica.

Chapter 5: Pirate or Privateer? What's in a Name?

Once he arrived back at the island, he thought he might have finally gone too far for Modyford to continue to support him, but to his pleasant surprise he was wrong. Modyford reprimanded him slightly, but he was still pleased with his work, especially when the Spaniards started making threats against Jamaica. This was all the excuse Modyford needed to act, and he soon commissioned Morgan as the commander-in-chief of the entire English fleet defending Jamaica. As such, he was authorized to lead men against any Spanish ship or village.

While the work would be hard and dangerous, there would be no pay from the government, all but implying that Morgan and his men could compensate themselves by stealing the treasure they managed to capture. Because they were given an official commission this time, Morgan and his crew were no longer considered outlaw pirates, but instead respectable privateers.

Morgan's commission contained the following specifics:

"1. You will with these Instructions receive my Commission which you are enjoyned with all expedition to publish and put in due execution, according to the full extent and import of the same, for the accomplishing whereof, you shall have all the assistance this Island can give you.

"2. You are to make known to me what strength you can possibly make, what your wants may be, that on due calculation of both, we may supply you with all possible speed.

"3. You are to take notice and advise your Fleet and Souldiers that you are on the old pleasing Account of no purchase no pay, and therefore that all which is got shall be divided amongst them according to accustomed Rules.

"4. In case you shall find it prudential, as by your Commission you are directed, to attain St. Jago of Cuba, and God blessing you with victory, you are hereby directed, in case you do it without any considerable hazards, to keep and make good the place and country thereabout, until you have advised me of your success and received my further Orders touching the same, lest your suddenly quitting and their suddenly returning, beget us new work, and put on new charges and hazards for the second defeating.

"5. In order to this you are to proclaim mercy and enjoyment of estates and liberty of customs to all the Spaniards that will submit and give assurance of their Loyalty to His Majesty, and Liberty to all the Slaves that will come in; and to such as by any good service may deserve the same; you are to give notice that their fugitive Masters' Plantations are to be divided amongst them as rewards for the same & make them sufficient Grants in writing, both for their Liberties and Estates, reserving to the Crown of England the fourth part of the produce to be yearly paid for the yearly maintenance of such Forces as shall defend those parts.

"6. In case you find that course to take approveable effect, you are as much as will stand with the same to preserve the Sugarworks and Canes; but if it otherwise appear to you, that in reason you cannot make good the place for any long time, and that the Spaniards and Slaves are deaf to your Proposals, you are then, with all expedition to destroy and burn all Habitations, and leave it as a Wilderness, putting the Men-Slaves to the Sword and making the Women-Slaves Prisoners to be brought hither, and sold for the account of your Fleet and Army, such of the men also that cannot speak Spanish, or any new Negro, you may preserve for the same account; or if any Ships be present to carry them for New England or Virginia, you may send them all on the same account.

"7. You are to enquire what usage our Prisoners have had, and what Quarter hath been given by the Enemy to such of ours as have fallen under their power, and being well informed, you are to give the same, or rather as our custom is to exceed in Civility and Humanity, endeavouring by all means to make all sorts of People sensible of your Moderation and good nature, and your inaptitude and loathing to spill the blood of men.

"8. You have hereby power to execute Marshall Law, according to such military Laws as have been made by me, and the Laws made by Act of Parliament for the government of the Fleet, which I approve of as fitting for the Service; and hereby authorise you to put them in execution against such as shall offend you, having first published the said Laws unto them, that none may pretend ignorance.

"9. If any Ship or Ships shall be present, which have not any Commissions, you are hereby impowered to Grant Commissions to them according to the form I have used, taking security of £1,000 for the performance of the same.

"10. What Ships in this Expedition you shall keep with you under your Command and them order and dispose for the best improvement of this Service, not suffering the takers or pretenders to sell them until they come into their Commission Port.

"11. In regard many things may happen in this Action which cannot be by me foreseen and provided for in these Instructions, therefore all such matters are left to your well known prudence and conduct, referring to you that are in the place to do therein what shall be needful, thus wishing you success and this Island made happy thereby.

Hungry for treasure, Morgan once again made his way to Cuba by working his way along the coast, attacking and pillaging every village and town he came across. He then decided to make good on his promise some years back to retrieve his gun from the governor of Panama. He first captured Santa Catalina, an island that the English had lost to the Spanish some years earlier. Then, on December 27, 1670, he captured San Lorenzo, a fortified position along the coast of Panama, killing almost all of the 323 men stationed there.

From San Lorenzo, Morgan sailed up the Chagres River toward the Pacific side of the country and the famous Panama City. He had 1,400 men with him, 200 more than the 1,200 soldiers stationed in Panama City. In order to conquer the city, he employed a classic pincer maneuver, dividing his forces into two groups. While one sailed up the river toward the city, the other came through the woods, preventing the Spanish from escaping into the countryside with their treasures.

Unfortunately for the pirates, they were unaware of the lack of resources that would be on hand to sustain them. Exquemelin explained:

"This day, about noon, they came near a post called Torna Cavallos: here the guide of the canoes cried out, that he perceived an ambuscade. His voice caused infinite joy to all the pirates, hoping to find some provisions to satiate their extreme hunger. Being come to the place, they found nobody in it, the Spaniards being fled, and leaving nothing behind but a few leathern bags, all empty, and a few crumbs of bread scattered on the ground where they had eaten. Being angry at this, they pulled down a few little huts which the Spaniards had made, and fell to eating the leathern bags, to allay the ferment of their stomachs, which was now so sharp as to gnaw their very bowels. Thus they made a huge banquet upon these bags of leather, divers quarrels arising concerning the greatest shares. By the bigness of the place, they conjectured about five hundred Spaniards had been there, whom, finding no victuals, they were now infinitely desirous to meet, intending to devour some of them rather than perish.

Having feasted themselves with those pieces of leather, they marched on, till they came about night to another post, called Torna Munni. Here they found another ambuscade, but as barren as the former. They searched the neighbouring woods, but could not find anything to eat, the Spaniards having been so provident, as not to leave anywhere the least crumb of sustenance, whereby the pirates were now brought to this extremity. Here again he was happy that had reserved since noon any bit of leather to make his supper of, drinking after it a good draught of water for his comfort. Some, who never were out of their mothers' kitchens, may ask, how these pirates could eat and digest those pieces of leather, so hard and dry? Whom I answer, that, could they once experiment what hunger, or rather famine, is, they would find the way as the pirates did. For these first sliced it in pieces, then they beat it between two stones, and rubbed it, often dipping it in water, to make it supple and tender. Lastly, they scraped off the hair, and broiled it. Being thus cooked, they cut it into small morsels, and ate it, helping it down with frequent gulps of water, which, by good fortune, they had at hand."

When Morgan attacked on January 28, 1671, he was greeted by a large contingent of ill trained Spanish soldiers who rushed headlong into his fire, rather than taking cover and waiting for the privateers to get closer. Exquemelin described the fighting:

"The pirates, now upon their march, came to the top of a little hill, whence they had a large prospect of the city and champaign country underneath. Here they discovered the forces of the people of Panama, in battle array, to be so numerous, that they were surprised with fear, much doubting the fortune of the day: yea, few or none there were but wished themselves at home, or at least free from the obligation of that engagement, it so nearly concerning their lives. Having been some time wavering in their minds, they at last reflected on the straits they had brought themselves into, and that now they must either fight resolutely, or die; for no quarter could be expected from an enemy on whom they had committed so many cruelties. Hereupon they encouraged one another, resolving to conquer, or spend the last drop of blood. Then they divided themselves into three battalions, sending before two hundred bucaniers, who were very dextrous at their guns. Then descending the hill, they marched directly towards the Spaniards, who in a spacious field waited for their coming. As soon as they drew nigh, the Spaniards began to shout and cry, 'Viva el rey!' 'God save the king!' and immediately their horse moved against the pirates: but the fields being full of quags, and soft underfoot, they could not wheel about as they desired. The two hundred bucaniers, who went before, each putting one knee to the ground, began the battle briskly, with a full volley of shot: the Spaniards defended themselves courageously, doing all they could to disorder the pirates. Their foot endeavoured to second the horse, but were constrained by the pirates to leave them. Finding themselves baffled, they attempted to drive the bulls against them behind, to put them into disorder; but the wild cattle ran away, frighted with the noise of the battle; only some few broke through the English companies, and only tore the colours in pieces, while the bucaniers shot every one of them dead.

The battle having continued two hours, the greatest part of the Spanish horse was ruined, and almost all killed: the rest fled, which the foot seeing, and that they could not possibly prevail, they discharged the shot they had in their muskets, and throwing them down, fled away, every one as he could. The pirates could not follow them, being too much harassed and wearied with their long journey. Many, not being able to fly whither they desired, hid themselves, for that present, among the shrubs of the sea-side, but very unfortunately; for most of them being found by the pirates, were instantly killed, without any quarter. Some religious men were brought prisoners before Captain Morgan; but he, being deaf to their cries, commanded them all to be pistolled, which was done. Soon after they brought a captain to him, whom he examined very strictly; particularly, wherein consisted the forces of those of Panama? He answered, their whole strength consisted in four hundred horse, twenty-four companies of foot, each of one hundred men complete; sixty Indians, and some negroes, who were to drive two thousand wild bulls upon the English, and thus, by breaking their files, put them into a total disorder: beside, that in the city they had made trenches, and raised batteries in several places, in all which they had placed many guns; and that at the entry of the highway, leading to the city, they had built a fort mounted with eight great brass guns, defended by fifty men.

Captain Morgan having heard this, gave orders instantly to march another way; but first he made a review of his men, whereof he found both killed and wounded a considerable number, and much greater than had been believed. Of the Spaniards were found six hundred dead on the place, besides the wounded and prisoners. The pirates, nothing discouraged, seeing their number so diminished, but rather filled with greater pride, perceiving what huge advantage they had obtained against their enemies, having rested some time, prepared to march courageously towards the city, plighting their oaths to one another, that they would fight till not a man was left alive. With this courage they recommenced their march, either to conquer or be conquered; carrying with them all the prisoners."

After three more hours of fighting, the pirates had forced the Spanish defenders to flee, leaving the city and all her treasures at Morgan's mercy. Morgan ordered his men not to drink the wine left by the inhabitants, not out of fear that they'd get drunk but because he was worried the Spanish had poisoned it. Much to Morgan's disappointment, these treasures did not prove to be as rich as he had hoped. Anticipating his attack, the Governor of Panama had ordered most of the city's wealth to be stored in a Spanish ship anchored out of sight in the Gulf of Panama. Eventually, a fire that may or may not have been set by Morgan's men burned most of the city and the inhabitants' person possessions. Though they tortured the men who survived their attack, Morgan's men found very little gold in the town.

Unbeknownst to Morgan, his attack on Panama City violated a peace treaty that had been signed between Spain and England the previous year, and this time, even his connections with Modyford could not save him. He was arrested and sent to England for trial, but once he was in court, Morgan was able to demonstrate that, owing to the slow way in which information crossed the Atlantic, he had no way of knowing about the treaty or its terms. As a result, he was not only found not guilty of the charges but even given a knighthood for his service to the crown. The following year, 1674, he returned to Jamaica, this time with an appointment as her lieutenant-governor.

Morgan served first as lieutenant-governor, and then as acting governor for the next seven years. However, his career was cut short by a change in politics. In 1681, Charles II replaced Morgan with Thomas Lynch, a weaker man more inclined to do his bidding. In August of that year, Morgan wrote the following letter to Sir Leoline Jenkins, in which he tried to determine what his next move should be. He began by drawing Jenkins' attention to the difference between what things are said to be and what they really are.

> Since my last 'I am by the public remour and vogue possessed' that the King has disbanded the two companies [of English soldiers] here. We have had such a report for a long time, but I have ever looked upon it as groundless, as I had no account of it from Court, and should much wonder if it were so, and so great a charge imposed on the Colony without intimation. It is said that Colonel Long induced the King to dismiss the companies as being useless here. I am much startled by the Colonel's allegation, seeing that our daily experience proves the contrary. They are constantly employed either at sea or ashore, in bringing in runaway or rebellious negroes or reducing of pirates, who, as I have already rebellious negroes or reducing of pirates, who, as I have already told you, are very numerous. Twenty of the soldiers are at this moment on board the Norwich in pursuit of a powerful and desperate pirate, and I hear that there has been an

encounter and that some of them are wounded, but I know no particulars.

He then reiterated his commitment to carrying out the King's will, if he would only be told what that actually is.

"By this you will judge of their usefulness. I urge nothing in favour of myself since I am daily in likelihood of being removed from the Government; it is for the King's service and for the good of the Island that I urge their continuance here, and I beg your good offices with the King in supporting my supplication that they may be continued."

After signing the letter, he received further information before he could mail it. Again, he pleads with Jenkins to give him clear instructions, and in turn reminds him of his faithful service to the Crown in the past.

"I have never received any advice from Court about them beyond a copy of a 'resulte' [resolution] of the Lords of Trade and Plantations, offering it as their opinion that they should be disbanded. This I received from my correspondent, and never thought it a sufficient order to disband the King's soldiers, raised by his commissions under his sign manual and signet. For it is a common maxim, nothing can cut a diamond but a diamond, so I humbly conceive I am not nor cannot be safe in doing of it except I receive the King's command under his hand and the seal of your office or of the Privy Council. I beg therefore once more to know the King's pleasure herein, for it is heavy upon me to maintain these men of my company, who are, whatever may have been said, a full hundred men, at my own charges, and much heavier on the other parties. 'God preserve your Honour' is and shall be the daily prayer of Henry Morgan."

Shortly after he returned to England, Morgan faced a new battle. In 1683, his former ship's surgeon, Alexandre Exquemelin, published a graphically detailed account of Morgan's piracy, which the knighted Sir Henry naturally considered a rather unflattering portrait of his actions. Morgan sued Exquemelin for libel and won an award of 200 pounds, as well as a retraction. But even though Exquemelin's history on pirates in the Americas was discredited in its day, historians continue to consider it one of the best contemporary historical sources for piracy in the 17th century. It also ensured that Morgan became known as one of the most cruel and bloodthirsty pirates in history.

Morgan died on August 25, 1688 of tuberculosis and possibly liver failure caused by his alcoholism. He left behind his wife, Mary Elizabeth, but no children. He left his property in Jamaica to his godsons Henry Archbold and Charles Byndloss, and he left a stipend to his sister Catherine Morgan Loyd.

Chapter 6: Morgan's Legacy

Perhaps the greatest irony of Morgan's legacy, and the manner in which it has become caricatured by rum makers and video game producers, is that Morgan has left a far more extensive historical record than just about every other famous pirate. While the tales and legends of pirates like Blackbeard, Anne Bonny, and Black Bart have all helped affix certain stereotypes about pirates into pop culture, the simple truth is that was made possible by the fact that the lives of most pirates were undocumented and thus full of mystery. People have been filling in the blanks with their imagination ever since.

With Morgan, on the other hand, his life and career were extensively covered by contemporaries, in part because he toed the line between being a pirate and privateer. Since at least one authority officially commissioned his expeditions, Morgan kept an account of his deeds, and one of his shipmates, Exquemelin, provided graphic details. What emerged was the portrait of a cunning, courageous, and convincing Captain who would do whatever it took to capture his objective.

People have long been fascinated by Morgan and his exploits, but the amount of information available has also made it possible for historians to try to actually find some of his lost ships. As recently as 2012, archaeologists were scouring waters near Panama for evidence of some of his shipwrecks, which occurred nearly 340 years ago, and some of the funding for the project was put forward by the spiced rum maker that uses Morgan as its namesake. Texas State University has even put together a "Lost Ships of Henry Morgan Project", whose mission, as member Fritz Hanselmann put it, is "telling the true story of Henry Morgan."As Hanselmann noted, "He was a real historic figure who played a significant role in the history of Panama and 17th century politics. Morgan was a legendary figure, even in his time. He pretty much ran amuck in the Spanish main, culminating in the sack of Panama City. He sacked a city no one thought could be sacked...Morgan was one of the most infamous privateers of all time, so for me, this is a chance to use archaeological research to bridge the gap between science and pop culture. Most people associate Captain Morgan with spiced rum, but he was also an iconic historical figure who accomplished incredible feats throughout the Caribbean."

With the help of the historical record, searches near the mouth of the Chagres River have turned up shipwrecks and cannons from the 17th century that might very well have been Morgan's ships. Archaeologists have also found booty on the seafloor, including, perhaps most fittingly, barrels of alcohol. While certain connections to Captain Morgan have yet to be made, The Lost Ships of Henry Morgan Project has vowed to keep at it, with Hanselmann stating, "Locating his lost ships and being able to properly preserve and share them with the public is our ultimate goal with this project. We're really close – and at the end of the day, his ships are down there and we're going to find them."

Bibliography

Breverton, Terry. Admiral Sir Henry Morgan: King of the Buccaneers (2005)

Exquemelin, A. O. and George A. Williams. The Pirates of Panama or, The Buccaneers of America; a True Account of the Famous Adventures and Daring Deeds of Sir Henry Morgan and Other Notorious Freebooters of the Spanish Main (2011)

Howard, Edward. Sir Henry Morgan, the buccaneer (v. 2) (1842)

Marrin, Albert. Terror of the Spanish Main: Sir Henry Morgan and His Buccaneers (1999)

Pope, Dudley. The Buccaneer King: The Biography of Sir Henry Morgan, 1635-1688 (1978)

Harry Morgan's Way: Biography Of Sir Henry Morgan 1635-1688 (2001)

Porter, Alexander. No Man Knows My Grave: Sir Henry Morgan, Captain William Kidd, Captain Woodes Rogers in the Great Age of Privateers and Pirates, 1665-1715, (1969)

Captain William Kidd

Chapter 1: Born to the Sea

Captain William Kidd was one of the most controversial men of the 17th century, and naturally there is controversy over where and when he was born. At the time of his execution, one of the ministers attending the execution wrote that Kidd was born in 1645, based on the fact that he estimated Kidd's age to be about 56. That led to some believing that he was born around 1645 in Greenock, Scotland. Today, however, modern scholars believe that William Kidd was born in January of 1654 around Dundee, Scotland. Records from one church parish in Dundee indicate a William Kidd was indeed baptized in 1654, and Kidd himself claimed he was born near Dundee that year when testifying in a court case. In fact, Kidd named his personal servant cabin boy "Dundee" while at sea. The discrepancy in the dates may have simply been a result of the fact that Kidd aged quickly while living a tough life at sea.

His family's origins are also somewhat mysterious. He was baptized in Dundee according to the rites of the Scottish Presbyterian Church, and his father John may have been a Presbyterian minister. What does seem certain is that John Kidd was a sea captain, and for that reason Kidd was often described by contemporaries as being "born to the sea". John Kidd apparently died at sea while William was still a child, and the family had to subsist off the generosity of their neighbors.

While there are records to indicate his existence at birth, Kidd goes off the historical record for nearly 30 years until reentering it around 1689. It is widely believed that Kidd began his career as a seaman's apprentice, which seems likely since his father had been a sea captain. However, the rumors that the ship he apprenticed on was in fact a pirating vessel seem unlikely. Not only would a parent be unlikely to apprentice her son to a pirate, but a pirate ship would also not be likely to accept a very young man who still needed training.

Sometime in the 1680s, Kidd joined a privateer crew made up of men from both England and France, and with them he sailed to the Caribbean to look for wealthy Spanish ships carrying gold and other treasure back to Europe from the Americas. While on this voyage, the crew commandeered a French ship and sailed it to Nevis, an English colonial island in the West Indies. When they arrived, the governor of the island, Christopher Cordrington, christened the ship *Blessed William*, presumably after King William III. Kidd was made captain of the ship, and his ship's assignment was to protect Nevis against the French. At the same time, the governor refused to pay them for their services, thereby implying that Kidd and his crew would have to make their money by taking from the French. In effect, Kidd was given carte blanche to raid enemy shipping.

Chapter 2: Privateer or Pirate

Exactly how Kidd became the captain remains the subject of speculation. Some say that the crew themselves elected him out of respect for his experience and sailing practice. Others say that Governor Christopher Codrington of Nevis chose him personally. What is known is that the *Blessed William*, her captain and her crew soon became part of a fleet of ships Codrington assembled to fight the French should they try to attack the English on Nevis. No matter who did the choosing, it is a testimony to the regard that those who knew Kidd held him in. Though he was only about 30 years old, he was already a seasoned sailor and respected leader.

When Kidd's mission started, the English and French were belligerents in the Nine Years' War, technically making him a privateer. On their first mission out, the crew of the *Blessed William* attacked Mariegalante, a French island near Nevis, and destroyed the island's only community. Kidd and his crew stole everything they could carry with them to their ship, including about 2,000 pounds of silver (worth about $300,000 today.). Every individual crew member took a share of booty worth about £2000, making them independently wealthy. The commander of the expedition that the *Blessed William* participated in, Captain Thomas Heweston, wrote that Kidd "was a mighty man who fought as well as any man I ever saw."

From Nevis, they sailed north to Massachusetts, where Kidd captured a French privateer and turned him in for ransom, in keeping with the instructions he had been given by the Crown. A few months later he was given a bonus by the British government for his success in fighting the French in the Caribbean.

After these initial successes raiding, Kidd was given orders to engage French warships, a far cry from raiding islands and commandeering small vessels. When Kidd told his crew about the orders, they heartily refused to join the squadron that was being sent to fight the French. With a major problem on his hands, Kidd confronted his upset crew by explaining to them it was their duty to obey orders of the Crown, since they were in the employ of the English as privateers. The effects of this confrontation may have played an important role in a similar and far more controversial event a decade later.

Before he had a chance to restore order, Kidd lost the *Blessed William* to Captain Culliford, a pirate well known for his treachery and deceit. Culliford discovered Kidd's ship anchored off the coast of Antigua in the West Indies. Learning that Kidd and most of the men had gone ashore, Culliford captured the ship and sailed it away, leaving Kidd and crew high and dry as well as thoroughly embarrassed. The captain was then forced to purchase a new ship, which he called the *Antigua*, in order to get back to New England. He was also told to try to find Culliford and the *Blessed William*, but it doesn't seem as though he ever did, because it wasn't the last time Culliford would make himself a menace in Kidd's life.

Chapter 3: Ashore

An illustration of Kidd's home at the corner of Pearl and Hanover streets on Manhattan

For reasons that remain unclear, Kidd took to shore for several years after sailing to New England, and he established himself as a well-respected member of New York City's society. He was married to the former Sarah Bradley, a wealthy young widow, and was an active member of the Trinity Church in New York. Incredibly, Kidd and Sarah had gotten a marriage license just a couple of days after Sarah's husband, the middle-aged John Oort, died suddenly. Naturally, this led to allegations against Kidd and his widowed bride, which would only grow stronger after Kidd earned more notoriety. Nevertheless, nobody could prove foul play, and thus the pair married without any issues and settled down in Manhattan.

Over the next few years, Kidd lived the life of a successful and well-connected businessman, including becoming close friends with the colony's royal governor, Col. Benjamin Fletcher. Fletcher himself was also acquainted with notorious pirates like Thomas Tew and Henry Every, operating under the belief that allowing the pirates a safe haven in New York City would help bolster his city's economy at the expense of other colonial cities like Philadelphia.

However, toward the end of the 17th century, Great Britain's attitude toward piracy began to shift. Whereas previous monarchs had turned a blind eye to piracy and corruption along the shores of North America, King William III considered them to be serious crimes. When he discovered that the governor of New York, Benjamin Fletcher, had been taking bribes from pirates in order to allow them to unload their treasure, the king replaced him with Richard Coote, the Earl of Bellomont.

The Earl of Bellomont

Despite Kidd's friendship with the previous governor, when Bellomont was looking for someone to help him stop piracy, he turned to the "trusty and well beloved Captain Kidd", commissioning him to hunt "pirates, free-booters and sea-rovers, being our subjects, or of other nations associated with them". At the same time, Kidd had permission to capture any French ships he might come across since the Nine Years' War was still raging. The Royal Commission read:

"William the Third, by the grace of God, King of England, Scotland, France and Ireland, defender of the faith, &c. To our trusty and well beloved ~

Capt. Robert Kidd, commander of the Adventure Galley with a crew of 80 men and mounting 30 guns.

Greeting: whereas we are informed, that Capt. Thomas Too, John Ireland, Capt.

Thomas Wake, and Capt. William Maze or Mace, and other subjects, natives or inhabitants of New-York, and elsewhere, in our plantations in America, have associated themselves with diverse others, wicked and ill-disposed persons, and do, against the law of nations, commit many and great piracies, robberies and depredations on the seas upon the parts of America, and in other parts, to the great hindrance and discouragement of trade and navigation, and to the great danger and hurt of our loving subjects, our allies, and all others, navigating the seas upon their lawful occasions.

Now know ye, that we being desirous to prevent the aforesaid mischief's, and as much as in us lies, to bring the said pirates, freebooters and sea-rovers to justice, have thought fit, and do hereby give and grant to the said Robert Kidd, to whom our commissioners for exercising the office of Lord High Admiral of England, have granted a commission as a private man-of-war, bearing date the 11th day of December, 1695, and unto the commander of the said ship for the time being, and unto the officers, mariners, and others which shall be under your command, full power and authority to apprehend, seize, and take into your custody as well the said Capt. Thomas Too, John Ireland, Capt. Thomas Wake and Capt. Wm. Maze or Mace, as all such pirates, free-booters, and searovers, being either our subjects, or of other nations associated with them, which you shall meet with upon the seas or coasts, with all their ships and vessels, and all such merchandises, money, goods, and wares as shall be found on board, or with them, in case they shall willingly yield themselves; but if they will not yield without fighting, then you are by force to compel them to yield.

And we also require you to bring, or cause to be brought, such pirates, freebooters, or sea-rovers, as you shall seize, to a legal trial, to the end they may be proceeded against according to the law in such cases. And we do hereby command all our officers, ministers, and other of our loving subjects whatsoever, to be aiding and assisting to you in the premises.

And we do hereby enjoin you to keep an exact journal of your proceedings in execution of the premises, and set down the names of such pirates, and of their officers and company, and the names of such ships and vessels as you shall by virtue of these presents take and seize, and the quantities of arms, ammunition, provision, and lading of such ships, and the true value of the same, as near as you can judge.

In witness whereof, we have caused our great seal of England to be affixed to these presents. Given at our court in Kensington, the 26th day of January, 1696, in the 7th year of our reign."

As far as funding for this project, most of the money was contributed by four of the most important men in England, including the Earl of Orford and the Duke of Shrewsbury. Kidd's letter of marque, which demanded that 10% of any treasure he found had to be given to the crown, was signed by none other than King William III himself. 80% of the financing was secured by New York's governor, Bellomont, through the four important backers, while Kidd and Robert Livingston, a confidant of the king who put Kidd in touch with these powerful men, would fund the other 20%. In addition to the King receiving 10%, 60% would go to the 4 backers, 15% would go to Kidd and Livingston, and 25% would go to Kidd's crew.

    It went without saying that all the parties involved in this arrangement realized and implicitly agreed that Kidd and his crew would "legally" plunder the riches of the Indian Ocean while ostensibly seeking out the notorious pirates like Tew who were operating there. In other words, the Crown would sanction Kidd to protect English ships from privateers and pirates by being the best privateer/pirate himself, and everyone would get rich off the booty Kidd and his crew stole. Given the extremely murky nature of the plan, the names of the people involved in Kidd's venture stayed anonymous at the time, and it was such a closely kept secret that Kidd would literally take their names to the grave.

Livingston

While all those men reached their understanding, Livingston was concerned about the fact that he and Kidd were on the hook to repay the other backers if the expedition was a failure. Thus, Livingston had Kidd sign another deal between the two of them and an acquaintance of Livingston's named Richard Blackham. In this deal, Livingston and Kidd sold some of their 15% for money upfront:

"Articles of Agreemt made this seaventh day of february 1695/6 between Robert Livingston Esqr. & Capt. Williame Kidd of the one part & Richard Blackham of the other part.

1st. The said Robert Livingston & Capt. William Kidd do joyntly & sevally agree with the said Richard Blackham, that in case the said Capt. Kidd do not meet with the Pirates, which went from new England Rode Island, New Yorke & Elsewhere, or do not take from any of the pyrates or from any the Kings Enemyes such goods mchandizes or [struck: other] any things of value as being devided as mentoned in Articles between the said Robert Livingston & Capt. William Kidd of the one part & Richard Earle of Bellomont on the other part bearing Date the 10th day of October 1695 shall fully recompense the said Richard Blackham for the money by him expended in buying the said one fifteenth part of the sd. Ship & primisses that thou they shall refund & repay to ye sd. Richard Blackham ye whole money by him to be advanced in Sterling money or money Equivalent thereunto on or before the 25th day of March wth shall be in the year of our Lord 1697 ye dangers of the seas & of the Enemy & mortality of the sd. Capt. Kidd allways excepted, upon paymt whereof ye said Robt. Livingston & Wm. Kidd are to have the sole pperty in ye sd. ship & furniture & this Indenture to be delivered up to them wth all other Covents & obligations thereunto belonging.

Robt. Livingston &

Wm Kidd

Sealed & delivered

In the p[re]ssence of us.

Samll. Spiser

Richd. Raper

John Wallis"

The secret contract between Kidd, Livingston and Blackham

Chapter 4: A Rocky Start

In his zeal for the adventure, the chance for riches, and the acceptance of the elite society and the King, Kidd overlooked or ignored the politically sensitive nature of his expedition. After all, if anything went wrong, his powerful backers would have to disavow their knowledge and connections with him to protect themselves and the King. Everything would have to go right for Kidd and his expedition.

In order to come up with the remainder of the funds needed to finance this voyage, Kidd sold the *Antigua* and bought instead the *Adventure Galley*, a large ship that was armed with 30 cannons and would hold 150 men. It also featured oars, which would allow it to be rowed in calm seas and would also make it more maneuverable. For her crew, Kidd chose only the best and brightest officers available.

Unfortunately, Kidd and his crew got off on the wrong foot with the British Royal Navy almost immediately. After Kidd had put the finishing touches on the plan in London, his expedition set out down the Thames toward open waters, but Kidd neglected to follow naval etiquette and fire a salute to a Navy yacht as he passed it at Greenwich. The yacht responded by firing a shot to remind them of their manners, but Kidd's crew only replied with further rudeness by pulling down their pants and slapping their backsides. Whether it was because Kidd and his crew were drunk or simply full of themselves given Kidd's connections to such important backers, the Royal Navy ship was hardly amused. Angered by this lack of respect, the sailors boarded the vessel and demanded, at gunpoint, that most of the crew leave Kidd's ship and enlist, on the spot, in the British Navy. Thus, Kidd was left short of men and bereft of his best officers as he set sail for New York.

In spite of these limitations, Kidd managed to capture at least one French ship on his way to America. Kidd arrived in New York in July 1696, but the agreement had required that he return to Boston with the plunder he had taken by March 1697, an impossible timeframe considering he would have to sail to the Indian Ocean and back. Once in New York, Kidd went about recruiting new members to his crew, but he had to make do with the fact that many of those that he found were themselves former pirates or at least had long criminal records.

Among those that he chose was Hendrick van der Heul, who became Kidd's quartermaster. Van der Heul is unique among the men sailing at that time because it's possible he may have been an African American, and if so, he would have been the first African American on record to have reached such a high rank on a European ship. He later became reached the rank of Master's Mate, and unlike many of the other men on the ship, there is no evidence to indicate he was ever charged with piracy. At the same time, the description of van der Heul as a "black man" in contemporary records may simply have meant he was swarthy; Bartholomew "Black Bart" Roberts was described the same way in Captain Charles Johnson's seminal pirate history in the early 18th century.

In September 1696, Kidd left New York and sailed south toward the Cape of Good Hope, only to encounter more trouble. On the way, he lost almost half his men to an outbreak of cholera on the island of Comoros. It is unclear whether he anchored at the island after some men became ill, or if they contracted the disease while on the island itself. Kidd was plagued with even more problems after losing so many of his men. His relatively new ship proved to be something of a lemon and began to spring leaks, forcing him to have to expend much of his crew's time and energy shoring up the hull. These setbacks were exasperated by the fact that he found none of the pirates he expected to capture in the seas around Madagascar.

As if that wasn't bad enough, Kidd had yet another run in with the Royal Navy that December.

On the night of December 12, 1696, Kidd spotted a Royal Navy squadron near the Cape of Good Hope and approached them to receive new sails, since he had lost several during his voyage. The squadron refused, even after Kidd pointed out that his Royal Commission mandated that the Royal Navy help him and fulfill his request. When the squadron's leader, Commander Warren, still refused to help, the two men got into a shouting match that ended with Warren telling Kidd he would impress some of Kidd's crew. Refusing to let that happen once again, Kidd sailed away from the squadron in the middle of the night, and now that he had crossed the Royal Navy yet again, he was fearful of stopping in Capetown as expected.

Chapter 5: Murder?

By the beginning of 1697, Kidd's expedition was in dire shape. In addition to having had to do more repairs on his ship and losing so many crew, Kidd's agreement called for him to be back in Boston in weeks with his booty, despite the fact he had still not captured a single ship. That also meant that his own crew had not been paid, and the longer that situation went on, the greater a chance of mutiny.

Still hoping to redeem the trip, Kidd headed for the Red Sea, having heard that pirates had gathered around the Strait of Bab-el-Mandeb. No doubt frustrated by everything that had happened so far, Kidd and his crew began haggling over whether to attack any target they came across. The crew argued that vessels were hiding their identity by flying false flags, making it impossible for them to determine whether it was a justifiable target, and thus they should simply start commandeering every vessel. Kidd, mindful of what had happened when he nearly failed to keep the peace with his crew a decade earlier, is rumored to have relented and thus attacked a Mughal convoy carrying Muslim pilgrims to Mecca. If this is indeed true, that was the first time that he actually participated in an attack that was not sanctioned by the English government. At the same time, it seems unlikely that they actually attacked that convoy, since such a success would have yielded extensive plunder that neither Kidd nor his crew ever mentioned.

Moreover, the notorious death of one of the crew members in October 1697 suggests Kidd and his crew were still at each other's throats as that year was closing. That month, Kidd was on the deck along with a crewman named William Moore when a Dutch ship came into sight. Moore, anxious for action, demanded that Kidd attack the ship. Kidd, however, felt that it was unwise to attack a ship from the native land of the English king who had given him his commission, so he refused. Moore became belligerent, and Kidd ended up calling him a "lousy dog." Moore replied, "If I am a lousy dog, you have made me so; you have brought me to ruin and many more."

That rejoinder left Kidd fuming, and he apparently lost his temper entirely. According to the charges later brought against him:

> "[Kidd]…feloniously, voluntarily, and of his malice aforethought, then and there did

make an assault in and upon one William Moore, in the peace of God and of our said sovereign lord the king, to wit then and there being, and to the ship aforesaid, called the Adventure-galley, then and there belonging; and that the aforesaid William Kidd, with a certain wooden bucket, bound with iron-hoops, of the value of eight pence, which he the said William Kidd then and there had and held in his right hand, did violently, feloniously, voluntarily, and of his malice aforethought, beat and strike the aforesaid William Moore in and upon the right part of the head of him the said William Moore, a little above the right ear of the said William Moore, then and there upon the high sea, in the ship aforesaid, and within the jurisdiction of the admiralty of England aforesaid, giving the said William Moore, then and there with the bucket aforesaid, in and upon the right part of the head of him the said William Moore, a little above the right ear of the said William Moore, one mortal bruise; of which mortal bruise the aforesaid William Moore…did die."

To be fair, English sea captains did have significant leeway during the 17th century when it came to disciplining their crews, but murder was still considered too extreme and therefore illegal. Kidd allegedly told the surgeon that he had "good friends in England, that will bring me off for that." If so, he clearly believed he would be protected by his connections.

By this time, there were other rumors of cruelty swirling around Kidd. Some of his crew would later tell tales of being hung by their arms from ropes while Kidd threatened them with a sword. Another time, his crew is said to have plundered a treading ship, the *Mary*, and tortured its crew while Kidd sat in his cabin visiting with her captain, Thomas Parker. For his part, Kidd claimed to have been furious when he learned what had happened and returned most of the plunder his men had taken.

Nonetheless, when these stories reached the Royal Navy, they were only too happy to believe them. Still smarting from Kidd's earlier insults, they quickly added his name to the list of men wanted for pirating. Though he had earlier authorized Kidd's actions, William III now withdrew his approval, mentioning Kidd specifically in a proclamation and forbidding him from receiving the clemency being offered to other pirates.

Moreover, Kidd and his desperate crew made a controversial decision in February 1698 by attacking the *Quedagh Merchant* off the coast of India. The giant merchant ship was full of valuable booty, including gold, jewels, and silk, and it would give Kidd the chance to placate his backers and possibly meet the terms of the agreement despite how late he would be in returning to Boston. However, *Quedagh Merchant* was not a pirate ship or a French ship; it was an Armenian ship owned by Indians carrying cargo from Persians and captained by an Englishman. Kidd ultimately determined it was a justifiable target because it was sailing with a French pass, but he was almost certainly aware of the kind of firestorm he was creating by plundering the ship. He was simply that desperate.

On April 1, 1698, Kidd finally reached Madagascar and found a pirate ship, the *Mocha Frigate*, captained by none other than Captain Culliford. According to his own account, written in the third person and referring to himself as the narrator:

…when he arrived in the said port, there was a pirate ship, called the Mocha Frigate, at an anchor, Robert Culliford, commander thereof; who with his men, left the same at his coming in, and ran into the woods : and the narrator proposed to his men to take the same, having sufficient power and authority so to do; but the mutinous crew told him, if he offered the same, they would rather fire two guns into him, than one into the other; and there upon ninety-seven deserted, and went into the Mocha Frigate, and sent into the woods for the said pirates, and brought the said Culliford, and his men, on board again ; and all the time she stayed in the said port, which was the space of four or five days, the said deserters, sometimes in great numbers, came on board the said galley and adventure prize, and carried away great guns, powder, shot, small arms, sails, anchors, cables, surgeons, chests, and what else they pleased; and threatened several times to murder the narrator, as he was informed, and advised to take care of himself; which they designed in the night to effect; but was prevented by him locking himself in his cabin at night, and securing himself with barricading the same with bales of goods; and, having about forty small arms, besides pistols, ready charged, kept them out.

That about the 15th july, the Mocha Frigate went away, being manned with about 130 men, and forty guns, bound out to take all nations : then it was that the narrator was left with only thirteen men; so that the moors he had to pump and keep the Adventure Galley above water, being carried away, she sunk in the harbor ; and the narrator, with the said thirteen men, went on board the Adventure Prize; where he was forced to stay five months for a fair wind; in the meantime, some passengers presented, that were bound for these parts; which he took on board, to help to bring the said Adventure Prize home."

This fateful encounter with Culliford would be argued about extensively during Kidd's trial, as Kidd sought to defend himself against charges that he had not only failed to attack the pirate ship but had actually traded with Culliford. After all, it made no sense that Culliford, who had earlier stolen one of Kidd's ships, would not have plundered the prize Kidd took just months earlier from the *Quedagh Merchant*.

Since Kidd's account is unbelievable, many have speculated that Kidd figured out a way to kill two birds with one stone. Since many of his crew wanted to stay around the Indian Ocean and take more booty, while Kidd himself wanted to return to New England and make good on his agreement, he simply traded a ship and crew to Culliford before returning west. This would have been a good deal for Culliford, since his own *Mocha Frigate* was badly damaged and needed repairs.

Chapter 6: The Trial

When Kidd was finally able to return to the Indies, more bad news was waiting for him, as he noted in his account: "That, about the beginning of april, 1699, the narrator arrived at Anguila in the West Indies, and sent his boat on shore; where his men had the news that he and his people were proclaimed pirates, which put them into such consternation, that they sought all opportunity to run the ship on shore upon some reef or shoal, fearing the narrator should carry them into some English port."

As Kidd's notoriety made its way around England, he became a millstone that the Tories tried to wrap around the necks of Whigs in Parliament. Even though Kidd's name was being tarnished across the Empire and there were orders for his arrest, Kidd was still relatively certain that he could beat the charges, perhaps due to the fact that he had reached an agreement with the king and other bigwigs. At the same time, realizing he was now a wanted man, Kidd left his remaining ship in the Caribbean and took an unnamed sloop to New York. Along the way, he is said to have buried some of his treasure on Gardenier's Island, perhaps hoping that he could later use the treasure to bribe officials if the need arose. It's also possible that he buried and hid some treasure for his own to avoid having to give his backers their fair share. Either way, he would hint at the fact that he had hidden some treasure during his trial.

As Kidd was making his way back to New England, several members involved in the original scheme became nervous. At this point, both Richard Livingston and Bellomont became concerned about how it would look for them if it was discovered they had been part of the scheme. When Kidd sent an attorney to meet with Bellomont in New York and feel him out, Kidd sent two French letters of marque that he had confiscated from the ships he had captured, which would help him prove that he was not a pirate and had abided by the conditions of the agreement. When Bellomont saw them, he simply took them and never reproduced them, leaving Kidd high and dry at trial. They would not resurface for several centuries.

Meanwhile, as Kidd kept sending Bellomont's wife gifts and trying to get a feel for things, Bellomont arranged to trick Kidd into coming to Boston, where he planned to have Kidd arrested and shipped to England in chains. He also ordered that Sarah Kidd be arrested too. After Kidd had been arrested, Bellomont had Kidd's treasure on Gardiner's Island dug up and confiscated, finding a treasure worth about £20,000, worth nearly $3 million today. Suspicions arose around the actions of the authorities on Gardiner's Island, since someone had to have been aware of the fact that Kidd was hiding such a huge treasure there. Gardiner himself claimed innocence before Bellomont, and that he was not there when the treasure was hidden because Kidd had told him to "take three Negroes, two boys and a girl, ashore, to keep till he, the said Kidd, should call for them". That way Gardiner could claim he was not present until after Kidd had hidden everything.

Before being sent back to England, Kidd was placed in solitary confinement in the infamous Stone Prison. The conditions there were so hard on the captain, who was accustomed to the open seas and open spaces, that Kidd had a nervous breakdown. For a time it was thought that he might not be sane enough to try, but after a year of confinement in Boston, Kidd was finally sent to London to be questioned by the English Parliament.

At that point, Kidd's case became a political football. The new Prime Minister, a Tory, knew that members of the Whig government had backed Kidd's voyages and hoped to disgrace them by associating their names' with that of the pirate. At the same time, Kidd was loyal and would not give the names of those who had hired him, figuring that he would eventually be rewarded and supported by his "friends".

While Kidd kept silent, some of the men who sailed with him were anything but. A record of the hearings that involved some of Kidd's cohorts kept for Bellomont explained the manner in which they lied to save their own lives:

"Richard Earl of Bellomont, Captain General and Governor in Chief of His Majesty's Province of Massachusetts Bay, New York and New Hampshire in America and the Territories therin depending and Vice Admiral of the same

TO ALL whom these presents shall come GREETING KNOW YE that the several examinations hereto annexed of the respective persons hereafter named that to say of :

Nicholas Churchill

James How

Robert Bradenham

James Brown

John Eldridge

Robert Hickman

Turlagh Sullivan

David Evans

Darby Mullins

Being all prisoners apprehended in the Government of the Province of East and West Jersesy and Pensilvania that on account of piracies by them committed and sent to Boston in the province of Massachusetts Bay above to be transported for England, were taken before Elisha Cooke and Issac Addington Esq. who are two members of His Majesties Council in the said Province of Massachusetts Bay and Justices of the Peace within the same

And that the said examinations are accordingly attested and signed by the said Elisha Cooke and Issac Addington as taken before them. In testimony whereof I have signed these presents and caused the seal of the province of Massachusetts Bay above said to be here unto affixed. Dated at Boston aforesaid the thirty first day of May 1700.

And in the twelfth year of His Majesties reign Boston in New England May 28th 1700 the examination of Nicholas Churchill of Lower Litchet neer Poole in Dorcetshire, seaman.

SAITH

That in the month of August 1696 the examinant sayled out of England in a shipp named the East India Merchant belonging to the Company of Burthen upwards of fifteen hundred tuns - Clarke Commander and in the voyage outward bound touching at the island of Joanna, this examinant left the ship by reason of the hard usage together with three others of the same company, and continued in the said island. And after some few weeks staying there Captain William Kidd Commander of the Adventure Galley came with his said shipp unto the island of Joanna.

And the examinant with his other three consorts took passage on the said Adventure Galley for Madagascar and were accordingly carried in the said shipp and landed on the island of St. Maries. He continued there and at Madagascar by the space of twelve or fourteen months waiting for an opportunity to get off and then took passage on the shipp Nassaw - Giles Shelly Commander for America.

And this examinant with diverse other passengers were put on shore at Cape May in Delaware River and from thence went to Burlington and after their arrival at Cape May they sent to Governor Bass to acquaint him thereof and that they came from Madagascar understanding that all who came from thence were taken up and had upon examination. And Governor Bass and Captain Snead Sub-Judge of the Admiralty came down to Cape May and ordered this examinant and three others with him to Burlington under custody of the Sheriff and there Governor Bass made out a warrant for their commitment to prison but the same was not executed upon them for the space of six months or more. They remaining all that while in the town and then they were commanded to prison where the examinant James How lay for seventeen or eighteen days and then were let out upon bail until the arrival of Colonel Hamilton appointed Governor of said place which was about three months afterwards and have been imprisoned ever since but no examination of them taken until now.

The examinant further saith he never was a privateering or at the taking of any prize nor had Captain Kidd any prize or prizes at the time when the examinant was passenger in his shipp nor had the examinant any other money or treasure than the value of the hundred pounds in dollars and pieces of eight that were given to him by Thomas Purdey one of his fellow passengers that died upon Shellys shipp and pay for his care and pains in tending and looking after him in his illness.

And saith Purdey gave the remainder of his money unto Captain Shelley which amounted unto more than one hundred and fifty pounds. The examinant has spent all that he had, none of his money was siezed.

Signed

Nicholas Churchill"

Furious that Kidd would not talk, the leaders of the Tory party ordered him to be tried in the High Court of Admiralty. Fearing that there might not be enough evidence to convict him of piracy, they focused much of their energy on the charge that he murdered William Moore. Some have speculated that Kidd did not fully realize the gravity of his situation when his trial began, but a careful reading of the transcript from the trial reveals that Kidd was concerned from the very beginning that his rights as an Englishman might be trampled.

Clerk of Arraignments : William Kidd, hold up thy hand.
Kidd : May it please your lordships, I desire you to permit me to have counsel.
Recorder : (Sir Salathiel Lovell) What would you have counsel for ?
Kidd : My lord, I have some matter of law relating to the indictment, and I desire I may have counsel to speak to it.
Dr. Oxenden : What matter of law can you have?
Cl. of Arr : How does he know what he is charged with? I have not told him.
Recorder : You must let the court know what those matters of law are, before you can have counsel assigned you.
Kidd : They be matters of law, my lord.
Recorder: Mr. Kidd, do you know what you mean by matters of law?
Kidd: I know what I mean; I desire to put off my trial as long as I can, till I can get my evidence ready.
Recorder: Mr. Kidd, you had best mention the matter of law you would insist on.
Dr. Oxenden (the judge): It cannot be matter of law, to put off your trial, but matter of fact.
Kidd: I desire your lordship's favour; I desire Dr. Oldish and Mr. Lemmon may be heard as to my case.
Kidd : I would beg that I may have my papers for my vindication.

Recorder : That is not matter of law. You have had long notice of your trial, and

might have prepared for it. How long have you had notice of your trial?
Kidd: A matter of a fortnight.
Dr. Oxenden : Can you tell the names of any persons that you would make use of in your defence ?
Kidd: I sent for them, but I could not have them.
Dr. Oxenden : Where were they then?
Kidd I brought them to my lord Bellamont in New England.
Recorder : What were their names? You cannot tell without book. Mr. Kidd, the court see no reason to put off your trial, therefore you must plead.
Cl. of Arr : W. Kidd, hold up thy hand.
Kidd: I beg your lordships I may have counsel admitted, and that my trial be put off; I am not really
prepared for it.
Recorder : Nor never will, if you can help it.
Dr. Oxenden : Mr. Kidd, you have had reasonable notice, and you knew you must be tried, and therefore you cannot plead you are not ready.

Then there was the matter of those who would be testifying against him, all of whom admitted that they had come into court based on the promised pardons offered by William III.

Cl. of Arr : Nicholas Churchill, hold up thy hand.
Churchill : My lord, I desire I may have the benefit of the proclamation; I came in upon the King's proclamation.
Recorder : If you do not plead, the court must pass judgment upon you. You can have no benefit in what you say, till you have pleaded. If you were indicted for felony, and you will not plead, the law takes it in nature of a confession, and judgment must pass, as if you were proved guilty.
Cl. of Arr : Nicholas Churchill, hold up thy hand. James Howe, hold up thy hand, Robert Lamley, hold up thy hand. (Which they did)
Recorder : W. Kidd has not held up his hand.
Cl. of Arr : He does hold up his hand. William Jenkins - hold up thy hand, Gabriel Loff - hold up thy hand, Hugh Parrot - hold up thy hand, Richard Barlicorn - hold up thy hand, Abel Owens - hold up thy hand.
Owens: I came in upon the King's proclamation, and entered myself into the King's service.
Recorder : You must plead first, and then if there be occasion, you will have the benefit of it. (Then he held up his hand)
Cl. of Arr : Darby Mullins, hold up thy hand.
Mullins : May it please your lordships, I came in voluntarily on the king's proclamation.
Recorder : This is the same case with Owens, you must speak to that afterwards.

The one piece of evidence that Kidd believed would clear him was not available to him at the beginning of the trial, thanks to the duplicity of Bellomont.

Cl. of Arr : W. Kidd, you stand indicted by the name of William Kidd. Art thou guilty or not guilty?
Kidd : I cannot plead to this indictment, till my French passes are delivered to me.
Cl. of Arr : Are you guilty or not guilty ?
Kidd : My lord, I insist upon my French papers; pray let me have them.
Recorder : That must not be now, till you have put yourself upon your trial.
Kidd : That must justify me.
Recorder : You may plead it then, if the court see cause.
Kidd : My justification depends on them.
Recorder : Mr. Kidd, I must tell you, if you will not plead, you must have judgment against you, as standing mute.
Cl. of Arr : What can he have counsel for, before he has pleaded?
Recorder : Mr. Kidd, the court tells you, you shall be heard what you have to say when you have pleaded to your indictment. If you plead to it, if you will, you may assign matter of law, if you have any; but then you must let the court know what you would insist on.
Kidd: I beg your lordship's patience till I can procure my papers. I had a couple of French passes, which I must make use of in order to my justification.
Kidd : If your lordships permit those papers to be read, they will justify me. I desire my counsel may be heard.
Mr. Coniers : We admit of no counsel for him.
Recorder : There is no issue joined; and therefore there can be no counsel assigned. Mr. Kidd, you must plead.
Kidd : I cannot plead till I have those papers that I insisted upon.
Mr. Lemmon : He ought to have his papers delivered to him, because they are very material for his defence. He has endeavoured to have them, but could not get them.
Mr. Coniers : You are not to appear for any one till he pleads, and that the court assigns you for his counsel.
Recorder : They would only put off the trial.
Mr. Coniers : He must plead to the indictment.
Cl. of Arr : Make silence.
Kidd : My papers were all seized, and I cannot make my defence without them. I desire my trial may be put off till I can have them.
Recorder : The court is of opinion they ought not to stay for all your evidence ; it may be they will never come. You must plead, and then if you can satisfy the court, that there is a reason to put off your trial, you may.

Kidd : My lord, I have business in law, and I desire counsel.

Recorder : Mr. Kidd, the course of courts is, when you have pleaded, the matter of trial is next: if you can then show there is cause to put off the trial, you may but now the matter is to plead.

Kidd : It is a hard case when all these things shall be kept from me, and I be forced to plead.

Recorder : If he will not plead, there must be judgment.

Kidd : My lord, would you have me plead, and not to have my vindication by me?

Cl. of Arr : Will you plead to the indictment ?

Kidd : I would beg that I may have my papers for my vindication.

Recorder : Mr. Kidd, I must tell you, if you will not plead, you must have judgment against you, as standing mute.

Kidd : I cannot plead till I have these papers; and I have not my witnesses here.

Recorder : You do not know your own interest; if you will not plead you must have judgment against you.

Kidd : If I plead I shall be an accessory to my own death, till I have persons to plead for me.

Recorder : You are an accessory to your own death, if you do not plead. We cannot enter into the evidence, unless you plead.

Cl. of Arr : Are you guilty or not guilty?

Recorder : He does not understand the law; you must read the statute to him.

Cl. of Arr : Mr. Kidd, are you guilty of this piracy, or not guilty?

Kidd : If you will give me a little time to find my papers, I will plead.

Cl. of Arr : There is no reason to give you time; will you plead or not?

Mr. Coniers : Be pleased to acquaint him with the danger he stands in by not pleading. Whatever he says, nothing can avail him till he pleads.

Recorder : He has been told so, but does not believe us.

Mr. Coniers : If there be any reason to put off his trial, it must be made appear after issue is joined.

Recorder : If you say guilty, there is an end of it; but if you say not guilty, the court can examine into the fact.

Officer : He says he will plead.

Cl. of Arr : W. Kidd, art thou guilty or not guilty ?

Kidd: Not guilty.

Cl. of Arr : How wilt thou be tried ?

Kidd.: By God and my country.

Cl. of Arr : God send thee a good deliverance (And so of all the rest)

Upon hearing this, Kidd once more pleaded for more time.

    Kidd : My lord, I beg I may have my trial put off for three or four days, till I have got my papers.
Recorder : The judges will be here by-and bye, and you may move the court then; we are only to prepare for your trial: We do not deny your motion; but when the court is full, they will consider of the reasons you have to offer.

    Cl. of Arr: W. Kidd, Hold up thy hand (which he did) Thou standest indicted in the name of William Kidd, late of London, mariner.

As it turns out, Kidd was correct about his need for the French passes. Scholars would later agree that he probably would have been acquitted had the court seen them. However, they were only found three centuries later, having been conveniently misfiled by a careless court archivist.

In addition to the piracy charges, Kidd also had to deal with the murder charge. Next, the court brought against Kidd the charge of murder in the death of William Moore. After the charge was read, the court asked for Kidd's plea. Kidd pled not guilty and then asked again for legal counsel.

    Kidd : My lord, I desire counsel may be assigned me.
Recorder : Captain Kidd, I told you it would be your time, when the jury was called, to offer what you had to offer; therefore, if you have anything now to say to the court, you had best say it.

Finally, Kidd had the opportunity to have counsel speak for him.

    Kidd : I beg I may have counsel. Dr. Oldish, and Mr. Lemmon, that they may be heard on my behalf.
Just. Powel : If he desires it, you may be counsel for him, provided there be any matter of law that he has to plead; otherwise he must be tried.
Dr. Oldish : My lord, he moves that his trial for piracy may be put off for several reasons; one is, there is one Davis, that is a necessary witness for him; he was taken a passenger into the ship, and therefore could not be concerned in any piracy: now this Davis stands indicted, so that he is deprived of this person, who is a necessary witness for him in this case.

    Mr. Coniers : He is not indicted yet; he may call him if he thinks fit.
Just. Powel : If he be indicted, yet he may be a witness.
Dr. Oldish : My lord, we desire he may be here.
Just. Powel : Where is he?
Cl. of Arr : He is in Newgate.

Just. Powel : Let him be sent for.
Dr. Oldish : My lord, it is very fit his trial should be delayed for some time, because he wants some papers very necessary for his defence. It is very true, he is charged with piracies in several ships; but they had French passes when the seizure was made. Now if there were French passes, it was a lawful seizure.
Just. Powel : Have you those passes?
Kidd : They were taken from me by my Lord Bellamont; and these passes would be my defence.
Dr. Oxenden : Had you any other passes when you took the Armenian ship?
Dr. Oldish : If those ships that he took had French passes, there was just cause of seizure, and it will excuse him from piracy.
Kidd : The passes were seized by my lord Bellamont, they we will prove my innocence as clear as the day.
Mr. Lemmon : My lord, I desire one word as to this circumstance; he was doing his king and country service, instead of being a pirate: for in this very ship there was a French pass, and it was shewn to Mr. Davis, and carried to my lord Bellamont, and he made a seizure of it. And there was a letter writ to testify it, which was produced before the parliament; and that letter has been transmitted from hand to hand, so that we cannot at present come by it. There are several other papers and letters that we cannot get; and therefore we desire the trial may be put off till we can procure them.
LCB Ward : Where are they?
Mr. Lemmon : We cannot yet tell whether they are in the Admiralty office, or whether Mr. Jodrell hath them.

Just. Powel : Let us see on which you go. You talk of French passes; you should have been prepared to make affidavit of it. What ship was that which had the French passes?
Mr. Lemmon : The same we were in, the same he is indicted for.
Just. Powel : Make out this, Mr. Lemmon.
Mr. Lemmon : My lord, we desire Mr. Davis may be sent for; he will prove it.
LCB Ward : Send for Edward Davis.
Mr. Fell : My lord, will you have him brought into Court?
L. C.B.Ward : Yes.
Sol. Gen : They have had a fortnight's notice to prepare for the trial.
Dr. Oldish : We petitioned for money, and the court ordered 50 pounds but the person that received it went away, and we had none till last night.
Dr. Oxenden : I ordered that the money might be paid into his own hands, that he might be sure to have it.
Mr. Crawley (Register) declared, that he paid the 50 pounds into his own hands on Tuesday morning.
LCB Ward : You ought to make it out, that there is a reasonable cause to put off the

trial, or else it cannot be allowed.
Mr. Lemmon : My lord, we will be ready tomorrow morning.
LCB Ward : They ought to have had due notice; what notice have they had?
Sol. Gen : A fortnight's notice, this day fortnight.
Dr. Oldish : My lord, he should have had his money delivered to him.
Kidd : I had no money nor friends to prepare for my trial till last night.
LCB Ward : Why did you not signify so much to the king's officers?
Sol. Gen : My lord, this we will do; let Davis be brought into court; and if that be a just excuse we
are contented. In the mean time, let him be tried for the murder, wherein there is no pretence of want
of witnesses or papers.
Officer : Davis is here, my lord.

For his part, Kidd never denied that he had killed the man. However, he had a different perspective on why he did it.

   LCB Ward : Then you may make your defence. You are charged with murder, and you have heard the evidence that has been given, what have you to say for yourself?
Kidd : I have evidence to prove it is no such thing, if they may be admitted to come hither. My lord, I will tell you what the case was : I was coming up within a league of the Dutchman, and some of my men were making a mutiny about taking her, and my gunner told the people he could put the captain in a way to take the ship, and be safe. Says I, How will you do that ? The gunner answered, We will get the captain and men aboard. And what then ? We will go aboard the ship, and plunder her, and we will have it under their hands that we did not take her. Says I, This is Judas like, I dare not do such a thing. Says he, We may do it, we are beggars already. Why says I, may we take this ship because we are poor? Upon that a mutiny arose: so I took up a bucket, and just throwed it at him and said you are a rogue to make such a motion. This I can prove, my lord.
LCB Ward : Call your evidence.
Kidd : They are prisoners, I desire they may be called up.
LCB Ward : Whatever other crimes they may be guilty of, they may be witnesses for him in this case.

Thus, Kidd was finally able to call witnesses in his defense. However, this attempt soon backfired.

     Kidd : Call Abel Owens. (Who appeared) Can you tell which way this bucket was thrown ?
     Just. Powel : What was the provocation of throwing this bucket?

Owens : I was in the cook-room and hearing some difference on the deck, I came out, and the gunner was grinding a chisel on a grind stone, and the captain and he had some words, and the gunner said to the captain, You have brought us to ruin, and we are desolate. And, the captain says how have I brought you to ruin? I have not brought you to ruin, I have not done an ill thing to ruin you, you are a saucy fellow to give me these words. And then he took up the bucket and did give him the blow.

Kidd : Was there not a mutiny among the men?

Owens : Yes, and the bigger part was for taking the ship; and the captain said, you that will take the Dutchman, you are the strongest, you may do what you please; if you will take her, you may take her; but if you go from aboard, you shall never come aboard this ship again.

LCB Ward : When was this mutiny you speak of?

Owens : When we were at sea.

LCB Ward : How long was it before this man's death?

Owens : About a month.

Just. Powel : At this time when the blow was given, did Moore the gunner endeavour to make any mutiny?

Owens : No.

Just. Powel : Was there any mutiny then?

Owens : None at all.

Kidd : Did not he say he could put me in a way to take the Dutchman, and be clear?

Owens : I know there were several of them would have done it, but you would not give consent to it.

Kidd : No; but this was the reason I threw the bucket at him.

LCB Ward : Captain Kidd, he tells you this was a month before you struck him.

LCB Ward : Captain Kidd, will you call anymore?

Kidd : Yes, my lord. Call Richard Barlicorn.

Just. Powel : What questions would you have him asked?

Kidd : R. Barlicorn, What was the reason that blow was given to the gunner?

Barlicorn : At first when you met with the ship, there was a mutiny, and two or three of the Dutchmen came aboard; And some said, she was a rich vessel, and they would take her; and the captain said. No, I will not take her. And there was a mutiny in the ship, and the men said, If you will not, we will. And he said. If you have a mind, you may; but they that will not, come along with me.

Kidd : Do you think William Moore was one of those that was for taking her ?

Barlicorn : Yes.

Kidd : He was going to make another mutiny, and I prevented him.

Just. Powel : Did Moore endeavour to make any mutiny at this time ?

Barlicorn : The ship was gone at that time.
Just. Powel : How long had she been gone?
Barlicorn : About a week.
Baron Hatsell : Was there any mutiny about the Dutch ship you saw?
Barlicorn : The Dutch ship? Not that I know of; but there was a mutiny aboard the Loyal Captain.
Kidd : Do you not know of another mutiny?
Baron Hatsell : Do you know of any other mutiny ? —
Barlicorn : No.
Kidd : At that very time they were going to make a mutiny.
LCB Ward : Will you ask him any more questions?
Kidd : What discourse had I with Moore at that time?
Barlicorn : I was aboard our ship, but did not see the blow given.
Kidd : They were saying they would take her, and he said he could put me in a way to take her, without coming to any harm.
LCB Ward : What occasion could those words be of a mutiny?
Barlicorn : There were many of the men would have gone with arms, and taken that ship without the captain's consent.
LCB Ward : At that time when this Moore was killed, was there any mutiny ?
Barlicorn : No.

After the prosecution gave its summary, Kidd once more tried to call a witness on his behalf.

Kidd : My lord, I have witnesses to produce for my reputation.
LCB Ward : Mr. Kidd, we gave you time to make your defence; why did not you produce them? You were asked more than once, if you had any more to say; and you said, you would call no more witnesses.
Kidd : I can prove what service I have done for the King.
LCB Ward : You should have spoken sooner; but what would that help in this case of murder? You said you had no more to say before I began.

His last hope of defense denied, the jury returned a verdict of guilty.

LCB Ward : He is to be tried according to law; the king's evidence hath been heard, and he has the liberty to produce what evidence he can for himself; will you put him to produce more evidence than he can? If he has any more to say, it will be his interest to say what he can; the court is willing to hear him as long as he hath any thing to offer for himself, either upon that account, or anything else.

At this point, Kidd knew he was beaten, and took one final stab at avoiding the gallows, claiming, "It was not designedly done, but in my passion, for which I am heartily sorry." At the same time, he kept reaching out to higher authorities, including offering a deal to the English government in one letter to the Speaker of the House of Commons:

"S'r,

The sence of my present Condition (being under Condemnation) and the thoughts of having bene imposed on by such as seek't my destruction thereby to fulfill their ambitious desires makes me uncapable of Expressing my selfe in those terms as I ought, therefore due most humbly pray that you will be pleased to represent to the Hon'bl. house of Comons that in my late proceedings in the Indies I have lodged goods and Tresure to the value of one hundred thousand pounds, which I desire the Government may have the benefitt of, in order thereto, I shall desire no manner of liberty but to be kept prisoner on board such shipp as may be appointed for that purpose, and only give the necessary directions and in case I faile therin I desire no favour but to be forthwith Executed acording to my Sentence. If y'r honbl. house will please to order a Comittee to come to me, I doubt not but to give such satisfaction as may obtaine mercy, most Humbly submitting to the wisdom of your great assembly I am

S'r Y'r Unfortunate humble servant

Wm Kidd"

All of it went for naught, and for whatever reason, Kidd never revealed the names of the people who had been part of his now notorious scheme. On May 23, 1701, Kidd, by this time an alcoholic, was afforded the "luxury" of being given so much rum and brandy that he could not stand up straight before being wheeled through the streets of London toward the Execution Dock in Wapping. Kidd continued to claim his innocence as he took his spot alongside two French pirates and Darby Mullins, the one crew member of his who had not attempted to save his own skin by selling out Kidd.

Even Kidd's execution proved to be a travesty of justice. On the first attempt to hang the 4 men, the rope around Kidd's neck broke and sent him crashing into the mud while the other 3 were successfully hanged. Such events were often considered cases of divine intervention by the courts and resulted in the man being set free, but for Kidd they simply brought in another rope and hanged him again.

As if that wasn't enough, pursuant to the maritime laws, the bodies of the 4 convicted pirates remained there until the tide had come and gone three times. After that, Kidd's corpse was tarred and then put in a cage at Tilbury Point along the Thames River, meant to serve as a warning against others who would contemplate piracy. Kidd's corpse would be displayed there for over two years, during which birds pecked at his rotting carcass until there was practically nothing left.

Illustration of Kidd gibbeted in chains

As fate would have it, Kidd would be the only participant in the scheme to be punished. Obviously the king would not be punished, and the four main financial backers maintained silence for the rest of their lives. Robert Livingston would become one of the richest men in New York and die of old age, while even Captain Culliford escaped major punishment by accepting the general amnesty afforded to every pirate not named William Kidd or Henry Every. After King William III's death, Queen Anne seized the remnants of Kidd's belongings and had them

publicly auctioned

Ultimately, Kidd left one of the most unique legacies among the best known pirates of history, especially since he insisted until the day he died that he was not a pirate at all. While it's clear that Kidd got a raw deal in his trial, it's also apparent that he likely committed illegal acts of piracy. At the very least, Kidd's life and death served as a reminder that there was an extremely fine line between privateers and pirates, one that authorities themselves would ignore if they needed to do so politically. For all of these reasons, it's ironic that Kidd became famous for burying treasure, one of the stereotypes most commonly associated with pirates despite the fact that Kidd is the only individual definitely known to have done so.

Howard Pyle's illustration of Kidd burying treasure

As the most famous individual of the Golden Age of Piracy to truly toe the line between piracy and privateering, English writer Harold Thompson may have summed it up best in calling Kidd "a man neither very good nor very bad, the fool of fortune and the tool of politicians, a pirate in spite of himself."

Kidd's Account of His Expedition

Boston, 17th July, 1699.

Mr. John Gardner of Gardner's Island presented this note to His Excellency in Council, which he made oath was delivered to him by Captain Kidd, as was wrote with the said Kidd's own hand on board his sloop, and all the particulars therein mentioned were committed to his custody.

Examined by Isaac Addington Secretary.

That the Journal of the said Captain Kidd, being violently taken from him in the Port of St. Marie's in Madagascar, and his life being many times threatened to be taken away from him by ninety seven of his men that deserted him there, he cannot give that exact account he otherwise could have done: but as far as his Memory will serve, is as followeth, viz..

That the said Adventure Galley was launched in Castle's Yard at Deptford, about the fourth of December 1695 and about the latter end of February the said Galley came to the buoy in the Nore and about the 1st Day of March following, his Men were pressed for him for the Fleet, which caused him to stay there for nineteen days and then sailed for the Downs, and arrived there about the Eighth or the Tenth Day of April 1696; and sailed thence for Plymouth; and on the Twenty-third Day of the said month of April he sailed on his intended voyage : and, some time in the month of May, met with a small French Vessel, with Salt and Fishing Tackle on board, bound for Newfoundland, which he took and made Prize of, and carried the same into New York, about the Fourth Day of July, when she was condemned as lawful Prize: The Produce whereof purchased provisions for the said Galley, and for her further intended Voyage.

That about the Sixth Day of September 1696, the said Captain Kidd sailed for the Madeiras, in company with one Joyner, Master of a Brigantine belonging to Bermudas, and arrived there about the 8th Day of October following: and thence to Bona vista, where they arrived about the nineteenth of the said month, and took in some salt, and stayed Three or Four Days; and sailed thence to St. Jago, and arrived there the Twenty-fourth of the said Month, where he took in some Water, and stayed about Eight or Nine Days; and thence sailed for the Cape of Good Hope; and in the Latitude of Thirty-two.

On the Twelfth Day of December 1696, met with Four English Men of War: Captain Warren was Commodore; and sailed a week in their Company ; and then parted, and sailed to Telere, a Port in the Island of Madagascar, and being there about the Twenty-ninth Day of January, came in a Sloop belonging to Barbadoes, loaded with Rum, Sugar, Powder and Shot, one French

Master, and Mr. Hatton and Mr. John Batt, Merchants ; and the said Hatton came on board the said Galley, and was suddenly taken ill and died in the Cabin: And, about the latter end of February, sailed for the Island of Johanna, the said Sloop keeping Company, and arrived there about the Eighteenth Day of March; where he found Four East India Merchantsmen outward bound ; and watered there all together, and staid about Four Days: And from thence, about the Twenty second of March, sailed for Mehila, an Island Ten Leagues distant from Johanna, where he arrived the next Morning, and there careened the said Galley; and about Fifty men died there in a Week's Time.

That on the 25th Day of April 1697, set sail for the Coast of India, and came upon the Coast of Mallabar, the Beginning of the Ninth of September; and went into Carwarr upon that Coast about the middle of the same Month, and watered there: And the Gentlemen of the English factory gave the Narrator an account, That the Portuguese were fitting out Two Men of War to take him; and advised him to put out to Sea, and to take Care of himself from them, and immediately to set sail thereupon; about the 12th of the said month of September; and the next morning, about Break of Day saw the said Two Men of War standing for the said Galley ; and spoke with him and asked him, Whence he was? Who replied from London; and they returned answer, From Goa; and so parted, wishing each other a good Voyage; And making still along the Coast, the Commodore of the said Man of War kept dogging the said Galley all the Night, waiting an Opportunity to board her; and in the Morning, without speaking a Word, Fired Six great Guns at the Galley, some whereof went through her, and wounded Four of his Men; and there upon he fired upon him again ; and the Fight continued all Day; and the narrator had Eleven Men wounded: the other Portuguese man of War lay some Distance off, and could not come up with the Galley, being calm; else would have likewise assaulted the same ; the said Fight was sharp, and the said Portuguese left the said Galley with such satisfaction, that the Narrator believes no Portuguese will ever attack the King's Colours again, in that Part of the World especially. And afterwards continued upon the same Coast, cruising upon the coast of Cameroone, for Pirates that frequent that Coast, till the Beginning of the month of November 1697, When he met with Captain How in the Loyal Captain, an English Ship belonging to Madeiras, bound to Surat, whom he examined; and finding his Pass good, designed to freely to let her pass about her Affairs; but, having Two Dutchmen on board, they told the Narrator's Men, That they had divers Greeks and Armenians on board, who had divers precious Stones and divers other rich Goods on board, which caused his Men to be very mutinous, and got up their Arms, and swore they would take the Ship : and two-thirds of his Men voted for the same: The narrator told them, the small Arms belonged to the Galley, and that he was not come to take any Englishmen, or lawful Traders; and that if they attempted any such thing, they should never come on board the Galley again, nor have the Boat, or small Arms; for he had no Commission to take any but the King's Enemies, and Pirates, and that he would attack them with the Galley, and drive them into Bombay; the other being a Merchantman, and having no Guns, might easily have done it with a few Hands; and, with all the Arguments and Menaces he could use, could scarce restrain them from their unlawful Design; but at last I prevailed, and with much ado I got him clear, and let him go about his Business. All which the said Captain How will attest, if living.

And that, about the 18th or 19th Day of the said month of November, met with a Moors Ship of about 200 Tons coming from Surat, bound to the Coast of Malabar, loaded with Two Horses, Sugar and Cotton, to trade there having about Forty Moors on board, with a Dutch Pilot, Boatswain, and Gunner; which said Ship the Narrator haled, and commanded on board; and with him came Eight or Nine Moors, and the said Three Dutchmen, who declared it was a Moors Ship ; and demanding their pass from Surat, which they shewed; and the same was a French Pass, which he believes was shewn by a Mistake; for the Pilot swore Sacrament she was a Prize, and staid on board the Galley; and would not return on board the Moor Ship ; but went in the Galley to the Port of St. Marie.

And that, about the First Day of February following, upon the same Coast, under French Colours with a Design to decoy, met with a Bengali Merchantman belonging to Surat, of the Burden of 4. or 500 Tons, 10 Guns; and he commanded the Master on board; and a Frenchman, Inhabitant of Surat, and belonging to the French Factory there, and Gunner of the said Ship, came on board as Master; and when he came on board, the Narrator caused the English Colours to be hoisted ; and the said Master was surprised, and said. You are all English; and asking, which was the Captain? Whom when he saw, said, Here is a good Prize, and delivered him the French Pass.

And that, with the said Two Prizes, sailed for the Port of St. Marie's in Madagascar; and, sailing thither, the said Galley was so leaky, that they feared she would have sunk every Hour, and it required Eight men every Two Glasses to keep her free ; and was forced to woold her round with Cables to keep her together; and with much ado carried her into the said Port of St. Mane's, where she arrived about the First of April, 1698: And about the 6th day of May, the lesser Prize was haled into the careening Island or Key, the other not being arrived; and ransacked and sunk by the mutinous men; who threatened the Narrator, and the men that would not join with them to burn and sink the other, that they might not go home and tell the news.

And that, when he arrived in the said Port, there was a Pirate Ship, called the Mocha Frigate, at an Anchor, Robert Culliford. Commander thereof; who with his Men, left the same at his coming in, and ran into the Woods : and the Narrator proposed to his men to take the same, having sufficient Power and Authority so to do; but the Mutinous Crew told him, If he offered the same, they would rather fire Two Guns into him, than one into the other ; and there upon Ninety-seven deserted, and went into the Mocha Frigate, and sent into the Woods for the said Pirates, and brought the said Culliford, and his Men, on board again ; and all the time she staid in the said Port, which was the Space of Four or Five Days, the said Deserters, sometimes in great Numbers, came on board the said Galley and Adventure Prize, and carried away great Guns, Powder, Shot, small Arms, Sails, Anchors, Cables, Surgeons, Chests, and what else they pleased; and threatened several times to murder the Narrator, as he was informed, and advised to take care of himself; which they designed in the Night to effect; but was prevented by him locking himself in his Cabin at Night, and securing himself with barricading the same with Bales of Goods; and, having about Forty small Arms, besides Pistols, ready charged, kept them out.

Their Wickedness was so great, after they had plundered and ransacked sufficiently, went Four Miles off to one Edward Welche's House, where his the Narrator's Chest was lodged, and broke it open; and took out Ten Ounces of Gold, 40 Pound of Plate, 370 Pieces of Eight, the Narrator's Journal, and a great many Papers that belonged to him, and the People of New York that fitted them out.

That about the 15th July, the Mocha Frigate went away, being manned with about 130 Men, and Forty Guns, bound out to take all Nations : Then it was that the Narrator was left with only Thirteen men; so that the Moors he had to pump and keep the Adventure Galley above Water, being carried away, she sunk in the Harbour ; and the Narrator, with the said Thirteen men, went on board the Adventure Prize; where he was forced to stay Five Months for a Fair Wind; In the meantime, some Passengers presented, that were bound for these Parts; which he took on board, to help to bring the said Adventure Prize home.

That, about the beginning of April, 1699, the Narrator arrived at Anguila in the West Indies, and sent his Boat on Shore; where his Men had the News That he and his People were proclaimed Pirates, which put them into such Consternation, That they sought all Opportunity to run the Ship on Shore upon some Reef or Shoal, fearing the Narrator should carry them into some English Port.

From Anguilla they came to St. Thomas'; where his Brother-in-law Samuel Bradley was put on shore, being sick; and Five more went away, and deserted him: Where he heard the same News, That the Narrator, and his Company, were proclaimed Pirates, which incensed the People more and more.

From St. Thomas set sail for Mona, an Island between Hispaniola and Porto Rico; where they met with a Sloop called the St, Anthony, bound for Antigua from Curacao, Mr. Wm. Boulton Merchant, and Samuel Wood, Master: The men on board then swore, they would bring the Ship no further. The Narrator then sent the said Sloop St. Anthony for Curacao for Canvas to make Sails for the Prize, she not being able to proceed; and she returned in Ten Days; and after the Canvas came, he could not persuade the Men to carry her for New England; but Six of them went and carried their Chests and Things on board of Two Dutch Sloops; bound for Curacao; and would not so much as heel the Vessel, or do anything, the Remainder of the men not being able to bring the Adventure Prize to Boston, the Narrator secured her in a good Harbour in some Part of Hispaniola and left in the Possession of Mr. Henry Boulton of Antigua. Merchant, the Maker, Three of the old Men, and Fifteen or Sixteen of the men that belonged to the said Sloop St. Anthony, and a Brigantine belonging to one Mr. Burt of Curacao.

That the Narrator bought the said Sloop St. Anthony off Mr. Boulton, for the Owner's Account; and after, he had given Directions to the said Boulton to be careful of the said Ship and Lading, and persuaded him to stay Three Months till he returned; and then made the best of his Way to New York; where he heard the Earl of Bellamont was, who was principally concerned in the Adventure Galley; and hearing his Lordship, was at Boston, came thither; and has now been 45 Days from the said Ship.

Signed : Wm. Kidd.

Boston. 7th July, 1699.

Further the Narrator saith. That the said Ship was left at St. Katharina, on the South East Part of Hispaniola, about Three Leagues to Leeward of the Westerly End of Savona: Whilst he lay at Hispaniola, he traded with Mr. Henry Boulton of Antigua, and Mr. Wm. Burt of Curacao, Merchants, to the Value of 11,200 Pieces of Eight; whereof he received the Sloop Antonio at 3000 Pieces of Eight, and 4200 Pieces of Eight by Bills of Exchange, drawn by Boulton and Burt upon Messieurs Gabriel and Lemont, Merchants in Curacao, made payable to Mr. Burt, who went himself to Curacao; and the Value of 4,000 Pieces of Eight more in Dust and Bar Gold; which Gold, with some more traded for at Madagascar, being Fifty Pounds Weight, or upwards, in Quantity, the Narrator left in Custody of Mr. Gardner of Gardner's Island, near the Eastern End of Long Island, fearing to bring it about by Sea: It is made up in a Bag put into a little Box, locked, nailed, corded about, and sealed: Saith he took no Receipt for it off Mr. Gardner.

The Gold that was seized at Mr. Campbell's, the Narrator, traded for at Madagascar, with what came out of Galley. Saith, That he carried in the Adventure Galley, from New York, 154 men : Seventy whereof came out of England with him. Some of his Sloop's Company put Two Bales of Goods on shore at Gardner's Island, being their own proper Goods. The Narrator delivered a Chest of Goods, viz.. Muslins, Latches, Romalls, and flowered Silk, unto Mr. Gardner of Gardner's Island aforesaid, to be kept there for the narrator : Put no Goods on shore anywhere else : Several of his Company landed their Chests, and other Goods, at several Places.

Further saith, He delivered a small Bale of coarse Calicoes unto a Sloop Man of Rhode Island, that he had employed there. The Gold seized at Mr. Campbells the Narrator intended for Presents to some, that he expected to do him Kindnesses. Some of his Company put their Chests and Bales on board a New York Sloop lying at Gardner's Island. Cc

Signed : Wm. Kidd.

Presented and taken, die praedict before his Excellency and Council.

Copy Examined by Isaac Addington, Secretary.

Bibliography

J.H. Temple and G. Sheldon. 1875. *History of the Town of Northfield.* Joel Munsell, Albany, N.Y.

Robert C. Ritchie. 1986. *Captain Kidd and the War against the Pirates.* Harvard Univ. Press, Cambridge, MA and London.

Exquemeling, John. 1684. *The Buccaneers of America.* London.

Arciniegas, G. 1946. *Caribbean, Sea of the New World.* Alfred A. Knopf, New York.

Henry Every

Chapter 1: Early Years

Perhaps not surprisingly, the early years of a man destined to become one of history's most successful pirates is wrapped in a shroud of uncertainty. Contemporary accounts placed his birthday anywhere between 1653 and 1665, but it's now believed (based in part on a confession by one of his crew) that he was born on August 23, 1659 in Newton Ferrers, a village in Devon, England. His parents, John and Anne, were wealthy, and it's believed his father was once a Royal Navy sailor who made his fortune in the liquor trade. Though it was once speculated that Henry Every was just a nickname and that his real name was Benjamin Bridgeman, the Royal Navy's records indicate he entered the service using the name Henry Every years before he ever became a pirate, meaning it was more likely Every was using the name Benjamin Bridgeman as an alias rather than the other way around.

Every was his parents' only child, and they were determined to give him the best education possible, but he quickly made it clear that he was more interested in being in a boat at sea than in an office on land. As soon as Every was old enough, he joined the Royal Navy, serving on various ships throughout his career. One of the first battles he may have participated in was the English attack on Algiers in 1671, and his first biographer also claimed that he later sailed around the Caribbean Sea as a privateer and transported resources in the New World through the Bay of Campeche.

Modern scholars continue to debate the veracity of those early accounts, but it's widely believed that Every first came into his own in the spring of 1689, shortly after the Nine Years War broke out in Europe. By this time he had worked his way up to the rank of midshipman aboard the HMS *Rupert*, and by then it appears he had also married and settled down. In fact, Every had a reputation for being a family man; he spent "little of his wages on extras such as tobacco and regularly consigned his pay to his family."

A few months into the war, the *Rupert* captured a French fleet just off the coast of Brest, and Every apparently conducted himself well enough during the battle to earn a promotion to the position of Master's Mate. When the ship's Captain, Sir Francis Wheeler, transferred to the HMS *Albemarle*, he took Every with him, and they would fight against the French navy at the Battle of Beachy Head a few weeks later in July 1690. Following the battle, a decisive defeat for the English, Every was discharged from the Navy.

Engraving depicting the Battle of Beachy Head by Jean Antoine Théodore de Gudin

After his naval career had ended, Every took up the ignominious career of slave trading, which marked the beginning of his illegal activities. From 1690-1692 Every captured men and women off the coast of Africa and shipped them in cramped ships to the Bahamas, which was not only immoral but also a violation of English law. At the time, England had given the Royal African Company the exclusive rights to ship slaves to England and her colonies, but like most illegal endeavors, the unlicensed slave trade was very profitable. Those seeking to make a lot of money attempted to circumvent the Royal African Company's monopoly on the slave trade, and so many "interlopers" sailed around the west coast of the African continent that the Royal Navy itself was compelled to get involved in protecting the company's interests.

Because trips to Africa itself were both expensive and dangerous, Every soon came up with his own method of acquiring slaves to sell. He would approach other English ships flying friendly colors, and as soon as Every's ship got close enough, he and his men would board the ships and take the captains and their cargoes hostage. By 1693, Every had become so notorious in the area that he was known by name among the agents of the Royal African Company and ship captains involved in the slave trade. Captain Thomas Phillips of the *Hannibal*, who clearly had at least one too many run-ins with Every, mentioned his piracy in one journal entry, writing, "I have no where upon the coast met the negroes so shy as here, which makes me fancy they have had tricks play'd them by such blades as Long Ben, alias Avery, who have seiz'd them and carry'd them away."

Chapter 2: Mutineer

As Every's early naval career suggested, a lot of the pirates that came to harass the European nations trading in the New World had first been enrolled in their own nations' navies, learning all about sailing and commanding boats and then putting these skills to use for their own good. When the European nations were officially at war with each other, they used private sailors as privateers to aid their cause. As a result, Every would soon find himself in the employ of Englishmen again, despite the fact he had menaced English slave traders in the preceding years. In early 1693, Sir James Houblon and several other English investors organized the Spanish Expedition Shipping venture. They purchased four warships that would sail to the Spanish West Indies, taking with them guns and cannon to sell to the Spaniards, and then fill their empty hulls with treasure plundered from the French. They recruited their crews aggressively, offering good wages paid in a timely manner.

Every's experience on both sides of the law earned him the position of First Mate in the new fleet, where he served under Admiral Sir Don Arturo O'Byrne of Ireland. Unfortunately, the company was plagued with bad luck from the very beginning. The trip to Spain, which should have taken two weeks, instead took five months, and when they finally did arrive, they found that their ship's paperwork had not been properly sent ahead and that they would have to wait to unload their cargo and get paid. This situation worsened as the months passed with no wages and less and less hope for them, until finally the men petitioned their captain and their wives back at home petitioned the company. Even still, no money was forthcoming, and tensions only rose as rumors spread that they might have even been sold to the Spanish as slaves.

The following May, word came that the ships were finally leaving port, but the men still had not been paid and began to talk of mutiny. One of the leaders of this movement was Henry Every himself, and according to later testimony, it was Every who walked "up and down, from ship to ship and persuaded the men to come on board [with] him, and he would carry them where they should get money enough." Due to his experience and the fact that he was more of their ilk than the captain, the men believed and trusted him.

By the evening of May 7, 1694, Every had his plan in place. When Admiral O'Byrne went ashore to stay with friends for the night, about 25 men led by Every rushed one of the ships, the *Charles II*, and took control from the bedridden captain. They were soon joined by other men from the *James*, and according to one historian, the following dialogue took place between Every and the Captain:

"Captain: What was the Matter?

Avery: Nothing.

Captain: Something's the Matter with the Ship, Does she drive? What Weather is it?

Avery: No, no, we're at Sea, with a fair Wind and good Weather.

Captain: At Sea! How can that be?

Avery: Come, don't be in a fright, but put on your clothes, and I'll let you into a secret: You must know, that I am captain of this ship now, and this is my cabin, therefore you must walk out; I am bound to Madagascar, with a design of making my own fortune, and that of all the brave fellows joined with me."

While it is unlikely that the conversation went so calmly, it is known that Every ran the probably intoxicated captain out of his own cabin and forced him to join the other sailors. When Captain Humphreys of that ship discovered what had happened, he fired on the *Charles II*, forcing Every and his men to make a run for it. Before the other two ships could be alerted, the *Charles II* disappeared into the moonless night.

In spite of his checkered past, Every was a reasonable man and even allowed those who were not part of the mutiny to leave the ship as soon as it got into port. He even went as far as to offer Gibson the captaincy of the ship, if he wanted it, but Gibson stayed loyal to his former employers and refused, instead opting to join the other men in the small ships headed for shore. Once they were gone, the mutineers elected Every as their captain and set sail for the Indian Ocean, renaming the *Charles II* the *Fancy*. They also agreed that every man on the crew would receive an equal portion of the treasure, with Every receiving a double portion, and thus turned their ship south toward Africa and the Cape of Good Hope.

Chapter 3: The Arch Pirate

18th century depiction of Every and the *Fancy*

Although they were obviously mutineers, the men were not yet pirates, but that would not last long. Shortly after heading south, Every and his crew attacked three English merchant ships bound home from Barbados off the Sotavento Islands in Cape Verde. Not only did they take much of the ships' cargo, they also convinced nine of the crew to join them on the *Fancy*, bringing the total crew to nearly 100.

According to the anonymous author of *A General History of the Pyrates* using the pseudonym Captain Charles Johnson:

"The Sloops Men were rejoiced at the new Ally, for their Vessels were so small, that they could not attack a Ship of any Force, so that hitherto they had not taken any considerable Prize, but now they hoped to fly at high Game; and Avery was as well pleased at this Reinforcement, to strengthen them, for any brave enterprise, and though the Booty must be lessened to each, by being divided into so many Shares, yet he found out an Expedient not to suffer by it himself as shall be shown in its Place.

Having consulted what was to be done, they resolved to sail out together upon a Cruize, the Galley and two Sloops; they therefore fell to work to get the Sloops off, which they soon effected, and steered towards the Arabian Coast; near the River Indus, the Man at the Mast-Head spied a Sail, upon which they gave Chace, and as they came nearer to her, they perceived her to be a tall Ship, and fancied she might be a Dutch East-India Man homeward bound; but she proved a better Prize; when they fired at her to bring too, she hoisted Mogul's Colours, and seemed to stand upon her Defence; Avery only canonaded at a Distance, and some of his Men began to suspect that he was not the Hero they took him for: However, the Sloops made Use of their Time, and coming one on the Bow, and the other on the Quarter, of the Ship, clapt her on Board, and enter'd her, upon which she immediately struck her Colours and yielded; she was one of the Great Mogul's own Ships, and there were in her several of the greatest Persons of his Court, among whom it was said was one of his Daughters, who were going on a Pilgrimage to Mecca, the Mahometans thinking themselves obliged once in their Lives to visit that Place, and they were carrying with them rich Offerings to present at the Shrine of Mahomet. It is known that the Eastern People travel with the utmost Magnificence, so that they had with them all their Slaves and Attendants, their rich Habits and Jewels, with Vessels of Gold and Silver, and great Sums of Money to defray the Charges of their Journey by Land; wherefore the Plunder got by this Prize, is not easily computed."

From Barbados, Every turned the *Fancy* toward Africa, and somewhere along the Guinea coast he persuaded an African chieftain into coming aboard his ship. He then took the man hostage, stole most of his property, and enslaved the chieftain and his men. From there, he proceeded up the coast to Bioko, where he refashioned the ship into a lighter, sleeker ship more suited to out sailing warships avoiding capture. By the time they were finished, the *Fancy* was one of the fastest ships in the European world.

With their now faster ship, Every and his pirates attacked two Danish ships near the Island of Principe, capturing their entire shipments of gold and ivory. Every also recruited 17 new men for his crew before moving on to Madagascar, where they put into St. Augustine's Bay to take on fresh supplies. After that stop, the *Fancy* moved on to the Comoros Islands, where they anchored for a while to rest. While there, they had the good fortune to capture a French pirate ship, and after looting it, they recruited about 40 of its crew members for their own ship.

In 1694, a poem was published in London. Reportedly written by Every himself, it gives the reader an interesting insight into the public's view of Every and his exploits.

"A Copy of Verses, composed by Captain Henry Every,
lately gone to sea to seek his fortune
Come all you brave Boys, whose Courage is bold,
Will you venture with me, I'll glut you with Gold?
Make haste unto Corona, a Ship you will find,
That's called the Fancy, will pleasure your mind.
Captain Every is in her, and calls her his own;
He will box her about, Boys, before he has done:
French, Spaniard and Portuguese, the Heathen likewise,
He has made a War with them until that he dies.
Her Model's like Wax, and she sails like the Wind,
She is rigged and fitted and curiously trimm'd,
And all things convenient has for his design;
God bless his poor Fancy, she's bound for the Mine.
Farewel, fair Plimouth, and Cat-down be damn'd,
I once was Part-owner of most of that Land;
But as I am disown'd, so I'll abdicate
My Person from England to attend on my Fate.
Then away from this Climate and temperate Zone,
To one that's more torrid, you'll hear I am gone,
With an hundred and fifty brave Sparks of this Age,
Who are fully resolved their Foes to engage.
These Northern Parts are not thrifty for me,
I'll rise the Anterhise, that some Men shall see
I am not afraid to let the World know,
That to the South-Seas and to Persia I'll go.
Our Names shall be blazed and spread in the Sky,
And many brave Places I hope to descry,
Where never a French man e'er yet has been,
Nor any proud Dut[c]h man can say he has seen.

My Commission is large, and I made it my self,
And the Capston shall stretch it full larger by half;
It was dated in Corona, believe it, my Friend,
From the Year Ninety three, unto the World's end.
I Honour St. George, and his Colours I were,
Good Quarters I give, but no Nation I spare,

> The World must assist me with what I do want,
> I'll give them my Bill, when my Money is scant.
> Now this I do say and solemnly swear,
> He that strikes to St. George the better shall fare;
> But he that refuses, shall sudenly spy
> Strange Colours abroad of my Fancy to fly.
> Four Chiviligies of Gold in a bloody Field,
> Environ'd with green, now this is my Shield;
> Yet call out for Quarter, before you do see
> A bloody Flag out, which our Decree,
> No Quarters to give, no Quarters to take,
> We save nothing living, alas 'tis too late;
> For we are now sworn by the Bread and the Wine,
> More serious we are than any Divine.
>
> Now this is the Course I intend for to steer;
> My false-hearted Nation, to you I declare,
> I have done thee no wrong, thou must me forgive,
> The Sword shall maintain me as long as I live."

Once they were safely in foreign waters, Every issued the following declaration to his fellow English captains:

"To all English Commanders let this satisfy that I was riding here at this instant in the ship Fancy, Man of War, formerly the Charles of the Spanish Expedition, who departed from Corunna the 7th of May, 1594, …and am now in a ship of 46 guns, 150 Men, and bound to seek our fortunes. I have never as yet wronged any English or Dutch, nor never intend [to,] while I am Commander. Wherefore, as I commonly speak with all ships, I desire whoever comes to the perusal of this to take this signal that if you or any whom you may inform are desirous to know what we are at, a distance then make your [ensign, flag] very prominent in a ball or bundle and hoist him at the Mizon Peek. The Mizon Being furled, I shall answer with the same and never molest you: for my men are hungry, stout and resolute, and should they exceed my desire, I cannot help my self.

As yet An Englishman's friend,

At [Anjouan] February 28th, 1695

Henry Every

There are 160 odd French armed men now at Mohilla who waits for opportunity of getting any ship, take care of your selves."

Obviously, Every was lying when he said that he had not attacked any English ships, but it probably didn't matter to him or the people to whom he was writing. No one was likely to take the word of a mutineer anyway, and even if some captains believed his offer to avoid ships that flew English colors, they had to have known based on his reputation and history that they were taking a big chance of being attacked and plundered if they got too close.

From his previous trips around the Indian Ocean, Every knew that Muslim pilgrims regularly made trips to Mecca sometime during the summer, so he took that into mind when he anchored off the coast of Perim, a small volcanic island, and waited for the Indian fleet to pass by. Because only the wealthiest Muslim leaders could afford to make their pilgrimage in the comfort of a sailing ship, pirates in the East knew that any pilgrim ship would yield great riches in jewelry and other personal property. However, the pilgrims also knew they were an attractive target and thus traveled in well protected fleets of ships.

In August 1695, Every met up with Thomas Tew, captain of the *Amity*, and four other pirate captains: Joseph Faro (captain of the *Portsmouth Adventure*), Richard Want (captain of the *Dolphin*), William Mayes (captain of the *Pearl*), and Thomas Wake (captain of the *Susanna*). Unlike Every, the other captains were privateers who had been commissioned by the Crown to attack foreign ships, but even though Every was not a privateer and was in fact wanted by the English authorities, they still chose him as their leader and admiral of the combined fleet. This put him in command of five captains, six ships and 440 men, but for a man of Every's experience and ego, this was not a problem.

Howard Pyle's depiction of Thomas Tew

Before long, Every's leadership was put to the test. A convoy of 25 ships, loaded with pilgrims and escorted by the well-armed *Fath Mahmamadi* began making their way past the pirate's island hide out. Because they were traveling quietly and at night, they almost got away without a fight, but the next morning Every and his men went after them. Unfortunately for the pirates, not all the ships were up for the chase; the *Dolphin* was not nearly fast enough to keep up with the other ships. As a result, Every ordered the ship scuttled and burned, and the crew brought aboard the *Fancy*, only for the *Amity* to fall behind the other pirate ships and never be seen again (possibly the result of Captain Tew being killed in battle against the fleet). The *Suzanna* also fell behind, but the ship was able to catch up in time to join in on the attack against the *Fath Mahmamadi*. Intimidated by Fancy's size and speed, she surrendered quickly. Her owner, Abdul Ghaffar, was one of the wealthiest merchants in the group, and the ship offered up a huge cargo of plunder into Every's eager hands estimated at being worth 60,000 pounds. One man who knew Ghaffar described his wealth, saying, "Abdul Ghafur, a Mahometan that I was acquainted with, drove a trade equal to the English East-India Company, for I have known him to fit out in a year, above twenty sail of ships, between 300 and 800 tons."

Although the booty stolen by the pirates could have bought them 50 pirate ships, when it was divided more than 400 ways among all the pirates, it did not amount to that much per man, or at least not enough to satisfy them. As a result, the ships once more went into hot pursuit and soon caught up with the *Ganj-i-sawai*, but her captain, Muhammad Ibrahim, would not be so easily intimidated and would not go quietly. Determined to fight, Ibrahim aimed most of his eight cannons at the remaining pirate ships, but the *Fancy* got off a lucky first shot to the mainmast and rendered the ship unmaneuverable. The sailors put up an initial fight but were soon defeated, not by Every, but by one of their own cannons, which exploded and killed many of them before Every's pirates could. Still, the hand-to-hand battle between the two crews lasted more than two hours before the Indian vessel surrendered.

Illustration depicting the fight between the *Fancy* and *Ganj-i-sawai*

Ironically, some of the worst criticism of how Ibrahim handled the battle came not from the English but from his own historians. Captain Ibrahim was blamed for cowardice, and even accused of hiding below decks and sending his own concubines up the stairs to defend him. One contemporary historian wrote, "The Christians are not bold in the use of the sword, and there were so many weapons on board the royal vessel that if the captain had made any resistance, they must have been defeated." Of course, Ibrahim would later defend his conduct, assuring others that he had indeed killed many of the pirates fighting against him.

Unfortunately, what happened after the plundering was horrifying, even by the low standards of pirates. Typically, Every and his men, like most pirates, would have been attacking ships manned by other sailors, with few or no women aboard. These ships, however, contained families, devout men and women who were making their way to center of their faith. Tragically, the pirates led by Every merely saw their weakness as an opportunity to inflict upon them all the horrors they could imagine. They raped the women, often repeatedly, before killing them. In order to avoid this fate that they considered worse than death, many women committed suicide, while those who survived the experience were taken as concubines back on to the *Fancy*.

Of course, the men onboard the ship fared no better. Many were tortured in the hopes that they would reveal the location of some previously hidden treasure, and those who survived the torture were subsequently killed along with the other men on the ship. Years later, John Sparkes, a hardened sailor who spent most of his life at sea, remembered with horror what had been done that week and said that it "still affected his soul." In a report filed by Sir John Gayer of the East India Company a few weeks after the incident, he wrote:

> "It is certain the pirates, which these people affirm were all English, did do very barbarously by the people of the Gunsway [an Anglicized version of the ship's name] and Abdul Gofor's Ship, to make them confess where their money was, and there happened to be a great Umbraws wife (as we hear) related to the king, returning from her pilgrimage to Mecca, in her old age. She they abused very much, and forced several other women, which caused one person of quality, his wife and nurse, to kill themselves to prevent the husbands seeing them (and their being) ravished."

One of the women Every took aboard may have been a princess, the daughter or granddaughter of the Emperor Aurangzeb, but it remains uncertain whether this particular story is true. What is certain is that the booty from the Ganj-i-sawai was the most ever taken by a pirate ship; while there is no way to know the exact value of the *Ganj-i-sawai*'s cargo, it had been estimated to have been as high as a million dollars. Of course, not all the treasure was Every's to keep, and upon having to try to divide it among all the men, an argument broke out between the crews of the *Pearl* and the *Fancy*. After much controversy, the matter was finally settled by giving Captain Mayes of the *Pearl* extra money to buy supplies, the group split up and went their own ways.

20th century depiction of Every and Emperor Aurangzeb's granddaughter.

After the audacious and successful attack on the Muslim fleet, the captains of the remaining pirate ships split up, with each going their own separate way. Every steered the *Fancy* for Bourbon, where he and his men divided the remainder of spoils, each man getting more than $1,500 ($200,000 in modern money). That was more money than they expected to earn during their entire lifetimes, but each member of the crew also got a substantial share of the valuable gemstones that the pirates that had taken from the ships. Not surprisingly, many of the men chose to retire after this haul and never sail again. This was especially true among the French and Danish members of his crew, with a majority opting to remain in Bourbon.

The ones who retired and went into hiding were the smart ones. Having taken in such a substantial haul, all pirates were technically criminals, but Every's deeds and the size of the treasure made him notorious. In August 1696, the Privy Council of Scotland put a £500 bounty on his head, and Every led his men to Nassau to hide. Even still, Every insisted on taking further steps to make even more money by investing some of the money for the purchase of 90 slaves before he left. Not only would the slaves be available to do the worst jobs during the voyage, but they could also be traded or sold once the ship arrived in the Bahamas. Best of all, from the pirate's point of view, buying and selling the slave worked as a sort of 17th century money laundering scheme.

During the very long voyage from the Indian Ocean to Nassau, the *Fancy* stopped for a short time at Ascension Island, where Every would add environmental genocide to his list of offenses. He and his men trapped and butchered more than 50 sea turtles. These became their food for the rest of the rest of their trip, and there would also be fewer mouths to feed because 17 pirates chose to stay on the desolate island rather than continue sailing to the other side of the world.

The attack on the Ganj-i-sawai could not have come at a worse time for the English government. For one thing, the East India Company had seen its profits drop by more than 90% over the past decade, and Every's attack made matters even worse because the Indian government prepared to retaliate against England for the sins of their countrymen. In Surat, the governor was forced to imprison the English people living there, both to punish them and protect them from mob violence, while the Indian emperor closed four English factories in the country and threw the company's officers in jail. He also threatened to attack Bombay, one of the few predominantly English cities in India.

Some historians have suggested that the East India Company initially tried to value the amount of the take on the low end in order to save money on the restitution by initially offering victims about $600,000 worth in reparations. However, they soon thought better of this and agreed to pay the full amount estimated by the Mughal leaders in the hope of smoothing things out with the Indian government. Meanwhile, Parliament declared Every and his men "enemies of the human race" and issued the following proclamation:

"Our privy council, messengers arms, our sheriffs in that part conjunctly and severally, especially constitute greeting, for as much as we are informed that Henry Every, alias Bridgeman, together with several other persons, Englishmen, Scotsmen, and foreigners, to the number of about one hundred and thirty, did steal, and runaway with the ship called the Phausie, alias Charles, of forty- six guns from the Port of Corunna in Spain, and commit several acts of piracy under English colors upon the Seas of India and Persia, contrary to the law of nations, and of this kingdom in particular; and that the said Henry Every, and several of his accomplices, since committing of the said acts of piracy, having left the ship in the island of providence, are returned to, and have dispersed themselves within this, our ancient kingdom, thinking and intending thereby to save and shelter themselves from the punishment and execution of law due to such heinous and notorious offenders; and we, being resolved, that outmost diligence shall be used for seizing and apprehending the persons of such open and villainous transgressions; do therefore, with advice of the lords of our privy council, require and command, the sheriffs of the several shires, stewards of stewardries, baillies of regalities and their respective deputies, magistrates of burghs, officers of our army, commanders of our forces and garrisons, and all others employed, or trusted by us in any station whatsoever, civil or military, within the kingdom, and our forces and garrisons, and all other employed, or trusted by us in any station whatsoever, civil or military, within this kingdom, and our good subjects, whatsoever within the same, to do their utmost endeavor and diligence to seize upon, and apprehend the persons of the said Henry Every, alias Bridgeman, together with …his accomplices, or any of them , and such others as were with them in the said ship (who may be probably known and discovered by the great quantities of Persian and Indian gold and silver, which they have with them) and deliver him or them prisoners to the next magistrate of any of our burghs, to be by them kept in safe custody until farther order be taken for bringing him or them to such consigned punishment as their crime does deserve, and out of detestation to such a horrid villainy, and to the effect the fame may not go unpunished; and for encouraging the magistrates above-named, and any other of our good subjects to search for, and apprehend such notorious rogues: we with advice foresaid do make offer, and assure the payment of the sum of five hundred pounds sterling for the said Henry Every, alias Bridgman, and fiftieth pounds sterling money foresaid for every one of the other persons above-named to any person or persons who shall seize and apprehend them or any of them, and deliver him or them prisoners to any of the magistrates of our burghs, which shall be truly and faithfully paid as a reward to the said person or persons who shall apprehend and deliver prisoner to any of our magistrates the said Henry Every, or any other of his accomplices above named, indemnifying hereby all and every one of our subjects from any hazard of slaughter, mutilation, or other acts of violence which they may commit against the said Henry Every, or any of his accomplices, or any persons that shall assist them, to hinder and oppose their being seized and taken: and we, with advice foresaid peremptorily inhibit and discharge all, and every one of our subjects whatsoever to shelter, harbor, conceal, or any ways assist, or supply the said Henry Every, or any of his accomplices above-named upon their highest peril. Our will is, therefore, and we charge you strictly, and command, that incontinent these our letters seen, the pass to the Mercat-Cross of Edinburgh, and remnant Mercat-Crosses of the head burghs of the several shires and stewartries within this kingdom, and there, in our name and authority make intimation hereof that none may pretend ignorance. And ordains these present to be printed."

The proclamation for the capture of Every

With that proclamation, the Crown put a 500 pound bounty on Every's head and also assured anyone who brought forth evidence against Every that they would be pardoned for any role they played in the event. Of course, Every was automatically excluded from any and all pardons of pirates that they might issue in the future. In addition to that bounty, the East India Company doubled the reward and offered to pay reparations to those harmed.

Chapter 4: Hunted Criminal

It is no surprise that the high bounty placed on Every's head made him the center of much interest among the pirating community. As the English would learn throughout the Golden Age of Piracy, one way to crack down on the number of pirates was by placing such a high bounty for their capture that the pirates would actually go after each other. As word spread about the bounty, many men, some of whom were former associates, began trying to track him down. They began their search in the English colonies around Central America but initially had no success; by this time, Every had anchored the *Fancy* off the coast of St. Thomas in the Virgin Islands, where he and his crew were able to discreetly sell some of their treasure to men who either did not know or did not care about its origins. During the early spring of 1696, he left St. Thomas and sailed to Royal Island, near Eleuthera.

Once they arrived at Eleuthera, Every and his crew were only 50 miles from the Bahamas, so he decided to contact the governor there and seek some sort of asylum. To that end, he dispatched four of his best men to New Providence, the capital city, with a letter for the governor, Sir Nicholas Trott. In the letter, Every explained his current situation, judiciously leaving out the part about raping and massacring a ship full of civilian pilgrims, and claimed he had just come from Africa and needed shore leave for himself and his men. Naturally, Every resorted to outright bribery. If Trott would allow them to come ashore, and ignore the little matter about the fact they were illegal slavers, Every and his crew would chip in to pay him more than 800 pounds. He also offered the governor ownership of the *Fancy* when he left.

Trott read the letter, signed "Henry Bridgeman," with great interest. On the one hand, he was the Royal Governor and responsible for maintaining English law on the island. On the other hand, England had shown little interest in the island over the last few years, he had been left primarily to his own designs, and the sum they were offering was equal to a year's salary. Then there was the matter of the French. Word had reached him that they had recently captured nearby Exuma and were headed his way. With fewer than 70 men currently living on the island, he knew that there was no way he could keep it out of French hands, but if he had help from Every and his crew, he might be able to use them to fight off the French navy. At the very least, the sight of the pirates would make them think twice about attacking the island. Perhaps just as importantly, there was also the issue of what this "Captain Bridgeman" might do if his request was turned down, since Trott did not have enough men to defend his island against 113 angry slavers.

Like most politicians facing a difficult decision, Trott decided to put the matter in the hands of a committee. He called in a council together to discuss the matter and put the matter before them, carefully omitting the detail of the offered bribe. They agreed to let the men come ashore, and Trott wrote to "Captain Bridgeman" telling him the good news. Once they arrived, Trott had a private meeting with Every, after which he received the ship and all that was left aboard it, including more than 50,000 pounds of ivory, several chests of guns and ammunition, and enough gunpowder to keep them firing for months. Strangest of all, however, was the assorted collection of ship anchors, taken no doubt after Every's many attacks.

If he had not already suspected it, seeing what the ship's hold contained, as well as the Indian coins with which he was paid, must have given Trott at least a clue that he was not dealing with run of the mill slavers. However, when he eventually heard about the hunt of Every and his men, Trott claimed plausible deniability, claiming he had had no idea who they were when he offered them shelter and free run of the island. He also claimed to have made no connection between the proclamation issued the previous year and the man he'd played host to. Fortunately for him, by the time the royal messengers arrived, he had removed and hidden all the ship's cargo and had it sunk off the coast of the island.

If Governor Trott later felt he had made a mistake in the bargain he struck, Every and his men came to feel likewise. While the Bahamas were beautiful and a tropical paradise, there was very little for them to do there. They had pockets full of money and nowhere to spend it except at a few small local pubs. They soon grew bored and restless.

Chapter 5: Man of Mystery

Once Trott received word about the price on Every's head, he had no choice but to issue a warrant for his arrest. He quickly contacted those in charge and told them where he had last seen Every, but naturally he did wait long enough to warn his "business partner" and send him on his way first. He could not risk Every being captured, as he had more to lose from the pirate's testimony than the pirate did.

As a result, Every and most of his crew escaped capture. Of the 24 men from Every's crew who were later captured, six of them were eventually hanged, but after escaping the Bahamas. Some of the pirates eventually bribed the governor of Pennsylvania, William Markham, and were allowed to live there, openly bragging about their exploits. Once again, they were protected by the fact that the royal governor had as much to lose by their capture as they did, and at one point the governor had to chide one of the magistrates for making a stink about the pirates' presence. That magistrate, Captain Robert Snead, would ultimately complain, "He called me rascal and dared me to issue my warrants against these men, saying that he had a good mind to commit me. I told him that were he not Governor I would not endure such language, and that it was hard to be so treated for doing my duty. He then ordered the constables not to serve any more of my warrants; moreover being greatly incensed he wrote a warrant with his own hand to the Sheriff to disarm me."

Meanwhile, Every disappeared into history and was never heard from again. It appeared that he had spent his time on the island planning his eventual escape, as he told different groups of men different stories about where he might be going. Thus, those who were later questioned were unable to give any sort of definitive details about where he should be sought.

The consensus is that he and some of his best men left the Bahamas aboard the *Sea Flower* and sailed to Ireland in the early summer of 1696. The author writing as Captain Charles Johnson speculated on what sort of home he might have built there:

> "In this Plan of Fortification they imitated one another, their Dwellings were rather Citadels than Houses; they made Choice of a Place overgrown with Wood, and scituate near a Water; they raised a Rampart or high Ditch round it, so strait and high, that it was impossible to climb it, and especially by those who had not the Use of scaling Ladders: Over this Ditch there was one Passage into the Wood; the Dwelling, which was a Hut, was built in that Part of the Wood which the Prince, who inhabited it, thought fit, but so covered that it could not be seen till you came at it; but the greatest Cunning lay in the Passage which lead to the Hut, which was so narrow, that no more than one Person could go a Breast, and contrived in so intricate a Manner, that it was a perfect Maze or Labyrinth, it being round and round, with several little cross Ways, so that a Person that was not well acquainted with the Way, might walk several Hours round and cross these Ways without being able to find the Hut; moreover all along the Sides of these narrow Paths, certain large Thorns which grew upon a Tree in that Country, were struck into the Ground with their Points uppermost, and the Path it self being made crooked and serpentine, if a Man should attempt to come near the Hut at Night, he would certainly have struck upon these Thorns, tho' he had been provided with that Clue which Ariadne gave to Theseus when he entered the Cave of the Minataur."

Johnson would go on to claim that Every died in Devon while he was still a young man, and that he settled there because merchants from nearby Bristol had cheated him out of his diamonds and gold. There is little evidence of that, however, leading many to consider it wishful thinking in the hope that fate would ultimately punish a man the law had been unable to touch. A similar theory also has Every returning to his home in Devon to live out his life under an assumed name. According to this theory, put forth in *The History and Lives of All the Most Notorious Pirates and their Crews*, he died of old age on June 10, 1714.

Of course, as long as anyone thought Every might still be alive, they continued to hunt for him. Over the decade following his disappearance, he was often sighted in various places along the English and American coasts. In 1709, an anonymous author took advantage of the public's continued interest in Every and published what was reported to be his memoirs. In this book, "Every" claimed to be the king of a colony of pirates living in Madagascar. Many in the public bought the book and believed the story, leading Every to become something of a romanticized figure in pirate history.

In a way, it was Every's career and that book about him that helped blaze the path for future pirates and society's perception of them. For centuries, pirates have been seen as somewhat romantic figures. From the heart of gold Long John Silver to the swashbuckling Errol Flynn, pirates have been considered something like naughty boys getting into harmless mischief and usually robbing the rich to give to the poor. Even those that seem to be mean or intimidating usually turn out to be merely misunderstood.

Pirates are even seen as charming fodder for children's literature. While Peter Pan's Captain Hook was a villain, he was a laughable and loveable bad guy, and completely harmless against the smart-aleck Peter. Today, Jake the Pirate is one of Disney's most popular shows, and entertains millions of pre-schoolers with his cute antics. Of course, the most famous pirate in modern time is the wickedly charming Jack Sparrow, hero of Disney's lucrative Pirates of the Caribbean franchise.

As Every's career suggests, however, the sad truth is that real pirates were typically neither charming nor funny. They were criminals who often killed for money, or even just for the fun of it, and of all the pirates who sailed during the 17th century, few were as wicked as Henry Every. While most pirates were content to attack similarly armed and manned ships, Every was just as happy to go after helpless civilians. In fact, he seemed to prefer them.

Every was clearly not of the same class as pirates like Francis Drake or Henry Morgan, who had their nation's blessing to cross the line, and he was much more cutthroat, both literally and figuratively. As a result, many historians now feel that Every's exploits, sanitized by the news accounts (or lack of them) of the time, became the inspiration for later pirates like Blackbeard and Black Bart Roberts. And one of Every's most significant contributions to piracy was the creation of the classic pirate flag, with the white skull and crossbones, which he personally put on a red background.

For better or worse, it's safe to say that pirates wouldn't have existed as the world knows and recognizes them today without him.

Bibliography

Fox, E. T. Henry Every. (2008)

Johnson, Charles. The Successful Pyrate. (1712). A tragi-comedic play based on the life of Henry Every.

General History. (1724)

Johnson, T. The Famous Adventures of Captain John Avery of Plymouth, a Notorious Pirate. (1809).

Rogoziski, Jan. Honor Among Thieves : Captain Kidd, Henry Every, and the Pirate Democracy in the Indian Ocean. (2000)

Van Broeck, Adrian. The Life and Adventures of Capt. John Avery; the Famous English

Pirate, Now in Possession of Madagascar. (1709). This largely fictionalized version of Every's life contributed to the mythology surrounding his life.

Blackbeard

Chapter 1: The Settlement of the New World

Though Blackbeard's origins are not very directly in the hands of Christopher Columbus, the famous explorer played an important role in Blackbeard's future. In 1492, of course, Columbus historic voyage across the Atlantic landed him in the West Indies. Columbus had discovered a New World that had been dormant in the Western imagination for nearly half a millenium. Not since the Norseman Leif Ericson landed in Newfoundland had a European ventured as far across the Atlantic.

Columbus' "discovery" set off a wave of interest in the New World, particularly from the Iberian Peninsula. Spaniards and the Portuguese rapidly raced to take away the riches that were present in Columbus' New World. Spanish colonization quickly took the lead, and just a year later permanent Spanish settlement began at Hispaniola in the year 1493. By 1511, Cuba was conquered by the Spanish, and much of the Caribbean was in the Empire's control.

By 1513, the Spanish were off the islands and on the American mainland. That year, Ponce De Leon conquered modern-day Florida, adding land to the empire, and less than a decade later, in 1521, Hernan Cortes completed his conquest of the Aztec Empire in modern-day Mexico, adding a huge swath of South and Central America to the Spanish Empire.

By the mid-1500's, the Spanish controlled much of the New World, with the Portuguese controlling small parts of it in the southern periphery. Quickly, though, other nations - namely, France and England - were taking note of Spain's rapid expansion. They, too, wanted a piece of the world's newest prize.

John Cabot was much more directly related to Blackbeard's future. Cabot, another Italian, was commissioned by the English crown to explore parts of the New World, specifically in North America. Cabot's dictate was to explore the north of the North American continent, and he thought, based on preliminary maps, that the distance between England and the New World was significantly shorter than that between Spain and its overseas possessions. Cabot thought the trip would be much easier, faster and more economical, and thus went to England first, and, to his surprise, quickly received a positive response.

Shortly thereafter, Cabot departed the Old World from Bistol, England, and in June 1497, the English voyage made landfall on the coast of modern-day Newfoundland. Cabot's exact landing spot remains uncertain, but Canada and the United Kingdom both recognize Cape Bonavista in Newfoundland as the "official" location of Cabot's landing.

Portrait of Cabot

Upon return to England, Cabot went directly to see the King and tell him of his discoveries, and the King gave him a significant sum, while also asking Cabot to conduct a second mission to North America to further explore the region.

John Cabot had found what was believed to be the fabled Northwest Passage, and throughout England the public clamored for the establishment of an English colonial empire. The recent Protestant Reformation had made enemies of England and Spain, with England controlled by Protestants and Spain by Catholics. England could no longer be so far behind its Spanish counterparts in the race to dominate the New World.

The origins of the English Empire lie squarely with Queen Elizabeth I. Her reign was marked by calmness at home: the Protestant Reformation, having ravaged England's political stability for decades, was now mostly settled. Some groups, namely the Separatists and the Puritans, remained dissatisfied, but they were for the most part on the periphery of English life.

Throughout the 1500's, England made claims to various territories across the New World, but did little to actively exploit them. In 1576, Baffin Island was claimed for England by Sir Francis Drake. Later, Elizabeth Island off Cape Horn was claimed. In 1583, St. John's on modern-day Newfoundland was claimed. The expansion was rapid but remained insignificant; England "claimed" multiple islands and locations, but it failed to either settle on them or actively take resources away, as the Spanish and Portuguese had been doing for nearly a century.

By 1584, it was apparent to Queen Elizabeth that her colonial ventures were going nowhere, and compared to Spain her nation was far behind. That year, she asked Sir Walter Raleigh to establish a colony in North America that would be named, in her honor, Virginia. He would have seven years to complete the mission or otherwise lose his charter.

Raleigh did not want to go on his own, however. He sent people, led by his distant cousins, to establish a colony in modern-day North Carolina named the Roanoke Colony. The colony, however, was riddled with problems, especially the fact that it was unable to protect and fend for itself thanks to tense relations with local Native Americans. The colony famously and mysteriously failed, coming to be known as the "Lost Colony", but other ventures were more successful. In the early 1600's, the colony of Bermuda was established on an island in the Atlantic. Jamestown was perhaps the most successful, founded in 1607 in the Virginia colony. It was the first permanent settlement in North America.

Later attempts to colonize took a different form. The earlier settlements were "proprietary" ventures, meaning they intended to make financial gains for the Crown, but later settlements, such as the Plymouth Colony and Massachusetts Bay, were more autonomous in their settlement. Though they benefited England, they also enjoyed a measure of their own sovereignty.

The area Blackbeard would later terrify the most - the Carolinas - was settled rather late in the history of English colonization. Whereas Virginia was settled in 1607, Massachusetts in 1620, and parts of Canada even in the late 1500's, the Carolina's were not settled until the 1660's. This was due in part to Spanish imperial claims over the region, which inhibited English expansion, but in 1663 Parliament issued a charter to a series of noblemen to establish the Province of Carolina south of Virginia. Not until 1729 was the area split into a South Carolina and a North Carolina.

A decade earlier, the Albemarle settlements became the first English settlement in the region. Immigrants from New England, Virginia, and Bermuda were responsible for settling the coastal area, but the settlement of the Carolinas remained coastal, with almost no inland settlement. This was unlike New England and Virginia, where settlement moved westward more quickly.

The government of the Province of Carolina was uniquely dictatorial among the English colonies of North America. Rather than have a popularly-elected colonial government, like Massachusetts and Virginia, Carolina was governed by a council of Lord Proprietors who appointed all the officials of government themselves. They were also particularly independent of the King himself and were able to govern without much intervention from London. By the time Blackbeard would wreak havoc across the Carolinas, this remained the method of governance in the two colonies. Lords appointed the officials of government, and almost no democratic rule existed. This made corruption rampant and enabled Blackbeard and other pirates to use the Carolinas as safe havens, even as the citizens of the colonies were displeased by the piracy.

The colonists upset with pirates could rely on one powerful ally. Around the time that the English colonies were settled in the New World, the country's navy was becoming the world's most powerful naval force. In the late 16th century, the Royal Navy managed to successfully defend against the invasion of the Spanish Armada by the Catholic King of Spain, who hoped to overthrow Queen Elizabeth and end Protestantism in England.

England's naval rise, however, caused conflict with other countries, especially the Netherlands. In the 1640's England passed a law known as the Navigation Acts, which required that all shipments to and from England were to be carried on English ships. The Dutch, however, were unhappy with this law, and declared war on England. The resulting First Anglo-Dutch War lasted from 1652 until 1654, but the war was inconclusive. A decade later, the Second Anglo-Dutch War erupted but again achieved largely inconclusive results. England's naval superiority in the Atlantic remained unmatched, enabling it to capture numerous critical locations and to ship ever more people overseas. This contrasted somewhat with the Spanish method of colonization, where a relatively few number of bureaucrats and crew moved to the New World and returned with gold and other resources to Spain.

At the same time, English expansion into the islands of the New World made the area somewhat lawless. Many nations from Europe attempted to gain control of the various islands of the Caribbean, leading to competition that mostly took place on the seas, leaving no single nation able to enforce law and order in the area. Naturally, piracy exploded in this environment, with many pirates igniting fear across the warm tropical seas of the middle Atlantic.

Chapter 2: Blackbeard's Early Life

Perhaps not surprisingly, the elusive Blackbeard's origins and early years are relatively unknown, and the mysterious beginnings added to the intrigue surrounding the subsequently famous English pirate. Though he is commonly referred to as Edward Teach, the name used most often today, there have historically been several other spellings of his last name, including Thatch, Thach, Thache, Thack, Tack, Thatche and Theach. It was also possible that Blackbeard intentionally obscured his real name to spare his family and anyone else who was unfortunate enough to have the same last name.

Though some undocumented accounts claim he was born in Jamaica, the place from which he would eventually launch his career on the seas, Blackbeard was more likely born in England, probably near Bristol, around the year 1680. Bristol is a port city in an inlet in the southeastern region of England and was an important one in the development of English colonization, since it was the port from which many early colonists departed. Bristol was also a center in the triangular slave trade route that now dominated the Atlantic Ocean, so as a young boy he would have likely seen this type of commerce developing in his home town, and he may have developed a fervent interest in the New World that was making his town and its people rich.

Shipping and the navy thus dominated the world in which the future pirate lived, and contemporary evidence suggests that he could read and write, meaning he at least came from a relatively modest family who could afford education. At the same time, the highest echelons of the shipping and naval trade were unavailable to most English save for the wealthy. It's assumed that these echelons were unavailable to the young boy in Bristol.

Because so little is known about his early life, it remains unclear when and why he left Bristol. The lack of opportunity available to the young man may have led him to go rogue and engage in piracy. Alternatively, the young boy may have taken haven in the Royal Navy, which was growing and was thus not particularly selective when it came to recruiting. It's this route - the Navy - where many think Edward Teach got his first experiences in shipping and seafaring, and it is presumed that he got these first experiences during Queen Anne's War.

The War of Spanish Succession broke out in the year 1702, and by then Spain was considered by many to be a declining power. It had a large territorial domain, but its technological advances over the past two centuries were few compared to its counterparts in Britain, France and even Italy. However, in 1702, the inheritance of the Spanish crown became uncertain because a sickly child had inherited the throne. The Hapsburgs of central Europe were now competing with the Bourbons of France, with both families claiming the right to rule all of Spain's realms.

Britain, meanwhile, preferred that the Spanish realms be ruled in a dispersed manner by multiple related monarchs; their unification into one unit was considered a threat. Other countries, including the Netherlands, Portugal, the remains of the Holy Roman Empire, and even some Spaniards loyal to King Charles, agreed with Britain. France, Spain and Bavaria wanted unification, because they would all be united together. The two sides eventually went to war.

In Europe, the war was called the War of Spanish Succession, since that was the substance of the war, but in North America it was known as Queen Anne's War. Each of the major belligerents - Spain, France and England - controlled critical pieces of North America, ultimately sucking them in despite the fact they were far removed from European thrones. In North America, the hostilities focused principally on various border disputes, and the Native Americans in the region were also actively involved in the development of the conflict.

During the war, another significant change took place. The English colonists in North America were no longer English - in 1707, with the Act of Union, they became British. That year, Queen Anne, Queen of England, Scotland and Ireland, which she ruled separately, had her three Parliaments agree to unite their countries into a single political unit - the United Kingdom of Great Britain and Ireland. Ironically, this type of political union was precisely what the Queen was fighting against in France and Spain

In North America, France and Spain allied against Britain, and each had Native American allies. The war was largely fought along territorial borders - in Spanish Florida, in New England, especially in modern-day Maine and in Southern Canada, and in Newfoundland, where a border dispute existed between France and England, until the war ended with the Treaty of Utrecht in 1713. France ceded parts of the Hudson Bay, Maine and Newfoundland to England, positive results for Britain's North American colonies.

In the famous pirate history written in the mid-18th century by someone using the pseudonym "Captain Charles Johnson", Teach is credited with being a privateer during Queen Anne's War, operating in and around Jamaica. The point of a privateer was either to augment a small government navy - which was not Britain's purpose - or to disrupt an enemy who was heavily dependent on trade. Spain's Empire was larger and more exploitive; the country reaped enormous fortunes out of North America while the Britain, meanwhile, had established small and dwindling societies across the Atlantic coast. Moreover, the British colonies were all relatively independent and did little to support Britain other than provide it with usable military territory. Britain thus made up the difference by having privateers steal from Spanish ships during Queen Anne's War.

It was presumably in this environment that Edward Teach first gained his knowledge of piracy and the sea. He is alleged to have been a very successful privateer throughout the duration of Queen Anne's War and was responsible for sacking and pillaging Spanish ships throughout the Southern Atlantic and the Caribbean. In addition to being successful at it, Edward Teach also took a liking to it, to the extent that the end of the war left Teach jobless and without a purpose. Captain Charles Johnson wrote that he "had often distinguished himself for his uncommon boldness and personal courage", and now he would have to find a new way of utilizing it.

Chapter 3: Becoming a Pirate

Depiction of Blackbeard in Johnsons's history of the pirates

Queen Anne's War ended in 1713, but contemporary histories state that Teach did not get into piracy until 1716. It is believed that he spent the next 3 years in New Providence. After the war, Teach decided to stick with the seafaring ways he had learned over the past few years, and now that he was no longer sanctioned by the British government, his conversion from privateer to pirate was complete. Teach got his start in piracy with Benjamin Hornigold, whose career in piracy also began immediately after the end of Queen Anne's War. Hornigold was a pirate leader who had been instrumental in helping implement what became known as a pirate republic in the West Indies, and as an Englishman he was concerned that Spanish boats would continue privateering even after the war. At the very least, he used that as a justification to begin attacking ships in and around the Bahamas, stealing resources and ships in high quantities. In the process, he acquired enough ships, including sloops and merchant vessels, to command an entire fleet of pirates, menacing the Caribbean.

Illustration depicting Hornigold

Hornigold's primary and most important ship was the *Ranger*, a well-armed vessel that was the most impressive and feared ship in the region during the period, and his second-in-command was none other than Edward Teach, who had command of the second largest sloop in Hornigold's fleet. It's still unclear how Teach managed to snag such a vaunted position; according to Charles Johnson's history, "[Teach] was never raised to any Command, till he went a-pyrating, which I think was at the latter End of the Year 1716, when Captain Benjamin Hornigold put him into a Sloop that he had made Prize of, and with whom he continued in Consortship till a little while before Hornigold surrendered." Another anti-piracy report claimed that Teach was in command of "a sloop 6 gunns [sic] and about 70 men".

Teach's piracy truly took off in 1717, beginning with Hornigold's fleet raiding a series of Spanish and Portuguese ships throughout the Caribbean, during which they stole tons of flour and white wine and later sold it at higher prices. While Blackbeard would gain a reputation for ferocity, and pirates would become known for making their prisoners walk the plank, the crews of the ships captured by Hornigold's fleet that spring were safely released. But he and his crew did fit one pirate stereotype; during their piracy, Teach and his crew became quite fond of the liquor they stole from other ships, especially Madeira wine, and their affinity for it became so strong that when they captured a ship called *Betty* in late September 1717, they only took the Madeira wine onboard before scuttling the ship with its crew and cargo.

That same month, Hornigold's fleet met with the notorious pirate Stede Bonnet, a well-to-do young man in the New World who decided to become a pirate in 1717 after marital troubles with his wife popped up. Known as "The Gentleman Pirate", Bonnet was ambitious but inexperienced, and though he and his crew had some successes capturing boats that year, his crew began pining for better leadership. Moreover, Bonnet had been seriously injured while attacking a Spanish ship. Thus, in September 1717, Bonnet acquiesced to letting Teach come onboard to command his ship, named *Revenge*, and with that Hornigold's fleet had added yet another ship. Johnson profiled Bonnet in his pirate history and explained how Bonnet became part of the pirate fleet:

"THE Major was a Gentleman of good Reputation in the Island of Barbadoes, was Master of a plentiful Fortune, and had the Advantage of a liberal Education. He had the least Temptation of any Man to follow such a Course of Life, from the Condition of his Circumstances. It was very surprizing to every one, to hear of the Major's Enterprize, in the Island were he liv'd; and as he was generally esteem'd and honoured, before he broke out into open Acts of Pyracy, so he was afterwards rather pitty'd than condemned, by those that were acquainted with him, believing that this Humour of going a pyrating, proceeded from a Disorder in his Mind, which had been but too visible in him, some Time before this wicked Undertaking; and which is said to have been occasioned by some Discomforts he found in a married State; be that as it will, the Major was but ill qualify'd for the Business, as not understanding maritime Affairs.

The Major was no Sailor as was said before, and therefore had been obliged to yield to many Things that were imposed on him, during their Undertaking, for want of a competent Knowledge in maritime Affairs; at length happening to fall in Company with another Pyrate, one Edward Teach, (who for his remarkable black ugly Beard, was more commonly called Black-Beard:) This Fellow was a good Sailor, but a most cruel hardened Villain, bold and daring to the last Degree, and would not stick at the perpetrating the most abominable Wickedness imaginable; for which he was made Chief of that execrable Gang, that it might be said that his Post was not unduly filled, Black-beard being truly the Superior in Roguery, of all the Company, as has been already related.

To him Bonnet's Crew joined in Consortship, and Bonnet himself was laid aside, notwithstanding the Sloop was his own; he went aboard Black-beard's Ship, not concerning himself with any of their Affairs."

Engraving depicting Stede Bonnet

One of the ways pirates of the era justified their piracy was by casting it as a patriotic venture that helped the Mother Country. Thus, Hornigold, an Englishman, refrained from attacking British ships, thinking that by doing so it would ultimately allow the pirate to be considered a privateer. It's just as likely that it intended to soothe Hornigold's conscience as he and his men continued attacking Spanish, French and Portugese ships. Attacking a British ship, however, would permanently leave him unable to gain legal protection if it was ever granted, so he continued to choose not to go after British boats.

His crew, however, thought otherwise. Aware of their status as pirates, the crew figured they may as well attack any ship carrying valuable cargo if possible, and they voted in late 1717 to begin attacking all ships, including those stationed out of Britain. It's unclear what if any role Teach played, or what position he advocated, but since Hornigold still opposed the idea, his crew was determined not to continue with him. Hornigold opted to head back to Jamaica, taking the *Ranger* with him. The fleet was now down to the *Revenge* and the sloop that Teach commanded before moving onto the *Revenge*.

Teach and Hornigold would never see each other again.

Chapter 4: Becoming Blackbeard

Teach's reaction to Hornigold's retirement from piracy is not entirely known, but its clear that he had absolutely no qualms about continuing his piracy. If anything, he became even more ambitious.

On November 28, 1717, Teach's *Revenge* and the other sloop conducted a daring attack against the slave ship *La Concorde* off the coast of French-controlled Saint Vincent. *La Concorde* had actually been a British frigate originally named *The Concord*, and it was a frigate equipped for warfare. It had undergone some adaptations that made it even better equipped for fighting during Queen Anne's War, but at the time it encountered Teach, dozens of crewmembers were ill with scurvy and dysentery.

Still, *La Concorde* was carrying a large cargo of slaves just recently obtained in Africa and was hardly willing to be taken without a fight, so when Teach's small fleet approached, *La Concorde* sailed into position to deliver a broadside of its own. Both ships fired at each other, killing an untold number on each side, but after firing a second volley Teach and his crew managed to subdue *La Concorde* and its crew. Instead of sailing to its destination as intended, the pirates commanded *La Concorde* to the Grenadines and dropped off its crew and cargo on the large island of Bequia.

The ship itself was another story. After all, it wasn't every day that pirates had a chance to commandeer a frigate, which posed a mortal danger to their own sloops as opposed to typical merchant vessels. The pirates had grand designs for *La Concorde*, and they began outfitting it with the intention of converting it for themselves. Once they were finished, Teach and his crew now had a new flagship, and *La Concorde* became *Queen Anne's Revenge*. Meanwhile, the French crew originally commanding *La Concorde* were given the pirates' smaller sloop, which they appropriately renamed *Mauvais Rencontre* (French for "Bad Encounter").

According to Charles Johnson, Teach had been given command of Queen Anne's Revenge with Hornigold's consent, suggesting that Hornigold had not yet been voted out and sent into retirement. Johnson wrote, "After cleaning on the Coast of Virginia, they returned to the West-Indies, and in the Latitude of 24, made Prize of a large French Guiney Man, bound to Martinico, which by Hornigold's Consent, Teach went aboard of as Captain, and took a Cruize in her; Hornigold returned with his Sloop to Providence, where, at the Arrival of Captain Rogers, the Governor, he surrendered to Mercy, pursuant to the King's Proclamation." However, it's widely believed that the attack on *La Concorde* was conducted only by Teach and his crew, suggesting that Hornigold was already out of the picture.

Whatever the case, the pirates now had a ship that was ideal for piracy. *Queen Anne's Revenge* was built as a frigate, a ship originally equipped for war, but by being converted to use for the slave trade it was also well-equipped to transport stolen goods. Thus, *Queen Anne's Revenge* could serve dual purposes, precisely what the pirates needed to destroy other ships and transport stolen goods.

18th century depiction of *Queen Anne's Revenge*

When Teach and his crew stole the ship, *La Concorde* was armed with about 14 guns, but *Queen Anne's Revenge* was armed with 40 guns, making it capable of attacking just about anything it wanted. It seemingly took no time for the pirates to utilize their new firepower; they attacked a big merchant ship called *Great Allen* near Saint Vincent, around where they captured *La Concorde*, and they won the battle against the well-equipped ship. The pirates ransacked the *Great Allen*, jettisoned the crew near shore, and burned and scuttled the vessel near the shore. The daring attack even found its way into newspapers as far north as Boston; the Boston News Letter noted the pirates had a "French ship of 32 Guns, a Briganteen of 10 guns and a Sloop of 12 guns." It's unclear when the pirates had acquired the Briganteen, but its addition meant Teach was in command of three ships and about 150 pirates.

In early December, the pirates tried their hand against the *Margaret* near the island of Anguilla in the British Virgin Islands, eventually commandeering the vessel. As Teach and his crew began stealing the goods from the *Margaret*, they forced the ship's crew to sit in captivity for about eight hours, and the ship's captain, Henry Bostock, was held aboard the *Queen Anne's Revenge*. After taking all the goods they wanted, the pirates let Bostock and his crew take back command of the *Margaret* and depart aboard their ship.

Whether Teach knew it or not, that was not the end of the matter, because Bostock went looking for some sort of justice. When he returned to his base on Saint Christopher Island, Bostock signed an affidavit with the Governor about the matter, during which he described Teach, the *Queen Anne's Revenge*, and more. Bostock noted that the pirate leader was a "tall spare man with a very black beard which he wore very long", the first contemporary reference to take note of Teach's most noticeable feature. Bostock claimed the pirates numbered 300, and the fleet consisted of a sloop and a large French guineaman with three dozen cannons. Bostock also noted that the flagship (*Queen Anne's Revenge*) contained a bunch of valuable (and presumably stolen) goods, including thousands of pounds of gold and silver. And whether it was true or just bluster intending to intimidate Bostock, Teach had told him the pirates had ransacked several other ships and intended to head to Hispaniola and ambush Spanish vessels.

Bostock's account has led some scholars to believe that Teach and his crew were responsible for attacking the *Monserrat Merchant*, which claimed to have encountered two ships and a sloop captained by men named Kentish and Edwards on November 30. Captain Edwards was an alias commonly used by Stede Bonnet, who was part of Teach's crew.

With Bostock having noted his long black beard, Teach shortly became known as Blackbeard, and descriptions of his beard became even more colorful over time. Several accounts described him as tying small ribbons of different colors into his beard, braiding it all the way around his ears, and in some cases lighting it on fire. Captain Johnson simply described Blackbeard as "a figure that imagination cannot form an idea of a fury from hell to look more frightful." The tall pirate was also described as wearing dark clothes, large boots, a big hat, and a colorful silk or velvet coat, and in battle Johnson wrote that he wore "a sling over his shoulders, with three brace of pistols, hanging in holsters like bandoliers; and stuck lighted matches under his hat." In essence, Blackbeard cut the very image that people today think of when picturing the pirates of this Golden Age of Piracy, and it's obvious that Blackbeard realized there was something to gain by appearing as intimidating as possible.

By the spring of 1718, the British government was referring to Teach as Blackbeard, and with that reports and accounts of his actions used the name Blackbeard as well. In conjunction, *Queen*

Anne's Revenge became the well-known flagship for Blackbeard and became synonymous with the terror associated with his fleet. The capture of *La Concorde* and its conversion into *Queen Anne's Revenge* may even have induced Blackbeard to grow out his famous beard. It's been suggested that prior to acquiring *Queen Anne's Revenge*, Blackbeard did not keep a long straggly beard but only started growing a fearsome beard once he had captured the fearsome frigate.

The more the pirate plundered, the more famous Blackbeard became across all of the British colonies in North America. Boston area newspapers followed Blackbeard's activities thereafter, even though he posed no threat to Boston, and naturally he garnered press in the Southern colonies, particularly around the coast of the Carolinas, which feared the pirate's advance into its waters. But like any legendary outlaw, Blackbeard was romanticized by some of the British colonists, who both feared the pirate and reveled in the colorful accounts of his conquests.

Chapter 5: The Legend and the Fleet Grows

The life of a pirate was not easy, and their fates were always up in the air, whether it was contracting a deadly illness while at sea or being captured and sent to the gallows. But in 1718 there were a couple of opportunities for pirates. In North America, Britain's Southern colonies braced themselves for a wave of piracy, but some residing there were not necessarily unhappy about such a wave, instead viewing it as a way to reap its profits. Meanwhile, the British government back in London began floating the possibility of combating piracy by offering pirates pardons that would offer them a way out of the lifestyle without being hanged. Pirates like Hornigold would choose one route, but others like Blackbeard would go the other way.

In February 1718, the Royal Navy was on the lookout for Blackbeard, and on February 6 the HMS *Scarborough* engaged a "Pyrate Ship of 36 Guns and 250 men, and a Sloop of 10 Guns and 100 men were Said to be Cruizing amongst the Leeward Islands". It is presumed this was Blackbeard's fleet. The *Scarborough*'s captain linked up with HMS *Seaford* to track and attack the pirates, but the *Queen Anne's Revenge* was so well-manned and well-armed that it could now go toe to toe with Britain's naval ships. Charles Johnson wrote, "A few Days after, Teach fell in with the Scarborogh Man of War, of 30 Guns, who engaged him for some Hours; but she finding the Pyrate well mann'd, and having tried her strength, gave over the Engagement, and returned to Barbadoes, the Place of her Station; and Teach sailed towards the Spanish America." The captain of the *Scarborough* reported that they last saw the pirate fleet headed "down the North side of Hispaniola", which would make sense given what Blackbeard had said to Bostock while capturing the *Margaret*.

According to Bostock's affidavit, Blackbeard was aware that authorities in London were planning to offer pardons to those pirates who would accept them, but in the early months of 1718, the swashbuckling pirate instead took huge strides to expand his crew and his fleet. While the Royal Navy and the British colonies in North America were on the lookout, Blackbeard sailed toward Central America in March, where his crew managed to stop a ship called the *Adventure* near Belize. But rather than sack the ship the pirates convinced the crew and the ship to join their fleet, possibly because the two pirate vessels themselves were taking on water and not fit for fighting. Charles Johnson credited the success to the intimidating appearance of the *Queen Anne's Revenge* and its famous flag: "At Turniff ten Leagues short of the Bay of Honduras, the Pyrates took in fresh Water; and while they were at an Anchor there, they saw a Sloop coming in, whereupon, Richards in the Sloop called the Revenge, slipped his Cable, and run out to meet her; who upon seeing the black Flag hoisted, struck his Sail and came to, under the Stern of Teach the Commadore. She was called the Adventure, from Jamaica, David Harriot Master. They took him and his Men aboard the great Ship, and sent a Number of other Hands with Israel Hands, Master of Teach's Ship, to Man the Sloop for the pyratical Account."

Whatever the reasons, David Harriot, an experienced ship captain, joined Blackbeard in his mission to destroy ships across the Caribbean, and the new group moved toward the Bay of Honduras, where they commandeered another ship and four sloops, adding them to Blackbeard's growing flotilla. Charles Johnson provided the details of Blackbeard's movements and additions during these early months:

"The 9th of April, they weighed from Turniff, having lain there about a Week, and sailed to the Bay, where they found a Ship and four Sloops, three of the latter belonged to Jonathan Bernard, of Jamaica, and the other to Captain James; the Ship was of Boston, called the Protestant Cæsar, Captain Wyar Commander. Teach hoisted his Black Colours, and fired a Gun, upon which Captain Wyar and all his Men, left their Ship, and got ashore in their Boat. Teach's Quarter-Master, and eight of his Crew, took Possession of Wyar's Ship, and Richards secured all the Sloops, one of which they burnt out of spight to the Owner; the Protestant Cæsar they also burnt, after they had plundered her, because she belonged to Boston, where some Men had been hanged for Pyracy; and the three Sloops belonging to Bernard they let go.

From hence the Rovers sailed to Turkill, and then to the Grand Caimanes, a small Island about thirty Leagues to the Westward of Jamaica, where they took a small Turtler, and so to the Havana, and from thence to the Bahama Wrecks, and from the Bahama Wrecks, they sailed to Carolina, taking a Brigantine and two Sloops in their Way."

With this sizable fleet, Blackbeard decided upon a rather ambitious objective: to blockade the port of Charleston, South Carolina. The early history of Charleston was riddled with problems. First, it was disputed territory between England and Spain. More importantly, it was under almost constant attack from nearby Native Americans hoping to avoid the fate of their northern counterparts, who had all but ceased to exist as a result of colonial expansion. But at the same time, its location ensured that it remained an important trading center between the English colonies in North America and the colonies in the islands of the Atlantic.

In May 1718, Blackbeard decided to blockade the famous port, which sounds suicidal until taking into account that the townspeople were busy fighting Native Americans on land and the port could not afford to have guard ships, leaving it vulnerable to attack. For about a week, Blackbeard and his crew stopped each and every ship that tried to enter or leave the harbor, detaining all the crew aboard their ships and plundering their goods. But this created another problem; with so many people onboard, some in poor condition, the pirates needed medical supplies. According to Johnson, Blackbeard had some of his pirates take one of the prisoners to the colony's leaders and demand medical supplies, threatening to murder every prisoner they had taken and deliver their severed heads to the Governor if their demand was not met. The pirate "ambassadors" also promised that Blackbeard would murder the prisoners if the colony did not allow them to return to their fleet. As a result, the pirates "walk'd the Streets publickly, in the Sight of all People, who were fired with the utmost Indignation, looking upon them as Robbers and Murtherers, and particularly the Authors of their Wrongs and Oppressions, but durst not so much as think of executing their Revenge, for fear of bringing more Calamities upon themselves, and so they were forced to let the Villains pass with Impunity."

Thanks to the pirate ambassadors' fondness for drinking, things nearly went awry even after the Governor agreed to the demands. The pirates were given a couple of days to collect the necessary medical supplies, but when they did not return, Blackbeard got nervous and moved his fleet and the detained ships to within sight of land, spreading even more panic. Eventually the prisoner they had taken along, a man Johnson called "Mr. Marks", returned and explained that the pirates had spent the last several days in Charleston getting drunk. Once the medical supplies and the pirates returned, Blackbeard released the ships and their crews, but without their goods.

After leaving Charleston, Blackbeard and his crew navigated north to an area known as Beaufort's Inlet in North Carolina, a move made primarily because they had gotten word that the British were sending a fleet of men-of-war to go after pirates across the West Indies and remove them from power. The British fleet was commanded by the famous privateer Woodes Rogers.

Woodes Rogers (right) receives a map of New Providence

In the process of trying to sail north, Blackbeard ran his prized flag ship aground in Beaufort Inlet. It has long been assumed that the *Queen Anne's Revenge* intended to hit sand and come to a stop but instead hit rock, cracking its main-mast and damaging much of its critical timbers. The ship began to take on water and would no longer be able to serve as Blackbeard's main base of operations. In an attempt to save the ship, Blackbeard ordered that numerous sloops throw ropes across the boat and try to pull it off the sandbar, but that only caused more problems because the sloops were destroyed in the process.

Scholars and other interested individuals have long tried to pinpoint the location where the *Queen Anne's Revenge* ran aground, and in the process there has been speculation that Blackbeard did it intentionally. David Herriot, captain of the *Adventure*, wrote that "the said Thatch's ship *Queen Anne's Revenge* run a-ground off of the Bar of Topsail-Inlet." Herriot also reported that the *Adventure* "run a-ground likewise about Gun-shot from the said Thatch". Captain Ellis Brand, commanding the HMS *Lyme*, reported in a letter to the Lords of Admiralty in July 1718, "On the 10th of June or thereabouts a large pyrate Ship of forty Guns with three Sloops in her company came upon the coast of North carolina ware they endeavour'd To goe in to a harbour, call'd Topsail Inlett, the Ship Stuck upon the barr att the entrance of the harbour and is lost; as is one of the sloops".

Without the *Queen Anne's Revenge*, the *Adventure*, and several of the sloops, Blackbeard and his crew was now unable to effectively fight or flee from the incoming force of pirate hunters. Aware that he could not escape royal authority, he thus looked toward accepting a royal pardon. Recently, the Crown had announced that all pirates, on condition that they stop their piracy in the Atlantic, would be offered a pardon on or before September 5, 1718 for all crimes committed before January 5, 1718. Blackbeard, of course, had committed some significant crimes - including the blockade of Charleston - after that date, but he apparently thought he could successfully negotiate and receive a pardon.

According to David Herriot, it was Blackbeard's goal all along to intentionally scuttle his fleet and break up his crew, which now numbered over 300 pirates, and it is widely believed that Blackbeard had told Stede Bonnet that he intended to receive a pardon. By intentionally destroying his ships and forcing his crew to split up, Blackbeard also ensured that he and the men who remained with him on his old boat, the *Revenge*, would gain a bigger share of the booty.

To test the waters, Blackbeard sent Stede Bonnet to see the Royal Governor of North Carolina, Charles Eden, to petition for a pardon, figuring that if Bonnet came back alive it meant Blackbeard could also receive a pardon. This petition was successful, and Bonnet was granted a pardon for all crimes, including those that occurred after January in Charleston, but as he set back to return to the *Revenge*, Bonnet found that Blackbeard had removed everything of value from the ship and marooned its crew before moving on. Bonnet and those men aimed to find Blackbeard but never did, and when they went back to being pirates, they were captured in late September and hanged.

Aware of Bonnet's success in receiving a pardon, Blackbeard took his much reduced fleet and crew to an area off the mainland of North Carolina and had his remaining ships anchored. He now let the rest of his crew in on his plan to obtain a pardon, likely doing this at sea so that in the event that his crew protested, they could not disperse. They were forced to stay with him or swim to land. Once his crew knew of his intent to request a pardon and thus give up piracy, he moved on to Bath, North Carolina, arriving there just days after Bonnet had received his pardon. Days later, Blackbeard and his crew received a pardon from Royal Governor Eden in North Carolina.

Blackbeard now found himself in an unusual place: on land.

Chapter 6: The Return of Blackbeard

Blackbeard had allegedly confided in Bonnet that he wished to receive a pardon, and he had indeed, allowing him to transfer to civilian life. But it's widely believed that Blackbeard never actually intended to do so, and that obtaining the pardon was merely a ploy. Charles Johnson asserted, "Teach goes up to the Governor of North-Carolina, with about twenty of his Men, surrender to his Majesty's Proclamation, and receive Certificates thereof, from his Excellency; but it did not appear that their submitting to this Pardon was from any Reformation of Manners, but only to wait a more favourable Opportunity to play the same Game over again."

Whether that was accurate or not, Blackbeard did settle for a time in Bath, traveling frequently between the town and his sloop at sea. Charles Johnson wrote that Blackbeard even married the 16 year old daughter of a local plantation owner while in Bath, although no documents of any kind have been able to verify it. What is known is that Blackbeard stayed in Bath for the duration of July and through most of August, maintaining his sloop anchored near Ocracoke Island. At the time, Bath was an extremely small settlement with just a handful of families, but it had long been an important port city due to its access to the Atlantic Ocean. Bath, however, was slowly on the wane, and by 1718 it was losing business to other ports, including Charleston, which attracted significantly more commerce.

While Blackbeard stayed in Bath, his crew had largely moved on to areas outside of Bath and were all dispersing across the North American mainland. What became of them is unknown, but Blackbeard was now planning to return to the sea, and his timing was perfect because war was about to break out between Britain and Spain. It's possible if not likely that Blackbeard had anticipated war coming when he decided to "give up" piracy and receive a pardon.

In the summer of 1718, the same concept that had ignited Queen Anne's War - the Spanish Crown's desire to also control the French Crown - came to the fore again. The "Sun King", King Louis XIV of France, had died in 1715, and his only surviving grandson was King Philip V of Spain. However, the terms that ended Queen Anne's War - also known as the War of Spanish Succession - excluded Philip from inheriting the throne. The Treaty of Utrecht thus gave the throne to Louis' childhood great grandson, King Louis XV. A few years later, however, Philip, who was born in France and seemed originally to be the rightful heir to the French crown, wanted to reclaim what he believed was due to him and thus declared war on France. In return, France allied with Great Britain, the Holy Roman Empire, the Dutch Republic and Savoy to form what would later be called the Quadruple Alliance, which united against Spain.

When the fighting started, privateers were needed once again, so Blackbeard went to speak with Governor Eden about being given the chance to become a British privateer. For his part, Eden recognized the chance of removing a potentially troublesome pirate by allowing him to head to Saint Thomas to seek out a position as a privateer. Thus, Blackbeard sailed off away from Bath on a sloop he renamed the *Adventure*.

Blackbeard never reached Saint Thomas, almost certainly because Blackbeard never had any intention of going there and becoming a privateer. Instead, he simply decided to move slightly north along the North American coast and resumed his piracy against colonial ships. With that turn of events, people began to believe Governor Eden was an ally of the Atlantic pirates, taking note of the fact that North Carolina had attracted numerous pirates along its shores and many of them were sent off to "secure privateering positions". Like Blackbeard, however, most of the pirates never actually did become privateers, instead returning to piracy and using North Caroline as their base.

Indeed, historians have noted that Eden engaged in illegal trade with the pirates, and he was about to do so with Blackbeard. Rather than move towards the Caribbean with just one sloop, Blackbeard decided to stay along the North Carolinian, Virginian and Delaware Coasts, during which he raided two French ships that were shipping goods south to the Caribbean. Blackbeard moved one of the ships' crews to the other ship and stole one of the two ships, but when asked by Eden he claimed that he found the ship deserted, even though it was carrying a considerable amount of sugar. An admiralty court judged that the ship was found derelict, allowing the sugar to be apportioned to Eden and Blackbeard himself.

Other colonial leaders, however, were not so happy to share in the spoils. One such Governor was the Governor of Pennsylvania, who issued a warrant for Blackbeard's arrest in late 1718. This, however, was relatively ineffective. Though Blackbeard had operated in Delaware Bay, which touched Philadelphia, he did not routinely go there. Worse, he was stationed far off from Pennsylvania, in North Carolina, and the Pennsylvania Governor had no authority to make an arrest in North Carolinian waters. Though the Governor of Pennsylvania sent sloops out towards the southern colonies to capture and arrest Blackbeard, they failed to find or confront the famous pirate. So long as Blackbeard remained away from Delaware Bay, he would be safe.

In the meantime, Blackbeard continued to anchor around Ocracoke Inlet off the coast near Bath, where he could both rely on Governor Eden and see ships coming in and out from a distance. But other colonial governors outside of North Carolina were beginning to worry about the dreadful pirate off their coasts, including Governor Alexander Spotswood of nearby Virginia. Many North Carolina citizens had petitioned the Virginia Governor for assistance in finding Blackbeard, since they believed their own Governor was secretly allied with the pirate and would do nothing to end his terror. But since some of Blackbeard's crew had begun residing in small port towns along Virginia's coast, this gave Spotswood a motive to issue a proclamation of arrest for their captain.

Governor Spotswood

However, Spotswood had some legal issues to deal with. When he learned that one of Blackbeard's men, a pirate named William Howard, was in Virginia territory, Spotswood had Howard arrested, only to have Howard's lawyers claim the Governor had no authority to arrest, detain, and try him. Spotswood responded by citing a statute that he claimed allowed the Governor to arrest criminals without trial if the situation was deemed urgent enough.

The situation with piracy seemed urgent enough to make this argument compelling, and Howard was sentenced to hang, but when word arrived from London that the British wanted all captured pirates to be allowed a chance to receive a pardon and give up piracy before July 23, 1718, Howard was pardoned. But in the process of pardoning Howard, Spotswood was able to obtain important information from him about Blackbeard's whereabouts. Moreover, for those pirates who would not accept a pardon, the British Crown put a price on their head. In November 1718, a proclamation offered a sizable reward to anyone who could help capture or kill Blackbeard:

"Whereas, by an Act of Assembly, made at a Session of Assembly, begun at the Capital in Williamsburgh, the eleventh Day of November, in the fifth Year of his

Majesty's Reign, entituled, An Act to encourage the apprehending and destroying of Pyrates: It is, amongst other Things enacted, that all and every Person, or Persons, who, from and after the fourteenth Day of November, in the Year of our Lord one thousand seven hundred and eighteen, and before the fourteenth Day of November, which shall be in the Year of our Lord one thousand seven hundred and nineteen, shall take any Pyrate, or Pyrates, on the Sea or Land, or in Case of Resistance, shall kill any such Pyrate…shall be entitled to have, and receive out of the publick Money, in the Hands of the Treasurer of this Colony, the several Rewards following; that is to say, for Edward Teach, commonly call'd Captain Teach, or Black-Beard, one hundred Pounds, for every other Commander of a Pyrate Ship, Sloop, or Vessel, forty Pounds…"

In addition to that, the Assembly of Virginia put a price on the capture of Blackbeard, and to help locate and capture or kill him, Governor Spotswood personally financed a mission headed by Lieutenant Robert Maynard to find the pirate off the coasts of North America. Some believe that Spotswood personally financed the mission in the hopes that the capture of Blackbeard would give him access to what he assumed would be a large horde of treasure, but whatever the motives Maynard took command of a small fleet on November 17, 1718 and set off to find Blackbeard. Maynard's two boats were named the *Jane* and *Ranger*, the last ironically sharing the name of Hornigold's pirate flagship in 1717.

On the evening of November 21, just days after beginning his search, Maynard found Blackbeard and his crew anchored off Ocracoke Inlet. Maynard had relied on information supplied by Howard, and this was Blackbeard's typical anchoring spot, so it was no surprise that Maynard found him there. Maynard went about preventing all traffic from entering or leaving the Ocracoke Inlet, but Blackbeard himself was entertaining guests on Ocracoke Island and was unaware Maynard had found him. Maynard had two ships and about 60 men, while Blackbeard had one sloop and about 25 men.

The following morning, Maynard saw Blackbeard aboard the *Adventure* and thus prepared to attack, but the element of surprise was lost. According to Charles Johnson, Blackbeard and Maynard engaged in legendary banter before the fight commenced:

"Damn you for Villains, who are you? And, from whence came you? The Lieutenant made him Answer, *You may see by our Colours we are no Pyrates. Black-beard* bid him send his Boat on Board, that he might see who he was; but Mr. *Maynard* reply'd thus; *I cannot spare my Boat, but I will come aboard of you as soon as I can, with my Sloop.* Upon this, *Black-beard* took a Glass of Liquor, and drank to him with these Words: *Damnation seize my Soul if I give you Quarters, or take any from you.* In Answer to which, Mr. *Maynard* told him, *That he expected no Quarters from him, nor should he give him any.*"

Once enemy ships came in range of the *Adventure*, it fired upon them, and Blackbeard maneuvered his sloop to bring his guns to bear against the *Ranger* and *Jane*. It's unclear whether the two sides fired guns at each other, but eventually they were in position to deliver broadside cannon attacks against each other. The broadsides on both sides delivered equally devastating results. Maynard would ultimately lose as much of a third of his men in the attack, and at some point, it's believed that shooting from Maynard's men destroyed the *Adventure*'s jib sheet, causing the crew to lose control of the sloop and have it run aground on a sandbar.

However it happened, Maynard's boats moved toward the *Adventure* until they came into contact, and Maynard had a trick up his sleeve. He kept many of his men below deck, anticipating early and damaging fire from Blackbeard, and the ruse worked. As the *Adventure* attacked the deck of Maynard's ships and found them empty, the confident pirates actually jumped off their own ship to board Maynard's. At that point, Maynard brought his men back on deck to counterattack, greatly surprising the pirates. The battle had now devolved into a one-on-one, man-on-man fight, complete with guns and swords.

While chaos ensued, Blackbeard and Maynard spotted each other and moved toward each other, engaging in a personal swordfight. But Maynard's men greatly outnumbered the pirates, and as Blackbeard tried to personally kill Maynard, he was slashed across the neck by one of Maynard's crew. Despite the severe wound, he continued until several of Maynard's men fell upon him and slashed and fired at him. Maynard later claimed Blackbeard had suffered five gunshot wounds and had been slashed at least 20 times.

"Here was an End of that couragious Brute, who might have pass'd in the World for a Heroe, had he been employ'd in a good Cause; his Destruction, which was of such Consequence to the Plantations, was entirely owing to the Conduct and Bravery of Lieutenant Maynard and his Men, who might have destroy'd him with much less Loss, had they had a Vessel with great Guns; but they were obliged to use small Vessels, because the Holes and Places he lurk'd in, would not admit of others of greater Draught; and it was no small Difficulty for this Gentleman to get to him, having grounded his Vessel, at least, a hundred times, in getting up the River, besides other Discouragements, enough to have turn'd back any Gentleman without Dishonour, who was less resolute and bold than this Lieutenant."

Capture of the Pirate, Blackbeard, 1718, **a 1920 painting by Jean Leon Gerome Ferris**

Upon Blackbeard's death, his pirates mostly stopped fighting. History's most famous pirate had finally been stopped. With Maynard's men finally victorious, Blackbeard's corpse was beheaded, and his body was thrown into the Atlantic Ocean, an appropriate resting place. Somehow, a legend persisted that his headless body swam around his sloop three times before sinking, but his head was definitely attached to the mast of Maynard's ship so the Lieutenant could provide proof of Blackbeard's death and thus collect both the Royal and Virginia awards. Of the pirates taken prisoner, all but two of them were hanged along Williamsburg's Capitol Landing and left to rot, providing a gruesome sight that ensured the location became known as "Gallows Road". The two pirates who survived successfully claimed that they were only present because they had been guests of Blackbeard's at a drinking party held on the *Adventure* the night before. Charles Johnson added an ironic twist to the story of the battle, writing, "What seems a little odd, is, that some of these Men, who behaved so bravely against Black-beard, went afterwards a pyrating themselves..."

Governor Eden, meanwhile, was embarrassed and angry by the attack. Governor Spotswood of Virginia had conducted the raid in undeniably North Carolinian waters. But Eden's perceived support of the pirates had depleted any clout he had with the colonists of North Carolina - or the British Crown - and he was unable to pursue much protest. Moreover, Charles Johnson wrote that while rummagine Blackbeard's sloop, Maynard and his men found personal correspondence between Blackbeard and Eden onboard.

Illustration of Blackbeard's head, from Charles Elles's *The Pirates Own Book* (1837)

Chapter 7: Blackbeard's Legacy

"We normally think about pirates as sort of blood-lusting, that they want to slash somebody to pieces. A pirate, just like a normal person, would probably rather not have killed someone, but pirates knew that if that person resisted them and they didn't do something about it, their reputation and thus their brand name would be impaired. So you can imagine a pirate rather reluctantly engaging in this behavior as a way of preserving that reputation." - Peter Leeson

Among historians, the era in which Blackbeard lived and died, 1670-1720 is often called the "Golden Age of Piracy," and Blackbeard himself plays a central role in that designation. His death in 1718 comes very close to the semi-official "end" of the Golden Age, hardly by coincidence.

Starting with Spain in the early 1500's, a series of other countries - France, England and the Netherlands primarily - followed Spain's lead over a hundred years later and began colonizing distant parts of the world. Of course, because of the long distances required, naval supremacy was a central part of this imperial expansion. With life on the high seas came piracy. Blackbeard's area of control was the central place in the birth of Western piracy. French buccaneers began the trend by seizing Spanish ships in the area and stealing their goods and treasures.

Though the era of the Golden Age of Piracy was long and varied - French buccaneers were very different from their English counterparts - Blackbeard has come to be the symbolic face of all pirates of the era. The disheveled, swashbuckling, eccentric pirate is indeed the stereotypical image Westerners hold of the pirates of the era, and Blackbeard's ability to fascinate generations of people is largely responsible for the ongoing popularity of the pirates as a subject of interest.

Even shortly after his death, Blackbeard was recognized for his prominence in Charles Johnson's 1724 pirate history, which was published that year in England and chronicled Blackbeard's life. From then on, Edward Teach assumed a central role in the history of Western piracy. Among the people of the West, Blackbeard is invariably the first pirate that comes to mind, and sometimes the only pirate an individual can name.

Like any legendary and mysterious figure, numerous superstitions abound surrounding the life and death of Blackbeard. These are especially prominent, unsurprisingly, in North Carolina and Virginia, where Blackbeard's piracy was most prevalent in 1718. In other ways, Blackbeard lives on in the public imagination through a series of myths, many of which are unsubstantiated and reflect the scarcity of information known about the actual man.

Some of Blackbeard's quirky characteristics have been recorded, but historians remain unsure the extent to which they are true. The tale of Blackbeard wearing lit matches under his hat to give his face extra glow and make him appear as a figure emerging from a shroud of smoke is colorful, but whether it's true or not, it serves to explain that Blackbeard was a truly fearless pirate who would do anything to intimidate his opponents.

The idea of pirates burying treasure all over also has its origins in Blackbeard, thanks to Robert Louis Stevenson's *Treasure Island*, but Blackbeard was all too happy to sell or drink his treasure and had little interest in burying it, especially because most of it consisted of perishable goods. In fact, few pirates actually buried any treasure. They stole treasure, and burying it and leaving it vulnerable didn't exactly make sense for their purposes of making money and achieving wealth.

While Blackbeard is the most famous pirate ever, he has often been characterized and remembered as the "greatest pirate ever" or the most successful. On the contrary, Blackbeard was only most successful when it came to capturing the imagination of the British, and later the West. Blackbeard was a mildly successful pirate who was hardly the best of his generation; many French buccaneers had captured and looted more treasure than Blackbeard had.

Today, superstition continues to create myths around Blackbeard's character. Throughout Virginia and North Carolina, mysterious lights are often seen, and locals refer to them as "Teach's Lights."

Accounts of Blackbeard's life have been fused with modern media and poetic license to turn Blackbeard into the archetypal pirate in film and literature. Pirate "language" originates with impressions of Blackbeard, as do pirate costumes, but contrary to popular belief the stereotypical pirate accent is not Scotch or Scotch-Irish. Instead, it's of West Country English origin. The particular accent of Southwestern English was very similar to that portrayed as the "pirate accent" today. The reason for that is simple: Blackbeard hailed from Bristol, a port town in Southwest England. When researchers for modern films decided how to make Blackbeard sound, they looked first to his place of origin. They then studied the accent of 18th-century Bristol and discovered unique words like "arr" and "matey." With that, pirates were invariably depicted as sounding like someone from Blackbeard's home. This was obviously not the case, but the idea stuck with the general public, and it owes its origins directly to Blackbeard.

That's not the whole story, though. When trying to research what an accent sounded like in the 18th century, historians needed to use written materials, since voices had not been recorded back then. They thus encountered some significant amount of error. As such, the likely accent of Blackbeard, the one known to all posterity, is inaccurate. Written accounts do not dispel the various differences among social classes and occupations that would have existed and changed Blackbeard's accent. Thus, knowing what Blackbeard would have sounded like is impossible.

However inaccurate the instantly recognizable "pirate accent" may be, it demonstrates powerfully how central Blackbeard is to the history of piracy in the West, and especially in North America. His words, though created without much substantive evidence, continue to define the meaning of piracy today.

Numerous books and films have been created, with Blackbeard as their primary subject. These include both fictional and nonfictional accounts of Blackbeard's life. Film accounts of Blackbeard go back to some of the earliest films ever made. In the 1950's, *Blackbeard the Pirate* was created and many similar renditions have been made over the years. As recently as the late 2000's, the Hallmark channel aired a multipart series entitled *Blackbeard*. The piece drew many viewers.

300 years after his death, Blackbeard continues to occupy an important place in the West, literally. In addition to being commemorated and remembered through films, television, and books, his life and piracy have been commemorated by monuments constructed explicitly to his memory. Each year, the famed Ocracoke Island hosts a reenactment of Blackbeard's death that attracts hundreds of spectators, who come to enjoy the frivolity and drama of the event.

Similarly, historians and archeologists continue to be fascinated by the prospect of finding out more about Blackbeard, who led a life that is largely unknown to contemporary historians. The North Carolina Maritime Museum, located in Beaufort, has many objects believed to be associated with Blackbeard and his piracy. The biggest historical discovery pertaining to Blackbeard came in the late 1990's when maritime archaeologists discovered the shipwreck believed to be *Queen Anne's Revenge*. The discovery was made off Fort Macon State Park in North Carolina, in relatively shallow waters in the Atlantic Ocean, and that shipwreck was discovered by recreating historical accounts of the incident and using them to track down a possible location for the ship. Underwater video of the capturing of the ship was uploaded to the internet for educational purposes, and artifacts have been brought to shore, many of them lending further credence to the idea that the ship really is *Queen Anne's Revenge*. This includes the fact that the ship had loaded cannons on board at the time of its sinking. Though still undergoing excavation, the National Geographic Society has explicitly stated its belief that the ship is *Queen Anne's Revenge*, and it has been slated for underwater preservation.

Though hated by many in his time, Blackbeard continues to fascinate people across the globe 3 centuries after his piracy. Movies, films and historical discoveries capture the attention of thousands of people every year, while legends terrify them along the Atlantic Coast. Blackbeard lives on in powerful ways, creating a worldwide image of 18th century piracy through one man alone.

Howell Davis and Black Bart Roberts

Chapter 1: The Cadogan

Like many pirates of his day, little is known about the origins of Howell Davis, aside from the fact that he was born in the coastal town of Milford Haven in Pembrokeshire, Wales in 1690. Little is known of his childhood, except that he became interested at a very young age in going to sea. That said, he apparently did not plan to become a pirate, despite the fact he had a particular skill set that made him the penultimate pirate, and a perfect fit for the stereotypical pirate that everyone thinks of today. While lying and bluffing may have led some people to an early death, perhaps at the hands of the state, those skills would make Davis both wealthy and famous.

Davis' first encounter with piracy occurred on July 11, 1718, while he was serving as First Mate on the slave ship *Cadogan*. The ship sailed from England bound to pick up slaves on the coast of Africa with a Captain named Skinner at her helm. Somewhere near Sierra Leone, the ship was attacked by pirates and commandeered by the pirate captain Edward England. Although pirates have a reputation for ruthlessly murdering people, pirate captains generally tried to impress sailors from captured ships to add to their crews. Unfortunately for Skinner, however, the *Cadogan* was captured by a pirate crew that had previously consisted of men who served under him. The anonymous writer who used the pseudonym Captain Charles Johnson explained:

> "It seems some Quarrel had happened between them, so that Skinner thought fit to remove these Fellows on Board of a Man of War, and at the same Time refused them their Wages; not long after they found Means to desert that Service, and shipping themselves aboard a Sloop in the West-Indies, was taken by a Pyrate, and brought to Providence, and sailed upon the same Account along with Captain England.
>
> As soon as Skinner had struck to the Pyrate, he was ordered to come on Board in his Boat, which he did, and the Person that he first cast his Eye upon, proved to be his old Boatswain, who star'd him in the Face like his evil Genius, and accosted him in this Manner.— *Ah, Captain Skinner! Is it you? The only Man I wished to see; I am much in your Debt, and now I shall pay you all in your own Coin.*
>
> The poor Man trembled every Joint, when he found into what Company he had fallen, and dreaded the Event, as he had Reason enough so to do; for the Boatswain immediately called to his Consorts, laid hold of the Captain, and made him fast to the Windless, and there pelted him with Glass Bottles, which cut him in a sad Manner; after which they whipp'd him about the Deck, till they were weary, being deaf to all his Prayers and Intreaties, and at last, because he had been a good Master to his Men, they said, he should have an easy Death, and so shot him thro' the Head."

After Captain England allowed Skinner to be murdered right there on deck, he invited the rest of the *Cadogan*'s men to join his crew. At first, Davis resisted England's offer and apparently told the pirate captain that he would rather be shot than become a pirate. But instead of enraging the pirate captain, England was so impressed by Davis' courage that he actually appointed him captain of the *Cadogan* in Skinner's place. England then cryptically gave Davis a sealed letter, but he ordered Davis upon pain of death to not open it until he had reached a certain latitude.

An 18th century woodcut depicting Captain England

When Davis and his ship reached the position that England had instructed him to sail to, he dutifully opened up the letter, only to find that it was a deed for the *Cadogan* and all its cargo, made out in his name. Whether or not Davis stopped to consider that, technically, the *Cadogan* was not Captain England's to give remains unclear, but the rest of the letter advised Davis to take his cargo to Brazil, where he would find the best prices for it, and then divide his profits with his men.

This situation marked a turning point in Davis' life: if he continued on the journey his first captain had ordered, he would have been in compliance with the law of the land. Though slave trading was hated by many, the Royal African Company had been chartered by the Crown to engage in the slave trade. However, if Davis changed course and went to Brazil, he would in essence be turning his back on the life he had known and throwing his lot in with pirates. In the end, Davis decided to skirt the law, which in this case might have actually been the morally superior decision. Trading in a life of human trafficking for one trafficking in stolen property, Davis started sailing toward Brazil. Even then, however, Davis appears not to have planned to remain a pirate; instead, he decided to sell the ship in Brazil.

Of course, it can't be said with certainty what Davis would have done in Brazil, because he never made it to South America. His crew decided that piracy was not for them and resisted his plans, despite his demands that they obey him and sail to Brazil. However, once the crew learned that some of the cargo on the ship was actually supposed to be delivered to Barbados, they threatened to mutiny as soon as they could, essentially turning Davis into a prisoner on his own ship. The *Cadogan* began sailing toward Barbados instead.

When they arrived in Barbados, the crew turned the cargo over to the merchant who had ordered them, and they handed Davis over to the police. They told the sad story of Skinner's death and accused Davis of piracy, inducing the police to quickly lock him up in the local jail, where he remained for the next three months. During that time, the military police came to determine that, no matter what his intentions may have been, he did not have the ship long enough to actually commit any acts of piracy. Thus they released him without ever bringing him to trial.

Many people have described jails as "schools for criminals", and this certainly proved to be the case for Howell Davis. Though he had never even stood trial, he sensed that his reputation would prevent him from finding a real job once he was released. Therefore he decided to travel to the island of New Providence once he was released, where he fully intended to join up with pirates at New Providence. Having "done the time," he seemed determined to do the crime.

Chapter 2: A Pirate

Ironically, now that Davis actually intended to become a pirate, his plans were thwarted once again; when he arrived in New Providence, he learned that most of the pirates had given up their piracy in favor of walking the straight and narrow path. Davis' timing happened to correspond with King William III offering clemency to any pirates who would turn themselves in and swear to give up piracy in the later stages of 1718. According to the proclamation:

"Whereas we have received information, that several persons, subjects of great Britain, have, since the twenty fourth day of June, in the year of our Lord one thousand, seven hundred and fifteen, committed diverse piracies and robberies upon the high seas in the West Indies, or adjoining to our plantations, which have, and may occasion, great damage to the merchants of Great Britain and others, trading into those parts; and though we have appointed such a force as we judge sufficient for suppressing the said piracies: yet the more effectually to put an end to the same, we have thought fit, by and with the advice of our privy council, to issue this our royal proclamation; and we do hereby promise and declare, that in case any of the said pirates shall, on or before the fifth day of September, in the year of our Lord one thousand, seven hundred and eighteen, surrender him or themselves to one of our principal secretaries of state in Great Britain or Ireland, or to any governor or deputy governor of any of our plantations or dominions beyond the seas, every such pirate and pirates, so surrendering him or themselves, as aforesaid, shall have our gracious pardon of and for such his or their piracy or piracies, by him or them."

In the case of New Providence Island, many of the pirates had taken the pardon brought by Captain Woodes Rogers, who had been sent by the King to round up as many pirates as possible and clean out the pirates' safe haven.

Rogers looking at a map of New Providence

In conjunction with the offer of a pardon, the Crown put out a proclamation in November 1718 that offered a sizable reward to anyone who helped capture or kill pirate captains:

> "Whereas, by an Act of Assembly, made at a Session of Assembly, begun at the Capital in Williamsburgh, the eleventh Day of November, in the fifth Year of his Majesty's Reign, entituled, An Act to encourage the apprehending and destroying of Pyrates: It is, amongst other Things enacted, that all and every Person, or Persons, who, from and after the fourteenth Day of November, in the Year of our Lord one thousand seven hundred and eighteen, and before the fourteenth Day of November, which shall be in the Year of our Lord one thousand seven hundred and nineteen, shall take any Pyrate, or Pyrates, on the Sea or Land, or in Case of Resistance, shall kill any such Pyrate…shall be entitled to have, and receive out of the publick Money, in the Hands of the Treasurer of this Colony, the several Rewards following…"

Upon seeing that there was not much hope of putting together a pirate crew at the time, many of the former pirates in the area instead started hunting other pirates, which was now potentially more lucrative and certainly safer. With that, Davis decided instead to join up with Governor Rogers, who was putting together crews for two sloops, the *Buck* and the *Mumvil Trader*, to capture pirates that had refused the King's offer of clemency. Along the way, he would also be transporting some pretty valuable items that he planned to trade with the Spanish and the French for information. While Davis still had not committed any actual acts of piracy, most of the other members of the crew were experienced pirates who had surrendered and accepted the pardon.

The two ships set out for Havana, Cuba, in the fall of 1718, carrying a letter of introduction from Captain Rogers to the Cuban government assuring the governor that the crew of the *Buck* and the *Mumvil Trader* were not pirates, but were on a mission of trade and pirate hunting. The captain, Jonathan Bass, was to deliver his cargo and then continue to Nassau, where he would attack any pirate ships and bring their crews to justice.

Though he had often been thwarted so far, Davis was secretly still determined to be a pirate, so when his sloop made landfall at Martinique, a French island in the West Indies, he conspired with six other pirates to form a mutiny. Working under the cover of night, they captured and restrained the captain of the *Buck* and took the ship for their own. Knowing that there were other similarly inclined crewmembers on the *Mumvil Trader*, they called to them and invited them aboard the *Buck* for a conference. After much talk, most of the men agreed to throw their lot in with Davis. Among those joining Davis that day were Thomas Anstis and Walter Kennedy. Anstis would go on to have a short but famous career of his own as a pirate, serving under Black Bart before taking a ship of his own. Kennedy would also serve under Black Bart before dying in 1721.

Though he did end up killing Captain Bass, Davis allowed those who did not want to join his crew to return to the *Mumvil Trader* and proceed on their way, but only after he and his men stole everything that ship had of value. With the captain dead and the other crew men gone, Davis called the remaining crew together to discuss what they should do next. He provided them with ample rations of rum while they discussed who should be chosen captain. Not surprisingly, the men soon agreed that Davis, the man who led them in the mutiny, should be their new captain. For his part, Davis was happy to accept the captaincy, but he also put together a list of rules that everyone on board had to swear to obey, including an excellent system that kept his men alert by offering the first man to spy a ship that was later plundered the chance to take the best pistols on board, in addition to his fair share of the plunder. Once everything was settled, Davis gave a rousing and inspirational speech which, according to Captain Charles Johnson, "was a Declaration of War against the whole world."

Knowing that they would need a swift boat to both pursue other vessels and escape capture, the men decided to put into port at Coxon's Hole on the east side of Cuba, where they could hide while making repairs and improvements to their sloop. Like many of the islands in the vicinity, the port could only be reached by a narrow channel that was both easily defensible and hard for

Royal Navy ships to enter. This was all necessary for the pirates, since they had failed to recruit a carpenter to join their crew and thus had their work cut out for them. After much struggle and arguing over to how to proceed, they completed their work and returned to the sea.

Sailing to Hispaniola, the newly formed pirate crew came across a French ship armed with twelve guns. This would be a challenge, because the ship and crew was twice as large as the *Buck*, but Davis and his pirates were running low on supplies and were on the verge of desperation. Despite the disadvantages, the pirates proceeded to attack the ship, and the French vessel quickly struck its colors. With a crew of just 35, Davis could only send all of 12 men aboard the ship to plunder her.

Just as they were enjoying the fruits of their first raid, they noticed another ship approaching. Threatening the crew with their lives, Davis asked the men on the French vessel what they knew about the other ship. One man admitted that he knew the ship and had spoken to the captain the previous day, and that it contained 24 guns and 60 crewmen. Davis wanted to go after the ship, despite the reluctance voiced by many of his crew that it might be too big a challenge, so he hatched a plan that would allow them to fool the ship's captain into surrendering.

First, he sent some of his crew members from the *Buck* onto the ship he had just taken and then ordered both ships to pursue the large vessel on their horizon. Sailing with the *Buck*, Davis brought the sloop alongside the vessel and raised his pirate colors, surprising the vessel with what seemed to be his foolishness. After Davis raised the colors, the other ship's captain replied to his audacity by ordering him to strike his colors and surrender. According to Captain Johnson Davis replied "that he intended to keep them in Play, till his Consort came up, who was able to deal with them, and that if they did not strike to him, they should have but bad Quarters; whereupon he gave them a Broad-Side, which they returned."

With that, the two ships ceased their fire and waited as the other ship, commandeered by some of Davis' pirates, approached. By this time, all the prisoners, in accordance with Davis' orders, had been forced to change out of their uniforms and into the white cotton shirts preferred by the pirates. They were then forced, at gunpoint, to stand on the deck and give the impression that they were part of the crew. Though the ship did not have a proper pirate flag, the crew had improvised by making one out of a piece of soiled fabric that was dirty enough to look black from a distance. When the ship fired a shot as it approached, Davis' ruse worked and the bigger ship surrendered, believing they were outmanned and outgunned. Incredibly, 35 pirates were now in possession of the *Buck* and two prize ships.

Once the other ship had surrendered, Davis ordered the captain of the French ship to come aboard the *Buck* along with a third of his crew, and he imprisoned the men below decks and held the captain in his own quarters. With only 40 men left aboard their new prize, Davis sent four more men on board the first ship with the pretense of ordering the French crew on board the new ship. However, he also sent aboard written instructions ordering them to behave themselves or face death. They were ordered to nail up the gun holes on the side of the ship so as to render them useless. They were also ordered to surrender all small weapons and ammunition they held on board and prepare to board the larger French ship.

Once the first ship was made useless, and its crew transferred to the larger ship, Davis ordered the members of the second ship aboard the first one. By incapacitating one of the prizes and keeping the crews confused and divided, he was able to guard the large number of prisoners with only a small number of men. They continued in this manner for the next two days, at the end of which Davis decided that the two ships were really too big and slow moving to make good pirating vessels. Thus, he returned them to their captains and crews, but only after the pirates had removed all the treasure, guns and ammunition. The two days of capture and confusion had placed such a strain upon the French captain that upon returning to his ship, he threatened to throw himself overboard, only to be restrained by his men until he regained his senses.

Chapter 3: Upping the Ante

Once he was finished with the French ships, Davis turned north toward the Cape de Verde Islands off the west coast of Africa, and along the way he captured and plundered a Spanish ship, but that was the only one he took before he arrived at St. Nicholas Island. When the Portuguese who ran the nearby islands saw Davis flying an English flag, they assumed he was a privateer and treated him quite well. They also allowed him to trade some of his ill-gotten goods for the supplies he needed to repair his ship.

Over the next five weeks, Davis and half his crew enjoyed a comfortable stay on the island, traveling inland on one occasion to Vila da Ribera Brava, where Davis, outfitted in his finest clothing, met with the governor and was cordially received. Davis and the pirates also enjoyed all the pleasantries the island could offer, including soft beds and hard liquor, and when they returned to the coast, Davis allowed the other half of his crew to make the trip, after reminding them that they must make sure not to give away their true backgrounds. Captain Charles Johnson would note that the amenities on the island were so nice that five of the pirates "were so charm'd with the Luxuries of the Place, and the free Conversation of some Women, that they staid behind; and one of them, whose Name was Charles Franklin, a Monmouthshire Man, married and settled himself."

Once all his men had returned to the coast, Davis spent the next few days overseeing the cleaning and refitting of his vessel. Leaving Saint Nicholas, they sailed southeast for the island of Boa Vista and dropped anchor in the harbor there while they looked around for something worth stealing. Finding nothing of value, they turned their sights and their sails south toward the Isle of May, where they found all the ships they could handle. Over the next several days, Davis and his men terrorized the coast, attacking and plundering several ships in the area. They also took on more crewmen, many of whom joined voluntarily, and Davis finally found a new ship that could sail with the *Buck* as a second pirate ship: the *King James*, a large sloop with 26 guns.

By the end of their stay off the coast of May, they had plenty of loot but very little fresh water, so they turned toward the island of Santiago, hoping to anchor there long enough to trade their booty for fresh supplies. Davis led the crew ashore in search first of a good supply of fresh water. However, before he could secure all that they needed, he was approached by the governor's men and questioned as to his background. On this occasion, his powers of deception failed him, and the governor soon became suspicious of his real intentions, even going so far as to accuse him outright of piracy. Davis feigned offense at this accusation and swore on his nonexistent honor that he was not a pirate, maintaining his innocence so steadfastly that the governor and his men withdrew a little ways to discuss his protestations of innocence. At that point, Davis and his men rushed back to their ships as fast and they could, but they were apparently undeterred by this close call, as Captain Charles Johnson explained:

> "Davis seemed mightily affronted, standing much upon his Honour, replying to the Governor, he scorn'd his Words; however, as soon as his Back was turn'd, for fear of Accidents, he got on Board again as fast as he could. Davis related what had happened, and his Men seemed to resent the Affront which had been offered him. Davis, upon this, told them, he was confident he could surprize the Fort in the Night; they agreed with him to attempt it…"

Deciding to take the island, Davis and his men again went ashore, though this time secretly and under the cover of darkness. They approached the fort that guarded the island and managed to subdue the guard before he could sound the alarm, and by the time the soldiers garrisoned there realized what was going on, it was too late to do much about it. The fort's garrison managed to fire one volley at Davis and his men, killing three of them, before they retreated to the governor's house and barricaded themselves inside. As the two sides exchanged fire, Davis found that he and his men were unable to break through the doors or walls, so the pirates lobbed several primitive grenades into the house, killing several of those therein and bringing the rest out to surrender.

By the time the sun rose, everyone on the island had discovered the pirates were on the island and had attacked the governor's home. The citizens rose to arms, compelling Davis and the pirates to retreat to their ships, but only after they took several cannons from the fort, along with other weapons and ammunition. After they successfully escaped the citizens of Santiago, Davis and the pirates spent the next several weeks continuing to harass Cape Verde's islands.

The location of Cape Verde relative to Africa

Once back at sea, Davis took stock of his situation. Counting the men he had recruited against those he had lost, he still had a total of 70 pirates to man the two ships. At this point, the captain asked the crew where they should go next, and after much discussion, with each man giving his opinion, they voted to sail toward Gambia, on the eastern coast of Africa. Davis agreed with their plans, knowing from experience that there was treasure to be had in that small country. Due to his time as a slaver, he knew that considerable treasure was kept in Gambia Castle, which served as the headquarters of the Royal African Company. Of course, that meant the castle was heavily guarded by well-armed and well-trained soldiers.

Figuring there was no way the pirates could successfully steal the treasure by fighting the guards, Davis assured his men that if they trusted him and let him put together a plan, they would all be rich. Had Davis not already proven himself cunning in these kinds of ruses, his men might have been more hesitant, but by now they had seen their captain in action so many times that they completely trusted his abilities. Therefore, they agreed to do as he instructed in all things without question.

Leaving the *Buck* at sea, Davis boarded the *King James* and set sail for Gambia. As they approached the site of the castle, he ordered all the men possible to go below decks and hide. Thus, as he approached the fort, the only thing the sentries on duty saw was a minimally manned ship with barely enough hands to keep her sailing, suggesting that it was a merchant vessel coming in to trade. The sentries allowed it to sail into the harbor and anchor right next to the castle itself.

Once there, Davis changed into his best suit of clothes and instructed his ship's surgeon and first officer to do the same. He also had six other members of the crew change into regular attire typically worn by sailors aboard a small merchant ship. After carefully instructing his men on what to say if questioned, he took the party ashore.

Though the little group appeared harmless, the governor was nonetheless cautious and sent a group of musketeers to escort them to his quarters. There he received them politely and asked them about their business, specifically where they were from and where they were going. Having already planned what to say, Davis claimed that they had recently arrived from Liverpool and were planning to sail up the Senegal River to the country by the same name. They further explained that they had hoped to trade there for ivory and gum, but that they had been chased off course by two French ships. Right on the spot, Davis made up a dramatic tale about their narrow escape and elaborated further about how they had decided to trade for some slaves to carry home instead.

When the governor asked him what he carried to trade for the slaves, Davis replied that they had a cargo of iron and metal plate. Interested in these items, which were difficult to get in colonial Africa, the governor offered to trade them slaves for their cargo, while slipping in the fact that what he really wanted was some good European liquor. Davis replied that, unfortunately, their supplies of that particular commodity were limited, but that he would be glad to send the governor a case of what they had on hand for his personal use.

With these kind exchanges, the governor became quite friendly toward the men and invited them to dine with him that evening. Davis demurred, saying that his duties as captain required that he return to the ship, at least for the evening. However, two of his officers would remain behind until he himself could return with the liquor he had promised. With that, Davis bid the governor adieu and boarded a rowboat to return to his ship.

Unbeknownst to the governor, Davis planned to return that evening with much more than alcohol. The entire time the governor had been entertaining him, Davis had been looking around the castle, making careful mental notes of all he saw. For instance, he noted that there was only one sentry on duty at the entrance, and that the guard house, where the men on duty waited to be called, stood right by it. He also noticed that when they were standing duty in the guard house, the men did not keep their weapons with them but instead laid them in a pile in the corner of the room. Upon entering the front hall of the governor's residence, he noticed that there were many guns displayed there, but not within easy reach of those in the castle who might need them.

Before he returned to his dinner with the governor, he called his men together and laid out his plan of attack. He warned them to stay sober and watchful all evening; as soon as they saw the flag over the castle lowered, they would know that he had control of the governor and that they should immediately send in 20 men to attack the castle. As a precaution, he also sent a small contingent of pirates to a nearby sloop to secure its captain and crew, lest they see what was going on and warn the castle.

With their plans carefully made, Davis armed himself with two hidden pistols and ordered each of his men to do likewise. He then directed them to walk casually into the guard house and strike up a friendly conversation with the guards. While chatting, they should keep an ear out for the sound of a single shot from his gun. This would be their signal to leap into action and secure the guards before they could act on what they heard.

When Davis arrived, the governor informed him that dinner was not yet ready and invited him to enjoy a drink or two while they waited. At this time, Davis volunteered one of his own men to wait on them, in the pretense of freeing up the governor's servants to finish dinner. This arrangement also allowed Davis' man free run of the castle, and he was soon able to report back to his captain, in hushed tones, that there were no other soldiers nearby. Upon hearing this, Davis quickly drew out his gun and stuck it in the governor's chest, demanding that he surrender the castle and all its treasures or be killed. Unprepared for this turn of events, the governor immediately acquiesced and assured Davis of his cooperation. While Davis continued to guard the governor, his men went into the hall and gathered all the guns displayed there, loading them and placing them in easy reach for the next phase of their plan.

When everything inside the castle was going according to plan, Davis fired one shot out the governor's window, signaling his men to execute their orders. They quickly pulled out their hidden weapons and rendered the soldiers in the guardhouse helpless without firing a single shot. They then removed all the weapons from the guardhouse and locked the soldiers in it. Meanwhile, another man went to the top of the castle roof and lowered the flag, calling the men from the ship to attack. They moved quickly and made the fort their own without any loss of life on either side.

At this point, Davis turned his attention to the soldiers he was holding. After berating them for their sloppy behavior, he offered any of them who were interested a place with his crew. Many of his victims were so impressed with his cunning that they agreed to join him. He loaded the rest up on the sloop he'd captured earlier and had all her sails and cables removed so they could not get away.

Davis and his crew spent the next day celebrating their victory in the castle, eating, drinking and shooting off salutes to the other pirates on the ships. The following day, however, they got back down to business and began searching the castle for treasure to carry away. At this point, they soon became disappointed, because it turned out that there was much less treasure left in the castle than they had originally believed. A recent shipment back to England had taken most of the anticipated wealth away. Of course, the pirates hardly walked away empty-handed; they found about 2,000 pounds of gold bars, as well as jewels and ivory. They took all they could carry, and then gave the rest to the master of the sloop they had "commandeered". They also returned the man's ship to him and thus sent him on his way richer than when he had arrived. They concluded their days at the castle by dismantling the remaining guns and armaments before blowing up the fort itself.

Not long after this split, Davis captured the man who was destined to succeed him as captain.

Chapter 4: Bartholomew Roberts and the Princess

The man who would become the most successful pirate in history was born John Roberts on May 17, 1682 in Casnewydd-Bach, Wales. His father, George Roberts, had grown up in Wales, as had his mother, but the historical record regarding his early years is almost completely scant. Nothing is known about his life until he was in his mid-30s, when he shows up as a member of the crew of a sloop sailing out of Barbados. Oral legends have it that Roberts had taken up a life at sea by his early teens, but when he did enter the historical record around 1718, he was going by the name Bartholomew Roberts, a name he may have chosen in honor of the then famous buccaneer Bartholomew Sharp.

In spite of his age and presumably decades of experience, Roberts had apparently not progressed very far in his nautical career, since he was only a third mate on the ship the *Princess*. In the early 18th century, the third mate was only 4th or 5th in line for command of the ship, and while there are several possible reasons for the fact he had only attained that rank, the most likely one was that he had problems with authority, which may have cost him promotions given to men who were his juniors. At the same time, he also seems to have been unable to save the amount of money he would need to purchase a ship of his own; Roberts was likely making about 3 pounds per month and no likely avenue of succeeding to the captaincy of the ship.

Ultimately, it may have been frustration with his career that drove him into a life of piracy. According to Captain Charles Johnson, "He could not plead Want of Employment, nor Incapacity of getting his Bread in an honest way, to favour so vile a Change, nor was he so much a Coward as to pretend it; but frankly own'd, it was to get rid of the disagreeable Superiority of some Masters he was acquainted with, and the Love of Novelty and Change, Maritime Peregrinations had accustom'd him to."

To make matters worse, the *Princess* was a slave ship, considered to be the lowest of the low in the sailing world, and Captain Plumb himself was not very well respected among other seaman, as slave trading was considered a profitable but disgusting business. The ships would regularly sail to Africa, where they would hire native Africans to capture and sell their countrymen, or even commandeer other slaver ships and simply steal their human cargos.

Ironically, Roberts' pirate career would be set in motion when his own ship was captured by pirates. On one of these slaving trips in June 1719, the *Princess* was captured by pirates while she was anchored off the Gold Coast near Annamaboa in West Africa. The captain of the two pirate ships that took her was Howell Davis, a well-known pirate himself. Like Roberts, Davis was from Wales, and he recognized the accent of his countryman. When Davis offered the crew members of the *Princess* a chance to join him, several of the men accepted his offer, including Roberts.

18th century woodcut depicting Howell Davis

Perhaps because of their shared heritage, Davis soon took a liking to Roberts and offered him the opportunity to try his hand as the ship's navigator. Though there is nothing to indicate that Roberts had ever served as a navigator on any of his previous voyages, he soon proved to have a knack for it and became one of Howell's most trusted confidants. They were able to speak to each other in Welsh, allowing them to discuss plans that they did not wish the rest of the crew to know about.

At first, Roberts was not interested in being a pirate. Though his work up to that time may not have been moral, it had at least been legal. However, after seeing the way in which his pirate captors lived, versus the type of lifestyle he had enjoyed on honest ships, Roberts lost most of his scruples against piracy. Captain Charles Johnson would quote Roberts in his history:

"*In an honest Service*, says he, *there is thin Commons, low Wages, and hard Labour; in this, Plenty and Satiety, Pleasure and Ease, Liberty and Power; and who would not ballance Creditor on this Side, when all the Hazard that is run for it, at worst, is only a sour Look or two at choaking. No, A merry Life and a short one, shall be my Motto.* Thus he preach'd himself into an Approbation of what he at first abhorr'd; and being daily regal'd with Musick, Drinking, and the Gaiety and Diversions of his Companions, these deprav'd Propensities were quickly edg'd and strengthen'd, to the extinguishing of Fear and Conscience."

Chapter 5: One Trick Too Many

Over the next several weeks, Davis continued sailing along the coast, arriving at Cape Appolonia, where he successfully captured three more ships, one from England and two from Scotland. Though he plundered each one, he did not keep them, allowing their captains and crews to sail safely away with their lives, if not their treasures. Next, he took on a large Dutch ship off the coast of Three Points Bay, and that large ship, with 30 cannons and 90 men, had no intention of going quietly. When the ship fired on Davis, her shot struck home and killed nine of his crew. The battle raged all afternoon and evening, ending the following morning around 9:00 a.m. when the Dutch ship finally surrendered.

Angered at the harm inflicted on his ship and crew by the battle, Davis decided to keep the Dutch ship for his own. He renamed the ship *Rover* and armed her with a total of 32 fixed cannons and 27 moveable guns. With the *James*, he sailed her up the coast to Anamaboe, where he entered the port at midday and discovered three ships anchored there: the Hink, the Plumb and the Morrice. He captured all three ships with little effort and plundered them. He then gave the Morrice to the Dutch sailors whose ship he had just previously taken and sent them on their way.

What Davis did not know was that several men had been in canoes sitting alongside the ship when he arrived. Seeing what was happening, they quietly sailed away, escaping to warn the fort that pirates were attacking. The fort fired in the direction of the Davis' ships, but they were too far away to hit. Nonetheless, Davis raised his pirate colors in an act of defiance and returned their fire for awhile before growing tired of the battle and sailing away toward Prince's Island.

While on their way there, the man in the crow's nest saw a distant ship, and the pirates went after this ship, which happened to be Dutch. Given the choice between facing the pirates and running aground, she chose the latter and would have crashed into the island had Davis not gotten in her way. He rigged his sails for pursuit and placed himself between the ship and the shore before firing on her, compelling the ship to surrender. This ship proved to be one of Davis' biggest prizes, consisting of 15,000 pounds of silver and other valuables. The most valuable prize, however, was human; the Governor of Acra Island was on board, along with all his property.

As was his custom, Davis offered safe passage to every member of the other crew who requested it. While he kept the *Morrice* for himself, he allowed the captains to return to the other two ships, but he kept 30 of their men (likely because they volunteered). However, he kept thirty of their men, presumably not against their wills. By this time, the King James had developed a serious leak, and Davis had abandoned her in High Cameroon. Years of sailing in the warm waters off of Africa and the Americas had allowed its hull to become eaten through by worms.

Next, Davis sailed for yet another island owned by the Portuguese, Principe, and as he approached it he flew his English flag, hoping to "come in under the radar." The soldiers protecting the island were suspicious, however, and sent a few men out to her to look the ship over. Davis met with them and claimed to be an English man-of-war sent by the King to hunt down pirates. He further added that he had received news there were pirates in the area and had come to investigate. The soldiers believed his report and brought him into the harbor with proper etiquette, allowing him to anchor just under their cannons. He then ordered 10 of his men to sail with him in a small dinghy to shore.

In honor of their visitor, the men of the fort sent him an armed escort to show Davis and his men to the governor, who received them warmly and assured them that he would be glad to assist them in any way he could. Davis in turn assured the governor that the bill for any supplies they took would be paid by the Crown before returning to his ship.

A short time after the pirates had arrived, a French ship pulled into the port, and it was a prize Davis found hard to resist. However, if he was going to steal the ship or its booty without blowing his cover, he needed a good story. This, of course, was right up his alley, and he soon convinced the governor that he had reason to believe that the ship had been trading with pirates. The governor not only allowed Davis to take everything of value from the ship over the protests of the French sailors but even offered him a commendation for his good work.

A few days later, Davis and his men again went ashore, this time with a more sinister purpose. They had heard that the governor and the leaders of the island kept their wives housed in separate buildings away from the shore in order to protect them from potential threats. Davis discovered where these houses were and led his men there, most likely with a plan of forcing themselves on the women. Somehow, word reached the ladies before the men arrived and they managed to escape, but Davis and his men, still under cover as Englishmen, were able to return to their ship.

Eventually, the crew had completed their work on the ship, and all that was left to do before returning to sea was plunder the island. However, Davis had been unable to discover where the governor kept his treasury. Having been unable to figure it out on shore, Davis decided to offer the governor a gift of 12 slaves and then invite him and his highest officials on board for a going away dinner. Once there, he intended to kidnap them and hold them for a sizable ransom.

Ultimately, this ruse would be Davis' last. The night before he planned to hatch his plot, one of the slaves on the ship escaped and swam ashore. The escapee somehow made his way to the governor and told him all that Davis had done and intended to do. Thus warned, the governor played his hand carefully, accepting Davis' invitation with good graces. However, when Davis arrived on shore to escort the governor to his ship, events took an unforeseen turn. He and some of his men began heading toward the governor's house with the intention of sharing a drink with him before they returned to the ship.

Captain Charles Johnson described what happened next:

> "The next Day Davis went on Shore himself, as if it were out of greater Respect to bring the Governor on Board: He was received with the usual Civility, and he, and other principal Pyrates, who, by the Way, had assumed the Title of Lords, and as such took upon them to advise or councel their Captain upon any important Occasion; and likewise held certain Priviledges, which the common Pyrates were debarr'd from, as walking the Quarter-Deck, using the great Cabin, going ashore at Pleasure, and treating with foreign Powers, that is, with the Captains of Ships they made Prize of; I say, Davis and some of the Lords were desired to walk up to the Governor's House, to take some Refreshment before they went on Board; they accepted it without the least Suspicion, but never returned again; for an Ambuscade was laid, a Signal being given, a whole Volley was fired upon them; they every Man dropp'd, except one, this one fled back, and escaped into the Boat, and got on Board the Ship: Davis was shot through the Bowels, yet he rise again, and made a weak Effort to get away, but his Strength soon forsook him, and he dropp'd down dead; just as he fell, he perceived he was followed, and drawing out his Pistols, fired them at his Pursuers; Thus like a game Cock, giving a dying Blow, that he might not fall unrevenged."

For his part, Davis was shot five times in the abdomen but was still able to keep fighting, firing on his enemies with every last ounce of dying strength. A report later asserted that one soldier finally cut Davis' throat to make sure he was dead. The date was June 19, 1719. Davis had been a pirate for less than one year.

Once word reached the crew that Davis had been killed, the men began to discuss who should be the next captain. Unlike many pirate ships, the *Princess* and the *Royal Rover* were strictly organized into two groups, much like the Houses of the British Parliament. In fact, they even called themselves the Houses of Lords and Commons, and Roberts had been elected as a Lord after just a few weeks onboard thanks to the fact he had found favor with Davis. Roberts' promotion was made all the more remarkable by the fact that he was still reportedly reluctant to engage in piracy after he had joined them.

The Lords had the right to choose the captain, and it was to them that Roberts made his case. Though he had only been with them a little more than a month, he still had more sailing experience than most of the men of the crew. According to one man who spoke on his behalf:

> "That it was not of any great signification who was dignified with title; for really and in truth, all good governments had (like theirs) the supreme power lodged with the

community, who might doubtless depute and revoke as suited interest or humor. We are the original of this claim (says he) and should a captain be so saucy as to exceed prescription at any time, why down with Him! it will be a caution after he is dead to his successors, of what fatal consequence any sort of assuming may be. However, it is my advice, that, while we are sober, we pitch upon a man of courage, and skilled in navigation, one, who by his council and bravery seems best able to defend this Commonwealth, and ward us from the dangers and tempests of an instable element, and the fatal consequences of anarchy; and such a one I take Roberts to be. A fellow I think, in all respects, worthy your esteem and favor."

However it happened, Roberts had left enough of an impression upon the crew that he was chosen as the new captain, truly making him a pirate in earnest. Up until this time, Roberts had continued to speak out openly against being a pirate, but he accepted the captaincy with a realization that he was now a pirate. According to Captain Charles Johnson, "He accepted of the Honour, saying, that since he had dipp'd his Hands in Muddy Water, and must be a Pyrate, it was better being a Commander than a common Man."

What made a group of pirates choose a recently captured merchant sailor for their captain, especially one who had up until that time been dubious about even becoming a pirate? Perhaps it was the fact that Roberts was so honest about where he stood that appealed to them. There was nothing underhanded about the way in which he dealt with the crew, and they felt that they could trust him. Perhaps more important, there were his skills as a navigator. For pirates who were dependent on being able to find places to hide quickly and easily, accurate navigation and record keeping were vitally important. In Roberts, they had a man they could trust to get them out of harm's way and keep them out of harm's way.

Perhaps to shows his strength, or perhaps to solidify his popularity among his men, the new Captain Roberts led his crew on an attack against the Portuguese fortress on Principe to avenge their previous captain's death. The pirates were even more successful than they anticipated in doing so. Johnson wrote that the group of about 30 pirates "march'd directly up under the Fire of their Ship Guns, and as soon as they were discover'd, the Portugueze quitted their Post and fled to the Town, and the Pyrates march'd in without Opposition, set Fire to the Fort, and threw all the Guns off the Hill into the Sea, which after they had done, they retreated quietly to their Ship."

In fact, their attack on the fort had been so successful that the now emboldened pirates were determined to burn the town itself, despite Roberts' hesitation:

"most of the Company were for burning the Town, which Roberts said he would yield to, if any Means could be proposed of doing it without their own Destruction, for the Town had a securer Scituation than the Fort, a thick Wood coming almost close to it, affording Cover to the Defendants, who under such an Advantage, he told them, it was to be fear'd, would fire and stand better to their Arms; besides, that bare Houses would be but a slender Reward for their Trouble and Loss. This prudent Advice prevailed; however, they mounted the French Ship, they seiz'd at this Place, with 12 Guns, and light'ned her, in order to come up to the Town, the Water being shoal, and battered down several Houses; after which they all returned on Board, gave back the French Ship to those that had most Right to her, and sailed out of the Harbour by the light of two Portuguese Ships, which they were pleased to set on Fire there."

Having avenged their former captain and enriching themselves, Roberts and his pirates set their sights on the sea once again. Days after attacking the town, Roberts and his crew attacked a Dutch man-of-war sailing off the coast of Guinea and captured the ship, plundering it before giving the ship back to its captain. Two days later, they captured the *Experiment*, a British ship that they came across while sailing west toward the Americas.

After these initial captures, Roberts led his men to Anamboe, an island where they could rest and reprovision. While there, he put the question to them as to where they should go next. The choice came down to between Brazil and the East Indies. After much discussion, the men voted to sail to Brazil.

While Black Bart gathered both men and crew during these exploits, the most important thing he gained was his crew's undying loyalty. Not only did his men respect him, they also began to think that he was invincible and "pistol proof", managing to escape death despite being conspicuously brave. As a result, his crew reasoned that if he somehow managed to stay safe, they would be safe as well. Roberts encouraged this perspective by designing a flag for his crew that featured a white outline of himself sharing an hour glass with Death, giving the impression that he had control over the date and time of his death. It was obvious to everyone that knew him that Roberts was a different sort of pirate captain.

Chapter 6: Heading West

On their way across the Atlantic Ocean to Brazil, Roberts and his men stopped off at the small uninhabited island of Ferdinando to execute some ship repairs and take on fresh water without fear of being caught and arrested. Upon leaving Ferdinando, they sailed on for Brazil, where they spent more than two months sailing up and down the coast looking for other ships. During their nearly 9 week venture, however, they found few ships and grew steadily discouraged. After much consultation, they decided to move on to the West Indies, where they hoped they might have better hunting.

Just as they were preparing to sail to the West Indies, their luck changed when they came across a group of 42 ships anchored in Todos os Santos' Bay. These ships were from Portugal and lay unguarded and fully loaded with treasure, waiting for a military escort to accompany them back home.

Unable to believe his luck, Roberts quickly captured the nearest ship and brought her master into his quarters and ordered him to tell him which of the 41 remaining ships carried the most treasure. Naturally, Roberts made the ship's master an offer he couldn't refuse: "The Portuguese being surprized at these Threats, and the sudden flourish of Cutlashes from the Pyrates, submitted without a Word, and the Captain came on Board; Roberts saluted him after a friendly manner, telling him, that they were Gentlemen of Fortune, but that their Business with him, was only to be informed which was the richest Ship in that Fleet; and if he directed them right, he should be restored to his Ship without Molestation, otherwise, he must expect immediate Death."

More concerned with his own survival than protecting another ship's cargo, the ship's master pointed out a large ship manned by 170 men and carrying 40 cannon. Others might have been intimidated by this discovery, but not Roberts and his men. Instead, they devised a strategy for taking the prize by subterfuge. According to Johnson:

> "Whereupon this Portuguese Master pointed to one of 40 Guns, and 150 Men, a Ship of greater Force than the Rover, but this no Ways dismayed them, they were Portuguese, they said, and so immediately steered away for him. When they came within Hail, the Master whom they had Prisoner, was ordered to ask, how Seignior Capitain did? And to invite him on Board, for that he had a Matter of Consequence to impart to him, which being done, he returned for Answer, That he would wait upon him presently: But by the Bustle that immediately followed, the Pyrates perceived, they were discovered, and that this was only a deceitful Answer to gain Time to put their Ship in a Posture of Defence; so without further Delay, they poured in a Broad-Side, boarded and grapled her; the Dispute was short and warm, wherein many of the Portuguese fell, and two only of the Pyrates. By this Time the Fleet was alarmed, Signals of Top-gallant Sheets flying, and Guns fired, to give Notice to the Men of War, who rid still at an Anchor, and made but scurvy hast out to their Assistance; and if what the Pyrates themselves related, be true, the Commanders of those Ships were blameable to the highest Degree, and unworthy the Title, or so much as the Name of Men: For Roberts finding the Prize to sail heavy, and yet resolving not to loose her, lay by for the headmost of them (which much out sailed the other) and prepared for Battle, which was ignominiously declined, tho' of such superior Force; for not daring to venture on the Pyrate alone, he tarried so long for his Consort as gave them both time leisurely to make off."

Through their surprise and daring, the pirates had taken an incredibly rich prize that included more than 40,000 gold pieces, as well as emeralds, diamonds and other gemstones, one of which was allegedly an elaborately designed cross made for the King of Portugal himself. The pirates were understandably thrilled with this major success, but they also had to flee the vicinity to avoid Portuguese reprisals. The *Rover* next sailed toward Guiana and Devil's Island, where they rested for a few weeks, living in luxury and spending as much of their newfound wealth as possible.

After spending some time there, the pirates found themselves refreshed but running out of booty, so they set sail again, this time toward the River Surinam. There they hoped to find more treasure and adventure, and in that they would not be disappointed. A short time after sailing up the river, they came across a small sloop that they quickly boarded and commandeered. They next came across a brigantine, but rather than continue sailing the *Rover* up the narrowing river, Roberts took 40 of his best men and sailed their newly acquired sloop in pursuit. Before they could reach the brigantine, however, the winds died down and the sloop was no longer able to move.

Eight days passed before the winds picked up sufficiently for Roberts to return to the *Rover*. There he found a shocking surprise: Walter Kennedy, the man he had left in command of the ship, had sailed off with the rest of the crew and all of the treasure. Kennedy and the pirates onboard the *Rover* wouldn't make it more than a year before many of them were arrested near Scotland and Kennedy had to go into hiding, only to be discovered and executed in 1721. Ironically, it was the lack of having a skilled navigator that did Kennedy and his men in; Captain Charles Johnson reported, "In this Company there was but one that pretended to any skill in Navigation, (for Kennedy could neither write nor read, he being preferred to the Command merely for his Courage, which indeed he had often signaliz'd, particularly in taking the Portuguese Ship,) and he proved to be a Pretender only; for shaping their Course to Ireland, where they agreed to land, they ran away to the North-West Coast of Scotland, and there were tost about by hard Storms of Wind for several Days, without knowing where they were, and in great Danger of perishing"

Walter Kennedy's "Jolly Roger" flag, which bore an obvious resemblance to Black Bart's

Meanwhile, the bloodied but unbowed Roberts renamed his new ship the *Fortune* and, taking his remaining men with him, sailed for Barbados. Having been deceived, Black Bart now codified his practices for running the ship by making a list of rules by which anyone who sailed with him would have to live. After Kennedy's treachery, Roberts and his men refused to abide any Irishmen onboard, and ironically, Roberts and his pirates swore to observe this new pirate code upon a Bible:

1. Every man shall have an equal vote in affairs of moment. He shall have an equal title to the fresh provisions or strong liquors at any time seized, and shall use them at pleasure unless a scarcity may make it necessary for the common good that a retrenchment may be voted.

2. Every man shall be called fairly in turn by the list on board of prizes, because over and above their proper share, they are allowed a shift of clothes. But if they defraud the company to the value of even one dollar in plate, jewels or money, they shall be marooned. If any man rob another he shall have his nose and ears slit, and be put ashore where he shall be sure to encounter hardships.

3. None shall game for money either with dice or cards.

4. The lights and candles should be put out at eight at night, and if any of the crew desire to drink after that hour they shall sit upon the open deck without lights.

5. Each man shall keep his piece, cutlass and pistols at all times clean and ready for action.

6. No boy or woman to be allowed amongst them. If any man shall be found seducing any of the latter sex and carrying her to sea in disguise he shall suffer death.

7. He that shall desert the ship or his quarters in time of battle shall be punished by death or marooning.

8. None shall strike another on board the ship, but every man's quarrel shall be ended on shore by sword or pistol in this manner. At the word of command from the quartermaster, each man being previously placed back to back, shall turn and fire immediately. If any man do not, the quartermaster shall knock the piece out of his hand. If both miss their aim they shall take to their cutlasses, and he that draw the first blood shall be declared the victor.

9. No man shall talk of breaking up their way of living till each has a share of 1,000. Every man who shall become a cripple or lose a limb in the service shall have 800 pieces of eight from the common stock and for lesser hurts proportionately.

10. The captain and the quartermaster shall each receive two shares of a prize, the master gunner and boatswain, one and one half shares, all other officers one and one quarter, and private gentlemen of fortune one share each.

11. The musicians shall have rest on the Sabbath Day only by right. On all other days by favor only.

Along the way to Barbados, Roberts and his crew were joined by Montigny la Palisse, a French pirate who was captain of the *Sea King*, a sloop similar in design to the *Fortune*. When the two sloops arrived in Barbados, however, they found the residents there less than willing to have them stay. Having had to deal with pirates for awhile by now, the residents on Barbados had outfitted two ships, the *Philipa* and the *Summerset*, to protect their coasts.

The two ships went after the pirates, hoping to capture or sink them, and successfully brought them to battle. The French ship had no stomach for battle and quickly fled the scene, but Black Bart chose to stay and fight. On February 26, 1720, he faced his two foes alone and fought well until excessive damage to his ships forced him to withdraw to the nearby island of Dominica. There he repaired his ship and nursed the many men of his crew who had been injured in the battle. The toll in human life proved to be very high, with 20 men dying of their wounds. Before long, word reached Roberts that two more ships had sailed out of Martinique in pursuit of him and his crew, but he still vowed not to rest until he had avenged his men's deaths.

As a visual symbol of his new mission in life, Roberts had a new flag created for his ships. It featured a crude drawing of him in white on a black background. Under his feet were two skulls, one labeled ABH for "A Barbadian's Head," and the other AMH for "A Martiniquian's Head."

Though Roberts was out for revenge, his men were able to convince him to take a long view of the situation. Rather than attempt immediate action against their enemies, they convinced him to sail north up the eastern coast of North America to Newfoundland. Along the way, they raided the small sea town of Canso, Nova Scotia, and they were also able to capture several ships anchored near Cape Breton and off the coast of Newfoundland. Once he arrived at his destination, Roberts attacked Ferryland, a coastal town in Newfoundland, and captured another 12 ships. Even the governor there would say about Roberts, "one cannot with-hold admiration for his bravery and courage"

In late June 1720, Roberts sailed into the harbor at Trepassey, terrifying both the captains and the crews of the ships anchored there. Unaccustomed to dealing with pirates, they immediately surrendered both their vessels and all their contents. As a result, Roberts was able to score his biggest success yet, capturing 22 ships and all their stores. While he was obviously thrilled with his success, Roberts was also furious at the way the captains had acted: he expected his opponents to at least put up a good fight against him. He sent out word that those who wanted to save their ships could do so only if they did as he said. Each morning, a gun would be fired that would inform that captains that they were to report to him on the *Fortune*, and any captain who failed to show up in a timely manner would have his ship burned to the waterline.

When the pirates left Bristol a few weeks later, they sailed away in a new ship they had chosen to replace the *Fortune*. They armed it with 16 guns taken from other vessels, burned the other ships remaining in the harbor, and rechristened their new boat the *Fortune*. Despite somewhat romanticizing the pirates in his pirate history, Captain Charles Johnson indicated just how merciless he considered Roberts to be in this episode. In addition to making a particularly harsh description of the scene, the anonymous writer noted just how much Black Bart and his pirates reveled in their deeds:

"It is impossible particularly to recount the Destruction and Havock they made here, burning and sinking all the shipping, except a Bristol Galley, and destroying the Fisheries, and Stages of the poor Planters, without Remorse or Compunction; for nothing is so deplorable as Power in mean and ignorant Hands, it makes Men wanton and giddy, unconcerned at the Misfortunes they are imposing on their Fellow Creatures, and keeps them smiling at the Mischiefs, that bring themselves no Advantage. They are like mad Men, that cast Fire-Brands, Arrows, and Death, and say, *are not we in Sport*?"

Roberts and his crew spent the next month sailing south, back toward the West Indies. On their way, they captured more than eight ships sailing from France to North America and chose the best of this lot to join their fleet, naming her the *Good Fortune*. The ship was aptly named, since the *Good Fortune* proved to be one of the best ships Roberts had owned thus far and allowed him to capture several more ships as they continued their journey south. Along the way, Roberts again encountered Montigny la Palisse, and invited his old French pal to once again join his fleet.

However, their journey was not without its trials. For the first time, his crew faced real danger of a non-military nature:

"In this Ship *Roberts* proceeded on his designed Voyage; but before they reached *Guiney*, he proposed to touch at *Brava*, the Southermost of *Cape Verd* Islands and clean. But here again by an intolerable Stupidity and want of Judgment, they got so far to Leeward of their Port, that despairing to regain it, or any of the Windward Parts of *Africa*, they were obliged to go back again with the Trade-Wind, for the *West-Indies*; which had very near been the Destruction of them all. *Surinam* was the Place now designed for, which was at no less than 700 Leagues Distance, and they had but one Hogshead of Water left to supply 124 Souls for that Passage; a sad Circumstance that eminently exposes the Folly and Madness among Pyrates, and he must be an inconsiderate Wretch indeed, who, if he could separate the Wickedness and Punishment from the Fact, would yet hazard his Life amidst such Dangers, as their want of Skill and Forecast made them liable to.

Their Sins, we may presume were never so troublesome to their Memories, as now, that inevitable Destruction seem'd to threaten them, without the least Glympse of Comfort or Alleviation to their Misery; for, with what Face could Wretches who had ravaged and made so many Necessitous, look up for Relief; they had to that Moment lived in Defiance of the Power that now alone they must trust for their Preservation, and indeed without the miraculous Intervention of Providence, there appeared only this miserable Choice, viz. a present Death by their own Hands, or a ling'ring one by Famine.

They continued their Course, and came to an Allowance of one single Mouthful of

Water for 24 Hours; many of them drank their Urine, or Sea Water, which, instead of allaying, gave them an inextinguishable Thirst, that killed them: Others pined and wasted a little more Time in Fluxes and Apyrexies, so that they dropped away daily. Those that sustain'd the Misery best, were such as almost starved themselves, forbearing all sorts of Food, unless a Mouthful or two of Bread the whole Day, so that those who survived were as weak as it was possible for Men to be and alive.

But if the dismal Prospect they set out with, gave them Anxiety, Trouble, or Pain, what must their Fears and Apprehensions be, when they had not one Drop of Water left, or any other Liquor to moisten or animate. This was their Case, when (by the working of Divine Providence, no doubt,) they were brought into Soundings, and at Night anchored in seven Fathom Water: This was an inexpressible Joy to them, and, as it were, fed the expiring Lamp of Life with fresh Spirits; but this could not hold long. When the Morning came, they saw Land from the Mast-Head, but it was at so great a Distance, that it afforded but an indifferent Prospect to Men who had drank nothing for the two last Days; however, they dispatch'd their Boat away, and late the same Night it return'd, to their no small Comfort, with a load of Water, informing them, that they had got off the Mouth of *Meriwinga* River on the Coast of *Surinam*.

One would have thought so miraculous an Escape should have wrought some Reformation, but alass, they had no sooner quenched their Thirst, but they had forgot the Miracle, till Scarcity of Provisions awakened their Senses, and bid them guard against starving; their allowance was very small, and yet they would profanely say, *That Providence which had gave them Drink, would, no doubt, bring them Meat also, if they would use but an honest Endeavour.*"

In September 1720, Roberts sailed the *Good Fortune* to Carriacou, a small island in the West Indies, where he had the ship completely refurbished and renamed the *Royal Fortune*. She would be the first of several ships that would bear this name, and she joined her sister ship, the *Fortune*, on a trip to St. Christopher's Island. There they sailed into Basse Terra Road, waving their pirate flags and playing their instruments for all they were worth. Their bravado made such an impact that every ship anchored in the Road immediately surrendered.

From St. Christopher's, Roberts sailed to St. Bartholomew Island, where he was greeted warmly by the French governor. Perhaps hoping that cooperation would spare his island, the governor allowed the pirates free reign on the island for several weeks, until they left on October 25. It appears that his strategy worked, since there were no reports of Roberts attacking that island or looting any of her ships.

Naturally, even when Roberts and his crew were taking time off, they were incredibly rowdy. As if to perpetuate the stereotype of pirates always being drunk, any member of the crew who didn't get drunk was actually suspected of betraying the crew. Captain Charles Johnson explained what happened to one unfortunate pirate who had a reputation for sobriety and made the mistake of going missing for a couple days:

"They passed some Time here, after they had got their Vessel ready, in their usual Debaucheries; they had taken a considerable Quanty of Rum and Sugar, so that Liquor was as plenty as Water, and few there were, who denied themselves the immoderate Use of it; nay, Sobriety brought a Man under a Suspicion of being in a Plot against the Commonwealth, and in their Sense, he was looked upon to be a Villain that would not be drunk. This was evident in the Affair of Harry Glasby, chosen Master of the Royal Fortune, who, with two others, laid hold of the Opportunity at the last Island they were at, to move off without bidding Farewel to his Friends. Glasby was a reserved sober Man, and therefore gave Occasion to be suspected, so that he was soon missed after he went away; and a Detachment being sent in quest of the Deserters, they were all three brought back again the next Day. This was a capital Offence, and for which they were ordered to be brought to an immediate Tryal.

Here was the Form of Justice kept up, which is as much as can be said of several other Courts, that have more lawful Commissions for what they do.—Here was no feeing of Council, and bribing of Witnesses was a Custom not known among them; no packing of Juries, no torturing and wresting the Sense of the Law, for bye Ends and Purposes, no puzzling or perplexing the Cause with unintelligible canting Terms, and useless Distinctions; nor was their Sessions burthened with numberless Officers, the Ministers of Rapine and Extortion, with ill boding Aspects, enough to fright Astræa from the Court. The Place appointed for their Tryals, was the Steerage of the Ship; in order to which, a large Bowl of Rum Punch was made, and placed upon the Table, the Pipes and Tobacco being ready, the judicial Proceedings began; the Prisoners were brought forth, and Articles of Indictment against them read; they were arraigned upon a Statute of their own making, and the Letter of the Law being strong against them, and the Fact plainly proved, they were about to pronounce Sentence, when one of the Judges mov'd, that they should first Smoak t'other Pipe; which was accordingly done.

All the Prisoners pleaded for Arrest of Judgment very movingly, but the Court had such an Abhorrence of their Crime, that they could not be prevailed upon to shew Mercy, till one of the Judges, whose Name was Valentine Ashplant, stood up, and taking his Pipe out of his Mouth, said, he had something to offer to the Court in behalf of one of the Prisoners; and spoke to this Effect.— By G—, Glasby shall not dye; d—n me if he shall. After this learned Speech, he sat down in his Place, and resumed his Pipe. This Motion was loudly opposed by all the rest of the Judges, in equivalent Terms; but Ashplant, who was resolute in his Opinion, made another pathetical Speech in the following Manner. G— d—n ye Gentlemen, I am as good a Man as the best of you; d—m my S—l if ever I turned my Back to any Man in my Life, or ever will, by

G—; Glasby is an honest Fellow, notwithstanding this Misfortune, and I love him, D—l d—n me if I don't: I hope he'll live and repent of what he has done; but d—n me if he must dye, I will dye along with him. And thereupon, he pulled out a pair of Pistols, and presented them to some of the learned Judges upon the Bench; who, perceiving his Argument so well supported, thought it reasonable that Glasby should be acquitted; and so they all came over to his Opinion, and allowed it to be Law.

But all the Mitigation that could be obtained for the other Prisoners, was, that they should have the Liberty of choosing any four of the whole Company to be their Executioners. The poor Wretches were ty'd immediately to the Mast, and there shot dead, pursuant to their villainous Sentence."

Chapter 7: History's Most Successful Pirate

From St. Bart's, Roberts sailed to St. Lucia and went on a pillaging spree, capturing and looting 15 ships from France and England in just three days. Among the ships that they took was the *Greyhound*, a sound vessel served by Chief Mate James Skyrme. Skyrme decided to join Roberts and his crew, and he later became the captain of the *Ranger*, one of Roberts' best ships.

It was during this period that Roberts finally had the opportunity to seek the revenge he had so longed for. While sailing off the coast of Martinique, he encountered the governor of the island on a man-of-war. Roberts ordered his crew to fly a flag of a French merchant ship and pull alongside. Having done so, he sent word to the governor that he knew the location of the infamous Captain Bartholomew Roberts. Intrigued, the governor let his guard down, allowing Roberts the chance to fire on the ship with both cannon and hand guns. When they had thoroughly cowed the crew, Roberts and his men boarded the ship and captured the governor. They then hauled him on to the deck of the *Royal Fortune*, and hung him from the nearest yardarm.

By the early spring of 1721, Robert's exploits in the West Indies had crippled trade between that part of the Americas and Europe almost entirely, to the extent that they were finding it hard to capture new ships. Moreover, the royal governors began to complain, and the crown sent ships to beef up the local navies. Hearing that they had become among the the most wanted pirates in the area, Roberts and his men wisely decided to leave the area and try their luck elsewhere. In April, the *Good Fortune* and the *Royal Fortune* sailed east toward Africa, but before they had gone very far, Thomas Anstis, the captain of the *Good Fortune*, decided to turn back and take his chances in the Caribbean. Captain Charles Johnson wrote that Anstis turned around due to some sort of hostility between Anstis and Roberts and blamed it on Roberts, but either way this left the *Royal Fortune* and the French *Sea King* to travel to Africa on their own.

By the time Roberts arrived at Cape Verde, the *Royal Fortune* had suffered so much damage that she was thought to be no longer salvageable. Thus, Roberts and his crew abandoned her and joined the crew of the *Sea King*, which they renamed the *Royal Fortune*. In this vessel, they landed at the mouth of the Senegal River on the coast of Guinea in June, and it was there that they encountered two French ships that attempted to chase them away. However, Roberts turned the tables on them and captured them instead. He renamed the largest of the two (the *Comte de Toulouse*) the *Ranger*, and he named the other the *Little Ranger*. The latter he used to store feed and supplies for the other, larger ships.

During this time, Roberts suffered one of the few challenges to his ship's peace, and Black Bart proved more than willing to enforce his code to deadly effect, especially against anyone willing to challenge his own authority:

> "Captain Roberts having been insulted by one of the drunken Crew, (whose Name I have forgot,) he, in the Heat of his Passion killed the Fellow on the Spot, which was resented by a great many others, put particularly one Jones, a brisk active young Man, who died lately in the Marshalsea, and was his Mess-Mate. This Jones was at that Time ashore a watering the Ship, but as soon as he came on Board, was told that Captain Roberts had killed his Comrade; upon which he cursed Roberts, and said, he ought to be served so himself. Roberts hearing Jones's Invective, ran to him with a Sword, and ran him into the Body; who, notwithstanding his Wound, seized the Captain, threw him over a Gun, and beat him handsomely. This Adventure put the whole Company in an Uproar, and some taking Part with the Captain, and others against him, there had like to have ensued a general Battle with one another, like my Lord Thomont's Cocks; however, the Tumult was at length appeas'd by the Mediation of the Quarter-Master; and as the Majority of the Company were of Opinion that the Dignity of the Captain, ought to be supported on Board; that it was a Post of Honour, and therefore the Person whom they thought fit to confer it on, should not be violated by any single Member; wherefore they sentenced Jones to undergo two Lashes from every one of the Company, for his Misdemeanour, which was executed upon him as soon as he was well of his Wound.

> This severe Punishment did not at all convince Jones that he was in the wrong, but rather animated him to some sort of a Revenge; but not being able to do it upon Roberts's Person, on Board the Ship, he and several of his Comrades, correspond with Anstis, Captain of the Brigantine, and conspire with him and some of the principal Pyrates on Board that Vessel, to go off from the Company. What made Anstis a Malecontent, was, the Inferiority he stood in, with Respect to Roberts, who carried himself with a haughty and magisterial Air, to him and his Crew, he regarding the Brigantine only as a Tender, and, as such, left them no more than the Refuse of their Plunder. In short, Jones and his Consort go on Board of Captain Anstis, on Pretence of a Visit, and there consulting with their Brethren, they find a Majority for leaving of Roberts, and so came to a Resolution to bid a soft Farewel, as they call it, that Night,

and to throw over-board whosoever should stick out; but they proved to be unanimous, and effected their Design as above-mentioned."

Fortunately for both captain and crew, the furor over this situation soon died down, and order returned to the ship. From Cape Verde, Roberts sailed for Sierra Leone, and when he arrived there on June 12, 1721, he learned that there were two ships from the British Royal Navy stationed there. Named the HMS *Swallow* and the HMS *Weymouth*, they were not in port at that time but were scheduled to return by the end of the year. Realizing their window of opportunity, Roberts and his crew sailed around the coast until August 8, when they encountered two large ships near Point Cestos, Liberia. The first, the *Onslow*, was full of soldiers being sent to Cape Coast Castle who were not entirely happy with life in the military and asked if they could join the pirate crew. This put Roberts in an awkward position. On the one hand, he could always use good men. On the other, these men were soldiers, not sailors, and he was unsure of how they would perform during a battle at sea. After consulting with his officers and crew, it was agreed that they should join the crew but would initially only receive quarter shares of any treasure gained.

With the infusion of new manpower, Roberts was able to outfit and man the *Onslow*, renaming it the *Royal Fortune*. He and his men continued to sail around the coast of Africa until the winter of that year, at which point they careened their ships at Cape Lopez and took their leisure. Sutton resigned as captain of the *Ranger* and Skyrme replaced him. They then turned their attention toward Ouidah, where they sailed into the harbor with their black pirate flags flapping in the sun. When they came into sight in January 1722, there were 11 ships there, and all of them surrendered without firing a single shot. Johnson described the scene:

"They came to Whydah with a St. George's Ensign, a black Silk Flag flying at their Mizen-Peek, and a Jack and Pendant of the same: The Flag had a Death in it, with an Hour-Glass in one Hand, and cross Bones in the other, a Dart by it, and underneath a Heart dropping three Drops of Blood.—The Jack had a Man pourtray'd in it, with a flaming Sword in his Hand, and standing on two Skulls, subscribed A B H and A M H i. e. a Barbadian's and a Martinican's Head, as has been before taken Notice of. Here they found eleven Sail in the Road, English, French and Portuguese; the French were three stout Ships of 30 Guns, and upwards of 100 Men each, yet when Roberts came to Fire, they, with the other Ships, immediately struck their Colours and surrendred to his Mercy. One Reason, it must be confess'd, of his easy Victory, was, the Commanders and a good Part of the Men being ashore, according to the Custom of the Place, to receive the Cargoes, and return the Slaves, they being obliged to watch the Seasons for it, which otherwise, in so dangerous a Sea as here, would be impracticable. These all, except the Porcupine, ransomed with him for eight Pound of Gold-Dust, a Ship, not without the trouble of some Letters passing and repassing from the Shore, before they could settle it; and notwithstanding the Agreement and Payment, they took away one of the French Ships, tho' with a Promise to return her, if they found she did not sail well, taking with them several of her Men for that End.

Some of the Foreigners, who never had Dealing this Way before, desired for Satisfaction to their Owners, that they might have Receipts for their Money, which were accordingly given, a Copy of one of them, I have here subjoined, viz.

'THIS is to certify whom it may or doth concern, that we GENTLEMEN OF FORTUNE, have received eight Pounds of Gold-Dust, for the Ransom of the Hardey, Captain Dittwitt Commander, so that we Discharge the said Ship,

Witness our Hands, this

13th of Jan. 1721-2.

Batt. Roberts'"

Of all the notorious actions Black Bart took in his pirate career, an episode involving one of these captured ships was probably his blackest. Johnson explained:

"But there was something so singularly cruel and barbarous done here to the Porcupine, Captain Fletcher, as must not be passed over without special Remark. This Ship lay in the Road, almost slaved, when the Pyrates came in, and the Commander being on Shore, settling his Accounts, was sent to for the Ransom, but he excused it, as having no Orders from the Owners; though the true Reason might be, that he thought it dishonourable to treat with Robbers; and that the Ship, separate from the Slaves, towards whom he could mistrust no Cruelty, was not worth the Sum demanded; hereupon, Roberts sends the Boat to transport the Negroes, in order to set her on Fire; but being in hast, and finding that unshackling them cost much Time and Labour, they actually set her on Fire, with eighty of those poor Wretches on Board, chained two and two together, under the miserable Choice of perishing by Fire or Water: Those who jumped overboard from the Flames, were seized by Sharks, a voracious Fish, in Plenty in this Road, and, in their Sight, tore Limb from Limb alive. A Cruelty unparalell'd! And for which had every Individual been hanged, few I imagine would think that Justice had been rigorous."

Chapter 8: Dead Men Tell No Tales

Like almost every pirate before and after him, Black Bart's luck eventually ran out, and it was due to the same courage and daring that had helped him capture hundreds of vessels in such a short time span. Roberts had captured nearly a dozen ships without having to fire a shot, but he had also knowingly done so in an area that was supposed to be defended by two Royal Navy ships:

"The Pyrates, indeed, were obliged to dispatch their Business here in hast, because they had intercepted a Letter from General Phips to Mr. Baldwin, the Royal African Company's Agent at Whydah, (giving an Account, that Roberts had been seen to Windward of Cape Three Points,) that he might the better guard against the Damages to the Company's Ships, if he should arrive at that Road before the Swallow Man of War, which he assured him, (at the Time of that Letter,) was pursuing them to that Place. Roberts call'd up his Company, and desired they would hear Phip's Speech, (for so he was pleased to call the Letter,) and notwithstanding their vapouring, perswaded them of the Necessity of moving; for, says he, such brave Fellows cannot be supposed to be frightned at this News, yet that it were better to avoid dry Blows, which is the best that can be expected, if overtaken."

On February 5, 1722, the HMS *Swallow* was on regular patrol off of Cape Lopez when she spotted three ships: the *Royal Fortune*, the *Ranger* and the *Little Ranger*. In a twist of fate, the *Swallow*'s captain, Chaloner Ogle, did not realize they were pirate ships and was prepared to pass on by, but he had to order his men to alter their course to avoid some rocky shoals. This maneuver attracted Roberts' attention and gave him the impression that the *Swallow* was actually a merchant ship trying to flee from him. As a result, he sent the *Ranger*, captained by James Skyrme, after her.

Both ships moved quickly and were soon out of the sight and hearing of the other two pirate ships. Realizing that a pirate ship was now coming after him and clearly mistaking the *Swallow* for a merchant ship, Ogle eventually had the *Swallow* turn and fire on the *Ranger*, killing 10 men immediately and blowing off Skyrme's leg. Skyrme ordered his men to tie on a tourniquet and place him in a chair on deck so he could continue to direct the fighting, but their cause was futile. In spite of his courage under fire, the *Ranger* was still forced to surrender. One particularly desperate group of pirates tried to kill themselves before being captured by gathering all the gunpowder they could, huddling around it, and firing a pistol at it, but this only resulted in burning a few of them before they were captured.

Ogle

While the *Ranger* was suffering its fate at the hands of the *Swallow*, Roberts continued to capture other ships while waiting for his other ship to return. On February 10, the *Swallow* was again patrolling the coast around Cape Lopez and again spotted the *Royal Fortune*. This time Ogle knew that she was indeed a pirate ship, and even that she was in the command of the famous Captain Roberts. What he did not know was that Roberts and his crew had captured the *Neptune* the day before and were still celebrating their success by drinking up her supplies of liquor. Unaware of what condition Roberts and his men were in, Ogle was determined to capture the ship and thus turned to attack her.

In addition to the fact the pirates were drunk, Ogle also had the element of surprise. When the man in the crow's nest of the *Royal Fortune* first spotted the *Swallow*, he reported that the *Ranger* was finally returning from battle. However, as the ship came closer, one of the crew, who had deserted from the *Swallow*, recognized the ship and warned Roberts that it was the *Swallow*. Unconcerned, he finished the breakfast he was enjoying with the captain of the recently captured *Neptune* and then returned to his quarters to change clothes. As Johnson noted, Black Bart dressed in his finest: "*Roberts* himself made a gallant Figure, at the Time of the Engagement, being dressed in a rich crimson Damask Wastcoat and Breeches, a red Feather in his Hat, a Gold Chain round his Neck, with a Diamond Cross hanging to it, a Sword in his Hand,

and two Pair of Pistols hanging at the End of a Silk Sling, flung over his Shoulders (according to the Fashion of the Pyrates;) and is said to have given his Orders with Boldness, and Spirit; coming, according to what he had purposed, close to the Man of War, received her Fire, and then hoisted his Black Flag, and returned it, shooting away from her, with all the Sail he could pack."

A depiction of Black Bart and his crew getting drunk before the battle

As Johnson's account suggests, Roberts had intended to escape by actually sailing across the *Sparrow* and trading broadsides with it, a particularly daring plan given that he was dealing with a Royal Navy frigate. After passing the *Sparrow* and exchanging fire with it, the *Royal Fortune* tried to make its break and escape while Ogle had to turn his boat around. Unfortunately for the pirates, however, Mother Nature intervened. The battle was fought in a tropical storm, and as the *Royal Fortune* was on the verge of escape, it actually hit the eye of the storm, completely killing the wind and leaving the *Royal Fortune* unable to sail away. This allowed the *Sparrow* to catch up and deliver a second broadside, which had a fatal effect on both the pirate ship and its captain:

> "[H]ad he took *Armstrong*'s Advice, to have gone before the Wind, he had probably escaped; but keeping his Tacks down, either by the Winds shifting, or ill Steerage, or both, he was taken a-back with his Sails, and the *Swallow* came a second Time very nigh to him: He had now perhaps finished the Fight very desperately, if Death, who took a swift Passage in a Grape-Shot, had not interposed, and struck him directly on the Throat. He settled himself on the Tackles of a Gun, which one *Stephenson*, from the Helm, observing, ran to his Assistance, and not perceiving him wounded, swore at him, and bid him stand up, and fight like a Man; but when he found his Mistake, and that his Captain was certainly dead, he gushed into Tears, and wished the next Shot might be his Lot."

Black Bart, the captain many had thought invincible, had been hit in the throat by artillery grapeshot, a ball no bigger than a penny, which severed his spine and killed him almost instantly. Because he knew that his life would almost certainly end in battle, Roberts had left instructions on how his body was to be treated. Thus, his crew "presently threw him over-board, with his Arms and Ornaments on, according to the repeated Request he made in his Life-time." True to form, the crew didn't even remove the opulent jewelry Roberts was wearing before weighing his body down and tossing it overboard.

Though Roberts was gone, his crew continued to fight. However, within a few hours, the *Swallow* took down *Royal Fortune's* main mast and the rest of the men were forced to surrender. Knowing what surely awaited them if they were captured, John Philips tried to blow up the ship, preventing the British from capturing the boat or any of the pirates, but his attempt failed and the crew of 272 was captured. Among those captured were 75 African men, who were sold into slavery, while the other 200 were taken to Cape Coast Castle and stood trial. Of these, 52 were convicted and hanged, while others were made indentured servants of the Royal African Company, which at the time owned a monopoly from the British government for slave trading. Ironically, many of Roberts' men were thus forced into the kind of career Roberts had been willing to break away from by becoming a pirate.

For his part, Ogle was hailed as a hero in the fight against piracy. Ogle was awarded a knighthood, making him the only naval officer to receive a special award for fighting pirates, and he was able to use gold he stole from Roberts' cabin to buy his way into the Admiralty.

Chapter 9: Black Bart's Legacy

Black Bart's legacy resonated both during his lifetime and well after it. In addition to all but shutting down trade in parts of the New World, the death of Black Bart is considered by many historians to have ended the Golden Age of Piracy. And among all the pirates in history, few helped shape the stereotypes and myths surrounding the pirates like Black Bart. During his very short three year career as a pirate, he and his crew captured nearly 475 ships, an average of about three ships a week, and Black Bart was one of the few pirate captains mentioned by name in Robert Louis Stevenson's famous *Treasure Island*.

At the same time, Black Bart's legacy owes much in part to the fact that so little was truly known about him. It is unclear what kind of childhood he had, or even when he took to the sea, and it's unclear when or why he decided to go by the name Bartholomew Roberts. Of course, the problem with separating the fact from fiction in his life centers around the very nature of piracy. From it very inception, this particular form of robbery has been romanticized by everyone from the pirates who were bragging about their exploits to the victims exaggerating their sense of terror. Then, of course, reporters writing for the newspapers of the day got in on the act, as well as authors writing tales of the high seas. By the time everyone had their say, there were more legends and myths than truth.

It was a mixture of fact and legend that turned Black Bart into one of history's most famous pirates. Though he was never referred to as Black Bart until after his death, the name suited him in both the color of his hair and the darkness of his character, but he was not nearly as bloodthirsty as many in his trade. He may not have been as kind as Howell Davis or Samuel Bellamy, but he was still more merciful than Edward Low. He did not mistreat his prisoners unless he or his men felt that they deserved it, and he also had a habit of giving those who cooperated gifts in the form of gold and jewelry from the ships he captured.

In addition to the colorful nickname, anyone who has read the pirate literature of the past few centuries instantly recognizes the influence Black Bart's personality has had. While he was popular among his men for being courageous, he also portrayed himself as a dashing and colorful character who enjoyed fine clothes and good food. He preferred drinking tea to swilling beer, and his pirate code suggests that he had some sort of strict religious upbringing since he ran his ships along Sabbattarian lines by allowing his musicians a day of rest. He was also strict about his men's sexual morality, forbidding them to bring either women or boys on board for illicit purposes. The creation of popular pirate characters like Jack Sparrow and Captain Hook have their origins in the way pirates like Black Bart were remembered and romanticized.

One of the most curious speculations about Black Bart was posited in 1997 by an author who claimed he was not even a man but a female transvestite. The only evidence that they cite is that he loved dressing well, and that his body was buried at sea, supposedly so no one would discover his secret. Naturally, historians have refuted the suggestion. First, the clothing worn by wealthy men during the early 18th century was often luxurious and ostentatious, especially by modern standards. Kings wore silk and velvet, as did landowners, Members of Parliament and even wealthy merchants. Men of even the lower classes might have a single silk handkerchief that was made by someone they loved for a special occasion.

Another problem with this argument is Roberts' own rules. Why would any sane individual help craft a law that would result in their own death if their secret was discovered? There were no such rules on other pirate ships, and though female passengers and crew were not the norm, they were not typically killed if they were discovered. While women like Anne Bonny and Mary Read would become famous as members of Calico Jack's crew, Roberts seems to have banned women strictly to enforce order.

Finally, there is the issue of Black Bart's body being thrown overboard rather than buried. This was not that uncommon a practice among pirate captains. They had lived their lives on the sea and preferred it for their final resting places. The more famous ones, such as Roberts, knew that there was a good chance that their bodies would be dug up and desecrated, should they be discovered buried on land. Therefore, there is nothing significant about his mode of burial.

In the end, speculation over Black Bart's sexuality merely overlooks the giant influence he had on his contemporaries and the even greater influence he had on the mythology of piracy.

Bibliography

Burl, Aubrey (2006) *Black Barty: Bartholomew Roberts and his pirate crew 1718-1723*. Sutton Publishing.

Cawthorne, Nigel (2005) *Pirates: An Illustrated History*. Capella.

Conlin, Dan (2009). *Pirates of the Atlantic: Robbery, Murder and Mayhem Off the Canadian East Coast*.

Cordingly, David (1999) *Life Among the Pirates: the Romance and the Reality*. Abacus.

Johnson, Charles (1724). *A General History of the Robberies and Murders of the Most Notorious Pyrates* (1998 ed.). Conway Maritime Press.

Richards, Stanley (1966) *Black Bart*. Christopher Davies.

Sanders, Richard (2007), *If a Pirate I Must Be ... The True Story of "Black Bart," King of the Caribbean Pirates*. Aurum Press, Ltd.

Yount, Lisa (2002) *Pirates*. Lucent Books.

Calico Jack, Anne Bonny and Mary Read

Chapter 1: Mary Read's Early Years

According to legend, Mary Read was born sometime between 1670-1698 in London, England. The sole contemporary account of her life, written anonymously by someone using the pseudonym Captain Charles Johnson, references Mary's husband as having died sometime around the Peace of Ryswick, which ended the Nine Years War in 1697. If that was correct, Mary had to have been born in the 1670s. Some modern historians believe it's more likely Mary's husband died sometime after the Treaty of Utrecht, which ended the War of the Spanish Succession in 1713. That makes Mary's date of birth more likely to be sometime around 1690.

Whatever the case, even from her earliest days of existence, Mary's life was shaped by the sea and the men who sailed on it. Her mother appears to have married a sailor while she was still rather young and became pregnant, but after he returned to the sea word eventually came back to her that he had met with an accident and died. Before she had time to fully cope, she had given birth to her first child, a son.

With her husband dead, the young Mrs. Read was forced to depend on her wealthy mother-in-law for support. However, this plan quickly fell through when she met another young man, probably a sailor, and found herself pregnant again. She knew that if the older woman found out what had happened, she would be left with no support at all and probably lose custody of her son in the process. Thus, she left town for a place where she could continue to pass herself off as a tragic young widow. She may have planned to put her new baby up for adoption and then return to her mother-in-law as if nothing had happened, or she may have hoped that, with her new reputation as the tragic widowed mother, she could find a new husband.

However, once Mrs. Read reached her new town tragedy struck once again, this time taking the life of her infant son. It was around this time that Mrs. Read came up with a cunning plan; if her new child was a boy, she could remain away long enough to let him "catch up" with the older baby's age and them pass him off as her first child, once more returning to her mother-in-law's good graces.

Unfortunately for Mrs. Read, fate had other plans, and she soon gave birth to a healthy baby girl named Mary. She may not have had the boy she desired, but the determined young woman saw no reason for the child's gender to thwart her plans, and she began to immediately dress young Mary in her dead brother's clothes. This was made easier by the fact that boys and girls in 17th century Europe both wore dresses until they were five or six years old. Her plan succeeded, and the elder Mrs. Read became once more enamored of her little grandson and continued to support them until her death.

As Mary's mother continued the ruse, little Mary found that she not only enjoyed dressing like a boy but also loved having access to the freedom that the life of a boy afforded her. Though her mother explained to her when she was old enough to understand that she was not actually a boy like other boys, Mary chose to continue to live as if she had been born male. After her grandmother died, her mother was again destitute and again hatched a plan to use her daughter to support her. Mary was by this time 13 years old, and when dressed in male clothing she looked very much the part of the effeminate footmen that the French nobility of that time preferred.

Before long, however, Mary grew tired of the restrictions of her life in the home of a nobleman and decided to seek her fortune elsewhere. She began by joining the crew of a British Man of War, but at first she found that life at sea was not to her particular liking. It may have been that she found it difficult to conceal her true gender within the cramped quarters of a sailing ship, but at the same time she was still just a teenager. She may very well have been intimidated by the rough and tumble life of a British sailor.

Whatever her reasons, she soon left the navy and joined the British army as a foot soldier. Though she did well in battle and was brave under fire, she soon realized that her family background was not sufficiently noble to earn her a commission as an officer in the infantry. As a result, she transferred again, this time to the cavalry, where she earned high praise for her ability to ride and shoot. It is unclear where she might have learned these skills, but the most likely place was while she was employed by the French nobleman.

It was while in the cavalry that Mary's life as a man came to an abrupt end. While she was in Holland she found herself fighting alongside a Flemish soldier and often spending evenings talking to him by the fireside. Before long, she found that she was no longer taking care of either her gear or herself, with her mind constantly wandering back to her Flemish comrade. She also found herself volunteering for increasingly dangerous missions, if for no reason than to fight by his side and help protect him. As Johnson quipped in *A General History of the Pyrates*, "Mars and Venus could not be served at the same Time."

As their feelings for each other intensified, the men with whom she served began to be suspicious, as did the object of her affection. When rumors began to fly about the camp that she might be homosexual, she decided to "come out of the closet" in a most unusual way: she admitted to her Flemish love that she was, in fact, a woman. The soldier, perhaps relieved that he had not fallen in love with another man, was thrilled to discover that she was in fact female, because it seemed to afford him the chance to take up his own personal mistress in camp. Johnson explained, "He was much surprized at what he found out, and not a little pleased, taking it for granted, that he should have a Mistress solely to himself, which is an unusual Thing in a Camp, since there is scarce one of those Campaign Ladies, that is ever true to a Troop or Company…"

While his initial intentions appear to have been strictly to make her his mistress, he soon discovered that she was not that willing to enter into a sexual relationship without the security of marriage. It's possible that Mary understood the price her mother paid for bearing her as an illegitimate daughter and was determined to avoid that fate herself.

For his part, her Flemish comrade eventually grew tired of waiting and proposed that they marry as soon as they could. Thus, when the army went into its summer quarters, they pooled their wages and bought her some simple, female clothing. Thus dressed, she broke the news to the company commander, who responded better than they had hoped and allowed her to leave the army with no blot on her record. Upon that, they were able to marry, and needless to say, the wedding between two former soldiers attracted much attention in the camp and led to the soldiers putting together, from their limited salaries, a sizable amount of cash for the newlyweds to begin their life together.

Using the money that they were given, as well as a little they had saved from their mutual salaries, the young couple bought an inn named The Three Horseshoes near Breda in Holland. Mary traded her breeches for petticoats and her gun for mugs of ale. There they did a good business, attracting many of their former brothers-in-arms, as well as others who heard their story and wanted to see the famous couple for themselves. But tragedy seemed to have an affinity for the Read family, and Mary's comfortably happy life ended when her husband died and left her a widow. Unable to continue to run the busy inn on her own, Mary returned to the only work she knew: soldiering. She cut her hair short again, pulled her sailor trousers out of the trunk and returned to Holland and the life of a foot soldier.

Mary obviously couldn't return to her cavalry division now that they knew her true gender, so instead she volunteered for out-of-the-way outposts with very few men, banking on the odds that she would not run into anyone who would recognize her. But this time, her plan to go to war was thwarted by peace. She soon realized that there was little hope of advancement within the confines of the peacetime military. Thus, instead of remaining in the army and waiting for her luck to run out, she boarded a merchant ship bound for the West Indies. In a new land, she might have reasoned, she would have new opportunities.

Chapter 2: Anne Cormac

18th century depiction of Anne Bonny

"Anne was not one of his legitimate Issue, which seems to cross an old Proverb, which says, that *Bastards have the best Luck*." – Captain Charles Johnston, *A General History of the Pyrates*

The story of Anne Bonny, and perhaps her ultimate fate, was set before she was even born. Her father, William Cormac, was a prominent Irish lawyer in County Cork who had been married a year or two when his wife gave birth to their first child. The birth was somewhat traumatic and it was decided that she would go to his mother's home to rest and recover. To keep the house running while his wife was gone, Cormac hired a young woman named Peg Brennan. During the wife's absence, Cormac and Brennan became romantically entangled, and not long after his wife returned, she discovered their misadventures and began to plan her revenge.

Her first step was to return to the home of the elder Mrs. Cormac and share with her what her son had been up to. Wife and mother then joined forces to see to it that Cormac lived to regret his actions. He was cut off from all his family's money and told that his wife would never return to him. The wife also accused Brennan of stealing some family silver and had her thrown in jail, where she remained for about six months. During this time the wife's anger against her waned, and after learning that the girl was pregnant, she dropped the charges against her. Brennan was released and returned to her own home, where she delivered a healthy baby girl, Anne, on March 8, 1702.

Not long after Anne was born, the younger Mrs. Cormac gave birth herself to twins, a boy and a girl. They appear to have been conceived during the short time between her return to Cork and her discovery of her husband's infidelity. By this time the, elder Mrs. Cormac was dying and called for her son to be reconciled to his wife for the sake of the two babies, but he refused and questioned if the children were even his, since they were born so soon after his wife's journey away from him.

Angered by her son's refusal to restore his family, the elder Mrs. Cormac changed her will, leaving all her money in trust for the care of her legitimate grandchildren and the younger Mrs. Cormac. She then died, still estranged from her son. Following her death, Cormac fell on hard times, so his wife, still feeling some affection, began to provide for him out of her inheritance.

Nevertheless, during this time Cormac had also kept up his relationship with Peg Brennan, though at something of a distance. They wrote to each other regularly, and he was kept well informed of the growth and development of young Anne. When the little girl was about five years old, he decided that he would like the chance to get to know her better, so he invited her to come and live with him. However, he knew that if his wife found out, she would not be pleased and might very well cut off his allowance.

To get around this potential problem, he hatched a cunning plan. He wrote to Brennan and told her to cut the child's hair and dress her as a boy. She could then send her to him by carriage but not come herself, and he would subsequently tell the community that Anne was actually the son of a distant relative who had been sent to apprentice as a law clerk. The plan worked for a while, and father and daughter finally got to know one another, but Mrs. Cormac eventually discovered that the boy was actually Brennan's daughter. This proved to be more than Mrs. Cormac could stand, and she immediately cut off her husband's allowance.

For his part, William realized that without the money he had nothing to lose, so instead of sending Anne back to live with her mother, he brought Peg to live with them. While this had the desired effect of upsetting and embarrassing his wife, it also brought him into public disrepute in the community and resulted in a serious decline in his law practice. When he was no longer able to support himself and figured that his life in Ireland was ruined, William decided to cut his losses and try his hand in the New World. He sold everything he had except the clothes on his back and, taking Peg and Anne with him, boarded a sailing ship bound for the Carolinas, ultimately settling in the Bahamas.

William quickly tried to establish a new law practice, but he discovered in short order that there was less demand for lawyers there in the early 18th century. Eventually William turned to merchandising, which suited him better, and for the next several years he and Peg lived together as man and wife while he bought and sold goods in the coastal town where they had landed. Before long, he had amassed a sufficient fortune that allowed him to purchase a rice plantation, where he and his family lived happily for a few more years until Peg's death. By this time, Anne was about 13 and considered a young woman more than capable of taking over her mother's duties as mistress of the plantation.

Chapter 3: Anne Bonny

"She was of a fierce and couragious Temper, wherefore, when she lay under Condemnation, several Stories were reported of her, much to her Disadvantage, as that she had kill'd an English Servant-Maid once in her Passion with a Case-Knife, while she look'd after her Father's House; but upon further Enquiry, I found this Story to be groundless: It was certain she was so robust, that once, when a young Fellow would have lain with her, against her Will, she beat him so, that he lay ill of it a considerable Time." – Captain Charles Johnson, *A General History of the Pyrates*

At 13, the slender and athletic Anne was considered very good looking. She had her parents' Irish coloring, with creamy skin, flaming red hair and pea green eyes. She also had a remarkable amount of grace and balance for a girl of her time, probably due in part to the fact she spent some of her early life romping and playing outdoors as a "boy" instead of sitting and sewing by the fire. But Anne also had a fiery temper to match her red hair, and she was known throughout the community for giving anyone that crossed her a piece of her mind. Sometimes, if they were not careful, they might get something else; on at least one occasion, she attacked a servant girl with a case knife, and the anonymous author who wrote *A General History of the Pyrates* under the pseudonym Captain Charles Johnson suggested that she actually killed the girl. And while Anne no longer dressed as a boy, it seems she still fought like one. On another occasion, when she was alone in the house or out for a walk, a young man attacked her with the intention of raping her. However, he soon regretted his attempt when she fought back so fiercely that she beat him unconscious. Though he survived the attack, he was apparently out of commission for some time and never tried anything like that with her again.

One might think that such a dangerous young woman would have a problem finding a husband, but in the early 18th century there were very few available women living in the Bahamas. As a result, those who were there had no problem finding young, single men to court them. Also, by this time, Anne was the only daughter of a wealthy plantation owner, making her all the more attractive as a match. Unfortunately for her father and potential suitors, Anne's temper and rebellious streak made her turn up her nose at all the nicer young men from good families that her father brought home to meet her. Fittingly, Anne was attracted to the shadier rogues instead, and when she was 16 years old, she fell in love with James Bonny, a poor sailor with rumored underworld connections.

When she told her father of her new beau, he flew into a rage and informed her that the word around the island was that Bonny was a pirate, and that he was probably only interested in her for her money. He forbade Anne to see him again and threatened to disinherit her if she did not end the relationship immediately. Of course, such threats meant nothing to the hard-headed girl, and her father's disapproval may well have made Bonny even more attractive to her.

For his part, it seems that Bonny was indeed interested in her money. While he probably found her fun and attractive, it was Anne's future inheritance that really set his heart racing. He continued to court her, hoping no doubt that her father would come around, but even when he did not, the two took their chances by eloping and running away to get married. William Cormac responded as promised and disowned her.

One legend has it that Anne was so incensed at being cut out of her father's will that she decided if she was not to have the plantation, no one would. The story claims Anne (and possibly Bonny) proceeded to sneak on to the grounds in the dark of night and tried to set fire to the fields and the house, but since there is no record of this event, it's likely either that Anne failed or never actually made the attempt.

Following their marriage, Anne and James moved to Nassau on what was then known as New Providence Island, hoping to find work there. When they arrived there, sometime between 1714 and 1718, it was a well-known haven for pirates, especially those from Britain. Over the previous century, many nations from Europe attempted to gain control of the various islands of the Caribbean, leading to competition that mostly took place on the seas and left no single nation able to enforce law and order in the area. Naturally, piracy exploded in this environment, with many pirates igniting fear across the warm tropical seas of the middle Atlantic.

Anne and her husband were arriving to New Providence Island right around the time Queen Anne's War was coming to an end. In Europe, the war was called the War of Spanish Succession, since that was the substance of the war, but in North America it was known as Queen Anne's War. Each of the major belligerents - Spain, France and England - controlled critical pieces of North America, ultimately sucking them in despite the fact they were far removed from European thrones. In North America, the hostilities focused principally on various border disputes, and the Native Americans in the region were also actively involved in the development of the conflict.

In a letter written by Governor Hamilton, English governor of the Bahamas, to the Council of Trade on April 10, 1716, he complained:

"In my former letter I acquainted your Lordships with Captain Soanes, H.M.S. Seahorse, who did design to leave this station and notwithstanding all the arguments that I have used, he does persist in his resolution of going home for Great Britain, before the arrival of the other ship of war to supply his place, and notwithstanding that we have now pirates among these Islands which I had an account of one of the Lieut. Governor of Antigua had been seen off for eight or ten days to the Windward part of that Island.

I therefore ordered the said Soanes to cruise five days to the East part of that Island between the latitude of sixteen and eighteen who is now returned but as I understand went only a little to the South East of that Island and so came down again not without some reflections on his being sent to cruise etc. Refers to enclosure, whereby he peremptorily resolves to leave this station, by which I shall be left without a man of war and if any pirates are or should continue among these Islands, it will not only prevent my going from Island to Island as H.M. service will require me, but very dangerous to the ships trading to and from these Islands."

As a result of this and similar complaints from other governors, King George I issued the following proclamation in the summer of 1717:

"Whereas we have received information, that several persons, subjects of great Britain, have, since the twenty fourth day of June, in the year of our Lord one thousand, seven hundred and fifteen, committed diverse piracies and robberies upon the high seas in the West Indies, or adjoining to our plantations, which have, and may occasion, great damage to the merchants of Great Britain and others, trading into those parts; and though we have appointed such a force as we judge sufficient for suppressing the said piracies: yet the more effectually to put an end to the same, we have thought fit, by and with the advice of our privy council, to issue this our royal proclamation; and we do hereby promise and declare, that in case any of the said pirates shall, on or before the fifth day of September, in the year of our Lord one thousand, seven hundred and eighteen, surrender him or themselves to one of our principal secretaries of state in Great Britain or Ireland, or to any governor or deputy governor of any of our plantations or dominions beyond the seas, every such pirate and pirates, so surrendering him or themselves, as aforesaid, shall have our gracious pardon of and for such his or their piracy or piracies, by him or them."

George I

Among those who took advantage of the king's offer of clemency was James Bonny, who promised to give up his pirating ways and walk a straight and narrow path. In return, the Crown and its representatives agreed not to prosecute him for any past crimes he was known or discovered to be associated with. This was common practice among many pirates at that time, especially the small time ones like Bonny.

Bonny, however, took it one step further. In the summer of 1718, he offered his services to the new governor, Woodes Rogers, as an informant. It is hard to say why he chose to do this, but the most likely answer, of course, is money. Bonny had never enjoyed hard work very much, and now that he had a wife to support, he had to find some way to earn a living.

On the other hand, there may have been another, more pressing reason why he wanted to get into the new governor's good graces. Anne was pregnant, and James had reason to believe that the birth of his first grandchild might soften old William Cormac's heart toward the young couple. In order to precipitate this, James needed to show that he had changed and was ready to be a responsible husband and father. He may have hoped that, by becoming a friend of the governor, he could persuade him to put in a good word for him with his father-in-law.

Chapter 4: The Vane Mutiny

Like many other shadowy characters of the Golden Age of Piracy, little is known about Jack Rackham's early years, and in Calico Jack's case, the historical record is even emptier than usual. The only information about his origins is that he was an Englishman who was born in Cuba around 1682, and there is no record of his ancestry or what his family was like. Part of the problem in finding information about Rackham's early life is due to difficulties related to his family name. As is often the case with the pirates of that era, there are discrepancies in the spelling of his name, which is hardly surprising given that pirates frequently used aliases to help evade authorities or subject their family to problems associated with being related to a criminal. Some documents refer to him as Rackam, while others spell it Rackum.

The first written record of Rackham's life comes from the log of the *Ranger*, a sloop Captained by Charles Vane. According to Vane's records, by 1718 Rackham had risen to the rank of quartermaster under his command, making him the second highest ranked officer on the ship behind the captain himself. Based on that log, it's likely that Calico Jack had been at sea for much of the first 30 years of his life, and since men rarely went to sea after a life on land, Rackham probably began his career as a cabin boy while still in his early teens.

18th century engraving that depicts Vane

By 1718, Charles Vane was one of the New World's most notorious pirates, and he had become famous for his success against Spanish galleons trying to safely move gold across the Gulf of Mexico. On a more personal level, Vane's name had become associated with torturing and murdering the crews he caught, cheating his own men out of booty, and mercilessly attacking any target he felt emboldened enough to take, including a 12-gun brigantine that he christened the *Ranger*.

Given his past, most historians believe that Vane and his shipmates (likely including Calico Jack) were initially English privateers, and Vane was at the height of his career in the beginning of 1718 when the King offered pardons to any pirates who would surrender themselves and promise to give up piracy. Before the pardon was offered by the King, Vane's crew had spent much of their time on shore at New Providence.

At the king's behest, Captain Woodes Rogers traveled to the West Indies to become governor of New Providence, and one of the goals of his governorship was to convince as many pirates as possible to accept the pardons, which would help him clean up New Providence that much faster. Rogers was backed up by two British men-of-war, which induced many pirates with lesser ships to take the pardon, but Rackham and the rest of Vane's crew refused the offer, preferring to take their chances on the open seas. In fact, Vane was so defiant that he had the *Ranger* fire at Rogers' ship as the pirate and his crew left the island.

Ironically, the pirates who accepted pardons were now put to use trying to capture the pirates who refused the offer, and many former pirates found it more lucrative to go after other pirates instead of merchant ships. As wanted men, Vane and his crew began sailing up and down the Eastern coast of the North America, hoping to trap ships sailing to or from England with supplies for the American colonies. In October, Vane and the crew even barely escaped capture and managed to spend a week off the coast of North Carolina with the most famous pirate of them all. The anonymous author writing under the pseudonym Captain Charles Johnson explained:

> "Vane cruised some Time off the Bar, in hopes to catch Yeats at his coming out again, but therein he was disappointed; however, he unfortunately for them, took two Ships from Charles-Town, bound home to England. It happen'd that just at this Time two Sloops well mann'd and arm'd, were equipp'd to go after a Pyrate, which the Governor of South-Carolina was informed, lay then in Cape Fear River, a cleaning: But Colonel Rhet, who commanded the Sloops, meeting with one of the Ships that Vane had plundered, going back over the Bar, for such Necessaries as had been taken from her, and she giving the Colonel an Account of her being taken by the Pyrate Vane, and also, that some of her Men, while they were Prisoners on Board of him, had heard the Pyrates say, they should clean in one of the Rivers to the Southward; he altered his first Design, and instead of standing to the Northward, in pursuit of the Pyrate in Cape Fear River, he turns to the Southward after Vane; who had ordered such Reports to be given

out, on purpose to send any Force that should come after him, upon a wrong Scent; for in Reality he stood away to the Northward, so that the Pursuit proved to be the contrary Way.

Colonel Rhet's speaking with this Ship, was the most unlucky Thing that could have happened, because it turned him out of the Road, which in all Probability, would have brought him into the Company of Vane, as well as of the Pyrate he went after; and so they might have been both destroy'd; whereas, by the Colonel's going a different Way, he not only lost the Opportunity of meeting with one, but if the other had not been infatuated, to lye six Weeks together at Cape Fear, he would have missed of him likewise: However, the Colonel having searched the Rivers and Inlets, as directed, for several Days, without Success, at length sailed in Prosecution of his first Design, and met with the Pyrate accordingly, whom he fought and took, as has been before spoken of, in the History of Major Bonnet.

Captain Vane went into an Inlet to the Northward, where he met with Captain Thatch, or Teach, otherwise call'd Black-beard, whom he saluted (when he found who he was) with his great Guns, loaded with Shot, (as is the Custom among Pyrates when they meet) which are fired wide, or up into the Air: Black-beard answered the Salute in the same Manner, and mutual Civilities passed for some Days; when about the Beginning of October, Vane took Leave, and sailed further to the Northward."

By this time, however, Vane's personality and discord among some of his shipmates resulted in one of his two pirate ships taking off without him:

"For Captain Vane, having always treated his Consort with very little Respect, assuming a Superiority over Yeats and his small Crew, and regarding the Vessel but as a Tender to his own; gave them a Disgust, who thought themselves as good Pyrates, and as great Rogues as the best of them; so they caball'd together, and resolved to take the first Opportunity to leave the Company; and accept of his Majesty's Pardon, or set up for themselves, either of which they thought more honourable than to be Servants to the former; and the putting aboard so many Negroes, where they found so few Hands to take Care of them, still aggravated the Matter, though they thought fit to conceal or stifle their Resentments at that Time.

A Day or two afterwards, the Pyrates lying off at Anchor, Yeats in the Evening slipp'd his Cable, and put his Vessel under Sail, standing into the Shore; which, when Vane saw, he was highly provoked, and got his Sloop under Sail to chase his Consort, who, he plainly perceived, had a Mind to have no further Affairs with him: Vane's Brigantine sailing best, he gained Ground of Yeats, and would certainly have come up with him, had he had a little longer Run for it; but just as he got over the Bar, when Vane came within Gun-shot of him, he fired a Broadside at his old Friend, (which did him no Damage,) and so took his Leave."

Now reduced to one ship, the crew of the *Ranger* encountered several ships along the coast of New York and attacked and plundered them, but on November 24, 1718, Vane and his crew sighted a ship and hoisted their pirate flag, figuring it would be enough to compel the target to surrender. They were greatly surprised when the ship instead hoisted colors that indicated it was a French man-of-war and fired a broadside at the *Ranger*. It was one of the largest ships the pirates had ever seen, and more than twice as large as the *Ranger*. Seeing how well it was armed, Vane thought it best to give the larger vessel a wide berth and stay out of her way, so he ordered his men to retreat where they would not be noticed and could avoid being attacked.

It was at this point that Calico Jack began making his mark on the Golden Age of Piracy. In opposition to Vane's plan, Rackham spoke up in favor of attacking, claiming he saw no reason not to attack and capture the larger ship. The pirates had a pattern of "trading up" to better ships by capturing them, and Rackham rightly pointed out that the huge French ship would likely be loaded with valuable cargo and could be a ship to use for future piracy. When Vane disagreed, Rackham told other members of the crew about his opinion, and most of the 90 pirates agreed with him, leading to a mutiny.

According to one historian:

"During this Chace, the Pyrates were divided in their Resolutions what to do: *Vane*, the Captain, was for making off as fast as he could, alledging the Man of War was too strong to cope with; but one *John Rackam*, who was an Officer, that had a kind of a Check upon the Captain, rose up in Defence of a contrary Opinion, saying, *That tho' she had more Guns, and a greater Weight of Mettal, they might board her, and then the best Boys would carry the Day. Rackam* was well seconded, and the Majority was for boarding; but *Vane* urged, *That it was too rash and desperate an Enterprize, the Man of War appearing to be twice their Force; and that their Brigantine might be sunk by her before they could reach on board.* The Mate, one *Robert Deal*, was of *Vane*'s Opinion, as were about fifteen more, and all the rest joined with *Rackam*, the Quarter-Master. At length the Captain made use of his Power to determine this Dispute, which, in these Cases, is absolute and uncontroulable, by their own Laws, *viz.* in *fighting, chasing*, or *being chased*; in all other Matters whatsoever, he is governed by a Majority; so the Brigantine having the Heels, as they term it, of the *French* Man, she came clear off.

But the next Day, the Captain's Behaviour was obliged to stand the Test of a Vote, and a Resolution passed against his Honour and Dignity, branding him with the Name of Coward, deposing him from the Command, and turning him out of the Company, with Marks of Infamy; and, with him, went all those who did not Vote for boarding the *French* Man of War. They had with them a small Sloop that had been taken by them some Time before, which they gave to *Vane*, and the discarded Members; and, that they might be in a Condition to provide for themselves, by their own honest Endeavours, they let them have a sufficient Quantity of Provisions and Ammunition along with them."

According to the records, Rackham set Vane and the fifteen men who had supported him afloat on the sloop, rather than killing them as many other mutineers had in the past. They even provided their former crewmates with enough food to survive and ammunition to defend themselves. Vane would eventually find his way back to piracy, but now Calico Jack was in charge.

Chapter 5: Captain Rackham

Following his rise to the captaincy, Rackham got off to a good start after sailing toward the Leeward Islands, where he and his crew of about 75 pirates captured several ships and plundered their cargo. Among those captured was a tavern keeper named Hosea Tisdall from Jamaica who pleaded with Rackham to allow him to return to his home. For whatever reason, Rackham agreed to their request, and as they made their way toward Jamaica, the *Ranger* captured a ship sailing from Madera, holding the captain for several days while plundering the ship. When they returned the ship to him, they allowed Tisdall to go with him so that he could make his way back to Jamaica. Rackham and the crew then proceeded on their way.

By this time it was nearly the end of the year, and the men were anxious for a break, so Rackham ordered them to drop anchor at a small island near Jamaica. There the pirates celebrated Christmas on shore, and they took advantage of their break by spending most of their time drinking, sleeping and chasing women. When they ran out of liquor and sobered up, they devoted the rest of their time to cleaning and repairing their ship. Captain Charles Johnson explained what prompted them to head back to sea: "After this Cruize, they went into a small Island and cleaned, and spent their Christmas ashore, drinking and carousing as long as they had any Liquor left, and then went to Sea again for more."

Though they sailed around the Caribbean for more than two months, Calico Jack and his crew did not have much luck in their pursuits. In fact, the only ship they ran into was a ship carrying criminals from the English prison at Newgate to work on the plantations being established in America. They kept the ship for a while, trying to decide what to do with her and her cargo, but before they reached a decision an English man-of-war approached, forcing them to turn the ship loose and make their own escape.

After finding little to interest them around Jamaica, Rackham and his crew made their way toward Bermuda, and along the way they captured a ship that had recently left the Carolinas and another ship sailing from New England. They took both ships to the Bahamas, where they cleaned and repaired both of them and the *Ranger*, after which they restocked all the ships and refitted them for a new voyage.

Calico Jack might have had 3 ships with which to prey on his targets, but apparently the pirates tarried in the Bahamas too long, because Captain Woodes Rogers, the governor of New Providence, got news of their presence there and sent a ship to capture them. The pirates managed to spot the English sloop far off shore, and after seeing that it appeared to be both well-armed and well-manned, the pirates decided to make a run for it. To ensure a speedy escape, they had to sacrifice the two prizes they had previously taken, and once again they only had the *Ranger*.

By the time Calico Jack and his pirates left shore, they had established something of a routine in the way they lived; they would sail around the Caribbean for a few months looking for ships to seize before returning to the island of Cuba, where many had unofficial families. One of those men was Rackham himself, who apparently had a common law wife and perhaps even a child or two living there. Thus, when the pirates left the Bahamas, they decided to return to Cuba and spend the booty they had taken before they abandoned the other ships.

Feeling safe on the large island, Calico Jack and his crew remained in Cuba for several months, spending most of their newly gained treasure on "wine, women and song." They also completed the work they had begun on the *Ranger* back in the Bahamas, and they were preparing to return to sea when their plans were interrupted by a man-of-war sailing toward Cuba's coast with a captured English sloop in tow. Seeing the pirates, the ship attacked, but before they could defeat the *Ranger* Calico Jack managed to sail into the shallower waters of a nearby island, where the larger ship could not safely follow them.

Unwilling to give up her potential prize so easily, the man-of-war sailed into the channel and dropped anchor, determined to wait until Rackham tried to make a run for it. Through his spy glass, Rackham could easily see his enemy, and the captain discussed the situation with his men to choose how the pirate ship would proceed. After much discussion, they came up with a plan that was both elegant in its simplicity and cunning in its execution. In the dark of the moonless night, Rackham sailed the *Ranger* up to the English sloop being towed in by the man-of-war and silently boarded her, getting the jump on the few sleeping Spaniards who were supposed to be guarding the sloop. The pirates woke each Spaniard by placing a knife to his throat and whispering that if he made so much as a sound, it would be his last. Within moments, Rackham and his men had complete possession of the English sloop that was being towed in by the man-of-war, and they quickly untied her from her Spanish captor and sailed her into open waters, leaving behind the tired old *Ranger* in her stead.

It was not until daylight that the men on the man-of-war realized what had happened, and they furiously fired on the *Ranger* hoping to kill anyone left aboard. Of course, the *Ranger* was empty, and her former crew had already disappeared past the horizon in a newer and faster ship. The man-of-war was thus left with only a now bullet riddled hull of an empty ship for their prize.

One of the things that enabled Rackham to move so quickly and silently against the man-of-war and its captured sloop was that his crew was significantly smaller than it had been in the past. Many of his men had chosen to stay behind in Cuba, so Rackham found himself sailing about the Caribbean with something resembling a skeleton crew. Nevertheless, as he sailed toward Jamaica, perhaps in hopes of recruiting more men, along the way he was able to attack and plunder several smaller vessels. While the booty on board provided the pirates with food and drink, Calico Jack and his crew had reached a breaking point; either he had to add to the crew or change his ways.

Chapter 6: Anne Bonny and Mary Read

Sometime in 1719, Calico Jack made his way back to Jamaica to add to his crew, and he would end up meeting one of the most famous pirates in history while he was there. During his stay in Jamaica, Rackham met a Frenchman named Pierre, who ran a popular salon that was frequented by the ladies of the island. One of those ladies was a young woman named Anne Bonny, the daughter of a prominent New World businessman. She was in her late teens but had already been married to James Bonny, a one-time pirate who had taken the pardon offer and was now a sailor for the Jamaican governor.

Although Anne Bonny may have been pregnant when she met Calico Jack, she was still young and pretty, and she had became bored with her life as the wife of a poor seaman. She found herself missing the social life that her father's home provided, but she was also too proud to return home and instead frequented the local pub for companionship instead. Little is known about Calico Jack's looks or his demeanor, but there was something about him that attracted young Anne. However, there was the delicate matter of her child and her husband. With Pierre's help, she found a place to live until she had her child, but as soon as she recovered from the birth, she left the boy with his father and took off to meet Rackham.

18th century engraving depicting Anne Bonny

In the early months of 1719, Anne, Calico Jack, and the rest of his crew sailed around the islands of the Bahamas, doing some minor pilfering and harassing local vessels. It's been alleged that Anne dressed up as a man as part of the crew, but it's unclear whether this is true, and after a few months Anne found herself pregnant again. When she shared the news with Rackham, he was not particularly pleased, since he enjoyed having her for a mistress but had no interest in being a father. Since she was not exactly the maternal type either, the two made a plan to deal with their unwanted pregnancy. When Anne's pregnancy would render her unfit for piracy, Calico Jack took her to Cuba and arranged for Anne to stay with his "Cuban family" until her child was delivered. He returned a few months later, picking Anne up from the island and leaving the child behind to be cared for, most likely with his half-siblings, by Rackham's former mistress. Rumor has it that he was later adopted by an English family by the name of Cunningham. What is clear, however, is that the child never saw either of his parents again.

Once she had recovered from childbirth, Anne returned to Rackham's ship, the *Revenge*. By this time she had been divorced by her husband, who cited abandonment for the grounds. It's also believed that Calico Jack offered to buy Anne in a "divorce by purchase," but she refused that arrangement herself. Either way, once she was divorced from Bonny, this left her free to marry Rackham, but there is no evidence that the two were ever legally wed.

As Calico Jack and his lover took to the seas once again, the King issued yet another offer of amnesty to those pirates who would turn themselves in and promise to walk the straight and narrow path of honest work. Despite the attempts of Rogers and other privateers, there was not enough success in 1718 to satisfy the Crown. Near the end of that year, on December 21, 1718, King George I issued yet another proclamation, this time reviewing his past offers of pardons and reiterating the bounty on the heads of the remaining pirates. The largest bounty was placed on Blackbeard's head, but a sizable bounty was also placed on the head of anybody else commanding a pirate ship.:

> "Whereas we did think fit, by and with the advice of our privy council, to issue our royal proclamation, bearing date the fifth day of September, one thousand, seven hundred and seventeen, in the fourth year of our reign, therein taking notice, that we had received information, that several persons, subjects of Great Britain, had, since the four and twentieth day of June, in the year of our lord one thousand, seven hundred and fifteen, committed divers piracies and robberies upon the high seas in the West Indies, or adjoining to our plantations, which had and might occasion great damage to the merchants of Great Britain, and others, trading into those parts: and we did thereby promise and declare, that in case any the said pirates should, on or before the fifth day of September, one thousand, seven hundred and eighteen, surrender him or themselves in manner as therein is directed, every such pirate and pirates, so surrendering him or themselves, as aforesaid, should have our gracious pardon of and for such his or their piracy or piracies, by him or them committed before the fifth day of January then next ensuing: and whereas several of the said pirates, not having had timely notice of our said proclamation, may not have surrendered themselves within the time therein appointed, and by reason thereof are incapable of receiving the benefit of our royal mercy and clemency intended thereby: and though we have appointed such a force, as we judge sufficient for suppressing the said piracies, yet the more effectually to put an end to the same, we have thought fit, by and with the advice of our privy-council, to issue this our royal proclamation; and we do hereby promise and declare, that in case any the said pirates shall, on or before the first day of July, in the year of our lord one thousand, seven hundred and nineteen, surrender him or themselves to one of our principal secretaries of state in Great Britain or Ireland, or to any governor or deputy-governor of any of our plantations or dominions beyond the seas, every such pirate and pirates, so surrendering him or themselves, as aforesaid, shall have our gracious pardon of and for such his or their piracy or piracies, by him or them committed before such time as they shall have received notice of this our royal proclamation; which pardon or pardons we have authorized and commanded our respective governors to grant

accordingly. And we do hereby strictly charge and command all our admirals, captains, and other officers at sea, and all our governors and commanders of any forts, castles, or other places in our plantations, and all others our officers civil and military, to seize and take such of the pirates, who shall refuse or neglect to surrender themselves accordingly. And we do hereby further declare, that in case any person or persons, on or after the first day of July, one thousand, seven hundred and nineteen, shall discover or seize, or cause or procure to be discovered or seized, any one or more of the said pirates, so neglecting or refusing to surrender themselves, as aforesaid, so as they may be brought to justice, and convicted of the said offence, such person or persons, so making such discovery or seizure, or causing or procuring such discovery or seizure to be made, shall have and receive as a reward for the same, (viz.) for every commander of any pirate-ship or vessel the sum of one hundred pounds; for every lieutenant, master, boatswain, carpenter, and gunner, the sum of forty pounds; for every inferior officer the sum of thirty pounds; and for every private man, the sum of twenty pounds; and if any person or persons, belonging to, and being part of the crew of any such pirate-ship or vessel, shall, on or after the said first day of July, one thousand, seven hundred and nineteen, seize and deliver, or cause to be seized and delivered, any commander or commanders of such pirate-ship or vessel, so as that he or they be brought to justice, and convicted of the said offence, such person or persons, as a reward for the same, shall receive for every such commander the sum of two hundred pounds; which said sums the lord treasurer, or the commissioners of our treasury for the time being, are hereby required and directed to pay accordingly.

Given at our court at St. James s, the twenty-first day of

December 1718. In the fifth year of our reign.

God save the king."

As a result of this bounty, hunting pirates suddenly became more lucrative than being one. After discussing the options with Anne and the rest of his crew, Rackham decided to give the honest life a try. Though he had rejected the previous pardon offer, his luck had not been too good lately, and he was ready to try something else. Calico Jack turned his ship toward the nearest fort, where he and his crew confessed to all (or at least most) of their piracy and swore to live out the rest of their days as honest sailors in the service of His Majesty.

Of course, the question arose as to how they were to make their living if not through piracy, but Rackham was one step ahead of his men. He explained that, as pirates themselves, they knew the hiding places and plans use by fellow pirates in the area. The King was offering a generous bounty for the capture of their former cohorts, so if they were no longer going to survive by being pirates, why not make their living by hunting them down?

Unfortunately, hunting pirates proved to be easier said than done. For one thing, many of the more serious captains were simply too smart to get caught. Likewise, the ones that could be easily found were few and far between. Many of them had taken the same path as Rackham and had become pirate hunters themselves. After a few months of trying to live their lives within the confines of the law, Rackham and his men gave up and returned to their former lives as pirates.

Chapter 7: Mary Read Joins the Crew

Upon heading west, it wouldn't take long for Mary to determine her new line of work. On her voyage across the Atlantic, her ship was captured by an unknown pirate ship sometime before they reached their island destination. Because Mary was the only English speaking sailor aboard that particular ship, the captain of the ship, thinking she was a man, offered her the opportunity to join his crew and become a pirate herself. Seeing the plunder that the men were taking for themselves, and the ease with which they took the ship, Mary took him up on this offer.

Mary likely traveled to the West Indies just as piracy was becoming rampant there, and it seems for the next few years she lived the life of a pirate while Calico Jack served under Vane and then captained his own ship. When the first clemency offer was made by the Crown, the pirate crew with whom Mary had been serving decided to surrender themselves and try living within the law for a change. For her part, Mary went to work back on shore, though it is unclear whether she did so as a man or woman, but before long a new sailing opportunity presented itself.

Once Calico Jack and Anne Bonny returned to piracy, Rackham lost no time in going after the next small ship he saw. During one of these voyages in 1719, Rackham came upon a moderately sized ship crewed by a bunch of men from the West Indies. After commandeering the ship, Calico Jack offered to let members of that boat join his crew, including an Englishman who he introduced to Anne. From the start Anne was fascinated by this new member of their crew, drawn to his delicately high pitched voice and clean shaven appearance. While most of the men wore beards or at least mustaches, this new man always kept his face clean shaven. As time went on, Anne found herself going out of her way to speak to him or work near him, and before long the two had become close friends.

As it turned out, the Englishman was no man at all. Like Calico Jack and Anne Bonny, Mary Read was a former pirate turned privateer, and it's unclear what choice she had but to join Rackham's crew after her ship was commandeered by the pirate. Mary would later insist that she had never intended to be a pirate but had simply fell into the life by accident, and that she only turned to the life after she was captured and forced to serve aboard a pirate ship. She further claimed that it was always her intention to abandon piracy as soon as she could. While all of that may have been possible, those statements would be made during her trial, when she was fighting for her life. Naturally, her trial was hardly the time to say that she had always wanted to be a pirate and could hardly wait to go back to it

For a time, Mary continued to keep her identity as a woman a secret from Anne, but as Anne continued to make sexual advances towards her, things were clearly complicated. Sensitive to the problems of being the new love of the captain's mistress, Mary chose to confide her true sex to Anne. According to legend, Anne did not lose her romantic interest in Mary when she found out she was a woman, and it is maintained by some that the two became lovers themselves, though initially keeping Mary's gender and their relationship a secret from Rackham.

Eventually, Calico Jack noticed his romantic rival, who he still thought was a man. As Johnson noted, "[T]his Intimacy so disturb'd Captain Rackam, who was the Lover and Gallant of Anne Bonny, that he grew furiously jealous, so that he told Anne Bonny, he would cut her new Lover's Throat…" After he had threatened to execute his rival, Anne, concerned about Mary's safety, decided to admit to Calico Jack that the other pirate was actually a woman. In a manner best left to the imagination, Rackham confirmed that this was true, and welcomed Mary to his crew and later, some say, his bed. As Johnson put it, "Captain Rackam, (as he was enjoined,) kept the Thing a Secret from all the Ship's Company, yet, notwithstanding all her Cunning and Reserve, Love found her out in this Disguise, and hinder'd her from forgetting her Sex."

It has long been speculated that the three of them all became lovers together. Whether this is true or not, the fact does remain that Mary and Anne remained very close to each during the rest of their time sailing together. But while Anne was known as the captain's woman and thus did not have to try to pass herself off as a man, Mary remained a female in hiding, living and working among the men as one of them.

Having established a pattern of almost group captaincy, Calico Jack, Anne Bonny and Mary Read began to work together to recruit more crew members, planning for long careers on the open seas. But they were doing so at a bad time; England, which had once turned a blind eye toward attacks on her enemy's vessels, was now joining with forces from other countries to hunt down pirates. Gone were the days when Grace O'Malley could meet with the queen, or when Francis Drake received a knighthood for attacking and pillaging Spanish vessels. Early 18th century Europe was colonial and business oriented. They needed safe waterways to guarantee their profits and keep tax revenue coming in from new products being brought to Europe from the Americas.

The sun was setting on the Golden Age of Piracy, and unbeknownst to them, their days of freedom were already numbered.

18th century depiction of Anne Bonny and Mary Read

Chapter 8: 1720

For the first few months of 1720, all went well for the Revenge, which continued to cruise around the coast of the Bahamas looking for ships that appeared to be transporting treasure. They would then fire a cannon ball over their bows and signal for them to surrender. Most did, and they quickly came alongside, boarded the ship and took what they wanted. Because Calico Jack still had a relatively small crew, they shied away from the biggest ships and thus never made a really big score like Black Bart or Blackbeard, and they were also not as bloodthirsty as some in their trade, typically allowing the captured crew to sail away to safety as soon as they got what they wanted.

Mary soon proved herself to be one of Calico Jack's best fighters. There are several reasons why this young woman proved to be so fierce. For one thing, Mary had had to become a good fighter in order to keep her identity secret. Homosexual relations among ships' crews were a natural occurrence given the lack of any available women, but Mary couldn't afford to potentially let the rest of the crew know she wasn't a man. Since she would definitely have been on of the most effeminate members of any crew she belonged to, she would have had to have been tough to fend off unwanted advances that might have given away her secret. Another reason for Mary's martial strength was that she had had plenty of practice defending herself through the years. She had made a living out of being a soldier, sailor, and even a member of a cavalry unit, all of which required her to be as strong and tough as the men she was serving alongside.

Similarly, according to the legends Anne was a fierce fighter and every bit as aggressive as Rackham himself. She was known to be a good shot and cool under pressure, and whenever there was a battle to be fought, she would be in the thick of it and would not quit until the job was done or the rest of the crew had decided to give up. Naturally, before long the tale of the two women pirates in Calico Jack's crew had made its way around the ships and pubs along the waterfront. Some claimed that it could not be possible that two women would be able to fight as well as men. Others, however, told a different tale. Those who had faced them in battle or fought alongside them on the *Revenge* were happy to tell tales of their exploits together.

In addition to taking each ship's cargo, the pirates were also inclined to take some of the more useful crew members. This was achieved in one of two ways. First, Calico Jack, after spotting a young man who had talents that he thought his crew could use, would approach him and suggest that he throw in his lot with them. Often the man in question would agree, and that would be that. However, some were more reluctant to give up their honest work. At this point, the pirate captain might reconsider his decision and let him remain on his own ship. But if Rackham still felt that he needed the man, he would force the man to join the crew.

Once on Calico Jack's ship, Mary had the first opportunity in her life to be who she truly was: a woman who enjoyed living her life as a man. But just as things had gotten complicated when Anne took an interest in her, things again got complicated when Mary took an interest in one of her crewmates, who had been forced into service on the *Revenge*. Before long, they were sharing the same table and slept near each other at night, igniting Mary's passions. If she made her feelings known without revealing her sex, she would obviously be misleading the other sailor, but if she did let him in on her secret and he was not interested, she would likely lose her place on the crew.

According to Johnson, Mary eventually revealed her sex to this new object of her affection, though whether it was intentional or not was unclear:

"In their Cruize they took a great Number of Ships belonging to Jamaica, and other Parts of the West-Indies, bound to and from England; and when ever they meet any good Artist, or other Person that might be of any great Use to their Company, if he was not willing to enter, it was their Custom to keep him by Force. Among these was a young Fellow of a most engageing Behaviour, or, at least, he was so in the Eyes of Mary Read, who became so smitten with his Person and Address, that she could neither rest, Night or Day; but as there is nothing more ingenious than Love, it was no hard Matter for her, who had before been practiced in these Wiles, to find a Way to let him discover her Sex: She first insinuated her self into his liking, by talking against the Life of a Pyrate, which he was altogether averse to, so they became Mess-Mates and strict Companions: When she found he had a Friendship for her, as a Man, she suffered the

Discovery to be made, by carelesly shewing her Breasts, which were very White. The young Fellow, who was made of Flesh and Blood, had his Curiosity and Desire so rais'd by this Sight, that he never ceased importuning her, till she confessed what she was."

After Mary admitted she was a woman, the two soon became lovers, though they kept their relationship a secret for both of their sakes. On the one hand, Mary wanted to remain known as a man. On the other, she made it clear that Calico Jack would not take it well if he discovered she was involved with another man.

For a while, they were able to keep their love a secret, but the young man still did not like the life of a pirate and was not settling in well with the crew. Before long, he so angered one of his fellow crew members that the man challenged him to a duel. Young and cocky, Mary's lover agreed and they planned to meet on the next island the ship stopped at. When they dropped anchor near one of the smaller islands in the West Indies, the men agreed to go ashore the next day and settle their quarrel.

Mary was obviously concerned about the fate of the man. While she could not stand the idea of him sacrificing his pride by refusing the challenge, she still hated to see him risk his life. In perhaps the most famous legend of Mary Read's life, she devised a clever way to intervene on his behalf herself. Because the crew still thought she was a man, she decided to pick her own fight with the man her lover was set to duel, going out of her way to offend him until he finally had enough and threatened her. In order to protect her lover's safety, Mary made sure that her own duel with the man came a few hours before he was set to duel her lover.

It has long been speculated that Captain Charles Johnson, the author of the pirate history, was a pirate himself, and the manner in which he described Mary Read's duel with this pirate certainly suggests he found the violence romantic:

"[H]er Passion was no less violent than his, and perhaps she express'd it, by one of the most generous Actions that ever Love inspired. It happened this young Fellow had a Quarrel with one of the Pyrates, and their Ship then lying at an Anchor, near one of the Islands, they had appointed to go ashore and fight, according to the Custom of the Pyrates: Mary Read, was to the last Degree uneasy and anxious, for the Fate of her Lover; she would not have had him refuse the Challenge, because, she could not bear the Thoughts of his being branded with Cowardise; on the other Side, she dreaded the Event, and apprehended the Fellow might be too hard for him: When Love once enters into the Breast of one who has any Sparks of Generosity, it stirs the Heart up to the most noble Actions; in this Dilemma, she shew'd, that she fear'd more for his Life than she did for her own; for she took a Resolution of quarreling with this Fellow her self, and having challenged him ashore, she appointed the Time two Hours sooner than that when he was to meet her Lover, where she fought him at Sword and Pistol, and killed him upon the Spot.

It is true, she had fought before, when she had been insulted by some of those Fellows, but now it was altogether in her Lover's Cause, she stood as it were betwixt him and Death, as if she could not live without him. If he had no regard for her before, this Action would have bound him to her for ever; but there was no Occasion for Ties or Obligations, his Inclination towards her was sufficient; in fine, they applied their Troth to each other, which Mary Read said, she look'd upon to be as good a Marriage, in Conscience, as if it had been done by a Minister in Church; and to this was owing her great Belly, which she pleaded to save her Life."

Indeed, Mary's actions eventually made her lover even fonder of her, but time was running out on the pirates. Months before they were ultimately captured, Calico Jack's crew were nearly captured, only to turn the tables in a daring plot. Captain Charles Johnson explained how the pirates captured one of their biggest prizes:

"They repaired to their Vessel, and was making ready to put Sea, when a Guarda del Costa came in with a small English Sloop, which she had taken as an Interloper on the Coast. The Spanish Guardship attack'd the Pyrate, but Rackam being close in behind a little Island, she could do but little Execution where she lay, therefore the Spaniard warps into the Channel that Evening, in order to make sure of her the next Morning. Rackam finding his Case desperate, and hardly any Possibility of escaping, resolved to attempt the following Enterprize: The Spanish Prize lying for better Security close into the Land, between the little Island and the Main; Rackam takes his Crew into the Boat, with their Pistols and Cutlashes, rounds the little Island, and falls aboard their Prize silently in the dead of the Night, without being discovered, telling the Spaniards that were aboard of her, that if they spoke a Word, or made the least Noise, they were dead Men, and so became Master of her; when this was done, he slipt her Cable, and drove out to Sea: The Spanish Man of War, was so intent upon their expected Prize, that they minded nothing else, and as soon as Day broke, made a furious Fire upon the empty Sloop, but it was not long before they were rightly apprized of the Matter, and cursed themselves for Fools, to be bit out of a good rich Prize, as she prov'd to be, and to have nothing but an old crazy Hull in the room of her.

Rackam and his Crew had no Occasion to be displeased at the Exchange, that enabled them to continue some Time longer in a Way of Life that suited their depraved Tempers."

In addition to taking each ship's cargo, the pirates were also inclined to take some of the more useful crew members. This was achieved in one of two ways. First, Calico Jack, after spotting a young man who had talents that he thought his crew could use, would approach him and suggest that he throw in his lot with them. Often the man in question would agree, and that would be that. However, some were more reluctant to give up their honest work. At this point, Rackham might reconsider his decision and let him remain on his own ship, but if he still felt that he needed the man, he would simply force the man to join the crew.

Over time, the men of Rackham's crew were quite aware that they had the dubious distinction of sailing alongside one of the only female pirates in the world in Anne Bonny. Though Mary continued to wear men's clothing, Anne would dress in either a feminine or a masculine style depending on how her mood and tasks for the day dictated. She had no fear of harassment, since Rackham made it clear that she was his mistress and therefore under his protection. Of course, Anne was also perfectly capable of taking care of herself, and it is unlikely that Rackham had to rise to her defense very often. At the same time, with Anne Bonny aboard his ship, the tales of Calico Jack and his female crew member were soon making their way through all the seaside pubs on both sides of the Atlantic. Some men refused to believe it was even true, while others maintained that there was no way a woman could work the sails and fight as well as men. However, those who would end up facing Anne Bonny and Mary Read in battle would tell a different story in 1720.

Seafaring superstition at that time maintained that it was unlucky to have a woman aboard a ship, and two women would have been twice as bad. While it is obvious that such superstitions were simply products of the male dominated nature of sea life during the 18th century, it didn't seem to faze Calico Jack. If Rackham ever felt embarrassed or awkward about his relationship with Bonny and Read, he mentioned it to no one, and he seems to have been secure enough in his own masculinity to not be troubled by what others thought. Calico Jack had likely spent decades at sea already, and if someone challenged his personal toughness, chances are that they would carry away more than a bruise or two to remind them not to ask again.

The crew also had similar success in September 1720, taking more booty and increasing the size of their crew at the same time. In early September, 1720, Rackham and his crew captured about eight small fishing boats near Harbour Island. These boats carried little of value accept their nets and fishing tackle, but the sale of these items did give the small crew enough capital to finance a trip to French Hispaniola. There they dropped anchor and went ashore looking for what they might steal, but all they found were some cattle roaming through the woods. They brought these on board, as well as several Frenchmen who were on the island hunting wild boar.

From Hispaniola, the small band made their way back to Jamaica, managing to plunder two more sloops while on their way. There, near Porto Maria Bay, they captured a schooner, captained by Thomas Spenlow, on October 19. The following morning, Rackham spotted another sloop, this one in dry dock near the coast. He fired a shot into the air, causing those who were working on her to run to the shore to see what was going on. While they were doing this, his own men slipped aboard and plundered the ship where it stood. When the men finally made it back to the sloop, they realized what had happened. With nothing left to work with, they sent word to Rackham that they knew they were beaten and would be just as happy to join his crew. Always in the market for new men, he accepted their offer and brought them aboard.

However, a month later, the *Revenge* was on a normal sailing expedition of the coast of Jamaica when their luck finally ran out. Unaware that he was being chased, Rackham sailed his ship hear Point Negril in the Bahamas. There he saw a small Pettiauger and went after it. Seeing that she was being chased, the Pettiauger ran ashore and landed her crew. They then hailed Rackham, and indicated by the flags that they were English. Recognizing his fellow countrymen, Rackham invited the men aboard for a drink. They agreed, and nine men joined him for beer and talk well into the night. By the time all was said and done, all the men on the ship were passed out from a combination of liquor and exhaustion.

The following morning, Mary, Anne and Calico Jack were on deck, perhaps talking or making plans for their next attack. Captain Charles Johnson explained:

"Rackam's coasting the Island in this Manner, proved fatal to him, for Intelligence came to the Governor, of his Expedition, by a Canoa which he had surprized ashore, in Ocho Bay; upon which a Sloop was immediately fitted out, and sent round the Island in quest of him, commanded by Captain Barnet, with a good Number of Hands. Rackam rounding the Island, and drawing near the Westermost Point, called Point Negril, saw a small Pettiauger, which at sight of the Sloop, run ashore and landed her Men; when one of them hailed her, Answer was made, They were English Men, and desired the Pettiauger's Men to come on Board, and drink a Bowl of Punch, which they were prevailed upon to do; accordingly the Company came all aboard of the Pyrate, consisting of nine Persons, in an ill Hour; they were armed with Muskets and Cutlashes, but, what was their real Design by so doing, I shall not take upon me to say; but they had no sooner laid down their Arms, and taken up their Pipes, but Barnet's Sloop, which was in Pursuit of Rackam's, came in Sight."

As always, the three were on alert for the sight of any other ships in the area, so when they saw a sloop approaching off their bow, they immediately sat up and took notice. As it got closer, Rackham pulled out his spy glass and took a look. That's when he saw the flag of the Governor of Jamaica flying stiffly in the breeze. The three immediately sprang into action, changing the sails and trying to make a speedy getaway. At first it seemed that they might avoid the other ship and perhaps slip by unnoticed, but before long they realized that they were spotted and the ship was giving chase.

Rackham called for all hands on deck, but nothing happened. He then sent Mary down to the hull to rouse the men, but she had little luck as they were all still pretty drunk. Returning to Anne and Calico Jack, she reported that it looked like the men were in no condition to fight. Their only option appeared to be to outrun the other ship. For the next few hours, the three tried with all their might to escape, steering and adjusting the rigging to make the maximum use of whatever wind there was. However, they soon realized that it was futile and prepared to fight.

Anne went below decks and tried herself to rouse the sleeping pirates. Again they ignored her or gave only lip service to coming upstairs. Things changed, however, when the first cannon ball flew over the bow of the ship and splashed in the water nearby. Rackham returned fire and the battle began in earnest. Some of the crew began to stumble up the stairs of the ship, squinting in the bright sunlight and asking what was going on.

Rackham gave them a quick rundown of the situation. No doubt reminding them that, if they were captured, many if not all of them would hang. This stirred up some interest among the crew, but they were still not in any physical condition to put up a serious fight. That left Rackham, Mary and Anne to fight off the ship alone. At first it seemed they might win. However, the final blow came when the sloop put a cannon ball through the hull of the *Revenge*, causing her to begin to take on water.

The roar of sea water rushing in and the spray of salt water on their faces soon roused the rest of the crew. By then, however, it was too late for them to fight. Instead, they focused their attention on trying to stop the ship from sinking. Some men tried to wrestle a patch into place to cover up the hole while others manned the pumps, desperately trying to return the water to the sea where it belonged.

Meanwhile, the captain and women were left on the upper decks, fighting the men boarding the ship alone. Many would later testify that the women were the fiercest fighters in this battle, and that they did more damage than any of the men of the crew. However, it soon became clear that they were outnumbered, outgunned and beaten. Rackham was forced to surrender his ship and his crew to Captain Jonathan Barnet, a privateer commissioned by the Governor of Jamaica to hunt down and capture pirates.

While that description of the fighting makes for a romantic and interesting story, it is doubtful that it actually went down that way. For one thing, it is unlikely that anyone would hide below decks of a ship taking on water. Indeed, the men may very well have been below trying to repair the hole or man the pumps. The women, with less physical strength, would have remained on the deck to carry on the fight. Once the ship was boarded, they would certainly have kept on fighting, even hand to hand if necessary.

No matter how the battle may have been fought, it certainly ended with the *Revenge* and her entire crew being captured by Barnet, who shipped them off to confinement at Spanish Town, Jamaica.

Chapter 9: Trials

Not surprisingly, when the infamous crew arrived at St. Jago de la Vega in Jamaica, they attracted more than their fair share of attention. Word soon spread around the community that the famous Calico Jack had been captured and that he did in fact have women in his crew. The guards in front of the fort were soon greeted by more than one curious face, arriving at the gate in the hopes of catching a glimpse of a member of this strange crew. At some point in time, either on their way to Spanish Town, or shortly after their arrival, it became known that Mary was actually a woman. Whether she was exposed by someone else or confessed it herself is unclear, but records indicate she and Anne were segregated from the men as soon as they arrived at Spanish Town.

Those hoping to see Bonny and Read stand trial would have to wait, because Calico Jack and his male crew members were tried first. On November 16, 1720, the Admiralty Court was called into session. The charges against them, specifically numerous counts of piracy, were read aloud, and the men were given a chance to enter their pleas. Though they pled not guilty, Captain Charles Johnson recorded that "they were all Guilty of the Pyracy and Felony they were charged with, which was, the going over with a pyratical and felonious Intent to John Rackam, &c. then notorious Pyrates, and by them known to be so, they all received Sentence of Death…" There was little doubt in anyone's mind that Calico Jack and his men had indeed done everything they were accused of.

The aptly named Sir Nicholas Laws presided over the court, which quickly found Rackham guilty as charged. They also convicted the ship's Master, George Fetherston, and her quartermaster, Richard Corner, as well as six crew men who had been with Rackham for the longest time: John Davis, John Howell, Patrick Carty, Thomas Earl, James Dobbin and Noah Harwood. Rackham, Fehterston, Corner, Davis and Howell were immediately sentenced to be executed the following day.

When asked if he had a last request, Rackham asked only to see Anne one more time. Unfortunately for him, he found his lover to be little comfort in the final hours of his life. According to tradition, she is said to have told him that she was sorry to see him in such a predicament, but that "if he had fought like a Man, he need not have been hanged like a dog." With those words ringing in his ears, he was carried off to the gallows and hanged in November 1720. To send a message, the authorities had Calico Jack's body gibbeted on a small islet near the entrance to Port Royal. There they remain for the next several years, their rotting corpses gruesome warnings to other who might consider entering the pirating life. However, Calico Jack had the last laugh. Today, the point in Port Royal where his body was hanged in disgrace is known as Rackham City.

The other four men who were convicted with Rackham were executed a few days later before the court recessed until after the Christmas holidays. The next group of nine pirates was tried on

January 24, 1721, and this particular group of sailors had come on the ship when they captured their last sloop. The prosecution offered only the flimsiest of evidence against them, saying:

"That the Prisoners at the Bar, viz. John Eaton, Edward Warner, Thomas Baker, Thomas Quick, John Cole, Benjamin Palmer, Walter Rouse, John Hanson, and John Howard, came aboard the Pyrate's Sloop at Negril Point, Rackam sending his Canoe ashore for that Purpose: That they brought Guns and Cutlashes on Board with them: That when Captain Barnet chased them, some were drinking, and others walking the Deck: That there was a great Gun and a small Arm fired by the Pyrate Sloop, at Captain Barnet's Sloop, when he chased her; and that when Captain Barnet's Sloop fired at Rackam's Sloop, the Prisoners at the Bar went down under Deck. That during the Time Captain Barnet chased them, some of the Prisoners at the Bar (but which of them he could not tell) helped to row the Sloop, in order to escape from Barnet: That they all seemed to be consorted together."

The men responded to the charges with a rather clever defense:

'That they had no Witnesses: That they had bought a Pettiauger in order to go a Turtleing; and being at Negril Point, and just got ashore, they saw a Sloop with a white Pendant coming towards them, upon which they took their Arms, and hid themselves in the Bushes: That one of them hail'd the Sloop, who answer'd, They were English Men, and desired them to come aboard and drink a Bowl of Punch; which they at first refused, but afterwards with much perswasion, they went on Board, in the Sloop's Canoe, and left their own Pettiauger at Anchor: That they had been but a short Time on Board, when Captain Barnet's Sloop heaved in Sight: That Rackam ordered them to help to weigh the Sloop's Anchor immediately, which they all refused: That Rackam used violent Means to oblige them; and that when Captain Barnet came up with them, they all readily and willingly submitted.

Next, two Frenchmen gave evidence on their behalf. This concluded the evidence against them, and the jury retired to consider what they had heard. In the end, this second group of men were also convicted and sentenced to execution. Some historians would later argue that this sentence appeared to have been a bit excessive, especially since there was so little substantive evidence against them. Nonetheless, Eaton, Quick, and Baker were all hanged on February 17 and Cole, Howard and Palmer followed them to the gallows the next day. It appears, however, that the rest of the male crew members survived their trials, though little is known of the rest of their lives.

Anne and Mary were tried last of all. When called to the stand, Mary swore that she had never wanted to be a pirate, that she had only come aboard Calico Jack's ship because he kidnapped her, and that she never fought against anyone. In addition to piracy, she was charged with sexual misconduct, a charge that suggests it was obvious she was pregnant. While she could not deny her condition, she did deny that she was a fornicator or adulteress. Instead, she maintained that she was actually married to the crewman who had fathered her child. However, when she was asked to give his name, she refused, saying only that the two of them hated the pirating life and had planned to leave the ship at the earliest possibility. She went on to try to convince the Justice of the Court that they already had plans for earning an honest living on land.

Meanwhile, Anne's father had heard of her capture and began to work to get her freed. He was still a prominent planter and had several friends in Jamaica on whom he called for help. He may have even found someone to speak on his daughter's behalf to the governor. However, it proved to be of little avail against the testimony of how Anne had conducted herself while on board, and especially during the final battle with Barnet's men

Unfortunately for Anne and Mary, the testimony of some of their crewmates sunk them, especially Mary's assertion that she did not want to continue in piracy. Several men, all of whom claimed to have been kidnapped themselves, swore that during battle no one fought as hard as Mary Read or Anne Bonny. At least one of them mentioned an occasion when the women not only refused to join the men in hiding below decks but also taunted the men for refusing to join them. It was also suggested that Mary even went below decks and threatened the men there with a loaded gun, and that when the men failed to move fast enough for her, she fired on them, killing one man and wounding several others.

According to one witness, when Barnet and his men attempted to board the ship, "the two women, prisoners at the bar, were then on board the said sloop, and wore men's jackets, and long trousers, and handkerchiefs tied about their heads; and that each of them had a machete and pistol in their hands, and cursed and swore at the men, to murder the deponent; and that they should kill her, to prevent her coming against them; and the deponent further said, that the reason of her knowing and believing them to be women then was by the largeness of their breasts."

Another witness said "that when they saw any vessel, gave chase, or attacked, they wore men's clothes; and at other times, they wore woman's clothes." This, of course, calls into question whether or not Mary actually concealed her identity as well as she is believed to have, but by now it was a moot point.

According to one historian, the most damning evidence against Mary actually came from a man she had once sailed with. One of the men who claimed to have been kidnapped by Rackham and forced into piracy said that he had often had conversations with Mary about how she came to be involved in piracy. He claimed that he was curious as to why anyone would pursue a life that was so filled with dangers and discomfort. He also testified that he sought her feelings about the possibility of dying in disgrace, either at the hands of the crown, or one of her enemies. According to this man's testimony, Mary replied to his question by answering:

"as to hanging, she thought it no great Hardship, for, were it not for that, every cowardly Fellow would turn Pyrate, and so infest the Seas, that Men of Courage must starve:— That if it was put to the Choice of the Pyrates, they would not have the punishment less than Death, the Fear of which, kept some dastardly Rogues honest; that many of those who are now cheating the Widows and Orphans, and oppressing their poor Neighbours, who have no Money to obtain Justice, would then rob at Sea, and the Ocean would be crowded with Rogues, like the Land, and no Merchant would venture out; so that the Trade, in a little Time, would not be worth following."

The court thus handed down the most dreaded sentence possible to both women, declaring:

"You, Mary Read, and Ann Bonny, alias Bonn, are to go from hence to the place from whence you came, and from thence to the place of execution; where you shall be severally hanged by the neck till you are severally dead. And god of his infinite mercy be merciful to both your souls."

At this point, the judge asked the women if they had anything to say for themselves. Both came forward and asked that their sentences be delayed because they were pregnant, since English law at that time forbade the execution of pregnant women to avoid killing their unborn child as well. Whether it was obvious they were pregnant or it was something that the court had to wait to confirm is unknown, but the judge decided to grant both women a stay of execution until they delivered their babies.

Mary did not live long enough to face either the gallows or childbirth, instead dying of some sort fever in early 1721. By this time she was so far along in her pregnancy that she either delivered the child right before her death or the doctors tried to save the child by delivering it through a quick caesarean section. Either way, they both died but were buried separately in St. Catherine parish in Jamaica. Ironically, the convicted criminal and the innocent child were among the first few people to be buried in that cemetery.

Pleading the belly ultimately proved to be useless to Mary Read, but it is widely believed the delay was enough to save Anne's life. While she remained in prison awaiting her child's birth, her father continued to speak to his friends on her behalf, and eventually he was able to arrange enough bribes to enough people to secure her release. Shortly after the birth of her baby, she disappeared from the history books, probably much to the relief of authorities who had no stomach for executing a woman with an infant child.

It remains unclear as to what exactly happened to Anne after her time in prison. Some believe that she returned to James Bonny and lived out the rest of her days as his wife, but that seems unlikely. For one thing, the two of them had been legally divorced, so it is likely that he had by this time married someone else. Also, Anne's father likely felt that he had put too much effort into her release to have her return to someone he had never cared much for anyway.

Others say that she returned to being a pirate, changing her name and joining another crew, but this seems even less likely. Unlike Mary Read, Anne Bonny never showed any particular love for life at sea. Her affection centered on Calico Jack, and it seems she did what she did just so she could be with him, simply following his path.

The final possibility is that which had the only documentary evidence to support it. According to records preserved by those claiming to be her descendants, Anne and her child returned with her father to Charleston, South Carolina, sailing quietly away on one of his merchant ships. If she was traveling illegally, he was able to grease enough palms to make sure that no one noticed or reported her. Because communication was more difficult at that time, he was able to use his influence and money to restore her reputation. She was still only 18 years old, and if rumors about her pirate career did reach anyone's ears they would likely disregard the stories as being wholly unlikely for a girl so young.

Not long after they returned to Charleston, Anne met a local man named Joseph Burleigh, who was somewhat older than her and was well known to her father. As they got to know each other, she may have told him about her checkered past or she may have simply portrayed herself as the young, pretty widow of a dead sea captain with whom she had a child. If Burleigh did have any misgivings about their future together, it is likely that Anne's father's fortune soon put those concerns to rest. The two married on December 21, 1721, when Anne was 19 years old.

Having sown her wild oats, Anne apparently settled down into the kind of domestic life she had previously been to restless to accept. According to the records, she and Burleigh lived the rest of their lives as happy, respected members of the Charleston community. She bore and raised 10 more children, living to see most of them grow to adulthood and marry. By the time she died, on April 22, 1782, she had grandchildren and great-grandchildren. She was buried in the Burleigh family plot in the York County Churchyard in York County, Virginia.

Chapter 10: Legacies

As pirates go, Calico Jack, Anne Bonny and Mary Read were not the meanest or kindest, nor were they the strongest or weakest. Calico Jack was not a successful pirate, and he is remembered more for his association with Anne Bonny and Mary Read than anything else. The same could be said for both Anne Bonny and Mary Read as well; their piracy was in no way remarkable aside from the fact that they were women.

While Calico Jack contributed to the stereotypes of pirates through the use of his "Jolly Roger" pirate flag and his colorful attire, the fact that Anne Bonny and Mary Read were women has become a legacy unto itself. Anne Bonny has passed down through history as a strong-willed independent girl who was fearless and wild enough to become just the kind of pirate people think of today when they hear the term. At the same time, her legend and reputation have a strong historical foundation Even by today's standards, to have been born the illegitimate daughter of a lawyer and his mistress is enough to turn heads. While modern political scandals have softened the public's sensibilities to such misdeeds as adultery, to bring a child into the picture is certain to call one's character into question. Likewise, to abandon one family and move half-way around the world to start another is more the thing of romance novels than it is of real life. And yet, that was precisely what Anne's formative years consisted of, along with being dressed like a boy and told to act like one.

Then there was the matter of her own personality. To harm or even threaten another person with a kitchen knife would land today's teenager in therapy at least, but Anne was simply ignored as the spoiled daughter of a wealthy plantation owner. Anne certainly wasn't encouraged to continue her rebellious ways, but she clearly didn't suffer any serious consequences for her actions either. Even Anne's decision to elope and run away is hardly an unusual story; plenty of young women have run away with men who were disliked by their families. And Anne's affinity for men who were rebellious like her also probably drew her to Calico Jack.

The story of a rebellious headstrong teenage girl who runs away with a bad boy is one that has played out in other settings and environments across history, but what makes Anne unique is that she happened to become a well-known pirate. While she was never a particularly effective one, and may not even have been interested in being one but for her feelings toward Calico Jack, the fact that Anne Bonny became known by name during the Golden Age of Piracy and the mystery surrounding her fate have helped maintain her legend. Throw in her association with another famous woman pirate like Mary Read, and the story becomes even better. To the degree that any pirate can be respected or celebrated, the stories and legends surrounding Anne Bonny have made her a unique and unlikely symbol for any independent woman striving to live outside of conventional society's norms and/or simply be as good as the boys at their own game.

The life, death, and legacy of Mary Read also captured the imaginations of everyone from historians to novelists, and feminists to masochists. There are a number of reasons why her story has been so fascinating in the past, and is likely to continue to be for years to come, beginning with the mystery of her childhood. It is well known that she was raised by her mother as if she had been a male child, and because she was illegitimate, many have speculated that her father may have himself been a sailor and maybe even a pirate. Was Mary born with a thirst for the sea and adventure, or was it simply a necessary evil for Mary's mother to support the family after her husband died?

Perhaps the most remarkable aspect of Mary's life was her sexual identity. At times, she embraced the male lifestyle that had been created for her and was perpetuated by her. During her brief marriage, she also seemed happy enough to live as a woman, only to return to the man's world and life at sea. In a similar vein, legend has it that Mary Read was openly bisexual, equally comfortable in romantic relationships with men and women, but it's also possible that stories of her romance with Anne Bonny were exaggerated just to add to the mystique of the female pirates. Likewise, there is no record of Anne Bonny being attracted to other women, while it is well documented that she had a long term affair with Calico Jack. And even if the three were at one time all lovers, Mary soon fell in love with the nameless seaman for whom she risked her life. Regardless of what is true and false, and what is documented history and unsubstantiated legend, Mary Read has captured the public imagination as being one of the only two well-documented female pirates in the so-called "Golden Age of Piracy."

In an age and society where the freedom of women was greatly restricted, Mary Read and Anne Bonny lived a life at sea as full members of a pirate crew. As subsequent generations increasingly romanticize piracy and the likes of Calico Jack, Anne Bonny and Mary Read, their stature continues to grow even further.

Bibliography

Brown, Douglas. (1962). *Anne Bonny, Pirate Queen: The True Saga of A Fabulous Female Buccaneer*. Monarch Books.

Creighton, Margartet and Lisa Norling. (1996). *Iron Men, Wooden Women: Gender and Seafaring in the Atlantic World, 1700-1920*. Gender Relations in the American Experience.

Defoe, Daniel and Manuel Schonhorn (1999). The General History of Pirates. New York: Dover Publications.

Eastman, Tamara J. and Constance Bond. (2000). The Pirate Trial of Anne Bonny and Mary Read. Fern Canyon Press.

Johnson, Captain Charles, ed. Hayward Arthur L., "A history of the robberies and murders of the most notorious pirates from their first rise and settlement in the island of Providence to the present year", George Routledge & Sons, Ltd. London.

Johnson, Pamela. (2009). Heart of a Pirate: A Novel of Anne Bonny. Stone Harbour Press.

Kaserman, James and Sarah. Florida Pirates: From the Southern Gulf Coast to the Keys and Beyond (The History Press) (Nov 16, 2011).

Meltzer, Milton; Waldman, Bruce (2001). *Piracy & Plunder: A Murderous Business*. New York: Dutton Children's Books.

Nash D. A. (2012) The Profligate: The Legend of Anne Bonny by D.A. NASH (Jun 5, 2012)

Nelson, James L. (2004). *The Only Life That Mattered: The Short and Merry Lives of Anne*

Bonny, Mary Read, and Calico Jack Rackam. McBooks Press.

Riley, Sandra. (2003). *Sisters of the Sea: Anne Bonny & Mary Read, Pirates of the Caribbean.* Riley Hall.

Sharp, Anne Wallace (2002). *Daring Pirate Women.* Minneapolis: Lerner Publications.

Utley, Stephen. (2012) *Anne Bonny.* CreateSpace Independent Publishing Platform.

Vantana, Karen and Becky Weaver (2010). *Anne Bonny: The Legend of a Female Pirate.* CreateSpace Independent Publishing Platform.

Weintraub, Aileen. (2005). *Anne Bonny and Mary Read: Fearsome Female Pirates of the Eighteenth Century.* Tony Stead Nonfiction Independent Reading Collections.

Williams, Jeffrey S. (2007). *Pirate Spirit: The Adventures of Anne Bonney.* iUniverse Star.

Captain Kidd's Entry in Captain Charles Johnson's Pirate History

Illustration of Captain Kidd

We are now going to give an account of one whose name is better known in England, than most of those whose histories we have already related; the person we mean is Captain Kid, whose public Trial and Execution here, rendered him the subject of all conversation.

In the beginning of King William's War, Captain Kid commanded a Privateer in the West-Indies, and by several adventurous actions acquired the reputation of a brave man, as well as an experienced seaman. About this time the Pirates were very troublesome in those parts, wherefore Captain Kid was recommended by the Lord Bellamont, then Governor of Barbadoes, as well as by several other persons, to the Government here, as a person very fit to be entrusted with the command of a Government Ship, and to be employed in cruising upon the Pirates, as knowing those Seas perfectly well, and being acquainted with their lurking places; but what reasons governed the politics of those times, I cannot tell, but this proposal met with no encouragement here, though it is certain it would have been of great consequence to the subject, our merchants suffering incredible damages by those robbers.

Upon this neglect the Lord Bellamont, and some others who knew what great captures had been made by the Pirates, and what a prodigious wealth must be in their possession, were tempted to fit out a ship at their own private charge, and to give the command of it to Captain Kid; and to give the thing a greater reputation, as well as to keep their seamen under the better command, they procured the King's Commission for the said Captain Kid.

Captain Kid had also another Commission, which was called a Commission of Reprisals; for it being then War time, this Commission was to justify him in the taking of French Merchant Ships, in case he should meet with any. He sail'd out of Plymouth in May 1696, in the Adventure Galley of thirty guns, and eighty men; the place he first design'd for was New York; in his Voyage thither he took a French Banker, but this was no Act of Piracy, he having a Commission for that purpose, as we have just observed.

When he arrived at New York he put up Articles for engaging more Hands, it being necessary to his Ship's crew, since he proposed to deal with a desperate enemy: The terms he offered were, that every man should have a share of what was taken, reserving for himself and Owners forty shares. Upon this encouragement he soon increas'd his company to a hundred and fifty five men.

With this company he first sail'd for Maderas, where he took in wine and some other necessaries; from thence he proceeded to Bonavist, one of the Cape de Verd Islands, to furnish the ship with salt, and from thence went immediately to St. Jago, another of the Cape de Verd Islands, in order to stock himself with provisions. When all this was done, he bent his course to Madagascar, the known rendezvous of Pirates; in this way he fell in with Captain Warren, Commodore of three Men-of-War; he acquainted them with his design, kept them company two or three days, and then leaving them, made the best way for Madagascar, where he arrived in February 1696, just nine months from his departure from Plymouth.

It does not appear all this while that he had the least design of turning Pirate; for near Mahala and Joanna both he met with several Indian ships richly laden, to which he did not offer the least violence, tho' he was strong enough to have done what he pleas'd with them; and the first outrage or depredation I find he committed upon mankind, was after his repairing his ship, and leaving Joanna; he touch'd at a place call'd Mabbee, upon the Red Sea, where he took some Guinea Corn from the natives, by force.

After this he sail'd to Bab's Key, a Place upon a little Island at the entrance of the Red Sea; here it was that he first began to open himself to his ship's company, and let them understand that he intended to change his measures; for, happening to talk of the Moca Fleet, which was to sail that way, he said We have been unsuccessful hitherto, but courage, my Boys, we'll make our fortunes out of this Fleet: And finding that none of them appear'd averse to it, he order'd a boat out, well mann'd, to go upon the coast to make discoveries, commanding them to take a prisoner and bring to him, or get intelligence any way they could. The boat return'd in a few days, bringing him word, that they saw fourteen or fifteen ships ready to sail, some with English, some with Dutch, and some with Moorish Colours. He therefore order'd a man continually to watch at the mast-head, least this Fleet should go by them; and about four days after, towards evening, it appear'd in sight, being convoy'd by one English and one Dutch Man-of-War. Kid soon fell in with them, and getting into the midst of them, fir'd at a Moorish ship which was next him; but the Men-of-War taking the Alarm, bore down upon Kid, and firing upon him, oblig'd him to sheer off, he not being strong enough to contend with them. Now he had begun hostilities, he resolv'd to go on, and therefore he went and cruis'd along the coast of Malabar; the first Prize he met was a small vessel belonging to Aden, the vessel was Moorish, and the Owners were Moorish Merchants, but the Master was an Englishman, his name was Parker. Kid forc'd him and a Portugueze that was call'd Don Antonio, which were all the Europeans on Board, to take on with them; the first he design'd as a pilot, and the last as an interpreter. He also used the men very cruelly, causing them to be hoisted up by the arms, and drubb'd with a naked cutlass, to force them to discover whether they had money on board, and where it lay; but as they had neither gold nor silver on board, he got nothing by his cruelty; however, he took from them a bale of pepper, and a bale of coffee, and so let them go.

Soon after this he came up with a Moorish Ship, the Master whereof was a Dutchman, call'd Schipper Mitchel, and chased her under French Colours, which they observing, hoisted French Colours too: When he came up with her, he hail'd her in French, and they having a Frenchman on board, answer'd him in the same language; upon which he order'd them to send their boat on board; they were oblig'd to do so, and having examin'd who they were, and from whence they came; he ask'd the Frenchman, who was a passenger, if he had a French pass for himself? The Frenchman gave him to understand that he had. Then he told the Frenchman he must pass for Captain, and by God, says he, you are the Captain: The Frenchman durst not refuse doing as he would have him: The meaning of this was, that he would seize the Ship as fair Prize, and as if she belonged to French Subjects, according to a commission he had for that purpose; tho', one would think, after what he had already done, that he need not have recourse to a quibble to give his actions a colour.

In short, he took the cargoe and sold it some time after, yet still he seem'd to have some fears upon him least these proceedings should have a bad end; for, coming up with a Dutch Ship some time, when his men thought of nothing but attacking her, Kid oppos'd it; upon which a mutiny arose, and the majority being for taking the said ship, and arming themselves to man the boat to go and seize her, he told them, such as did, never should come on Board him again; which put an end to the design, so that he kept company with the said ship some time, without offering her any violence: However, this dispute was the occasion of an accident, upon which an indictment was afterwards grounded against Kid; for Moor, the Gunner, being one day upon deck, and talking with Kid about the said Dutch Ship, some words arose betwixt them, and Moor told Kid, that he had ruin'd them all; upon which, Kid, calling him Dog, took up a bucket and struck him with it, which breaking his skull, he died the next day.

But Kid's penitential fit did not last long, for coasting along Malabar, he met with a great number of boats, all which he plunder'd. Upon the same Coast he also lit upon a Portugueze Ship, which he kept possession of a week, and then having taking out of her some chests of Indian goods, thirty jars of butter, and some wax, iron, and a hundred bags of rice, he let her go.

The Adventure Galley was now so old and leaky, that they were forced to keep two pumps continually going, wherefore Kid shifted all the guns and tackle out of her into the Queda Merchant, intending her for his Man-of-War; and as he had divided the Money before, he now made a division of the remainder of the cargo: Soon after which, the greatest part of the company left him, some going on board Captain Culliford, and others absconding in the Country, so that he had not above forty men left.

He put to sea and happened to touch at Amboyna, one of the Dutch Spice Islands, where he was told, that the news of his Actions had reach'd England, and that he was there declared a Pirate.

The truth on't is, his Piracies so alarmed our Merchants, that some motions were made in Parliament, to enquire into the commission that was given him, and the persons who fitted him out: These proceedings seem'd to lean a little hard upon the Lord Bellamont, who thought himself so much touch'd thereby, that he published a Justification of himself in a pamphlet after Kid's execution. In the mean time, it was thought advisable, to publish a Proclamation, offering the King's free Pardon to all such Pirates as should voluntarily surrender themselves, whatever Piracies they had been guilty of at any time, before the last day of April, 1699—That is to say, for all Piracies committed Eastward of the Cape of Good Hope, to the Longitude and Meridian of Socatora, and Cape Camorin. In which Proclamation, Avery and Kid were excepted by Name.

When Kid left Amboyna he knew nothing of this Proclamation, for certainly had he had notice of his being excepted in it, he would not have been so infatuated, to run himself into the very jaws of danger; but relying upon his interest with the Lord Bellamont, and fancying, that a French Pass or two he found on board some of the ships he took, would serve to countenance the matter, and that part of the booty he got would gain him new friends—I say, all these things made him flatter himself that all would be hushed, and that justice would but wink at him. Wherefor he sail'd directly for New York, where he was no sooner arrived, but by the Lord Bellamont's orders, he was secured with all his papers and effects. Many of his fellow-adventurers who had forsook him at Madagascar, came over from thence passengers, some to New England and some to Jersey; where hearing of the King's Proclamation for pardoning of Pirates, they surrendered themselves to the Governor of those places: At first they were admitted to bail, but soon after were laid in strict confinement, where they were kept for some time, till an opportunity happened of sending them with their Captain over to England to be tried.

Accordingly a Sessions of Admiralty being held at the Old Baily, in May, 1701, Captain Kid, Nicholas Churchill, James How, Robert Lumley, William Jenkins, Gabriel Loff, Hugh Parrot, Richard Barlicorn, Abel Owens, and Darby Mullins, were arraingn'd for Piracy and Robbery on the High Seas, and all found guilty, except three; these were Robert Lumley, William Jenkins, and Richard Barlicorn, who proving themselves to be apprentices to some of the officers of the ship, and producing their Indentures in Court, were acquitted.

Kid was tried upon an indictment of Murder also, viz. for killing Moor the Gunner, and found guilty of the same. Nicholas Churchill and James How pleaded the King's Pardon, as having surrendered themselves within the time limited in the Proclamation, and Colonel Bass, Governor of West Jersey, to whom they surrendered, being in Court, and called upon, proved the same; however, this plea was over-ruled by the Court, because there being four Commissioners named in the Proclamation, it was adjudged no other person was qualified to receive their surrender, and that they could not be intitled to the benefit.

As to Captain Kid's Defence, he insisted much upon his own innocence, and the villany of his men; he said he went out in a laudable employment and had no occasion, being then in good circumstances, to go a-Pirating; that the men often mutinied against him, and did as they pleas'd; that he was threatened to be shot in his cabin, and that ninety five left him at one time, and set fire to his boat, so that he was disabled from bringing his ship home, or the Prizes he took, to have them regularly condemn'd, which he said were taken by virtue of a commission under the broad seal, they having French Passes—The Captain called one Col. Hewson to his Reputation, who gave him an extraordinary character, and declared to the Court, that he had served under his command, and been in two engagements with him against the French, in which he fought as well as any man he ever saw; that there were only Kid's Ship and his own against Monsieur du Cass, who commanded a squadron of six sail, and they got the better of him, but this being several years before the facts mentioned in the Indictment were committed, prov'd of no manner of service to the Prisoner on his Trial.

As to the friendship shown to Culliford, a notorious Pirate, Kid denied, and said, he intended to have taken him, but his men being a parcel of rogues and villains refused to stand by him, and several of them ran away from his ship to the said Pirate.—But the evidence being full and particular against him, he was found Guilty as before mentioned.

When Kid was asked what he had to say why Sentence should not pass against him, he answered, That he had nothing to say, but that he had been sworn against by perjured wicked People. And when Sentence was pronounced, he said, My Lord it is a very hard Sentence. For my part I am the innocentest Person of them all, only I have been sworn against by perjured Persons.

Wherefore about a week after, Capt. Kid, Nicholas Churchill, James How, Gabriel Loff, Hugh Parrot, Abel Owen, and Darby Mullins, were executed at Execution Dock, and afterwards hung up in Chains, at some distance from each other, down the river, where their Bodies hung exposed for many years.

Henry Every's Entry in A General History of the Pyrates

NONE of these bold Adventurers were ever so much talked of, for a while, as Avery; he made as great a Noise in the World as Meriveis does now, and was looked upon to be a Person of as great Consequence; he was represented in Europe, as one that had raised himself to the Dignity of a King, and was likely to be the Founder of a new Monarchy; having, as it was said, taken immense Riches, and married the Great Mogul's Daughter, who was taken in an Indian Ship, which fell into his Hands; and that he had by her many Children, living in great Royalty and State; that he had built Forts, erected Magazines, and was Master of a stout Squadron of Ships, mann'd with able and desperate Fellows of all Nations; that he gave Commissions out in his own Name to the Captains of his Ships, and to the Commanders of his Forts, and was acknowledged by them as their Prince. A Play was writ upon him, called, the Successful Pyrate; and, these Accounts obtained such Belief, that several Schemes were offered to the Council for fitting out a Squadron to take him; while others were for offering him and his Companions an Act of Grace, and inviting them to England, with all their Treasure, least his growing Greatness might hinder the Trade of Europe to the East-Indies.

Yet all these were no more than false Rumours, improved by the Credulity of some, and the Humour of others who love to tell strange Things; for, while it was said, he was aspiring at a Crown, he wanted a Shilling; and at the same Time it was given out he was in Possession of such prodigious Wealth in Madagascar, he was starving in England.

No doubt, but the Reader will have a Curiosity of knowing what became of this Man, and what were the true Grounds of so many false Reports concerning him; there fore, I shall, in as brief a Manner as I can, give his History.

He was born in the West of England near Plymouth in Devonshire, being bred to the Sea, he served as a Mate of a Merchant-Man, in several trading Voyages: It happened before the Peace of Ryfwick, when there was an Alliance betwixt Spain, England, Holland, &c. against France, that the French in Martinico, carried on a smugling Trade with the Spaniards on the Continent of Peru, which by the Laws of Spain, is not allowed to Friends in Time of Peace, for none but native Spaniards are permitted to Traffick in those Parts, or set their Feet on Shore, unless at any Time they are brought as Prisoners; wherefore they constantly keep certain Ships cruising along the Coast, whom they call Guarda del Costa, who have the Orders to make Prizes of all ships they can light of within five Leagues of Land. Now the French growing very bold in Trade, and the Spaniards being poorly provided with Ships, and those they had being of no Force, it often fell out, that when they light of the French Smuglers, they were not strong enough to attack them, therefore it was resolv'd in Spain, to hire two or three stout foreign Ships for their Service, which being known at Bristol, some Merchants of that City, fitted out two Ships of thirty odd Guns, and

120 Hands each, well furnished with Provision and Ammunition, and all other Stores; and the Hire being agreed for, by some Agents for Spain, they were commanded to sail for Corunna or the Groine, there to receive their Orders, and to take on Board some Spanish Gentlemen, who were to go Passengers to New-Spain.

Of one of these Ships, which I take to be call'd the Duke, Capt. Gibson Commander, Avery was first Mate, and being a Fellow of more Cunning than Courage, he insinuated himself into the good Will of several of the boldest Fellows on Board the other Ship, as well as that which he was on Board of; having sounded their Inclinations before he opened himself, and finding them ripe for his Design, he, at length, proposed to them, to run away with the Ship, telling them what great Wealth was to be had upon the Coasts of India. It was no sooner said than agreed to, and they resolved to execute their Plot at Ten a Clock the Night following.

It must be observ'd, the Captain was one of those who are mightily addicted to Punch, so that he passed most of his Time on Shore, in some little drinking Ordinary; but this Day he did not go on Shore as usual; however, this did not spoil the Design, for he took his usual Dose on Board, and so got to Bed before the Hour appointed for the Business: The Men also who were not privy to the Design, turn'd into their Hammocks, leaving none upon Deck but the Conspirators, who, indeed, were the greatest Part of the Ship's Crew. At the Time agreed on, the Dutchess's Long-Boat appear'd, which Avery hailing in the usual Manner, was answered by the Men in her, Is your drunken Boatswain on Board? Which was the Watch-Word agreed between them, and Avery replying in the Affirmative, the Boat came aboard with sixteen stout Fellows, and joined the Company.

When our Gentry saw that all was clear, they secured the Hatches, so went to work; they did not slip the Anchor, but weigh'd it leisurely, and so put to Sea without any Disorder or Confusion, tho' there were several Ships then lying in the Bay, and among them a Dutch Frigate of forty Guns, the Captain of which was offered a great Reward to go out after her; but Mynheer, who perhaps would not have been willing to have been served so himself could not be prevail'd upon to give such Usage to another, and so let Mr. Avery pursue his Voyage, whither he had a Mind to.

The Captain, who by this Time, was awaked, either by the Motion of the Ship, or the Noise of working the Tackles, rung the Bell; Avery and two others went into the Cabin; the Captain, half asleep, and in a kind of Fright, ask'd, What was the Matter? Avery answered cooly, Nothing; the Captain replied, something's the Matter with the Ship, Does she drive? What Weather is it? Thinking nothing less then that it had been a Storm, and that the Ship was driven from her Anchors: No, no, answered Avery, we're at Sea, with a fair Wind and good Weather. At Sea! says the Captain, How can that be? Come, says Avery, don't be in a Fright, but put on your Cloaths, and I'll let you into a Secret: — You muse know, that I am Captain of this Ship now, and this is my Cabin, therefore you must walk out; I am bound to Madagascar, with a Design of making my own Fortune, and that of all the brave Fellows joined with me.

The Captain having a little recovered his Senses, began to apprehend the meaning; however, his Fright was as great as before, which Avery perceiving, bad him fear nothing, for, says he, if you have a Mind to make one of us, we will receive you, and if you'll turn sober, and mind your Business, perhaps in Time I may make you one of my Lieutenants, if not, here's a Boat a-longside, and you shall be set ashore.

The Captain was glad to hear this, and therefore accepted of his Offer, and the whole Crew being called up, to know who was willing to go on Shore with the Captain, and who to seek their Fortunes with the rest; there were not above five or six who were willing to quit this Enterprize; wherefore they were put into the Boat with the Captain that Minute, and made their Way to the Shore as well as they could.

They proceeded on their Voyage to Madagascar, but I do not find they took any Ships in their Way; when they arrived at the N. E. Part of that Island, they found two Sloops at Anchor, who, upon seeing them, slip'd their Cables and run themselves ashore, the Men all landing, and running into the Woods; these were two Sloops which the Men had run away with from the West-Indies, and seeing Avery, they supposed him to be some Frigate sent to take them, and therefore not being of Force to engage him, they did what they could to save themselves.

He guessed where they were, and sent some of his Men on Shore to let them know they were Friends, and to offer they might join together for their common Safety; the Sloops Men were well arm'd, and had posted themselves in a Wood, with Centinels just on the out-side, to observe whether the Ship landed her Men to pursue them, and they observing only two or three Men to come towards them without Arms, did not oppose them, but having challenged them, and they answering they were Friends, they lead them to their Body, where they delivered their Message; at first, they apprehended it was a Stratagem to decoy them on Board, but when the Ambassadors offered that the Captain himself, and as many of the Crew as they should name, would meet them on Shore without Arms, they believed them to be in Earnest, and they soon entered into a Confidence with one another; those on Board going on Shore, and some of those on Shore going on Board.

The Sloops Men were rejoiced at the new Ally, for their Vessels were so small, that they could not attack a Ship of any Force, so that hitherto they had not taken any considerable Prize, but now they hop'd to fly at high Game; and Avery was as well pleased at this Reinforcement, to strengthen them, for any brave Enterprize, and tho' the Booty must be lessened to each, by being divided into so many Shares, yet he found out an Expedient not to suffer by it himself as shall be shewn in its Place.

Having consulted what was to be done, they resolved to sail out together upon a Cruize, the Galley and two Sloops; they therefore fell to work to get the Sloops off, which they soon effected, and steered towards the Arabian Coast; near the River Indus, the Man at the Mast-Head spied a Sail, upon which they gave Chace, and as they came nearer to her, they perceived her to be a tall Ship, and fancied she might be a Dutch East-India Man homeward bound; but she proved a better Prize; when they fired at her to bring too, she hoisted Mogul's Colours, and seemed to stand upon her Defence; Avery only canonaded at a Distance, and some of his Men began to suspect that he was not the Hero they took him for: However, the Sloops made Use of their Time, and coming one on the Bow, and the other on the Quarter, of the Ship, clapt her on Board, and enter'd her, upon which she immediately struck her Colours and yielded; she was one of the Great Mogul's own Ships, and there were in her several of the greatest Persons of his Court, among whom it was said was one of his Daughters, who were going on a Pilgrimage to Mecca, the Mahometans thinking themselves obliged once in their Lives to visit that Place, and they were carrying with them rich Offerings to present at the Shrine of Mahomet. It is known that the Eastern People travel with the utmost Magnificence, so that they had with them all their Slaves and Attendants, their rich Habits and Jewels, with Vessels of Gold and Silver, and great Sums of Money to defray the Charges of their Journey by Land; wherefore the Plunder got by this Prize, is not easily computed.

   Having taken all the Treasure on Board their own Ships, and plundered their Prize of every Thing else they either wanted or liked, they let her go; she not being able to continue her Voyage, returned back: As soon as the News came to the Mogul, and he knew that they were English who had robbed them, he threatened loud, and talked of sending a mighty Army with Fire and Sword, to extirpate the English from all their Settlements on the Indian Coast. The East-India Company in England, were very much alarmed at it; however, by Degrees, they found Means to pacify him, by promising to do their Endeavours to take the Robbers, and deliver them into his Hands; however, the great Noise this Thing made in Europe, as well as India, was the Occasion of all these romantick Stories which were formed of Avery's Greatness.

   In the mean Time our successful Plunderers agreed to make the best of their Way back to Madagascar, intending to make that Place their Magazine or Repository for all their Treasure, and to build a small Fortification there, and leave a few Hands always ashore to look after it, and defend it from any Attempts of the Natives; but Avery put an End to this Project, and made it altogether unnecessary.

   As they were Steering their Course, as has been said, he sends a Boat on Board of each of the Sloops, desiring the Chief of them to come on Board of him, in order to hold a Council; they did so, and he told them he had something to propose to them for the common Good, which was to provide against Accidents; he bad them consider the Treasure they were possess'd of, would be sufficient for them all if they could secure it in some Place on Shore; therefore all they had to fear, was some Misfortune in the Voyage; he bad them consider the Consequences of being separated by bad Weather, in which Case, the Sloops, if either of them should fall in with any Ships of Force, must be either taken or sunk, and the Treasure on Board her lost to the rest, besides the common Accidents of the Sea; as for his Part he was so strong, he was able to make his Party good with any Ship they were like to meet in those Seas; that if he met with any Ship of such Strength, that he could not take her, he was safe from being taken, being so well mann'd; besides his Ship was a quick Sailor, and could carry Sail, when the Sloops could not, wherefore, he proposed to them, to put the Treasure on Board his Ship, to seal up each Chest with 3 Seals, whereof each was to keep one, and to appoint a Rendezvous, in Case of Separation.

Upon considering this Proposal, it appeared so seasonable to them, that they readily came into it, for they argued to themselves, that an Accident might happen to one of the Sloops and the other escape, wherefore it was for the common Good. The Thing was done as agreed to, the Treasure put on Board of Avery, and the Chests seal'd; they kept Company that Day and the next, the Weather being fair, in which Time Avery tampered with his Men, telling them they now had sufficient, to make them all easy, and what should hinder them from going to some Country, where they were not known, and living on Shore all the rest of their Days in Plenty; they understood what he meant: And in short, they all agreed to bilk their new Allies, the Sloop's Men, nor do I find that any of them felt any Qualms of Honour rising in his Stomach, to hinder them from consenting to this Piece of Treachery. In fine, they took Advantage of the Darkness that Night, steer'd another Course, and, by Morning, lost Sight of them.

I leave the Reader to judge, what Swearing and Confusion there was among the Sloop's Men, in the Morning, when they saw that Avery had given them the Slip; for they knew by the Fairness of the Weather, and the Course they had agreed to steer, that it must have been done on purpose: But we leave them at present to follow Mr. Avery.

Avery, and his Men, having consulted what to do with themselves, came to a Resolution, to make the best of their Way towards America; and none of them being known in those Parts, they intended to divide the Treasure, to change their Names, to go ashore, some in one Place, some in other, to purchase some Settlements, and live at Ease. The first Land they made, was the Island of Providence, then newly settled; here they staid some Time, and having considered that when they should go to New-England, the Greatness of their Ship, would cause much Enquiry about them; and possibly some People from England, who had heard the Story of a Ship's being run away with from the Groine, might suspect them to be the People; they therefore took a Resolution of disposing of their Ship at Providence: Upon which, Avery pretending that the Ship being fitted out upon the privateering Account, and having had no Success, he had received Orders from the Owners, to dispose of her to the best Advantage, he soon met with a Purchaser, and immediately bought a sloop.

In this Sloop, he and his Companions embarq'd, they touch'd at several Parts of America, where no Person suspected them; and some of them went on Shore, and dispersed themselves about the Country, having received such Dividends as Avery would give them; for he concealed the greatest Part of the Diamonds from them, which in the first Hurry of plundering the Ship, they did not much regard, as not knowing their Value.

At length he came to Boston, in New-England, and seem'd to have a Desire of settling in those Parts, and some of his Companions went on Shore there also, but he changed his Resolution, and proposed to the few of his Companions who were left, to sail for Ireland, which they consented to: He found out that New-England was not a proper Place for him, because a great deal of his Wealth lay in Diamonds; and should he have produced them there, he would have certainly been seiz'd on Suspicion of Pyracy.

In their Voyage to Ireland, they avoided St. George's Channel, and sailing North about, they put into one of the Northern Ports of that Kingdom; there they disposed of their Sloop, and coming on Shore they separated themselves, some going to Cork, and some to Dublin, 18 of whom obtain'd their Pardons afterwards of K. William. When Avery had remain'd some Time in this Kingdom, he was afraid to offer his Diamonds to sale, least an Enquiry into his Manner of coming by them should occasion a Discovery; therefore considering with himself what was best to be done, he fancied there were some Persons at Bristol, whom he might venture to trust; upon which, he resolved to pass over into England; he did so, and going into Devonshire, he sent to one of these Friends to meet him at a Town called Biddiford; when he had communicated himself to his Friends, and consulted with him about the Means of his Effects, they agreed, that the safest Method would be, to put them in the Hands of some Merchants, who being Men of Wealth and Credit in the World, no Enquiry would be made how they came by them; this Friend telling him he was very intimate with some who were very fit for the Purpose, and if he would but allow them a good Commission would do the Business very faithfully. Avery liked the Proposal, for he found no other Way of managing his Affairs, since he could not appear in them himself; therefore his Friend going back to Bristol, and opening the Matter to the Merchants, they made Avery a Visit at Biddiford, where, after some Protestations of Honour and Integrity, he delivered them his Effects, consisting of Diamonds and some Vessels of Gold; they gave him a little Money for his present Subsistance, and so they parted.

He changed his Name and lived at Biddiford, without making any Figure, and therefore there was no great Notice taken of him; yet let one or two of his Relations know where he was, who came to see him. In some Time his little Money was spent, yet he heard nothing from his Merchants; he writ to them often, and after much Importunity they sent him a small Supply, but scarce sufficient to pay his Debts: In fine, the Supplies they sent him from Time to Time, were so small, that they were not sufficient to give him Bread, nor could he get that little, without a great deal of Trouble and Importunity, wherefore being weary of his Life, he went privately to Bristol, to speak to the Merchants himself, where instead of Money he met a most shocking Repulse, for when he desired them to come to an Account with him, they silenced him by threatening to discover him, so that our Merchants were as good Pyrates at Land as he was at Sea.

Whether he was frightened by these Menaces, or had seen some Body else he thought knew him, is not known; but he went immediately over to Ireland, and from thence sollicited his Merchants very hard for a Supply, but to no Purpose, for he was even reduced to beggary: In this Extremity he was resolved to return and cast himself upon them, let the Consequence be what it would. He put himself on Board a trading Vessel, and work'd his Passage over to Plymouth, from whence he travelled on Foot to Biddiford, where he had been but a few Days before he fell sick and died; not being worth as much as would buy him a Coffin.

Thus have I given all that could be collected of any Certainty concerning this Man; rejecting the idle Stories which were made of his fantastick Greatness, by which it appears, that his Actions were more inconsiderable than those of other Pyrates, since him, though he made more Noise in the World.

Now we shall turn back and give our Readers some Account of what became of the two Sloops.

We took Notice of the Rage and Confusion, which must have seized them, upon their missing of Avery; however, they continued their Course, some of them still flattering themselves that he had only out sailed them in the Night, and that they should find him at the Place of Rendezvous: But when they came there, and could hear no Tydings of him, there was an End of Hope. It was Time to consider what they should do with themselves, their Stock of Sea Provision was almost spent, and tho' there was Rice and Fish, and Fowl to be had ashore, yet these would not keep for Sea, without being properly cured with Salt, which they had no Conveniency of doing; therefore, since they could not go a Cruizing any more, it was Time to think of establishing themselves at Land; to which Purpose they took all Things out of the Sloops, made Tents of the Sails, and encamped themselves, having a large Quantity of Ammunition, and abundance of small Arms.

Here they met with several of their Countrymen, the Crew of a Privateer Sloop which was commanded by Captain Thomas Tew; and since it will be but a short Digression, we will give an Account how they came here.

Captain George Dew and Captain Thomas Tew, having received Commissions from the then Governor of Bermudas, to sail directly for the River Gambia in Africa; there, with the Advice and Assistance of the Agents of the Royal African Company, to attempt the taking the French Factory at Goorie, lying upon that Coast. In a few Days after they sailed out, Dew in a violent Storm, not only sprung his Mast, but lost Sight of his Consort; Dew therefore returned back to refit, and Tew instead of proceeding on his Voyage, made for the Cape of Good Hope, and doubling the said Cape, shaped his Course for the Straits of Babel Mandel, being the Entrance into the Red Sea. Here he came up with a large Ship, richly laden, bound from the Indies to Arabia, with three hundred Soldiers on Board, besides Seamen; yet Tew had the Hardiness to board her, and soon carried her; and, 'tis said, by this Prize, his Men shared near three thousand Pounds a Piece: They had Intelligence from the Prisoners, of five other rich Ships to pass that Way, which Tew would have attacked, tho' they were very strong, if he had not been over-ruled by the Quarter-Master and others.—This differing in Opinion created some ill Blood amongst them, so that they resolved to break up pyrating, and no Place was so fit to receive them as Madagascar; hither they steered, resolving to live on Shore and enjoy what they got.

As for Tew himself, he with a few others in a short Time went off to Rhode Island, from whence he made his Peace.

Thus have we accounted for the Company our Pyrates met with here.

It must be observed that the Natives of Madagascar are a kind of Negroes, they differ from those of Guiney in their Hair, which is long, and their Complexion is not so good a Jet; they have innumerable little Princes among them, who are continually making War upon one another; their Prisoners are their Slaves, and they either sell them, or put them to death, as they please: When our Pyrates first settled amongst them, their Alliance was much courted by these Princes, so they sometimes joined one, sometimes another, but wheresoever they sided, they were sure to be Victorious; for the Negroes here had no Fire-Arms, nor did they understand their Use; so that at length these Pyrates became so terrible to the Negroes, that if two or or three of them were only seen on one Side, when they were going to engage, the opposite Side would fly without striking a Blow.

By these Means they not only became feared, but powerful; all the Prisoners of War, they took to be their Slaves; they married the most beautiful of the Negroe Women; not one or two, but as many as they liked; so that every one of them had as great a Seraglio as the Grand Seignior at Constantinople: Their Slaves they employed in planting Rice, in Fishing, Hunting, &c. besides which, they had abundance of others, who lived, as it were, under their Protection, and to be secure from the Disturbances or Attacks of their powerful Neighbours; these seemed to pay them a willing Homage. Now they began to divide from one another, each living with his own Wives, Slaves and Dependants, like a separate Prince; and as Power and Plenty naturally beget Contention, they sometimes quarrelled with one another, and attacked each other at the Head of their several Armies; and in these civil Wars, many of them were killed; but an Accident happened, which obliged them to unite again for their common Safety.

It must be observed that these sudden great Men, had used their Power like Tyrants, for they grew wanton in Cruelty, and nothing was more common, than upon the slightest Displeasure, to cause one of their Dependants to be tied to a Tree and shot thro' the Heart, let the Crime be what it would, whether little or great, this was always the Punishment; wherefore the Negroes conspired together, to rid themselves of these Destroyers, all in one Night; and as they now lived separate, the Thing might easily have been done, had not a Woman, who had been Wife or Concubine to one of them, run near twenty Miles in three Hours, to discover the Matter to them: Immediately upon the Alarm they ran together as fast as they could, so that when the Negroes approached them, they found them all up in Arms; wherefore they retired without making any Attempt.

This Escape made them very cautious from that Time, and it will be worth while to describe the Policy of these brutish Fellows, and to shew what Measures they took to secure themselves.

They found that the Fear of their Power could not secure them against a Surprize, and the bravest Man may be kill'd when he is asleep, by one much his inferior in Courage and Strength, therefore, as their first Security, they did all they could to foment War betwixt the neighbouring Negroes, remaining Neuter themselves, by which Means, those who were overcome constantly lied to them for Protection, otherwise they must be either killed or made Slaves. They strengthened their Party, and tied some to them by interest; when there was no War, they contrived to spirit up private Quarrels among them, and upon every little Dispute or Misunderstanding, push on one Side or other to Revenge; instruct them how to attack or surprize their Adversaries, and lend them loaded Pistols or Firelocks to dispatch them with; the Consequence of which was, that the Murderer was forced to fly to them for the safety of his Life, with his Wives, Children and Kindred.

Such as these were fast Friends, as their Lives depended upon the safety of his Protectors; for as we observed before, our Pyrates were grown so terrible, that none of their Neighbours had Resolution enough to attack them in an open War.

By such Arts as these, in the Space of a few Years, their Body was greatly increased, they then began to separate themselves, and remove at a greater Distance from one another, for the Convenience of more Ground, and were divided like Jews, into Tribes, each carrying with him his Wives and Children, (of which, by this Time they had a large Family,) as also their Quota of Dependants and Followers; and if Power and Command be the Thing which distinguish a Prince, these Ruffians had all the Marks of Royalty about them, nay more, they had the very Fears which commonly disturb Tyrants, as may be seen by the extream Caution they took in fortifying the Places where they dwelt.

In this Plan of Fortification they imitated one another, their Dwellings were rather Citadels than Houses; they made Choice of a Place overgrown with Wood, and scituate near a Water; they raised a Rampart or high Ditch round it, so strait and high, that it was impossible to climb it, and especially by those who had not the Use of scaling Ladders: Over this Ditch there was one Passage into the Wood; the Dwelling, which was a Hut, was built in that Part of the Wood which the Prince, who inhabited it, thought fit, but so covered that it could not be seen till you came at it; but the greatest Cunning lay in the Passage which lead to the Hut, which was so narrow, that no more than one Person could go a Breast, and contrived in so intricate a Manner, that it was a perfect Maze or Labyrinth, it being round and round, with several little cross Ways, so that a Person that was not well acquainted with the Way, might walk several Hours round and cross these Ways without being able to find the Hut; moreover all along the Sides of these narrow Paths, certain large Thorns which grew upon a Tree in that Country, were struck into the Ground with their Points uppermost, and the Path it self being made crooked and serpentine, if a Man should attempt to come near the Hut at Night, he would certainly have struck upon these Thorns, tho' he had been provided with that Clue which Ariadne gave to Theseus when he entered the Cave of the Minataur.

Thus Tyrant like they lived, fearing and feared by all; and in this Scituation they were found by Captain Woods Rogers, when he went to Madagascar, in the Delicia, a Ship of forty Guns, with a Design of buying Slaves in order to sell to the Dutch at Batavia or New-Holland: He happened to touch upon a Part of the Island, where no Ship had been seen for seven or eight Years before, where he met with some of the Pyrates, at which Time, they had been upon the Island above 25 Years, having a large motly Generation of Children and Grand-Children descended from them, there being about that Time, eleven of them remaining alive.

Upon their first seeing a Ship of this Force and Burthen, they supposed it to be a Man of War sent to take them; they therefore lurked within their Fastnesses, but when some from the Ship came on Shore, without any shew of Hostility, and offering to trade with the Negroes, they ventured to come out of their Holes, attended like Princes; and since they actually are Kings De Facto, which is a kind of a Right, we ought to speak of them as such.

Having been so many Years upon this Island, it may be imagined, their Cloaths had long been worn out, so that their Majesties were extreamly out at the Elbows; I cannot say they were ragged, since they had no Cloaths, they had nothing to cover them but the Skins of Beasts without any tanning, but with all the Hair on, nor a Shoe nor Stocking, so they looked like the Pictures of Hercules in the Lion's Skin; and being overgrown with Beard, and Hair upon their Bodies, they appeared the most savage Figures that a Man's Imagination can frame.

However, they soon got rigg'd, for they sold great Numbers of those poor People under them, for Cloaths, Knives, Saws, Powder and Ball, and many other Things, and became so familiar that they went aboard the Delicia, and were observed to be very curious, examining the inside of the Ship, and very familiar with the Men, inviting them ashore. Their Design in doing this, as they afterwards confessed, was to try if it was not practicable to surprize the Ship in the Night, which they judged very easy, in case there was but a slender Watch kept on Board, they having Boats and Men enough at Command, but it seems the Captain was aware of them, and kept so strong a Watch upon Deck, that they found it was in vain to make any Attempt; wherefore, when some of the Men went ashore, they were for inveigling them, and drawing them into a Plot, for seizing the Captain and securing the rest of the Men under Hatches, when they should have the Night-Watch, promising a Signal to come on Board to join them; proposing, if they succeeded, to go a Pyrating together, not doubting but with that Ship they should be able to take any Thing they met on the Sea: But the Captain observing an intimacy growing betwixt them and some of his Men, thought it could be for no good, he therefore broke it off in Time, not suffering them so much as to talk together; and when he sent a Boat on Shore with an Officer to treat with them about the Sale of Slaves, the Crew remained on Board the Boat, and no Man was suffered to talk with them, but the Person deputed by him for that Purpose.

Before he sailed away, and they found that nothing was to be done, they confessed all the Designs they had formed against him. Thus he left them as he found them, in a great deal of dirty State and Royalty, but with fewer Subjects than they had, having, as we observed, sold many of them; and if Ambition be the darling Passion of Men, no doubt they were happy. One of these great Princes had formerly been a Waterman upon the Thames, where having committed a Murder, he fled to the West-Indies, and was of the Number of those who run away with the Sloops; the rest had been all foremast Men, nor was there a Man amongst them, who could either read or write, and yet their Secretaries of State had no more Learning than themselves. This is all the Account we can give of these Kings of Madagascar, some of whom it is probable are reigning to this Day.

Blackbeard's Entry in A General History of the Pyrates

It has long been believed that *A General History of the Robberies and Murders of the most notorious Pyrates* was authored by Daniel Defoe under the alias "Captain Charles Johnson", but modern scholars have suggested other potential authors. As noted by pirate researcher Colin Woodard in his book *The Republic of Pirates*, "Recently, Arne Bialuschewski of the University of Kiel in Germany has identified a far more likely candidate: Nathaniel Mist, a former sailor, journalist, and publisher of the Weekly Journal. The book's first publisher of record, Charles Rivington, had printed many books for Mist, who lived just a few yards from his office. More importantly, the General History was registered at Her Majesty's Stationery Office in Mist's name. As a former seaman who had sailed the West Indies, Mist, of all London's writer-publishers, was uniquely qualified to have penned the book...Mist was also a committed Jacobite...which could explain the General History's not entirely unsympathetic account of the maritime outlaws."

In fact, the sympathetic and overexaggerated nature of the author's profiles of various pirates is responsible for creating the lore that still surrounds pirates like Blackbeard today. The history is rife with anecdotes about pirates missing legs, burying treasure, missing eyes, and sailing aboard notorious ships like the Jolly Roger. While most of the profiles relied on the available facts, it was the artistic poetic license that has helped the history and its subjects endure.

One of those profiles, of course, was Blackbeard. The profile for Blackbeard is reproduced below:

Edward Teach was a Bristol Man born, but had sailed some Time out of Jamaica in Privateers, in the late French War; yet tho' he had often distinguished himself for his uncommon Boldness and personal Courage, he was never raised to any Command, till he went a-pyrating, which I think was at the latter End of the Year 1716, when Captain Benjamin Hornigold put him into a Sloop that he had made Prize of, and with whom he continued in Consortship till a little while before Hornigold surrendered.

In the Spring of the Year 1717, Teach and Hornigold sailed from Providence, for the Main of America, and took in their Way a Billop from the Havana, with 120 Barrels of Flower, as also a Sloop from Bermuda, Thurbar Master, from whom they took only some Gallons of Wine, and then let him go; and a Ship from Madera to South-Carolina, out of which they got Plunder to a considerable Value.

After cleaning on the Coast of Virginia, they returned to the West-Indies, and in the Latitude of 24, made Prize of a large French Guiney Man, bound to Martinico, which by Hornigold's Consent, Teach went aboard of as Captain, and took a Cruize in her; Hornigold returned with his Sloop to Providence, where, at the Arrival of Captain Rogers, the Governor, he surrendered to Mercy, pursuant to the King's Proclamation.

Aboard of this Guiney Man Teach mounted no Guns, and named her the Queen Ann's Revenge; and cruising near the Island of St. Vincent, took a large Ship, called the Great Allen, Christopher Taylor Commander; the Pyrates plundered her of what they though fit, put all the Men ashore upon the Island above mentioned, and then set Fire to the Ship.

A few Days after, Teach fell in with the Scarborogh Man of War, of 30 Guns, who engaged him for some Hours; but she finding the Pyrate well mann'd, and having tried her strength, gave over the Engagement, and returned to Barbadoes, the Place of her Station; and Teach sailed towards the Spanish America.

In his Way he met with a Pyrate Sloop of ten Guns, commanded by one Major Bonnet, lately a Gentleman of good Reputation and Estate in the Island of Barbadoes, whom he joyned; but in a few Days after, Teach, finding that Bonnet knew nothing of a maritime Life, with the Consent of his own Men, put in another Captain, one Richards, to Command Bonnet's Sloop, and took the Major on aboard his own Ship, telling him, that as he had not been used to the Fatigues and Care of such a Post, it would be better for him to decline it, and live easy and at his Pleasure, in such a Ship as his, where he should not be obliged to perform Duty, but follow his own Inclinations.

At Turniff ten Leagues short of the Bay of Honduras, the Pyrates took in fresh Water; and while they were at an Anchor there, they saw a Sloop coming in, whereupon, Richards in the Sloop called the Revenge, slipped his Cable, and run out to meet her; who upon seeing the black Flag hoisted, struck his Sail and came to, under the Stern of Teach the Commadore. She was called the Adventure, from Jamaica, David Harriot Master. They took him and his Men aboard the great Ship, and sent a Number of other Hands with Israel Hands, Master of Teach's Ship, to Man the Sloop for the pyratical Account.

The 9th of April, they weighed from Turniff, having lain there about a Week, and sailed to the Bay, where they found a Ship and four Sloops, three of the latter belonged to Jonathan Bernard, of Jamaica, and the other to Captain James; the Ship was of Boston, called the Protestant Cæsar, Captain Wyar Commander. Teach hoisted his Black Colours, and fired a Gun, upon which Captain Wyar and all his Men, left their Ship, and got ashore in their Boat. Teach's Quarter-Master, and eight of his Crew, took Possession of Wyar's Ship, and Richards secured all the Sloops, one of which they burnt out of spight to the Owner; the Protestant Cæsar they also burnt, after they had plundered her, because she belonged to Boston, where some Men had been hanged for Pyracy; and the three Sloops belonging to Bernard they let go.

From hence the Rovers sailed to Turkill, and then to the Grand Caimanes, a small Island about thirty Leagues to the Westward of Jamaica, where they took a small Turtler, and so to the Havana, and from thence to the Bahama Wrecks, and from the Bahama Wrecks, they sailed to Carolina, taking a Brigantine and two Sloops in their Way, where they lay off the Bar of Charles-Town for five or six Days. They took here a Ship as she was coming out, bound for London, commanded by Robert Clark, with some Passengers on Board for England; the next Day they took another Vessel coming out of Charles-Town, and also two Pinks coming into Charles-Town; likewise a Brigantine with 14 Negroes aboard; all which being done in the Face of the Town, struck a great Terror to the whole Province of Carolina, having just before been visited by Vane, another notorious Pyrate, that they abandoned themselves to Dispair, being in no Condition to resist their Force. They were eight Sail in the Harbour, ready for the Sea, but none dared to venture out, it being almost impossible to escape their Hands. The inward bound Vessels were under the same unhappy Dilemma, so that the Trade of this Place was totally interrupted: What made these Misfortunes heavier to them, was a long expensive War, the Colony had had with the Natives, which was but just ended when these Robbers infested them.

Teach detained all the Ships and Prisoners, and, being in want of Medicines, resolves to demand a Chest from the Government of the Province; accordingly Richards, the Captain of the Revenge Sloop, with two or three more Pyrates, were sent up along with Mr. Marks, one of the Prisoners, whom they had taken in Clark's Ship, and very insolently made their Demands, threatning, that if they did not send immediately the Chest of Medicines, and let the Pyrate-Ambassadors return, without offering any Violence to their Persons, they would murder all their Prisoners, send up their Heads to the Governor, and set the Ships they had taken on Fire.

Whilst Mr. Marks was making Application to the Council, Richards, and the rest of the Pyrates, walk'd the Streets publickly, in the Sight of all People, who were fired with the utmost Indignation, looking upon them as Robbers and Murtherers, and particularly the Authors of their Wrongs and Oppressions, but durst not so much as think of executing their Revenge, for fear of bringing more Calamities upon themselves, and so they were forced to let the Villains pass with Impunity. The Government were not long in deliberating upon the Message, tho' 'twas the greatest Affront that could have been put upon them; yet for the saving so many Mens Lives, (among them, Mr. Samuel Wragg, one of the Council;) they comply'd with the Necessity, and sent aboard a Chest, valued at between 3 and 400 l. and the Pyrates went back safe to their Ships.

Blackbeard, (for so Teach was generally called, as we shall hereafter shew) as soon as he had received the Medicines and his Brother Rogues, let go the Ships and the Prisoners; having first taken out of them in Gold and Silver, about 1500 l. Sterling, besides Provisions and other Matters.

From the Bar of Charles-Town, they sailed to North-Carolina; Captain Teach in the Ship, which they called the Man of War, Captain Richards and Captain Hands in the Sloops, which they termed Privateers, and another Sloop serving them as a Tender. Teach began now to think of breaking up the Company, and securing the Money and the best of the Effects for himself, and some others of his Companions he had most Friendship for, and to cheat the rest: Accordingly, on Pretence of running into Topsail Inlet to clean, he grounded his Ship, and then, as if it had been done undesignedly, and by Accident; he orders Hands's Sloop to come to his Assistance, and get him off again, which he endeavouring to do, ran the Sloop on Shore near the other, and so were both lost. This done, Teach goes into the Tender Sloop, with forty Hands, and leaves the Revenge there; then takes seventeen others and Marroons them upon a small sandy Island, about a League from the Main, where there was neither Bird, Beast or Herb for their Subsistance, and where they must have perished if Major Bonnet had not two Days after taken them off.

Teach goes up to the Governor of North-Carolina, with about twenty of his Men, surrender to his Majesty's Proclamation, and receive Certificates thereof, from his Excellency; but it did not appear that their submitting to this Pardon was from any Reformation of Manners, but only to wait a more favourable Opportunity to play the same Game over again; which he soon after effected, with greater Security to himself, and with much better Prospect of Success, having in this Time cultivated a very good understanding with Charles Eden, Esq; the Governor above mentioned.

The first Piece of Service this kind Governor did to Black-Beard, was, to give him a Right to the Vessel which he had taken, when he was a pyrating in the great Ship called the Queen Ann's Revenge; for which purpose, a Court of Vice-Admiralty was held at Bath-Town; and, tho' Teach had never any Commission in his Life, and the Sloop belonging to the English Merchants, and taken in Time of Peace; yet was she condemned as a Prize taken from the Spaniards, by the said Teach. These Proceedings shew that Governors are but Men.

Before he sailed upon his Adventures, he marry'd a young Creature of about sixteen Years of Age, the Governor performing the Ceremony. As it is a Custom to marry here by a Priest, so it is there by a Magistrate; and this, I have been informed, made Teach's fourteenth Wife, whereof, about a dozen might be still living. His Behaviour in this State, was something extraordinary; for, while his Sloop lay in Okerecock Inlet, and he ashore at a Plantation, where his Wife lived, with whom after he had lain all Night, it was his Custom to invite five or six of his brutal Companions to come ashore, and he would force her to prostitute her self to them all, one after another, before his Face.

In June 1718, he went to Sea, upon another Expedition, and steered his Course towards Bermudas; he met with two or three English Vessels in his Way, but robbed them only of Provisions, Stores and other Necessaries, for his present Expence; but near the Island aforementioned, he fell in with two French Ships, one of them was loaden with Sugar and Cocoa, and the other light, both bound to Martinico; the Ship that had no Lading he let go, and putting all the Men of the loaded Ship aboard her, he brought home the other with her Cargo to North-Carolina, where the Governor and the Pyrates shared the Plunder.

When Teach and his Prize arrived, he and four of his Crew went to his Excellency, and made Affidavit, that they found the French Ship at Sea, without a Soul on Board her; and then a Court was called, and the Ship condemned: The Governor had sixty Hogsheads of Sugar for his Dividend, and one Mr. Knight, who was his Secretary, and Collector for the Province, twenty, and the rest was shared among the other Pyrates.

The Business was not yet done, the Ship remained, and it was possible one or other might come into the River, that might be acquainted with her, and so discover the Roguery; but Teach thought of a Contrivance to prevent this, for, upon a Pretence that she was leaky, and that she might sink, and so stop up the Mouth of the Inlet or Cove where she lay, he obtained an Order from the Governor, to bring her out into the River, and set her on Fire, which was accordingly executed, and she was burnt down to the Water's Edge, her Bottom sunk, and with it, their Fears of her ever rising in Judgment against them.

Captain Teach, alias Black-beard, passed three or four Months in the River, sometimes lying at Anchor in the Coves, at other Times sailing from one Inlet to another, trading with such Sloops as he met, for the Plunder he had taken, and would often give them Presents for Stores and Provisions took from them; that is, when he happened to be in a giving Humour; at other Times he made bold with them, and took what he liked, without saying, by your Leave, knowing well, they dared not send him a Bill for the Payment. He often diverted himself with going ashore among the Planters, where he revelled Night and Day: By these he was well received, but whether out of Love or Fear, I cannot say; sometimes he used them courteously enough, and made them Presents of Rum and Sugar, in Recompence of what he took from them; but, as for Liberties (which 'tis said) he and his Companions often took with the Wives and Daughters of the Planters, I cannot take upon me to say, whether he paid them ad Valorem, or no. At other Times he carried it in a lordly Manner towards them, and would lay some of them under Contribution; nay, he often proceeded to bully the Governor, not, that I can discover the least Cause of Quarrel betwixt them, but it seemed only to be done, to shew he dared do it.

The Sloops trading up and down this River, being so frequently pillaged by Black-beard, consulted with the Traders, and some of the best of the Planters, what Course to take; they, saw plainly it would be in vain to make any Application to the Governor of North-Carolina, to whom it properly belonged to find some Redress; so that if they could not be relieved from some other Quarter, Black-beard would be like to reign with Impunity, therefore, with as much Secrecy as possible, they sent a Deputation to Virginia, to lay the Affair before the Governor of that Colony, and to solicit an armed Force from the Men of War lying there, to take or destroy this Pyrate.

This Governor consulted with the Captains of the two Men of War, viz. the Pearl and Lime, who had lain in St. James's River, about ten Months. It was agreed that the Governor should hire a couple of small Sloops, and the Men of War, should Man them; this was accordingly done, and the Command of them given to Mr. Robert Maynard, first Lieutenant of the Pearl, an experienced Officer, and a Gentleman of great Bravery and Resolution, as will appear by his gallant Behaviour in this Expedition. The Sloops were well mann'd and furnished with Ammunition and small Arms, but had no Guns mounted.

About the Time of their going out, the Governor called an Assembly, in which it was resolved to publish a Proclamation, offering certain Rewards to any Person or Persons, who, within a Year after that Time, should take or destroy any Pyrate: The original Proclamation being in our Hands, is as follows:

By his Majesty's Lieutenant Governor, and, Commander in Chief, of the Colony and Dominion of Virginia,

A PROCLAMATION,

Publishing the Rewards given for apprehending, or killing, Pyrates.

Whereas, by an Act of Assembly, made at a Session of Assembly, begun at the Capital in Williamsburgh, the eleventh Day of November, in the fifth Year of his Majesty's Reign, entituled, An Act to encourage the apprehending and destroying of Pyrates: It is, amongst other Things enacted, that all and every Person, or Persons, who, from and after the fourteenth Day of November, in the Year of our Lord one thousand seven hundred and eighteen, and before the fourteenth Day of November, which shall be in the Year of our Lord one thousand seven hundred and nineteen, shall take any Pyrate, or Pyrates, on the Sea or Land, or in Case of Resistance, shall kill any such Pyrate, or Pyrates, between the Degrees of thirty four, and thirty nine, of Northern Latitude, and within one hundred Leagues of the Continent of Virginia, or within the Provinces of Virginia, or North-Carolina, upon the Conviction, or making due Proof of the killing of all, and every such Pyrate, and Pyrates, before the Governor and Council, shall be entitled to have, and receive out of the publick Money, in the Hands of the Treasurer of this Colony, the several Rewards following; that is to say, for Edward Teach, commonly call'd Captain Teach, or Black-Beard, one hundred Pounds, for every other Commander of a Pyrate Ship, Sloop, or Vessel, forty Pounds; for every Lieutenant, Master, or Quarter-Master, Boatswain, or Carpenter, twenty Pounds; for every other inferior Officer, sixteen Pounds, and for every private Man taken on Board such Ship, Sloop, or Vessel, ten Pounds; and, that for every Pyrate, which shall be taken by any Ship, Sloop or Vessel, belonging to this Colony, or North-Carolina, within the Time aforesaid, in any Place whatsoever, the like Rewards shall be paid according to the Quality and Condition of such Pyrates. Wherefore, for the Encouragement of all such Persons as shall be willing to serve his Majesty, and their Country, in so just and honourable an Undertaking, as the suppressing a Sort of People, who may be truly called Enemies to Mankind: I have thought fit, with the Advice and Consent of his Majesty's Council, to issue this Proclamation, hereby declaring, the said Rewards shall be punctually and justly paid, in current Money of Virginia, according to the Directions of the said Act. And, I do order and appoint this Proclamation, to be published by the Sheriffs, at their respective County-Houses, and by all Ministers and Readers, in the several Churches and Chappels, throughout this Colony.

Given at our Council-Chamber at Williamsburgh, this 24th Day of November, 1718, in the fifth Year of his Majesty's Reign.

GOD SAVE THE KING.

A. SPOTSWOOD.

The 17th of November, 1718, the Lieutenant sail'd from Kicquetan, in James River in Virginia, and, the 21st in the Evening, came to the Mouth of Okerecock Inlet, where he got Sight of the Pyrate. This Expedition was made with all imaginable Secrecy, and the Officer manag'd with all the Prudence that was necessary, stopping all Boats and Vessels he met with, in the River, from going up, and thereby preventing any Intelligence from reaching Black-Beard, and receiving at the same time an Account from them all, of the Place where the Pyrate was lurking; but notwithstanding this Caution, Black-beard had Information of the Design, from his Excellency of the Province; and his Secretary, Mr. Knight, wrote him a Letter, particularly concerning it, intimating, That he had sent him four of his Men, which were all he could meet with, in or about Town, and so bid him be upon his Guard. These Men belonged to Black-beard, and were sent from Bath-Town to Okerecock Inlet, where the Sloop lay, which is about 20 Leagues.

Black-beard had heard several Reports, which happened not to be true, and so gave the less Credit to this, nor was he convinced till he saw the Sloops: Whereupon he put his Vessel in a Posture of Defence; he had no more than twenty five Men on Board, tho' he gave out to all the Vessels he spoke with, that he had 40. When he had prepared for Battle, he set down and spent the Night in drinking with the Master of a trading Sloop, who, 'twas thought, had more Business with Teach, than he should have had.

    Lieutenant Maynard came to an Anchor, for the Place being shoal, and the Channel intricate, there was no getting in, where Teach lay, that Night; but in the Morning he weighed, and sent his Boat a-head of the Sloops to sound; and coming within Gun-Shot of the Pyrate, received his Fire; whereupon Maynard hoisted the King's Colours, and stood directly towards him, with the best Way that his Sails and Oars could make. Black-beard cut his Cable, and endeavoured to make a running Fight, keeping a continual Fire at his Enemies, with his Guns; Mr. Maynard not having any, kept a constant Fire with small Arms, while some of his Men laboured at their Oars. In a little Time Teach's Sloop ran a-ground, and Mr. Maynard's drawing more Water than that of the Pyrate, he could not come near him; so he anchored within half Gun-Shot of the Enemy, and, in order to lighten his Vessel, that he might run him aboard, the Lieutenant ordered all his Ballast to be thrown over-board, and all the Water to be staved, and then weigh'd and stood for him; upon which Black-beard hail'd him in this rude Manner: Damn you for Villains, who are you? And, from whence came you? The Lieutenant made him Answer, You may see by our Colours we are no Pyrates. Black-beard bid him send his Boat on Board, that he might see who he was; but Mr. Maynard reply'd thus; I cannot spare my Boat, but I will come aboard of you as soon as I can, with my Sloop. Upon this, Black-beard took a Glass of Liquor, and drank to him with these Words: Damnation seize my Soul if I give you Quarters, or take any from you. In Answer to which, Mr. Maynard told him, That he expected no Quarters from him, nor should he give him any.

    By this time Black-beard's Sloop fleeted, as Mr. Maynard's Sloops were rowing towards him, which being not above a Foot high in the Waste, and consequently the Men all exposed, as they came near together, (there being hitherto little or no Execution done, on either Side,) the Pyrate fired a Broadside, charged with all Manner of small Shot. ——A fatal Stroke to them! The Sloop the Lieutenant was in, having twenty Men killed and wounded, and the other Sloop nine. This could not be help'd, for there being no Wind, they were oblig'd to keep to their Oars, otherwise the Pyrate would have got away from him, which, it seems, the Lieutenant was resolute to prevent.

    After this unlucky Blow, Black-beard's Sloop fell Broadside to the Shore; Mr. Maynard's other Sloop, which was called the Ranger, fell a-stern, being, for the present, disabled; so the Lieutenant finding his own Sloop had Way, and would soon be on Board of Teach, he ordered all his Men down, for fear of another Broadside, which must have been their Destruction, and the loss of their Expedition. Mr. Maynard was the only Person that kept the Deck, except the Man at the Helm, whom he directed to lye down snug, and the Men in the Hold were ordered to get their Pistols and their Swords ready for close fighting, and to come up at his Command; in order to which, two Ladders were placed in the Hatch-Way for the more Expedition. When the Lieutenant's Sloop boarded the other, Captain Teach's Men threw in several new fashioned sort of Grenadoes, viz. Case Bottles fill'd with Powder, and small Shot, Slugs, and Pieces of Lead or Iron, with a quick Match in the Mouth of it, which being lighted without Side, presently runs into the Bottle to the Powder, and as it is instantly thrown on Board, generally does great Execution, besides putting all the Crew into a Confusion; but by good Providence, they had not that Effect here; the Men being in the Hold, and Black-beard seeing few or no Hands aboard, told his Men, That they were all knock'd on the Head, except three or four; and therefore, says he, let's jump on Board, and cut them to Pieces.

Whereupon, under the Smoak of one of the Bottles just mentioned, Black-beard enters with fourteen Men, over the Bows of Maynard's Sloop, and were not seen by him till the Air cleared; however, he just then gave a Signal to his Men, who all rose in an Instant, and attack'd the Pyrates with as much Bravery as ever was done upon such an Occasion: Black-beard and the Lieutenant fired the first Pistol at each other, by which the Pyrate received a Wound, and then engaged with Swords, till the Lieutenant's unluckily broke, and stepping back to cock a Pistol, Black-beard, with his Cutlash, was striking at that Instant, that one of Maynard's Men gave him a terrible Wound in the Neck and Throat, by which the Lieutenant came off with a small Cut over his Fingers.

They were now closely and warmly engaged, the Lieutenant and twelve Men, against Black-beard and fourteen, till the Sea was tinctur'd with Blood round the Vessel; Black-beard received a Shot into his Body from the Pistol that Lieutenant Maynard discharg'd, yet he stood his Ground, and fought with great Fury, till he received five and twenty Wounds, and five of them by Shot. At length, as he was cocking another Pistol, having fired several before, he fell down dead; by which Time eight more out of the fourteen dropp'd, and all the rest, much wounded, jump'd over-board, and call'd out for Quarters, which was granted, tho' it was only prolonging their Lives for a few Days. The Sloop Ranger came up, and attack'd the Men that remain'd in Black-beard's Sloop, with equal Bravery, till they likewise cry'd for Quarters.

Here was an End of that couragious Brute, who might have pass'd in the World for a Heroe, had he been employ'd in a good Cause; his Destruction, which was of such Consequence to the Plantations, was entirely owing to the Conduct and Bravery of Lieutenant Maynard and his Men, who might have destroy'd him with much less Loss, had they had a Vessel with great Guns; but they were obliged to use small Vessels, because the Holes and Places he lurk'd in, would not admit of others of greater Draught; and it was no small Difficulty for this Gentleman to get to him, having grounded his Vessel, at least, a hundred times, in getting up the River, besides other Discouragements, enough to have turn'd back any Gentleman without Dishonour, who was less resolute and bold than this Lieutenant. The Broadside that did so much Mischief before they boarded, in all Probability saved the rest from Destruction; for before that Teach had little or no Hopes of escaping, and therefore had posted a resolute Fellow, a Negroe whom he had bred up, with a lighted Match, in the Powder-Room, with Commands to blow up when he should give him Orders, which was as soon as the Lieutenant and his Men could have entered, that so he might have destroy'd his Conquerors: and when the Negro found how it went with Black-beard, he could hardly be perswaded from the rash Action, by two Prisoners that were then in the Hold of the Sloop.

What seems a little odd, is, that some of these Men, who behaved so bravely against Black-beard, went afterwards a pyrating themselves, and one of them was taken along with Roberts; but I do not find that any of them were provided for, except one that was hanged; but this is a Digression.

The Lieutenant caused Black-beard's Head to be severed from his Body, and hung up at the Bolt-sprit End, then he sailed to Bath-Town, to get Relief for his wounded Men.

It must be observed, that in rummaging the Pyrate's Sloop, they found several Letters and written Papers, which discovered the Correspondence betwixt Governor Eden, the Secretary and Collector, and also some Traders at New-York, and Black-beard. It is likely he had Regard enough for his Friends, to have destroyed these Papers before the Action, in order to hinder them from falling into such Hands, where the Discovery would be of no Use, either to the Interest or Reputation of these fine Gentlemen, if it had not been his fixed Resolution to have blown up together, when he found no possibility of escaping.

When the Lieutenant came to Bath-Town, he made bold to seize in the Governor's Store-House, the sixty Hogsheads of Sugar, and from honest Mr. Knight, twenty; which it seems was their Dividend of the Plunder taken in the French Ship; the latter did not long survive this shameful Discovery, for being apprehensive that he might be called to an Account for these Trifles, fell sick with the Fright, and died in a few Days.

After the wounded Men were pretty well recover'd, the Lieutenant sailed back to the Men of War in James River, in Virginia, with Black-beard's Head still hanging at the Bolt-sprit End, and fiveteen Prisoners, thirteen of whom were hanged. It appearing upon Tryal, that one of them, viz. Samuel Odell, was taken out of the trading Sloop, but the Night before the Engagement. This poor Fellow was a little unlucky at his first entering upon his new Trade, there appearing no less than 70 Wounds upon him after the Action, notwithstanding which, he lived, and was cured of them all. The other Person that escaped the Gallows, was one Israel Hands, the Master of Black-beard's Sloop, and formerly Captain of the same, before the Queen Ann's Revenge was lost in Topsail Inlet.

The aforesaid Hands happened not to be in the Fight, but was taken afterwards ashore at Bath-Town, having been sometime before disabled by Black-beard, in one of his savage Humours, after the following Manner.—One Night drinking in his Cabin with Hands, the Pilot, and another Man; Black-beard without any Provocation privately draws out a small Pair of Pistols, and cocks them under the Table, which being perceived by the Man, he withdrew and went upon Deck, leaving Hands, the Pilot, and the Captain together. When the Pistols were ready, he blew out the

Candle, and crossing his Hands, discharged them at his Company; Hands, the Master, was shot thro' the Knee, and lam'd for Life; the other Pistol did no Execution. —Being asked the meaning of this, he only answered, by damning them, that if he did not now and then kill one of them, they would forget who he was.

Hands being taken, was try'd and condemned, but just as he was about to be executed, a Ship arrives at Virginia with a Proclamation for prolonging the Time of his Majesty's Pardon, to such of the Pyrates as should surrender by a limited Time therein expressed: Notwithstanding the Sentence, Hands pleaded the Pardon, and was allowed the Benefit of it, and is alive at this Time in London, begging his Bread.

Now that we have given some Account of Teach's Life and Actions, it will not be amiss, that we speak of his Beard, since it did not a little contribute towards making his Name so terrible in those Parts.

Plutarch, and other grave Historians have taken Notice, that several great Men amongst the Romans, took their Sir-Names from certain odd Marks in their Countenances; as Cicero, from a Mark or Vetch on his Nose; so our Heroe, Captain Teach, assumed the Cognomen of Blackbeard, from that large Quantity of Hair, which, like a frightful Meteor, covered his whole Face, and frightened America more than any Comet that has appeared there a long Time.

This Beard was black, which he suffered to grow of an extravagant Length; as to Breadth, it came up to his Eyes; he was accustomed to twist it with Ribbons, in small Tails, after the Manner of our Ramilies Wiggs, and turn them about his Ears: In Time of Action, he wore a Sling over his Shoulders, with three brace of Pistols, hanging in Holsters like Bandaliers; and stuck lighted Matches under his Hat, which appearing on each Side of his Face, his Eyes naturally looking fierce and wild, made him altogether such a Figure, that Imagination cannot form an Idea of a Fury, from Hell, to look more frightful.

If he had the look of a Fury, his Humours and Passions were suitable to it; we shall relate two or three more of his Extravagancies, which we omitted in the Body of his History, by which it will appear, to what a Pitch of Wickedness, human Nature may arrive, if it's Passions are not checked.

In the Commonwealth of Pyrates, he who goes the greatest Length of Wickedness, is looked upon with a kind of Envy amongst them, as a Person of a more extraordinary Gallantry, and is thereby entitled to be distinguished by some Post, and if such a one has but Courage, he must certainly be a great Man. The Hero of whom we are writing, was thoroughly accomplished this Way, and some of his Frolicks of Wickedness, were so extravagant, as if he aimed at making his Men believe he was a Devil incarnate; for being one Day at Sea, and a little flushed with drink:—Come, says he, let us make a Hell of our own, and try how long we can bear it; accordingly he, with two or three others, went down into the Hold, and closing up all the

Hatches, filled several Pots full of Brimstone, and other combustible Matter, and set it on Fire, and so continued till they were almost suffocated, when some of the Men cried out for Air; at length he opened the Hatches, not a little pleased that he held out the longest.

The Night before he was killed, he set up and drank till the Morning, with some of his own Men, and the Master of a Merchant-Man, and having had Intelligence of the two Sloops coming to attack him, as has been before observed; one of his Men asked him, in Case any thing should happen to him in the Engagement with the Sloops, whether his Wife knew where he had buried his Money? He answered, That no Body but himself and the Devil, knew where it was, and the longest Liver should take all.

Those of his Crew who were taken alive, told a Story which may appear a little incredible; however, we think it will not be fair to omit it, since we had it from their own Mouths. That once upon a Cruize, they found out that they had a Man on Board more than their Crew; such a one was seen several Days amongst them, sometimes below, and sometimes upon Deck, yet no Man in the Ship could give an Account who he was, or from whence he came; but that he disappeared little before they were cast away in their great Ship, but, it seems, they verily believed it was the Devil.

One would think these Things should induce them to reform their Lives, but so many Reprobates together, encouraged and spirited one another up in their Wickedness, to which a continual Course of drinking did not a little contribute; for in Black-beard's Journal, which was taken, there were several Memorandums of the following Nature, sound writ with his own Hand.— Such a Day, Rum all out:—Our Company somewhat sober:—A damn'd Confusion amongst us!—Rogues a plotting;—great Talk of Separation.—So I look'd sharp for a Prize;—such a Day took one, with a great deal of Liquor on Board, so kept the Company hot, damned hot, then all Things went well again.

Thus it was these Wretches passed their Lives, with very little Pleasure or Satisfaction, in the Possession of what they violently take away from others, and sure to pay for it at last, by an ignominious Death.

The Names of the Pyrates killed in the Engagement, are as follow.

Edward Teach, Commander.

Phillip Morton, Gunner.

Garrat Gibbens, Boatswain.

Owen Roberts, Carpenter.

Thomas Miller, Quarter-Master.

John Husk,

Joseph Curtice,

Joseph Brooks,

Nath. Jackson.

All the rest, except the two last, were wounded and afterwards hanged in Virginia.

John Carnes, Joseph Philips,

Joseph Brooks, James Robbins,

James Blake, John Martin,

John Gills, Edward Salter,

Thomas Gates, Stephen Daniel,

James White, Richard Greensail.

Richard Stiles, Israel Hands, pardoned.

Cæsar, Samuel Odel, acquited.

There were in the Pyrate Sloops, and ashore in a Tent, near where the Sloops lay, 25 Hogsheads of Sugar, 11 Teirces, and 145 Bags of Cocoa, a Barrel of Indigo, and a Bale of Cotton; which, with what was taken from the Governor and Secretary, and the Sale of the Sloop, came to 2500 l. besides the Rewards paid by the Governor of Virginia, pursuant to his Proclamation; all which was divided among the Companies of the two Ships, Lime and Pearl, that lay in James River; the brave Fellows that took them coming in for no more than their Dividend amongst the rest, and was paid it within these three Months.

Howell Davis' Entry in Captain Charles Johnson's *A General History of the Pyrates*

Captain Howel Davis was born at Milford, in Monmouthshire, and was from a Boy brought up to the Sea. The last Voyage he made from England, was in the Cadogan Snow of Bristol, Captain Skinner Commander, bound for the Coast of Guiney, of which Snow Davis was chief Mate: They were no sooner arrived at Sierraleon on the aforesaid Coast, but they were taken by the Pyrate England, who plunder'd them, and Skinner was barbarously murdered, as has been related before in the Story of Captain England.

After the Death of Captain Skinner, Davis pretended that he was mightily sollicited by England to engage with him; but that he resolutely answered, he would sooner be shot to Death than sign the Pyrates Articles. Upon which, England, pleased with his Bravery, sent him and the rest of the Men again on Board the Snow, appointing him Captain of her, in the Room of Skinner, commanding him to pursue his Voyage. He also gave him a written Paper sealed up, with Orders to open it when he should come into a certain Latitude, and at the Peril of his Life follow the Orders therein set down. This was an Air of Grandeur like what Princes practice to their Admirals and Generals.—It was punctually complied with by Davis, who read it to the Ship's Company; it contained no less than a generous Deed of Gift of the Ship and Cargoe, to Davis and the Crew, ordering him to go to Brasil and dispose of the Lading to the best Advantage, and to make a fair and equal Dividend with the rest.

Davis proposed to the Crew, whether they were willing to follow their Directions, but to his great Surprize, found the Majority of them altogether averse to it, wherefore in a Rage, he bad them be damn'd, and go where they would. They knew that Part of their Cargoe was consigned to certain Merchants at Barbadoes, wherefore they steered for that Island. When they arrived, they related to these Merchants the unfortunate Death of Skinner, and the Proposal which had been made to them by Davis; upon which Davis was seized and committed to Prison, where he was kept three Months; however, as he had been in no Act of Pyracy, he was discharged without being brought to any Tryal, yet he could not expect any Employment there; wherefore knowing that the Island of Providence was a kind of Rendevouz of Pyrates, he was resolved to make one amongst them, if possible, and to that Purpose, found Means of shipping himself for that Island; but he was again disappointed, for when he arrived there, the Pyrates had newly surrendered to Captain Woods Rogers, and accepted of the Act of Grace, which he had just brought from England.

However, Davis was not long out of Business, for Captain Rogers having fitted out two Sloops for Trade, one called the Buck, the other the Mumvil Trader; Davis found an Employment on Board of one of them; the Lading of these Sloops was of considerable Value, consisting of European Goods, in order to be exchanged with the French and Spaniards; and many of the Hands on Board of them, were the Pyrates lately come in upon the late Act of Grace. The first Place they touched at, was the Island of Martinico, belonging to the French, where Davis having conspired with some others, rise in the Night, secured the Master and seized the Sloop; as soon as this was done, they called to the other Sloop, which lay a little Way from them, among whom they knew there were a great many Hands ripe for Rebellion, and ordered them to come on Board of them; they did so, and the greatest Part of them agreed to join with Davis; those who were otherwise inclined, were sent back on Board the Mumvil Sloop, to go where they pleased, Davis having first taken out of her, every Thing which he thought might be of Use.

After this, a Counsel of War was called over a large Bowl of Punch, at which it was proposed to chuse a Commander; the Election was soon over, for it fell upon Davis by a great Majority of legal Pollers, there was no Scrutiny demanded, for all acquiesced in the Choice: As soon as he was possess'd of his Command, he drew up Articles, which were signed and sworn to by himself and the rest, then he made a short Speech, the sum of which, was, a Declaration of War against the whole World.

After this they consulted about a proper Place where they might clean their Sloop, a light Pair of Heels being of great Use either to take, or escape being taken; for this purpose they made Choice of Coxon's Hole, at the East End of the Island of Cuba, a Place where they might secure themselves from Surprize, the Entrance being so narrow, that one Ship might keep out a hundred.

Here they cleaned with much Difficulty, for they had no Carpenter in their Company, a Person of great Use upon such Exigencies; from hence they put to Sea, making to the North-Side of the Island of Hispaniola. The first Sail which fell in their Way, was a French Ship of twelve Guns; it must be observed, that Davis had but thirty five Hands, yet Provisions began to grow short with him; wherefore he attacked this Ship, she soon struck, and he sent twelve of his Hands on Board of her, in order to plunder: This was no sooner done, but a Sail was spied a great Way to Windward of them; they enquired of the French Man what she might be, he answered, that he had spoke with a Ship, the Day before, of 24 Guns and 60 Men, and he took this to be the same.

Davis then proposed to his Men to attack her, telling them, she would be a rare Ship for their Use, but they looked upon it to be an extravagant Attempt, and discovered no Fondness for it, but he assured them he had a Stratagem in his Head would make all safe; wherefore he gave Chace, and ordered his Prize to do the same. The Prize being a slow Sailor, Davis first came up with the Enemy, and standing along Side of them, shewed his pyratical Colours: They, much surpriz'd, called to Davis, telling him, they wondered at his Impudence in venturing to come so near them, and ordered him to strike; but he answered, that he intended to keep them in Play, till his Consort came up, who was able to deal with them, and that if they did not strike to him, they should have but bad Quarters; whereupon he gave them a Broad-Side, which they returned.

In the mean Time the Prize drew near, who obliged all the Prisoners to come upon Deck in white Shirts, to make a Shew of Force, as they had been directed by Davis; they also hoisted a dirty Tarpawlin, by Way of black Flag, they having no other, and fir'd a Gun: The French Men were so intimidated by this Appearance of Force, that they struck. Davis called out to the Captain to come on Board of him, with twenty of his Hands; he did so, and they were all for the greater Security clapt into Irons, the Captain excepted: Then he sent four of his own Men on Board the first Prize, and in order still to carry on the Cheat, spoke aloud, that they should give his Service to the Captain, and desire him to send some Hands on Board the Prize, to see what they had got; but at the same Time gave them a written Paper, with Instructions what to do. Here he ordered them to nail up the Guns in the little Prize, to take out all the small Arms and Powder, and to go every Man of them on Board the second Prize; when this was done, he ordered that more of the Prisoners should be removed out of the great Prize, into the little one, by which he secured himself from any Attempt which might be feared from their Numbers; for those on Board of him were fast in Irons, and those in the little Prize had neither Arms nor Ammunition.

Thus the three Ships kept Company for 2 Days, when finding the great Prize to be a very dull Sailor, he thought she would not be fit for his Purpose, wherefore he resolved to restore her to the Captain, with all his Hands; but first, he took Care to take out all her Ammunition, and every Thing else which he might possibly want. The French Captain was in such a Rage, at being so outwitted, that when he got on Board his own Ship, he was going to throw himself over-board, but was prevented by his Men.

Having let go both his Prizes, he steered Northward, in which Course he took a small Spanish Sloop; after this, he made towards the Western Islands, but met with no Booty thereabouts; then he steered for the Cape de Verde Islands, they cast Anchor at St. Nicholas, hoisting English Colours; the Portuguese inhabiting there, took him for an English Privateer, and Davis going ashore, they both treated him very civilly, and also traded with him. Here he remained five Weeks, in which Time, he and half his Crew, for their Pleasure, took a Journey to the chief Town of the Island, which was 19 Miles up the Country: Davis making a good Appearance, was caressed by the Governor and the Inhabitants, and no Diversion was wanting which the Portuguese could shew, or Money could purchase; after about a Week's Stay, he came back to the Ship, and the rest of the Crew went to take their Pleasure up to the Town, in their Turn.

At their Return they clean'd their Ship, and put to Sea, but not with their whole Company; for five of them, like Hannibal's Men, were so charm'd with the Luxuries of the Place, and the free Conversation of some Women, that they staid behind; and one of them, whose Name was Charles Franklin, a Monmouthshire Man, married and settled himself, and lives there to this Day.

From hence they sailed to Bonevista, and looked into that Harbour, but finding nothing, they steer'd for the Isle of May: When they arrived here, they met with a great many Ships and Vessels in the Road, all which they plundered, taking out of them whatever they wanted; and also strengthen'd themselves with a great many fresh Hands, who most of them enter'd voluntarily. One of the Ships they took to their own Use, mounted her with twenty six Guns, and call'd her the King James. There being no fresh Water hereabouts, they made towards St. Jago, belonging to the Portuguese, in order to lay in a Store; Davis, with a few Hands, going ashore to find the most commodious Place to water at, the Governor, with some Attendants, came himself and examined who they were, and whence they came? And not liking Davis's Account of himself, the Governor was so plain to tell them, he suspected them to be Pyrates. Davis seemed mightily affronted, standing much upon his Honour, replying to the Governor, he scorn'd his Words; however, as soon as his Back was turn'd, for fear of Accidents, he got on Board again as fast as he could. Davis related what had happened, and his Men seemed to resent the Affront which had been offered him. Davis, upon this, told them, he was confident he could surprize the Fort in the Night; they agreed with him to attempt it, and accordingly, when it grew late, they went ashore well arm'd; and the Guard which was kept, was so negligent, that they got within the Fort before any Alarm was given: When it was too late there was some little Resistance made, and three Men killed on Davis's Side. Those in the Fort, in their Hurry, run into the Governor's House to save themselves, which they barricadoed so strongly, that Davis's Party could not enter it; however, they threw in Granadoe-Shells, which not only ruin'd all the Furniture, but kill'd several Men within.

When it was Day the whole Country was alarm'd, and came to attack the Pyrates; wherefore it not being their Business to stand a Siege, they made the best of their Way on Board their Ship again, after having dismounted the Guns of the Fort. By this Enterprize they did a great Deal of Mischief to the Portuguese, and but very little Good to themselves.

Having put to Sea they muster'd their Hands, and found themselves near seventy strong; then it was proposed what Course they should steer, and differing in their Opinions, they divided, and by a Majority it was carried for Gambia on the Coast of Guiney; of this Opinion was Davis, he having been employ'd in that Trade, was acquainted with the Coast: He told them, that there was a great deal of Money always kept in Gambia Castle, and that it would be worth their while to make an Attempt upon it. They ask'd him how it was possible, since it was garrisoned? He desired they would leave the Management of it to him, and he would undertake to make them Masters of it. They began now to conceive so high an Opinion of his Conduct, as well as Courage, that they thought nothing impossible to him, therefore they agreed to obey him, without enquiring further into his Design.

Having come within Sight of the Place, he ordered all his Men under Deck, except as many as were absolutely necessary for working the Ship, that those from the Fort seeing a Ship with so few Hands, might have no Suspicion of her being any other than a trading Vessel; then he ran close under the Fort, and there cast Anchor; and having ordered out the Boat, he commanded six Men in her, in old ordinary Jackets, while he himself, with the Master and Doctor, dressed themselves like Gentlemen; his Design being, that the Men should look like common Sailors, and they like Merchants. In rowing ashore he gave his Men Instructions what to say in Case any Questions should be asked them.

Being come to the landing Place, he was received by a File of Musqueteers, and conducted into the Fort, where the Governor accosting them civilly, ask'd them who they were, and whence they came? They answered they were of Liverpool, bound for the River of Sinnegal, to trade for Gum and Elephants Teeth, but that they were chaced on that Coast by two French Men of War, and narrowly escaped being taken, having a little the Heels of them; but now they were resolved to make the best of a bad Market, and would Trade here for Slaves; then the Governor ask'd them, what was the chief of their Cargo? They answered, Iron and Plate, which were good Things there; the Governor told him he would Slave them to the full Value of their Cargoe, and asked them, if they had any European Liquor on Board? they answered, a little for their own Use; however, a Hamper should be at his Service. The Governor then very civilly invited them all to stay and dine with him; Davis told him, that being Commander of the Ship, he must go on Board to see her well moored, and give some other Orders, but those two Gentlemen might stay, and that he himself would also return before Dinner, and bring the Hamper of Liquor with him.

While he was in the Fort, his Eyes were very busy in observing how Things lay; he took Notice there was a Centry at the Entrance, and a Guard-House just by it, where the Soldiers upon Duty commonly waited, their Arms standing in a Corner, in a Heap; he saw also a great many small Arms in the Governor's Hall; now when he came on Board, he assured his Men of Success, desiring them not to get drunk, and that as soon as they saw the Flag upon the Castle struck, they might conclude he was Master, and send twenty Hands immediately ashore; in the mean Time, there being a Sloop at Anchor near them, he sent some Hands in a Boat, to secure the Master and all the Men, and bring them on Board of him, least they observing any Bustle or arming in his Ship, might send ashore and give Intelligence.

These Precautions being taken, he ordered his Men, who were to go in the Boat with him, to put two Pair of Pistols each under their Cloaths, he doing the like himself, and gave them Directions to go into the Guard-Room, and to enter into Conversation with the Soldiers, and observe when he should fire a Pistol thro' the Governor's Window, to start up at once and secure the Arms in the Guard-Room.

When Davis arrived, Dinner not being ready, the Governor proposed that they should pass their Time in making a Bowl of Punch till Dinner-Time: It must be observed, that Davis's Coxen waited upon them, who had an Opportunity of going about all Parts of the House, to see what Strength they had, he whispered Davis, there being no Person then in the Room, but he, (Davis) the Master, the Doctor, the Coxen and Governor; Davis on a sudden drew out a Pistol, clapt it to the Governor's Breast, telling him, he must surrender the Fort and all the Riches in it, or he was a dead Man. The Governor being no Ways prepared for such an Attack, promised to be very Passive, and do all they desired, therefore they shut the Door, took down all the Arms that hung in the Hall, and loaded them. Davis fires his Pistol thro' the Window, upon which his Men, without, executed their Part of the Scheme, like Heroes, in an Instant; getting betwixt the Soldiers and their Arms, all with their Pistols cock'd in their Hands, while one of them carried the Arms out. When this was done, they locked the Soldiers into the Guard-Room, and kept Guard without.

In the mean Time one of them struck the Union Flag on the Top of the Castle, at which Signal those on Board sent on Shore a Reinforcement of Hands, and they got Possession of the Fort without the least Hurry or Confusion, or so much as a Man lost of either Side.

Davis harangued the Soldiers, upon which a great many of them took on with him, those who refused, he sent on Board the little Sloop, and because he would not be at the Trouble of a Guard for them, he ordered all the Sails and Cables out of her, which might hinder them from attempting to get away.

This Day was spent in a kind of Rejoycing, the Castle firing her Guns to salute the Ship, and the Ship the Castle; but the next Day they minded their Business, that is, they fell to plundering, but they found Things fall vastly short of their Expectation; for they discovered, that a great deal of Money had been lately sent away; however, they met with the Value of about two thousand Pounds Sterling in Bar Gold, and a great many other rich Effects: Every Thing they liked, which was portable, they brought aboard their Ship; some Things which they had no Use for, they were so generous to make a Present of, to the Master and Crew of the little Sloop, to whom they also returned his Vessel again, and then they fell to work in dismounting the Guns, and demolishing the Fortifications.

After they had done as much Mischief as they could, and were weighing Anchor to be gone, they spy'd a Ship bearing down upon them in full Sail; they soon got their Anchor's up, and were in a Readiness to receive her. This Ship prov'd to be a French Pyrate of fourteen Guns and sixty four Hands, half French, half Negroes; the Captain's Name was La Bouche; he expected no less than a rich Prize, which made him so eager in the Chace; but when he came near enough to see their Guns, and the Number of their Hands upon Deck, he began to think he should catch a Tartar, and supposed her to be a small English Man of War; however, since there was no escaping, he resolved to do a bold and desperate Action, which was to board Davis. As he was making towards her, for this Purpose, he fired a Gun, and hoisted his black Colours; Davis returned the Salute, and hoisted his black Colours also. The French Man was not a little pleased at this happy Mistake; they both hoisted out their Boats, and the Captains went to meet and congratulate one another with a Flag of Truce in their Sterns; a great many Civilities passed between them, and La Bouche desired Davis, that they might sail down the Coast together, that he (La Bouche) might get a better Ship: Davis agreed to it, and very courteously promised him the first Ship he took, fit for his Use, he would give him, as being willing to encourage a willing Brother.

The first Place they touch'd at, was Sierraleon, where at first going in, they spied a tall Ship at Anchor; Davis being the best Sailor first came up with her, and wondering that she did not try to make off, suspected her to be a Ship of Force. As soon as he came along Side of her, she brought a Spring upon her Cable, and fired a whole Broadside upon Davis, at the same Time hoisted a black Flag; Davis hoisted his black Flag in like Manner, and fired one Gun to Leeward.

In fine, she proved to be a Pyrate Ship of twenty four Guns, commanded by one Cocklyn, who expecting these two would prove Prizes, let them come in, least his getting under Sail might frighten them away.

This Satisfaction was great on all Sides, at this Junction of Confederates and Brethren in Iniquity; two Days they spent in improving their Acquaintance and Friendship, the third Day Davis and Cocklyn, agreed to go in La Bouche's Brigantine and attack the Fort; they contrived it so, as to get up thither by high Water; those in the Fort suspected them to be what they really were, and therefore stood upon their Defence; when the Brigantine came within Musket-Shot, the Fort fired all their Guns upon her, the Brigantine did the like upon the Fort, and so held each other in Play for several Hours, when the two confederate Ships were come up to the Assistance of the Brigantine; those who defended the Fort, seeing such a Number of Hands on Board these Ships, had not the Courage to stand it any longer, but abandoning the Fort, left it to the Mercy of the Pyrates.

They took Possession of it, and continued there near seven Weeks, in which Time they all cleaned their Ships. We should have observed, that a Galley came into the Road while they were there, which Davis insisted should be yielded to La Bouche, according to his Word of Honour before given; Cocklyn did not oppose it, so La Bouche went into her, with his Crew, and cutting away her half Deck, mounted her with twenty four Guns.

Having called a Counsel of War, they agreed to sail down the Coast together, and for the greater Grandeur, appointed a Commadore, which was Davis; but they had not kept Company long, when drinking together on Board of Davis, they had like to have fallen together by the Ears, the strong Liquor stirring up a Spirit of Discord among them, and they quarrelled, but Davis put an End to it, by this short Speech:—Heark ye, you Cocklin and La Bouche, I find by strengthening you, I have put a Rod into your Hands to whip my self, but I'm still able to deal with you both; but since we met in Love, let us part in Love, for I find, that three of a Trade can never agree.—Upon which the other two went on Board their respective Ships, and immediately parted, each steering a different Course.

Davis held on his Way down the Coast, and making Cape Appollonia, he met with two Scotch and one English Vessel, which he plundered, and then let go. About five Days after he fell in with a Dutch Interloper of thirty Guns and ninety Men, (half being English,) off Cape Three Points Bay; Davis coming up along Side of her, the Dutch Man gave the first Fire, and pouring in a broad-Side upon Davis, killed nine of his Men, Davis returned it, and a very hot Engagement followed, which lasted from one a Clock at Noon, till nine next Morning, when the Dutch Man struck, and yielded her self their Prize.

Davis fitted up the Dutch Ship for his own Use, and called her the Rover, aboard of which he mounted thirty two Guns, and twenty seven Swivels, and proceeded with her and the King James, to Anamaboe; he entered the Bay betwixt the Hours of twelve and one at Noon, and found there three Ships lying at Anchor, who were trading for Negroes, Gold and Teeth: The Names of these Ships were the Hink Pink, Captain Hall Commander, the Princess, Captain Plumb, of which Roberts, who will make a considerable Figure in the sequel of this History, was second Mate, and the Morrice Sloop, Captain Fin; he takes these Ships without any Resistance, and having plundered them, he makes a Present of one of them, viz. the Morrice Sloop, to the Dutch Men, on Board of which alone were found a hundred and forty Negroes, besides dry Goods, and a considerable Quantity of Gold-Dust.

It happened there were several Canoes along Side of this last, when Davis came in, who saved themselves and got ashore; these gave Notice at the Fort, that these Ships were Pyrates, upon which the Fort fired upon them, but without any Execution, for their Mettle was not of Weight enough to reach them; Davis therefore, by Way of Defiance, hoisted his black Flag and returned their Compliment.

The same Day he sail'd with his three Ships, making his Way down the Coast towards Princes, a Portuguese Colony: But, before we proceed any farther in Davis's Story, we shall give our Reader an Account of the Portuguese Settlements on this Coast, with other curious Remarks, as they were communicated to me by an ingenious Gentleman, lately arrived from those Parts.

A Description of the Islands of St. THOME, DEL PRINCIPE, and ANNOBONO.

AS the Portuguese were the great Improvers of Navigation, and the first Europeans who traded too and settled on the Coasts of Africa, even round to India, and made those Discoveries, which now turn so much to the Advantage of other Nations, it may not be amiss, previously to a Description of those Islands, to hint on that wonderful Property of the Loadstone, that a little before had been found out, and enabled them to pursue such new and daring Navigations.

The attractive Power of the Loadstone, was universally known with the Ancients, as may be believed by its being a native Fossil of the Grecians, (Magnes a Magnesia) but its directive, or polar Virtue, has only been known to us within this 350 Years, and said to be found out by John Goia of Malphi, in the Kingdom of Naples, Prima dedit nautis usum magnetis Amalphi; tho' others think, and assure us, it was transported by Paulus Venetus from China to Italy, like the other famous Arts of modern Use with us, PRINTING and the Use of GUNS.

The other Properties of Improvements of the Magnet, viz. Variation, or its Defluction from an exact N. or S. Line, Variation of that Variation, and its Inclination, were the Inventions of Sebastian Cabot, Mr. Gellibrand, and Mr. Norman; the Inclination of the Needle, or that Property whereby it keeps an Elevation above the Horizon, in all Places but under the Equator, (where its Parallel) is as surprizing a Phænomenon as any, and was the Discovery of our Countrymen; and could it be found regular, I imagine would very much help towards the Discovery of Longitude, at least would point out better Methods than hitherto known, when Ships drew nigh Land, which would answer as useful an End.

Before the Verticity and Use of the Compass, the Portuguese Navigations had extended no farther than Cape Non, (it was their ne plus ultra,) and therefore so called; distress of Weather, indeed, had drove some Coasters to Porto Santo, and Madera, before any certain Method of steering was invented; but after the Needle was seen thus inspired, Navigation every Year improved under the great Incouragements of Henry, Alphonsus, and John II. Kings of Portugal, in Part of the 14th and in the 15th Century.

King Alphonsus was not so much at leasure as his Predecessor, to pursue these Discoveries, but having seen the Advantages accrued to Portugal by them, and that the Pope had confirmed the perpetual Donation of all they should discover between Cape Bajadore and India, inclusively, he resolved not to neglect the proper Assistance, and farmed the Profits that did or might ensue to one Bernard Gomez, a Citizen of Lisbon, who was every Voyage obliged to discover 100 Leagues, still farther on: And about the Year 1470 made these Islands, the only Places (of all the considerable and large Colonies they had in Africa,) that do now remain to that Crown.

St. Thome is the principal of the three, whose Governour is stiled Captain General of the Islands, and from whom the other at Princes receives his Commission, tho' nominated by the Court of Portugal: It is a Bishoprick with a great many secular Clergy who appear to have neither Learning nor Devotion, as may be judged by several of them being Negroes: One of the Chief of them, invited us to hear Mass, as a Diversion to pass Time away, where he, and his inferior Brethren acted such affected Gestures and Strains of Voice, as shewed to their Dishonour, they had no other Aim than pleasing us; and what I think was still worse, it was not without a View of Interest; for as these Clergy are the chief Traders, they stoop to pitiful and scandalous Methods for ingratiating themselves: They and the Government, on this trading Account, maintain as great Harmony, being ever jealous of each other, and practising little deceitful Arts to monopolize what Strangers have to offer for sale, whether Toys or Cloaths, which of all Sorts are ever Commodious with the Portuguese, in all Parts of the World; an ordinary Suit of Black will sell for seven or eight Pound; a Turnstile Wig of four Shillings, for a Moidore; a Watch of forty Shillings, for six Pound, &c.

The Town is of mean Building, but large and populous, the Residence of the greater Part of the Natives, who, thro' the whole Island, are computed at 10000, the Militia at 3000, and are in general, a rascally thievish Generation, as an old grave Friend of mine can Witness; for he having carried a Bag of second hand Cloaths on Shore, to truck for Provisions, seated himself on the Sand for that Purpose, presently gathered a Crowd round him, to view them; one of which desired to know the Price of a black Suit, that unluckily lay uppermost, and was the best of them, agreeing to the Demand, with little Hesitation, provided it would but fit him; he put them on immediately, in as much hurry as possible, without any co-licentia Seignor; and when my Friend was about to commend the Goodness of the Suit, and Exactness they set with, not dreaming of the Impudence of running away from a Crowd, the Rascal took to his Heels, my Friend followed and bawled very much, and tho' there was 500 People about the Place, it served to no other End but making him a clear Stage, that the best Pair of Heels might carry it; so he lost the Suit of Cloaths, and before he could return to his Bag, others of them had beat off his Servant, and shared the rest.

Most of the Ships from Guiney, of their own Nation, and frequently those of ours, call at one or other of these Islands, to recruit with fresh Provisions, and take in Water, which on the Coast are not so good, nor so conveniently to come by: Their own Ships likewise, when they touch here, are obliged to leave the King his Custom for their Slaves, which is always in Gold, at so much a Head, without any Deduction at Brasil, for the Mortality that may happen afterwards; this by being a constant Bank to pay off the civil and military Charges of the Government, prevents the Inconveniency of Remittances, and keeps both it and Princes Isle rich enough to pay ready Money for every Thing they want of Europeans.

Their Beefs are small and lean, (two hundred Weight or a little more,) but the Goats, Hogs and Fowls very good, their Sugar course and dirty, and Rum very ordinary; as these Refreshments lay most with People who are in want of other Necessaries, they come to us in Way of bartering, very cheap: A good Hog for an old Cutlash; a fat Fowl for a Span of Brasil Tobacco, (no other Sort being valued, &c.) But with Money you give eight Dollars per Head for Cattle; three Dollars for a Goat; six Dollars for a grown Hog; a Testune and a Half for a Fowl; a Dollar per Gallon for Rum; two Dollars a Roove for Sugar; and half a Dollar for a Dozen of Paraquets: Here is Plenty likewise of Corn and Farine, of Limes, Citrons and Yamms.

The Island is reckoned nigh a Square, each Side 18 Leagues long, hilly, and lays under the Æquinoctial, a wooden Bridge just without the Town, being said not to deviate the least Part of a Minute, either to the Southward or Northward; and notwithstanding this warm Scituation, and continual vertical Suns, the Islanders are very healthy, imputed by those who are disposed to be merry, in a great Measure to the Want of even so much as one Surgeon or Physician amongst them.

Isle Del Principe, the next in Magnitude, a pleasant and delightful Spot to the grave, and thoughtfull Disposition of the Portuguese, an Improvement of Country Retirement, in that, this may be a happy and uninterrupted Retreat from the whole World.

I shall divide what I have to say on this Island, into Observations made on our Approach to it, on the Seas round it, the Harbour, Produce of the Island and Seasons, Way of Living among the Inhabitants, some Custom of the Negroes, with such proper Deductions on each as may illustrate the Description, and inform the Reader.

We were bound hither from Whydah, at the latter Part of the Month July, when the Rains are over, and the Winds hang altogether S. W. (as they do before the Rains, S. E.) yet with this Wind (when at Sea) we found the Ship gained unexpectedly so far to the Southward, (i. e. Windward,) that we could with ease have weathered any of the Islands, and this seems next to impossible should be, if the Currents, which were strong to Leeward, in the Road of Whydah, had extended in like Manner cross the Bite of Benin: No, it must then have been very difficult to have weathered even Cape Formosa: On this Occasion, I shall farther expatiate upon the Currents on the whole Coast of Guiney.

The Southern Coast of Africa runs in a Line of Latitude, the Northern on an Eastern Line, but both strait, with the fewest Inlets, Gulphs or Bays, of either of the four Continents; the only large and remarkable one, is that of Benin and Calabar, towards which the Currents of each Coast tend, and is strongest from the Southward, because more open to a larger Sea, whose rising it is (tho' little and indiscernable at any Distance from the Land,) that gives rise to these Currents close in Shore, which are nothing but Tides altered and disturbed by the Make and Shape of Lands.

For Proof of this, I shall lay down the following Observations as certain Facts. That in the Rivers of Gambia and Sierraleon, in the Straits and Channels of Benin, and in general along the whole Coast, the Flowings are regular on the Shores, with this Difference; that, in the abovemention'd Rivers, and in the Channels of Benin, where the Shore contract the Waters into a narrow Compass, the Tides are strong and high, as well as regular; but on the dead Coast, where it makes an equal Reverberation, slow and low, (not to above two or three Foot,) increasing as you advance towards Benin; and this is farther evident in that at Cape Corso, Succonda and Commenda, and where the Land rounds and gives any Stop, the Tides flow regularly to four Foot and upwards; when on an evener Coast, (tho' next adjoining,) they shall not exceed two or three Foot; and ten Leagues out at Sea, (where no such Interruption is,) they become scarcely, if at all, perceptible.

What I would deduce from this, besides a Confirmation of that ingenious Theory of the Tides, by Captain Halley; is first, that the Ships bound to Angola, Cabenda, and other Places on the Southern Coast of Africa, should cross the Æquinoctial from Cape Palmas, and run into a Southern Latitude, without keeping too far to the Westward; and the Reason seems plain, for if you endeavour to cross it about the Islands, you meet Calms, southerly Winds and opposite Currents; and if too far to the Westward, the trade Winds are strong and unfavourable; for it obliges you to stand into 28 or 30° Southern Latitude, till they are variable.

Secondly, On the Northern Side of Guiney, if Ships are bound from the Gold-Coast to Sierraleon, Gambia, or elsewhere to Windward, considering the Weakness of these Currents, and the Favourableness of Land Breezes, and Southerly in the Rains, Turnadoes, and even of the Trade Wind, when a-breast of Cape Palmas, it is more expeditious to pursue the Passage this Way, than by a long perambulatory Course of 4 or 500 Leagues to the Westward, and as many more to the Northward, which must be before a Wind can be obtained, that could recover the Coast.

Lastly, it is, in a great Measure, owning to this want of Inlets, and the Rivers being small and unnavigable, that the Seas rebound with so dangerous a Surff thro' the whole Continent.

Round the Shores of this Island, and at this Season, (July, August and September,) there is a great Resort of Whale-Fish, tame, and sporting very nigh the Ships as they sail in, always in Pairs, the Female much the smaller, and often seen to turn on their Backs for Dalliance, the Prologue to engendring: It has an Enemy, called the Thresher, a large Fish too, that has its Haunts here at this Season, and encounters the Whale, raising himself out of the Water a considerable Heighth, and falling again with great Weight and Force; it is commonly said also, that there is a Sword Fish in these Battles, who pricks the Whale up to the Surface again, but without this, I believe, he would suffocate when put to quick Motions, unless frequently approaching the Air, to ventilate and remove the impediments to a swifter Circulation: Nor do I think he is battled for Prey, but to remove him from what is perhaps the Food of both. The Number of Whales here has put me sometimes on thinking an advantageous Fishery might be made of it, but I presume they (no more than those of Brasil) are the Sort which yield the profitable Part, called Whale-Bone: All therefore that the Islanders do, is now and then to go out with two or three Canoes, and set on one for Diversion.

The Rocks and outer Lines of the Island, are the Haunts of variety of Sea-Birds, especially Boobies and Noddies; the former are of the Bigness of a Gull, and a dark Colour, named so from their Simplicity, because they often sit still and let the Sailors take them up in their Hands; but I fancy this succeeds more frequently from their Weariness, and the Largeness of their Wings, which, when they once have rested, cannot have the Scope necessary to raise and float them on the Air again. The Noddies are smaller and flat footed also.

What I would remark more of them, is, the admirable Instinct in these Birds, for the proper Seasons, and the proper Places for Support. In the aforemention'd Months, when the large Fish were here, numerous Flocks of Fowl attend for the Spawn and Superfluity of their Nourishment; and in January few of either; for the same Reason, there are scarce any Sea Fowl seen on the African Coast; Rocks and Islands being generally their best Security and Subsistance.

The Harbour of Princes is at the E. S. E. Point of the Island; the North-Side has gradual Soundings, but here deep Water, having no Ground at a Mile off with 140 Fathom of Line. The Port (when in) is a smooth narrow Bay, safe from Winds, (unless a little Swell when Southerly) and draughted into other smaller and sandy Ones, convenient for raising of Tents, Watering, and hawling the Seam; the whole protected by a Fort, or rather Battery, of a dozen Guns on the Larboard-Side. At the Head of the Bay stands the Town, about a Mile from the anchoring Place, and consists of two or three regular Streets, of wooden built Houses, where the Governor and chief Men of the Island reside. Here the Water grows shallow for a considerable Distance, and the Natives, at every Ebb, (having before encompassed every convenient Angle with a Rise of Stones, something like Weirs in England) resort for catching of Fish, which, with them, is a daily Diversion, as well as Subsistance, 500 attending with Sticks and wicker Baskets; and if they cannot dip them with one Hand, they knock them down with the other. The Tides rise regularly 6 Foot in the Harbour, and yet not half that Heighth without the Capes that make the Bay.

Here are constantly two Missionaries, who are sent for six Years to inculcate the Christian Principles, and more especially attend the Conversion of the Negroes; the present are Venetians, ingenious Men, who seem to despise the loose Morals and Behaviour of the Seculars, and complain of them as of the Slaves, ut Color Mores sunt nigri. They have a neat Conventual-

House and a Garden appropriated, which, by their own Industry and Labour, not only thrives with the several Natives of the Soil, but many Exoticks and Curiosities. A Fruit in particular, larger than a Chesnut, yellow, containing two Stones, with a Pulp, or clammy Substance about them, which, when suck'd, exceeds in Sweetness, Sugar or Honey, and has this Property beyond them, of giving a sweet Taste to every Liquid you swallow for the whole Evening after. The only Plague infesting the Garden, is a Vermin called Land-Crabs, in vast Numbers, of a bright red Colour, (in other Respects like the Sea ones) which burrough in these sandy Soils like Rabbets, and are as shy.

The Island is a pleasant Intermixture of Hill and Valley; the Hills spread with Palms, Coco-Nuts, and Cotton-Trees, with Numbers of Monkeys and Parrots among them; the Valleys with fruitful Plantations of Yamms, Kulalu, Papas, Variety of Sallating, Ananas, or Pine-Apples, Guavas, Plantanes, Bonanas, Manyocos, and Indian Corn; with Fowls, Guinea Hens, Muscovy Ducks, Goats, Hogs, Turkies, and wild Beefs, with each a little Village of Negroes, who, under the Direction of their several Masters, manage the Cultivation, and exchange or sell them for Money, much after the same Rates with the People of St. Thome.

I shall run a Description of the Vegetables, with their Properties, not only because they are the Produce of this Island, but most of them of Africa in general.

The Palm-Trees are numerous on the Shores of Africa, and may be reckoned the first of their natural Curiosities, in that they afford them Meat, Drink and Cloathing; they grow very straight to 40 and 50 Foot high, and at the top (only) have 3 or 4 Circles of Branches, that spread and make a capacious Umbrella. The Trunk is very rough with Knobs, either Excrescencies, or the Healings of those Branches that were lopped off to forward the Growth of the Tree, and make it answer better in its Fruit. The Branches are strongly tied together with a Cortex, which may be unravelled to a considerable Length and Breadth; the inward Lamella of this Cortex, I know are wove like a Cloath at Benin, and afterwards died and worn: Under the Branches, and close to the Body of the Tree, hang the Nuts, thirty Bunches perhaps on a Tree, and each of thirty Pound Weight, with prickly Films from between them, not unresembling Hedge-Hogs; of these Nuts comes a liquid and pleasant scented Oyl, used as Food and Sauce all over the Coast, but chiefly in the Windward Parts of Africa, where they stamp, boil and skim it off in great Quantities; underneath, where the Branches fasten, they tap for Wine, called Cockra, in this Manner; the Negroes who are mostly limber active Fellows, encompass themselves and the Trees with a Hoop of strong With, and run up with a great deal of Agility; at the Bottom of a Branch of Nuts, he makes an Excavation of an Inch and a half over, and tying fast his Calabash, leaves it to destil, which it does to two or three Quarts in a Night's Time, when done he plugs it up, and chooses another; for if suffered to run too much, or in the Day Time, the Sap is unwarily exhausted, and the Tree spoiled: The Liquor thus drawn, is of a wheyish Colour, intoxicating and sours in 24 Hours, but when new drawn, is pleasantest to thirst and hunger both: It is from these Wines they draw their Arack in India. On the very Top of the Palm, grows a Cabbage, called so, I believe, from some resemblance its Tast is thought to have with ours, and is used like it; the Covering has a Down that makes the best of Tinder, and the Weavings of other Parts are drawn out into strong Threads.

Coco-Nut-Trees are branch'd like, but not so tall as, Palm Trees, the Nut like them, growing under the Branches, and close to the Trunk; the milky Liquor they contain, (to half a Pint or more,) is often drank to quench Thirst, but surfeiting, and this may be observed in their Way of Nourishment, that when the Quantity of Milk is large, the Shell and Meat are very thin, and harden and thicken in Proportion, as that loses.

Cotton Trees also are the Growth of all Parts of Africk, as well as the Islands, of vast Bigness, yet not so incremental as the Shrubs or Bushes of five or six Foot high; these bear a Fruit (if it may be so called) about the Bigness of Pigeons Eggs, which as the Sun swells and ripens, bursts forth and discovers three Cells loaded with Cotton, and Seeds in the Middle of them: This in most Parts the Negroes know how to spin, and here at Nicongo and the Island St. Jago, how to weave into Cloths.

Yamms are a common Root, sweeter but not unlike Potato's: Kulalu, a Herb like Spinnage: Papa, a Fruit less than the smallest Pumkins; they are all three for boiling, and to be eat with Meat; the latter are improved by the English into a Turnip or an Apple Tast, with a due Mixture of Butter or Limes.

Guava's, a Fruit as large as a Pipin, with Seeds and Stones in it, of an uncouth astringing Tast, tho' never so much be said in Commendation of it, at the West-Indies, it is common for Cræolians, (who has tasted both,) to give it a Preference to Peach or Nectarine, no amazing Thing when Men whose Tasts are so degenerated, as to prefer a Toad in a Shell, (as Ward calls Turtle,) to Venison, and Negroes to fine English Ladies.

Plantanes and Bonano's are Fruit of oblong Figure, that I think differ only secundum Major & Minus, if any, the latter are preferable, and by being less, are juicier; they are usually, when stripped of their Coat, eat at Meals instead of Bread: The Leaf of this Plantane is an admirable Detergent, and, externally applied, I have seen cure the most obstinate scorbutick Ulcers.

Manyoco. A Root that shoots its Branches about the heighth of a Currant Bush; from this Root the Islanders make a Farine or Flower, which they sell at three Ryals a Roove, and drive a considerable Trade for it with the Ships that call in. The manner of making it, is first to press the Juice from it, (which is poisonous) done here with Engines, and then the Negroe Women, upon a rough Stone, rub it into a granulated Flower, reserved in their Houses, either to boil, as we do our Wheat, and is a hearty Food for the Slaves; or make it into a Bread, fine, white, and well tasted, for themselves. One thing worth taking Notice about Manyoco in this Island, is, that the Woods abound with a wild poisonous and more mortiferous Sort, which sometimes Men, unskilled in the Preparation of it, feed on to their Destruction: This the Missionaries assured me they often experimented in their Hogs, and believed we did in the Mortality of our Sailors.

Indian Corn, is likewise as well as the Farine de Manyoco and Rice, the common Victualling of our Slave Ships, and is afforded here at 1000 Heads for two Dollars. This Corn grows eight or nine Foot high, on a hard Reed or Stick, shooting forth at every six Inches Heighth, some long Leaves; it has always an Ear, or rather Head, at top, of, perhaps, 400 Fold Increase; and often two, three, or more, Midway.

Here are some Tamarind Trees; another called Cola, whose Fruit, or Nut (about twice the Bigness of a Chestnut, and bitter) is chewed by the Portugueze, to give a sweet Gust to their Water which they drink; but above all, I was shewn the Bark of one (whose Name I do not know) gravely affirm'd to have a peculiar Property of enlarging the Virile Member; I am not fond of such Conceits, nor believe it in the Power of any Vegetables, but must acknowledge, I have seen Sights of this kind among the Negroes very extraordinary; yet, that there may be no Wishes among the Ladies for the Importation of this Bark, I must acquaint them, that they are found to grow less merry, as they encrease in Bulk. I had like to have forgot their Cinnamon Trees; there is only one Walk of them, and is the Entrance of the Governor's Villa; they thrive extreemly well, and the Bark not inferior to our Cinnamon from India; why they and other Spice, in a Soil so proper, receive no farther Cultivation, is, probably, their Suspicion, that so rich a Produce, might make some potent Neighbour take a Fancy to the Island.

They have two Winters, or rather Springs, and two Summers: Their Winters, which are the rainy Seasons, come in September and February, or March, and hold two Months, returning that Fatness and generative Power to the Earth, as makes it yield a double Crop every Year, with little Sweat or Labour.

Hic Ver Assiduum atque Alienis Mensibus Æstas —Bis gravidæ Pecudes, bis Pomis utilis arbos.

Their first coming is with Travado's, i. e. sudden and hard Gusts of Wind, with Thunder, Lightning and heavy Showers, but short; and the next new or full Moon at those Times of the Year, infallibly introduces the Rains, which once begun, fall with little Intermission, and are observed coldest in February. Similar to these are rainy Seasons also over all the Coast of Africa: If there may be allowed any general Way of calculating their Time, they happen from the Course of the Sun, as it respects the Æquinoctial only; for if these Æquinoxes prove rainy Seasons all over the World (as I am apt to think they are) whatever secret Cause operates with that Station of the Sun to produce them, will more effectually do it in those vicine Latitudes; and therefore, as the Sun advances, the Rains are brought on the Whydah and Gold Coast, by April, and on the Windwardmost Part of Guiney by May: The other Season of the Sun's returning to the Southward, make them more uncertain and irregular in Northern Africa; but then to the

Southward again, they proceed in like manner, and are at Cape Lopez in October, at Angola in November, &c.

The Manner of living among the Portugueze here is, with the utmost Frugality and Temperance, even to Penury and Starving; a familiar Instance of Proof is, in the Voracity of their Dogs, who finding such clean Cupboards at home, are wild in a manner with Hunger, and tare up the Graves of the Dead for Food, as I have often seen: They themselves are lean with Covetousness, and that Christian Vertue, which is often the Result of it, Selfdenyal; and would train up their Cattle in the same way, could they fetch as much Money, or had not they their Provision more immediately of Providence. The best of them (excepting the Governor now and then) neither pay nor receive any Visits of Escapade or Recreation; they meet and sit down at each others Doors in the Street every Evening, and as few of them, in so small an Island, can have their Plantations at any greater Distance, than that they may see it every Day if they will, so the Subject of their Talk is mostly how Affairs went there, with their Negroes, or their Ground, and then part with one another innocently, but empty.

The Negroes have yet no hard Duty with them, they are rather Happy in Slavery; for as their Food is chiefly Vegetables, that could no way else be expended, there is no Murmurs bred on that account; and as their Business is Domestick, either in the Services of the House, or in Gardening, Sowing, or Planting, they have no more than what every Man would prefer for Health and Pleasure; the hardest of their Work is the Carriage of their Pateroons, or their Wives, to and from the Plantations; this they do in Hammocks (call'd at Whydah, Serpentines) slung cross a Pole, with a Cloath over, to screen the Person, so carried, from Sun and Weather, and the Slaves are at each End; and yet even this, methinks, is better than the specious Liberty a Man has for himself and his Heirs to work in a Coal Mine.

The Negroes are, most of them, thro' the Care of their Patroons, Christians, at least nominal, but excepting to some few, they adhere still to many silly Pagan Customs in their Mournings and Rejoycings, and in some Measure, powerful Majority has introduced them with the Vulgar of the Mulatto and Portugueze Race.

If a Person die in that Colour, the Relations and Friends of him meet at the House, where the Corpse is laid out decently on the Ground and covered (all except the Face) with a Sheet; they sit round it, crying and howling dreadfully, not unlike what our Countrymen are said to do in Ireland: This Mourning lasts for eight Days and Nights, but not equally intense, for as the Friends, who compose the Chorus, go out and in, are weary, and unequally affected, the Tone lessens daily, and the Intervals of Grief are longer.

In Rejoycings and Festivals they are equally ridiculous; these are commonly made on some Friend's Escape from Shipwreck, or other Danger: They meet in a large Room of the House, with a Strum Strum, to which one of the Company, perhaps, sings wofully; the rest standing round the Room close to the Petitions, take it in their Turns (one or two at a time) to step round, called Dancing, the whole clapping their Hands continually, and hooping out every Minute Abeo, which signify no more, than, how do you. And this foolish Mirth will continue three or four Days together at a House, and perhaps twelve or sixteen Hours at a time.

The Portugueze, tho' eminently abstemious and temperate in all other Things, are unbounded in their Lusts; and perhaps they substitute the former in room of a Surgeon, as a Counterpoison to the Mischiefs of a promiscuous Salacity: They have most of them Venereal Taints, and with Age become meager and hectick: I saw two Instances here of Venereal Ulcers that had cancerated to the Bowels, Spectacles that would have effectually perswaded Men (I think) how Salutary the Restriction of Laws are.

Annobono is the last, and of the least Consequence of the three Islands; there are Plenty of Fruits and Provisions, exchanged to Ships for old Cloaths and Trifles of any Sort; they have a Governor nominated from St. Thome, and two or three Priests, neither of which are minded, every one living at Discretion, and fill'd with Ignorance and Lust.

To return to Davis, the next Day after he left Anamaboe, early in the Morning, the Man at the Mast-Head espied a Sail. It must be observed, they keep a good Look-out; for, according to their Articles, he who first espies a Sail, if she proves a Prize, is entitled to the best Pair of Pistols on Board, over and above his Dividend, in which they take a singular Pride; and a Pair of Pistols has sometimes been sold for thirty Pounds, from one to another.

Immediately they gave Chace, and soon came up with her; the Ship proved to be a Hollander, and being betwixt Davis and the Shore, she made all the Sail she could, intending to run aground; Davis guessed her Design, and putting out all his small Sails, came up with her before she could effect it, and fired a Broad-side, upon which she immediately struck, and called for Quarter. It was granted, for according to Davis's Articles, it was agreed, that Quarter should be given whenever it was called for, upon Pain of Death. This Ship proved a very rich Prize, having the Governor of Acra on Board, with all his Effects, going to Holland; there was in Money to the Value of 15000 l. Sterling, besides other valuable Merchandizes, all which they brought on Board of themselves.

Upon this new Success, they restored Captain Hall and Captain Plumb, before-mentioned, their Ships again, but strengthened their Company with thirty five Hands, all white Men, taken out of these two and the Morrice Sloop; they also restored the Dutch their Ship, after having plunder'd her, as is mentioned.

Before they got to the Island of Princes, one of their Ships, viz. that call'd the King James, sprung a Leak; Davis order'd all Hands out of her, on Board his own Ship, with every thing else of Use, and left her at an Anchor at High Cameroon. As soon as he came in Sight of the Island, he hoisted English Colours; the Portuguese observing a large Ship sailing towards them, sent out a little Sloop to examine what she might be; this Sloop hailing of Davis, he told them he was an English Man of War, in Quest of Pyrates, and that he had received Intelligence there were some upon that Coast; upon this they received him as a welcome Guest, and piloted him into the Harbour. He saluted the Fort, which they answered, and he came to an Anchor just under their Guns, and hoisted out the Pinnace, Man of War Fashion, ordering nine Hands and a Coxen in it, to row him ashore.

The Portugueze, to do him the greater Honour, sent down a File of Musqueteers to receive him, and conduct him to the Governor. The Governor not in the least suspecting what he was, received him very civilly, promising to supply him with whatever the Island afforded; Davis thanked him, telling him, the King of England would pay for whatever he should take; so after several Civilities pass'd between him and the Governor, he returned again on Board.

It happened a French Ship came in there to supply it self with some Necessaries, which Davis took into his Head to plunder, but to give the Thing a Colour of Right, he persuaded the Portugueze, that she had been trading with the Pyrates, and that he found several Pyrates Goods on Board, which he seized for the King's Use: This Story passed so well upon the Governor, that he commended Davis's Diligence.

A few Days after, Davis, with about fourteen more, went privately ashore, and walk'd up the Country towards a Village, where the Governor and the other chief Men of the Island kept their Wives, in tending, as we may suppose, to supply their Husbands Places with them; but being discovered, the Women fled to a neighbouring Wood, and Davis and the rest retreated to their Ship, without effecting their Design: The Thing made some Noise, but as no body knew them, it passed over.

Having cleaned his Ship, and put all Things in Order, his Thoughts now were turned upon the main Business, viz. the Plunder of the Island, and not knowing where the Treasure lay, a Stratagem came into his Head, to get it (as he thought) with little Trouble, he consulted his Men upon it, and they liked the Design: His Scheme was, to make a Present to the Governor, of a Dozen Negroes, by Way of Return for the Civilities received from him, and afterwards to invite him, with the chief Men, and some of the Friers, on Board his Ship, to an Entertainment; the Minute they came on Board, they were to be secured in Irons, and there kept till they should pay a Ransom of 40000 l. Sterling.

But this Stratagem proved fatal to him, for a Portugueze Negroe swam ashore in the Night, and discovered the whole Plot to the Governor, and also let him know, that it was Davis who had made the Attempt upon their Wives. However, the Governor dissembled, received the Pyrates Invitation civilly, and promised that he and the rest would go.

The next Day Davis went on Shore himself, as if it were out of greater Respect to bring the

Governor on Board: He was received with the usual Civility, and he, and other principal Pyrates, who, by the Way, had assumed the Title of Lords, and as such took upon them to advise or councel their Captain upon any important Occasion; and likewise held certain Priviledges, which the common Pyrates were debarr'd from, as walking the Quarter-Deck, using the great Cabin, going ashore at Pleasure, and treating with foreign Powers, that is, with the Captains of Ships they made Prize of; I say, Davis and some of the Lords were desired to walk up to the Governor's House, to take some Refreshment before they went on Board; they accepted it without the least Suspicion, but never returned again; for an Ambuscade was laid, a Signal being given, a whole Volley was fired upon them; they every Man dropp'd, except one, this one fled back, and escaped into the Boat, and got on Board the Ship: Davis was shot through the Bowels, yet he rise again, and made a weak Effort to get away, but his Strength soon forsook him, and he dropp'd down dead; just as he fell, he perceived he was followed, and drawing out his Pistols, fired them at his Pursuers; Thus like a game Cock, giving a dying Blow, that he might not fall unrevenged.

Black Bart's Entry in A General History of the Pyrates

Bartholomew Roberts sailed in an honest Employ, from London aboard of the Princess, Captain Plumb Commander, of which Ship he was second Mate: He left England, November 1719, and arrived at Guiney about February following, and being at Anamaboe, taking in Slaves for the West-Indies, was taken in the said Ship by Captain Howel Davis, as mentioned in the preceeding Chapter. In the beginning he was very averse to this sort of Life, and would certainly have escaped from them, had a fair Opportunity presented it self; yet afterwards he changed his Principles, as many besides him have done upon another Element, and perhaps for the same Reason too, viz. Preferment,—and what he did not like as a private Man he could reconcile to his Conscience as a Commander.

Davis being cut off in the manner beforementioned, the Company found themselves under a Necessity of filling up his Post, for which there appear'd two or three Candidates among the select Part of them, that were distinguish'd by the Title of Lords, such were Sympson, Ashplant, Anstis, &c. and on canvassing this Matter, how shatter'd and weak a Condition their Government must be without a Head, since Davis had been remov'd, in the manner beforemention'd, my Lord Dennis propos'd, its said, over a Bowl to this Purpose.

That it was not of any great Signification who was dignify'd with Title; for really and in Truth, all good Governments had (like theirs) the supream Power lodged with the Community, who might doubtless depute and revoke as suited Interest or Humour. We are the Original of this Claim (says he) and should a Captain be so sawcy as to exceed Prescription at any time, why down with Him! it will be a Caution after he is dead to his Successors, of what fatal Consequence any sort of assuming may be. However, it is my Advice, that, while we are sober, we pitch upon a Man of Courage, and skill'd in Navigation, one, who by his Council and

Bravery seems best able to defend this Commonwealth, and ward us from the Dangers and Tempests of an instable Element, and the fatal Consequences of Anarchy; and such a one I take Roberts to be. A Fellow! I think, in all Respects, worthy your Esteem and Favour.

This Speech was loudly applauded by all but Lord Sympson, who had secret Expectations himself, but on this Disappointment, grew sullen, and left them, swearing, he did not care who they chose Captain, so it was not a Papist, for against them he had conceiv'd an irreconcileable Hatred, for that his Father had been a Sufferer in Monmouth's Rebellion.

Roberts was accordingly elected, tho' he had not been above six Weeks among them, the Choice was confirm'd both by the Lords and Commoners, and he accepted of the Honour, saying, That since he had dipp'd his Hands in muddy Water, and must be a Pyrate, it was better being a Commander than a common Man.

As soon as the Government was settled, by promoting other Officers in the room of those that were kill'd by the Portugueze, the Company resolv'd to revenge Captain Davis's Death, he being more than ordinarily respected by the Crew for his Affability and good Nature, as well as his Conduct and Bravery upon all Occasions; and pursuant to this Resolution, about 30 Men were landed in order to make an Attack upon the Fort, which must be ascended to by a steep Hill against the Mouth of the Cannon. These Men were headed by one Kennedy, a bold daring Fellow, but very wicked and profligate; they march'd directly up under the Fire of their Ship Guns, and as soon as they were discover'd, the Portugueze quitted their Post and fled to the Town, and the Pyrates march'd in without Opposition, set Fire to the Fort, and threw all the Guns off the Hill into the Sea, which after they had done, they retreated quietly to their Ship.

But this was not look'd upon as a sufficient Satisfaction for the Injury they received, therefore most of the Company were for burning the Town, which Roberts said he would yield to, if any Means could be proposed of doing it without their own Destruction, for the Town had a securer Scituation than the Fort, a thick Wood coming almost close to it, affording Cover to the Defendants, who under such an Advantage, he told them, it was to be fear'd, would fire and stand better to their Arms; besides, that bare Houses would be but a slender Reward for their Trouble and Loss. This prudent Advice prevailed; however, they mounted the French Ship, they seiz'd at this Place, with 12 Guns, and light'ned her, in order to come up to the Town, the Water being shoal, and battered down several Houses; after which they all returned on Board, gave back the French Ship to those that had most Right to her, and sailed out of the Harbour by the light of two Portuguese Ships, which they were pleased to set on Fire there.

Roberts stood away to the Southward, and met with a Dutch Guiney Man, which he made Prize of, but after having plundered her, the Skipper had his Ship again: Two Days after, he took an English Ship, called the Experiment, Captain Cornet, at Cape Lopez, the Men went all into the Pyrate Service, and having no Occasion for the Ship, they burnt her, and then steered for St. Thome, but meeting with nothing in their Way, they sailed for Annabona, and there water'd, took in Provisions, and put it to a Vote of the Company, whether their next Voyage should be, to the East-Indies, or to Brasil; the latter being resolved on, they sailed accordingly, and in 28 Days arrived at Ferdinando, an uninhabited Island, on that Coast: Here they water'd, boot-top'd their Ship, and made ready for the designed Cruise.

Now that we are upon this Coast, I think it will be the proper Place to present our Readers with a Description of this Country, and some ingenious Remarks of a Friend, how beneficial a Trade might be carried on here by our West-India Merchants, at a little Hazard.

BRASIL (a Name signifying the holy Cross) was discovered for the King of Portugal, by Alvarez Cabral, Ann. Dom. 1501. extending almost from the Æquinoctial to 28° South. The Air is temperate and cool, in comparison of the West-Indies, from stronger Breezes and an opener Country, which gives less Interruption to the Winds.

The northernmost Part of it stretching about 180 Leagues, (a fine fertile Country,) was taken from the Portuguese by the Dutch West-India Company, Anno. 1637 or thereabouts; but the Conquerors, as is natural where there is little or no Religion subsisting, made such heavy Exactions on the Portuguese, and extended such Cruelty to the Natives, that prepared them both easily to unite for a Revolt, facilitated by the Dutch Mismanagement: For the States being at this Time very intent on their India Settlements, not only recalled Count Morrice their Governor, but neglected Supplies to their Garrisons; however, tho' the others were countenanced with a Fleet from Portugal, and had the Affection of the Natives, yet they found Means to withstand and struggle with this superior Power, from 1643 to 1660, and then was wholly abandoned by them, on Articles dishonourable to the Portuguese, viz.

That the Dutch, on Relinquishing, should keep all the Places they had conquered in India from Portugal. That they should pay the States 800000 l. and permit them still the Liberty of Trade to Africa and Brasil, on the same Custom and Duties with the King of Portugal's Subjects. But since that Time, new Stipulations and Treaties have been made; wherein the Dutch, who have been totally excluded the Brasil Trade, have, in lieu thereof, a Composition of 10 per Cent. for the Liberty of trading to Africa; and this is always left by every Portuguese Ship (before she begins her Slaving) with the Dutch General of the Gold-Coast, at Des Minas.

There are only three principal Towns of Trade on the Brasil Coast, St. Salvadore, St. Sebastian, and Pernambuca.

St. Salvadore in the Bahia los todos Santos, is an Archbishoprick and Seat of the Viceroy, the chief Port of Trade for Importation, where most of the Gold from the Mines is lodged, and whence the Fleets for Europe generally depart. The Seas about it abound with Whale-Fish, which in the Season they catch in great Numbers; the Flesh is salted up generally to be the Victualling of their Slave-Ships, and the Train reserved for Exportation, at 30 and 35 Millrays a Pipe.

Rio Janeiro (the Town St. Sebastian) is the Southernmost of the Portuguese, the worst provided of Necessaries, but commodious for a Settlement, because nigh the Mine, and convenient to supervise the Slaves, who, as I have been told, do usually allow their Master a Dollar per Diem, and have the Overplus of their Work (if any) to themselves.

The Gold from hence is esteemed the best, (for being of a copperish Colour,) and they have a Mint to run it into Coin, both here and at Bahia; the Moidors of either having the initial Letters of each Place upon them.

Pernambuca (tho' mention'd last) is the second in Dignity, a large and populous Town, and has its rise from the Ruins of Olinda, (or the handsome,) a City of a far pleasanter Situation, six Miles up the River, but not so commodious for Traffick and Commerce. Just above the Town the River divides it self into two Branches, not running directly into the Sea, but to the Southward; and in the Nook of the Island made by that Division, stands the Governor's House, a square plain Building of Prince Maurice's, with two Towers, on which are only this Date inscribed, Anno 1641. The Avenues to it are every way pleasant, thro' Visto's of tall Coco-Nut Trees.

Over each Branch of the River is a Bridge; that leading to the Country is all of Timber, but the other to the Town (of twenty six or twenty eight Arches) is half of Stone, made by the Dutch, who in their Time had little Shops and gaming Houses on each Side for Recreation.

The Pavements also of the Town are in some Places of broad Tiles, the remaining Fragments of their Conquest. The Town has the outer Branch of the River behind it, and the Harbour before it, jetting into which latter are close Keys for the weighing and receiving of Customage on Merchandize, and for the meeting and conferring of Merchants and Traders. The Houses are strong built, but homely, letticed like those of Lisbon, for the Admission of Air, without Closets, and what is worse, Hearths; which makes their Cookery consist all in frying and stewing upon Stoves; and that they do till the Flesh become tender enough to shake it to Pieces, and one Knife is then thought sufficient to serve a Table of half a Score.

The greatest Inconvenience of Pernambuca is, that there is not one Publick-House in it; so that Strangers are obliged to hire any ordinary one they can get, at a Guinea a Month: And others who come to transact Affairs of Importance, must come recommended, if it were only for the sake of Privacy.

The Market is stocked well enough, Beef being at five Farthings per l. a Sheep or Goat at nine Shillings, a Turkey four Shillings, and Fowls two Shillings, the largest I ever saw, and may be procured much Cheaper, by hiring a Man to fetch them out of the Country. The dearest in its kind is Water, which being fetch'd in Vessels from Olinda, will not be put on Board in the Road under two Crusado's a Pipe.

The Portuguese here are darker than those of Europe, not only from a warmer Climate, but their many Intermarriages with the Negroes, who are numerous there, and some of them of good Credit and Circumstances. The Women (not unlike the Mulatto Generation every where else) are fond of Strangers; not only the Courtezans, whose Interest may be supposed to wind up their Affections, but also the marryed Women who think themselves obliged, when you favour them with the Secrecy of an Appointment; but the Unhappiness of pursuing Amours, is, that the generallity of both Sexes are touched with veneral Taints, without so much as one Surgeon among them, or any Body skilled in Physick, to cure or palliate the progressive Mischief: The only Person pretending that Way, is an Irish Father, whose Knowledge is all comprehended in the Virtues of two or three Simples, and those, with the Salubrity of the Air and Temperance, is what they depend on, for subduing the worst of Malignity; and it may not be unworthy Notice, that tho' few are exempted from the Misfortune of a Running, Eruptions, or the like, yet I could hear of none precipitated into those deplorable Circumstances we see common in unskillful mercurial Processes.

There are three Monasteries, and about six Churches, none of them Rich or Magnificent, unless one dedicated to St. Antonio, the Patron of their Kingdom, which shines all over with exquisite Pieces of Paint and Gold.

The Export of Brasil (besides Gold) is chiefly Sugars and Tobacco; the latter are sent off in Rowls of a Quintal Weight, kept continually moistened with Mulossus, which, with the Soil it springs from, imparts a strong and peculiar Scent, more sensible in the Snuff made from it, which tho' under Prohibition of importing to Lisbon, sells here at 2 s. per l. as the Tobacco does at about 6 Millraies a Rowl. The finest of their Sugars sells at 8 s. per Roove, and a small ill tasted Rum drawn from the Dregs and Mulossus, at two Testunes a Gallon.

Besides these, they send off great Quantities of Brasil Wood, and Whale Oyl, some Gums and Parrots, the latter are different from the African in Colour and Bigness, for as they are blue and larger, these are green and smaller; and the Females of them ever retain the wild Note, and cannot be brought to talk.

In lieu of this Produce, the Portugueze, once every Year by their Fleet from Lisbon, import all manner of European Commodities; and whoever is unable or negligent of supplying himself at that Season, buys at a very advanced Rate, before the Return of another.

To transport Passengers, Slaves, or Merchandize from one Settlement to another, or in Fishing; they make use of Bark-Logs, by the Brasilians called Jingadahs: They are made of four Pieces of Timber (the two outermost longest) pinned and fastened together, and sharpened at the Ends: Towards each Extremity a Stool is fixed to sit on for paddling, or holding by, when the Agitation is more than ordinary; with these odd sort of Engines, continually washed over by the Water, do these People, with a little triangular Sail spreeted about the Middle of it, venture out of Sight of Land, and along the Coasts for many Leagues, in any sort of Weather; and if they overset with a Squall (which is not uncommon) they swim and presently turn it up right again.

The Natives are of the darkest Copper Colour, with thin Hair, of a square strong make, and muscular; but not so well looking as the Wooley Generation: They acquiesce patiently to the Portugueze Government, who use them much more humanly and Christian-like than the Dutch did, and by that Means have extended Quietness and Peace, as well as their Possessions, three or four hundred Miles into the Country. A Country abounding with fine Pastures and numerous Herds of Cattle, and yields a vast Increase from every thing that is sown: Hence they bring down to us Parrots, small Monkies, Armadillos and Sanguins, and I have been assured, they have, (far In-land,) a Serpent of a vast Magnitude, called Siboya, able, they say, to swallow a whole Sheep; I have seen my self here the Skin of another Specie full six Yards long, and therefore think the Story not improbable.

The Harbour of Pernambuca is, perhaps, singular, it is made of a Ledge of Rocks, half a Cables length from the Main, and but little above the Surface of the Water, running at that equal Distance and Heighth several Leagues, towards Cape Augustine, a Harbour running between them capable of receiving Ships of the greatest Burthen: The Northermost End of this Wall of Rock, is higher than any Part of the contiguous Line, on which a little Fort is built, commanding the Passage either of Boat or Ship, as they come over the Bar into the Harbour: On the Starboard Side, (i. e. the Main) after you have entered a little way, stands another Fort (a Pentagon) that would prove of small Account, I imagine, against a few disciplined Men; and yet in these consists all their Strength and Security, either for the Harbour or Town: They have begun indeed a Wall, since their removing from Olinda, designed to surround the latter; but the slow Progress they make in raising it, leaves Room to suspect 'twill be a long time in finishing.

The Road without, is used by the Portugueze, when they are nigh sailing for Europe, and wait for the Convoy, or are bound to Bahia to them, and by Strangers only when Necessity compels; the best of it is in ten Fathom Water, near three Miles W. N. W. from the Town; nigher in, is foul with the many Anchors lost there by the Portugueze Ships; and farther out (in 14 Fathom) corally and Rocky. July is the worst and Winter Season of this Coast, the Trade Winds being then very strong and dead, bringing in a prodigious and unsafe Swell into the Road, intermixed every Day with Squalls, Rain, and a hazey Horizon, but at other times serener Skies and Sunshine.

In these Southern Latitudes is a Constellation, which from some Resemblance it bears to a Jerusalem Cross, has the Name of Crosiers, the brightest of this Hemisphere, and are observed by, as the North Star is in Northern Latitudes; but what I mention this for, is, to introduce the admirable Phænomenon in these Seas of the Megellanick Clouds, whose Risings and Sittings are so regular, that I have been assured, the same Nocturnal Observations are made by them as by the Stars; They are two Clouds, small and whitish, no larger in Appearance than a Man's Hat, and are seen here in July in the Latitude of 8° S. about four of the Clock in the Morning; if their Appearance should be said to be the Reflection of Light, from some Stellary Bodies above them, yet the Difficulty is not easily answered, how these, beyond others, become so durable and regular in their Motions.

From these casual Observations on the Country, the Towns, Coast, and Seas of Brasil, it would be an Omission to leave the Subject, without some Essay on an interloping Slave Trade here, which none of our Countrymen are adventurous enough to pursue, though it very probably, under a prudent Manager, would be attended with Safety and very great Profit; and I admire the more it is not struck at, because Ships from the Southern Coast of Africa, don't lengthen the Voyage to the West-Indies a great deal, by taking a Part of Brasil in their Way.

The Disadvantages the Portugueze are under for purchasing Slaves, are these, that they have very few proper Commodities for Guiney, and the Gold, which was their chiefest, by an Edict in July 1722, stands now prohibited from being carried thither, so that the Ships employed therein are few, and insufficient for the great Mortality and Call of their Mines; besides, should they venture at breaking so destructive a Law, as the abovementioned (as no doubt they do, or they could make little or no Purchace) yet Gold does not raise its Value like Merchandize in travelling (especially to Africa) and when the Composition with the Dutch is also paid, they may be said to buy their Negroes at almost double the Price the English, Dutch, or French do, which necessarily raises their Value extravagantly at Brasil; (those who can purchase one, buying a certainer Annuity than South-Sea Stock.)

Thus far of the Call for Slaves at Brasil; I shall now consider and obviate some Difficulties objected against any Foreigners (suppose English) interposing in such a Trade, and they are some on theirs, and some on our Side.

On their Side it is prohibited under Pain of Death, a Law less effectual to the Prevention of it than pecuniary Mulcts would be, because a Penalty so inadequate and disproportioned, is only In terrorem, and makes it merciful in the Governor, or his Instruments, to take a Composition of eight or ten Moidors, when any Subject is catched, and is the common Custom so to do as often as they are found out.

On our Side it is Confiscation of what they can get, which considering, they have no Men of War to guard the Coast, need be very little, without supine Neglect and Carelessness.

I am a Man of War, or Privateer, and being in Want of Provisions, or in Search of Pyrates, put in to Pernambuca for Intelligence, to enable me for the Pursuit: The Dread of Pyrates keeps every one off, till you have first sent an Officer, with the proper Compliments to the Governor, who immediately gives Leave for your buying every Necessary you are in want of, provided it be with Money, and not an Exchange of Merchandize, which is against the Laws of the Country.

On this first time of going on Shore, depends the success of the whole Affair, and requires a cautious and discreet Management in the Person entrusted: He will be immediately surrounded at landing with the great and the small Rabble, to enquire who? and whence he comes? and whether bound? &c. and the Men are taught to answer, from Guiney, denying any thing of a Slave on Board, which are under Hatches, and make no Shew; nor need they, for those who have Money to lay out will conclude on that themselves.

By that time the Compliment is paid to the Governor, the News has spread all round the Town, and some Merchant addresses you, as a Stranger, to the Civility of his House, but privately desires to know what Negroes he can have, and what Price. A Governor may possibly use an Instrument in sifting this, but the Appearance of the Gentleman, and the Circumstance of being so soon engaged after leaving the other, will go a great way in forming a Man's Judgment, and leaves him no room for the Suspicion of such a Snare; however, to have a due Guard, Intimations will suffice, and bring him, and Friends enough to carry off the best Part of a Cargo in two Nights time, from 20 to 30 Moidors a Boy, and from 30 to 40 a Man Slave. The Hazard is less at Rio Janeiro.

There has been another Method attempted, of settling a Correspondence with some Portugueze Merchant or two, who, as they may be certain within a Fortnight of any Vessels arriving on their Coast with Slaves, might settle Signals for the debarquing them at an unfrequented Part of the Coast, but whether any Exceptions were made to the Price, or that the Portuguese dread Discovery, and the severest Prosecution on so notorious a Breach of the Law, I cannot tell but it has hither to proved abortive.

However, Stratagems laudable, and attended with Profit, at no other Hazard (as I can perceive) then loss of Time, are worth attempting; it is what is every Day practised with the Spaniards from Jamaica.

Upon this Coast our Rovers cruiz'd for about nine Weeks, keeping generally out of Sight of Land, but without seeing a Sail, which discourag'd them so, that they determined to leave the Station, and steer for the West-Indies, and in order thereto, stood in to make the Land for the taking of their Departure, and thereby they fell in, unexpectedly, with a Fleet of 42 Sail of Portuguese Ships, off the Bay of los todos Santos, with all their Lading in for Lisbon, several of them of good Force, who lay too waiting for two Men of War of 70 Guns each, their Convoy. However, Roberts thought it should go hard with him, but he would make up his Market among them, and thereupon mix'd with the Fleet, and kept his Men hid till proper Resolutions could be form'd; that done, they came close up to one of the deepest, and ordered her to send the Master on Board quietly, threat'ning to give them no Quarters, if any Resistance, or Signal of Distress was made. The Portuguese being surprized at these Threats, and the sudden flourish of Cutlashes from the Pyrates, submitted without a Word, and the Captain came on Board; Roberts saluted him after a friendly manner, telling him, that they were Gentlemen of Fortune, but that their Business with him, was only to be informed which was the richest Ship in that Fleet; and if he directed them right, he should be restored to his Ship without Molestation, otherwise, he must expect immediate Death.

Whereupon this Portuguese Master pointed to one of 40 Guns, and 150 Men, a Ship of greater Force than the Rover, but this no Ways dismayed them, they were Portuguese, they said, and so immediately steered away for him. When they came within Hail, the Master whom they had Prisoner, was ordered to ask, how Seignior Capitain did? And to invite him on Board, for that he had a Matter of Consequence to impart to him, which being done, he returned for Answer, That he would wait upon him presently: But by the Bustle that immediately followed, the Pyrates perceived, they were discovered, and that this was only a deceitful Answer to gain Time to put their Ship in a Posture of Defence; so without further Delay, they poured in a Broad-Side, boarded and grapled her; the Dispute was short and warm, wherein many of the Portuguese fell, and two only of the Pyrates. By this Time the Fleet was alarmed, Signals of Top-gallant Sheets flying, and Guns fired, to give Notice to the Men of War, who rid still at an Anchor, and made but scurvy hast out to their Assistance; and if what the Pyrates themselves related, be true, the Commanders of those Ships were blameable to the highest Degree, and unworthy the Title, or so much as the Name of Men: For Roberts finding the Prize to sail heavy, and yet resolving not to loose her, lay by for the headmost of them (which much out sailed the other) and prepared for Battle, which was ignominiously declined, tho' of such superior Force; for not daring to venture on the Pyrate alone, he tarried so long for his Consort as gave them both time leisurely to make off.

They found this Ship exceeding rich, being laden chiefly with Sugar, Skins, and Tobacco, and in Gold 40000 Moidors, besides Chains and Trinckets, of considerable Value; particularly a Cross set with Diamonds, designed for the King of Portugal; which they afterwards presented to the Governor of Caiana, by whom they were obliged.

Elated with this Booty, they had nothing now to think of but some safe Retreat, where they might give themselves up to all the Pleasures that Luxury and Wantonness could bestow, and for the present pitch'd upon a Place called the Devil's Islands, in the River of Surinam, on the Coast of Caiana, where they arrived, and found the civilest Reception imaginable, not only from the Governor and Factory, but their Wives, who exchanged Wares and drove a considerable Trade with them.

They seiz'd in this River a Sloop, and by her gained Intelligence, that a Brigantine had also sailed in Company with her, from Rhode-Island, laden with Provisions for the Coast. A Welcome Cargo! They growing short in the Sea Store, and as Sancho says, No Adventures to be made without Belly-Timber. One Evening as they were rumaging (their Mine of Treasure) the Portuguese Prize, this expected Vessel was descry'd at Mast-Head, and Roberts, imagining no Body could do the Business so well as himself, takes 40 Men in the Sloop, and goes in pursuit of her; but a fatal Accident followed this rash, tho' inconsiderable Adventure, for Roberts thinking of nothing less than bringing in the Brigantine that Afternoon, never troubled his Head about the Sloop's Provision, nor inquired what there was on Board to subsist such a Number of Men; but out he sails after his expected Prize, which he not only lost further Sight of, but after eight Days contending with contrary Winds and Currents, found themselves thirty Leagues to Leeward. The Current still opposing their Endeavours, and perceiving no Hopes of beating up to their Ship, they came to an Anchor, and inconsiderately sent away the Boat to give the rest of the Company Notice of their Condition, and to order the Ship to them; but too soon, even the next Day, their Wants made them sensible of their Infatuation, for their Water was all expended, and they had taken no thought how they should be supply'd, till either the Ship came, or the Boat returned, which was not likely to be under five or six Days. Here like Tantalus, they almost famished in Sight of the fresh Streams and Lakes; being drove to such Extremity at last, that they were forc'd to tare up the Floor of the Cabin, and patch up a sort of Tub or Tray with Rope Yarns, to paddle ashore, and fetch off immediate Supplies of Water to preserve Life.

After some Days, the long-wish'd-for Boat came back, but with the most unwellcome News in the World, for Kennedy, who was Lieutenant, and left in Absence of Roberts, to Command the Privateer and Prize, was gone off with both. This was Mortification with a Vengeance, and you may imagine, they did not depart without some hard Speeches from those that were left, and had suffered by their Treachery: And that there need be no further mention of this Kennedy, I shall leave Captain Roberts, for a Page or two, with the Remains of his Crew, to vent their Wrath in a few Oaths and Execrations, and follow the other, whom we may reckon from that Time, as steering his Course towards Execution Dock.

Kennedy was now chosen Captain of the revolted Crew, but could not bring his Company to any determined Resolution; some of them were for pursuing the old Game, but the greater Part of them seem'd to have Inclinations to turn from those evil Courses, and get home privately, (for there was no Act of Pardon in Force,) therefore they agreed to break up, and every Man to shift for himself, as he should see Occasion. The first Thing they did, was to part with the great Portugueze Prize, and having the Master of the Sloop (whose Name I think was Cane) aboard, who they said was a very honest Fellow, (for he had humoured them upon every Occasion,) told them of the Brigantine that Roberts went after; and when the Pyrates first took him, he complemented them at an odd Rate, telling them they were welcome to his Sloop and Cargo, and wish'd that the Vessel had been larger, and the Loading richer for their Sakes: To this good natured Man they gave the Portugueze Ship, (which was then above half loaded,) three or four Negroes, and all his own Men, who returned Thanks to his kind Benefactors, and departed.

Captain Kennedy in the Rover, sailed to Barbadoes, near which Island, they took a very peaceable Ship belonging to Virginia; the Commander was a Quaker, whose Name was Knot; he had neither Pistol, Sword, nor Cutlash on Board; and Mr. Knot appearing so very passive to all they said to him, some of them thought this a good Opportunity to go off; and accordingly eight of the Pyrates went aboard, and he carried them safe to Virginia; They made the Quaker a Present of 10 Chests of Sugar, 10 Rolls of Brasil Tobacco, 30 Moidors, and some Gold-Dust, in all to the value of about 250 l. They also made Presents to the Sailors, some more, some less, and lived a jovial Life all the while they were upon their Voyage, Captain Knot giving them their

Way; nor indeed could he help himself, unless he had taken an Opportunity to surprize them, when they were either drunk or asleep; for awake they wore Arms aboard the Ship, and put him in a continual Terror; it not being his Principle (or the Sect's) to fight, unless with Art and Collusion; he managed these Weapons well till he arrived at the Capes, and afterwards four of the Pyrates went off in a Boat, which they had taken with them, for the more easily making their Escapes, and made up the Bay towards Maryland, but were forced back by a Storm into an obscure Place of the Country, where meeting with good Entertainment among the Planters, they continued several Days without being discovered to be Pyrates. In the mean Time Captain Knot leaving four others on Board his Ship, (who intended to go to North-Carolina,) made what hast he could to discover to Mr. Spotswood the Governor, what sort of Passengers he had been forced to bring with him, who by good Fortune got them seized; and Search being made after the others, who were revelling about the Country, they were also taken, and all try'd, convicted and hang'd, two Portuguese Jews who were taken on the Coast of Brasil, and whom they brought with them to Virginia, being the principal Evidences. The latter had found Means to lodge Part of their Wealth with the Planters, who never brought it to Account: But Captain Knot surrendered up every Thing that belonged to them, that were taken aboard, even what they presented to him, in lieu of such Things as they had plundered him of in their Passage, and obliged his Men to do the like.

Some Days after the taking of the Virginia Man last mentioned, in cruising in the Latitude of Jamaica, Kennedy took a Sloop bound thither from Boston, loaded with Bread and Flower; aboard of this Sloop went all the Hands who were for breaking the Gang, and left those behind that had a Mind to pursue further Adventures. Among the former were Kennedy, their Captain, of whose Honour they had such a dispicable Notion, that they were about to throw him overboard, when they found him in the Sloop, as fearing he might betray them all, at their return to England; he having in his Childhood been bred a Pick-pocket, and before he became a Pyrate, a House-breaker; both Professions that these Gentlemen have a very mean Opinion of. However, Captain Kennedy, by taking solemn Oaths of Fidelity to his Companions, was suffered to proceed with them.

In this Company there was but one that pretended to any skill in Navigation, (for Kennedy could neither write nor read, he being preferred to the Command merely for his Courage, which indeed he had often signaliz'd, particularly in taking the Portuguese Ship,) and he proved to be a Pretender only; for shaping their Course to Ireland, where they agreed to land, they ran away to the North-West Coast of Scotland, and there were tost about by hard Storms of Wind for several Days, without knowing where they were, and in great Danger of perishing: At length they pushed the Vessel into a little Creek, and went all ashore, leaving the Sloop at an Anchor for the next Comers.

The whole Company refresh'd themselves at a little Village about five Miles from the Place where they left the Sloop, and passed there for Ship-wreck'd Sailors, and no doubt might have travelled on without Suspicion; but the mad and riotous Manner of their Living on the Road, occasion'd their Journey to be cut short, as we shall observe presently.

Kennedy and another left them here, and travelling to one of the Sea-Ports, ship'd themselves for Ireland, and arrived there in Safety. Six or seven wisely withdrew from the rest, travelled at their leasure, and got to their much desired Port of London, without being disturbed or suspected; but the main Gang alarm'd the Country where-ever they came, drinking and roaring at such a Rate, that the People shut themselves up in their Houses, in some Places, not daring to venture out among so many mad Fellows: In other Villages, they treated the whole Town, squandering their Money away, as if, like Æsop, they wanted to lighten their Burthens: This expensive manner of Living procured two of their drunken Stragglers to be knocked on the Head, they being found murdered in the Road, and their Money taken from them: All the rest, to the Number of seventeen as they drew nigh to Edinburgh, were arrested and thrown into Goal, upon Suspicion, of they knew not what; However, the Magistrates were not long at a Loss for proper Accusations, for two of the Gang offering themselves for Evidences were accepted of; and the others were brought to a speedy Tryal, whereof nine were convicted and executed.

Kennedy having spent all his Money, came over from Ireland, and kept a common B—y-House on Deptford Road, and now and then, 'twas thought, made an Excursion abroad in the Way of his former Profession, till one of his Houshold W—s gave Information against him for a Robbery, for which he was committed to Bridewell; but because she would not do the Business by halves, she found out a Mate of a Ship that Kennedy had committed Pyracy upon, as he foolishly confess'd to her. This Mate, whose Name was Grant, paid Kennedy a Visit in Bridewell, and knowing him to be the Man, procured a Warrant, and had him committed to the Marshalsea Prison.

The Game that Kennedy had now to play was to turn Evidence himself; accordingly he gave a List of eight or ten of his Comrades; but not being acquainted with their Habitations, one only was taken, who, tho' condemn'd, appeared to be a Man of a fair Character, was forc'd into their Service, and took the first Opportunity to get from them, and therefore receiv'd a Pardon; but Walter Kennedy being a notorious Offender, was executed the 19th of July, 1721, at Execution Dock.

The rest of the Pyrates who were left in the Ship Rover, staid not long behind, for they went ashore to one of the West-India Islands; what became of them afterwards, I can't tell, but the Ship was found at Sea by a Sloop belonging to St. Christophers, and carried into that Island with only nine Negroes aboard.

Thus we see what a disastrous Fate ever attends the Wicked, and how rarely they escape the Punishment due to their Crimes, who, abandon'd to such a profligate Life, rob, spoil, and prey upon Mankind, contrary to the Light and Law of Nature, as well as the Law of God. It might have been hoped, that the Examples of these Deaths, would have been as Marks to the

Remainder of this Gang, how to shun the Rocks their Companions had split on; that they would have surrendered to Mercy, or divided themselves, for ever from such Pursuits, as in the End they might be sure would subject them to the same Law and Punishment, which they must be conscious they now equally deserved; impending Law, which never let them sleep well, unless when drunk. But all the Use that was made of it here, was to commend the Justice of the Court, that condemn'd Kennedy, for he was a sad Dog (they said) and deserved the Fate he met with.

But to go back to Roberts, whom we left on the Coast of Caiana, in a grievous Passion at what Kennedy and the Crew had done; and who was now projecting new Adventures with his small Company in the Sloop; but finding hitherto they had been but as a Rope of Sand, they formed a Set of Articles, to be signed and sworn to, for the better Conservation of their Society, and doing Justice to one another; excluding all Irish Men from the Benefit of it, to whom they had an implacable Aversion upon the Account of Kennedy. How indeed Roberts could think that an Oath would be obligatory, where Defiance had been given to the Laws of God and Man, I can't tell, but he thought their greatest Security lay in this, That it was every one's Interest to observe them if they were minded to keep up so abominable a Combination.

The following, is the Substance of the Articles, as taken from the Pyrates own Informations.

I.

Every Man has a Vote in Affairs of Moment; has equal Title to the fresh Provisions, or strong Liquors, at any Time seized, and use them at pleasure, unless a Scarcity (no uncommon Thing among them) make it necessary, for the good of all, to vote a Retrenchment.

II.

Every Man to be called fairly in turn, by List, on Board of Prizes, because, (over and above their proper Share,) they were on these Occasions allowed a Shift of Cloaths: But if they defrauded the Company to the Value of a Dollar, in Plate, Jewels, or Money, MAROONING was their Punishment. This was a Barbarous Custom of putting the Offender on Shore, on some desolate or uninhabited Cape or Island, with a Gun, a few Shot, a Bottle of Water, and a Bottle of Powder, to subsist with, or starve. If the Robbery was only between one another, they contented themselves with slitting the Ears and Nose of him that was Guilty, and set him on Shore, not in an uninhabited Place, but somewhere, where he was sure to encounter Hardships.

III.

No Person to Game at Cards or Dice for Money.

IV.

The Lights and Candles to be put out at eight o'Clock at Night: If any of the Crew, after that

Hour, still remained inclined for Drinking, they were to do it on the open Deck; which Roberts believed would give a Check to their Debauches, for he was a sober Man himself, but found at length, that all his Endeavours to put an End to this Debauch, proved ineffectual.

V.

To keep their Piece, Pistols, and Cutlash clean, and fit for Service: In this they were extravagantly nice, endeavouring to outdo one another, in the Beauty and Richness of their Arms, giving sometimes at an Auction (at the Mast,) 30 or 40 l. a Pair, for Pistols. These were slung in Time of Service, with different coloured Ribbands, over their Shoulders, in a Way peculiar to these Fellows, in which they took great Delight.

VI.

No Boy or Woman to be allowed amongst them. If any Man were sound seducing anny of the latter Sex, and carried her to Sea, disguised, he was to suffer Death; so that when any fell into their Hands, as it chanced in the Onslow, they put a Centinel immediately over her to prevent ill Consequences from so dangerous an Instrument of Division and Quarrel; but then here lies the Roguery; they contend who shall be Centinel, which happens generally to one of the greatest Bullies, who, to secure the Lady's Virtue, will let none lye with her but himself.

VII.

To Desert the Ship, or their Quarters in Battle, was punished with Death, or Marooning.

VIII.

No striking one another on Board, but every Man's Quarrels to be ended on Shore, at Sword and Pistol, Thus; The Quarter-Master of the Ship, when the Parties will not come to any Reconciliation, accompanies them on Shore with what Assistance he thinks proper, and turns the Disputants Back to Back, at so many Paces Distance: At the Word of Command, they turn and fire immediately, (or else the Piece is knocked out of their Hands:) If both miss, they come to their Cutlashes, and then he is declared Victor who draws the first Blood.

IX.

No Man to talk of breaking up their Way of Living, till each had shared a 1000 l. If in order to this, any Man should lose a Limb, or become a Cripple in their Service, he was to have 800 Dollars, out of the publick Stock, and for lesser Hurts, proportionably.

X.

The Captain and Quarter-Master to receive two Shares of a Prize; the Master, Boatswain, and

Gunner, one Share and a half, and other Officers, one and a Quarter.

XI.

The Musicians to have Rest on the Sabbath Day, but the other six Days and Nights, none without special Favour.

These, we are assured, were some of Roberts's Articles, but as they had taken Care to throw over-board the Original they had sign'd and sworn to, there is a great deal of Room to suspect, the remainder contained something too horrid to be disclosed to any, except such as were willing to be Sharers in the Iniquity of them; let them be what they will, they were together the Test of all new Comers, who were initiated by an Oath taken on a Bible, reserv'd for that Purpose only, and were subscrib'd to in Presence of the worshipful Mr. Roberts. And in Case any Doubt should arise concerning the Construction of these Laws, and it should remain a Dispute whether the Party had infring'd them or no, a Jury is appointed to explain them, and bring in a Verdict upon the Case in Doubt.

Since we are now speaking of the Laws of this Company, I shall go on, and, in as brief a Manner as I can, relate the principal Customs, and Government, of this roguish Common-Wealth; which are pretty near the same with all Pyrates.

For the Punishment of small Offences, which are not provided for by the Articles, and which are not of Consequence enough to be left to a Jury, there is a principal Officer among the Pyrates, called the Quarter-Master, of the Mens own chusing, who claims all Authority this Way, (excepting in Time of Battle:) If they disobey his Command, are quarrelsome and mutinous with one another, misuse Prisoners, plunder beyond his Order, and in particular, if they be negligent of their Arms, which he musters at Discretion, he punishes at his own Arbitrement, with drubbing or whipping, which no one else dare do without incurring the Lash from all the Ships Company: In short, this Officer is Trustee for the whole, is the first on Board any Prize, separating for the Company's Use, what he pleases, and returning what he thinks fit to the Owners, excepting Gold and Silver, which they have voted not returnable.

After a Description of the Quarter-Master, and his Duty, who acts as a sort of a civil Magistrate on Board a Pyrate Ship; I shall consider their military Officer, the Captain; what Privileges he exerts in such anarchy and unrulyness of the Members: Why truly very little, they only permit him to be Captain, on Condition, that they may be Captain over him; they separate to his Use the great Cabin, and sometimes vote him small Parcels of Plate and China, (for it may be noted that Roberts drank his Tea constantly) but then every Man, as the Humour takes him, will use the Plate and China, intrude into his Apartment, swear at him, seize a Part of his Victuals and Drink, if they like it, without his offering to find Fault or contest it: Yet Roberts, by a better Management than usual, became the chief Director in every Thing of Moment, and it happened thus:—The Rank of Captain being obtained by the Suffrage of the Majority, it falls on one superior for Knowledge and Boldness, Pistol Proof (as they call it,) and can make those fear, who do not love him; Roberts is said to have exceeded his Fellows in these Respects, and when advanced, enlarged the Respect that followed it, by making a sort of Privy-Council of half a Dozen of the greatest Bullies; such as were his Competitors, and had Interest enough to make his Government easy; yet even those, in the latter Part of his Reign, he had run counter to in every Project that opposed his own Opinion; for which, and because he grew reserved, and would not drink and roar at their Rate, a Cabal was formed to take away his Captainship, which Death did more effectually.

The Captain's Power is uncontroulable in Chace, or in Battle, drubbing, cutting, or even shooting any one who dares deny his Command. The same Privilege he takes over Prisoners, who receive good or ill Usage, mostly as he approves of their Behaviour, for tho' the meanest would take upon them to misuse a Master of a Ship, yet he would controul herein, when he see it, and merrily over a Bottle, give his Prisoners this double Reason for it. First, That it preserved his Precedence; and secondly, That it took the Punishment out of the Hands of a much more rash and mad Sett of Fellows than himself. When he found that Rigour was not expected from his People, (for he often practised it to appease them,) then he would give Strangers to understand, that it was pure Inclination that induced him to a good Treatment of them, and not any Love or Partiality to their Persons; for, says he, there is none of you but will hang me, I know, whenever you can clinch me within your Power.

And now seeing the Disadvantages they were under for pursuing the Account, viz. a small Vessel ill repaired, and without Provisions, or Stores; they resolved one and all, with the little Supplies they could get, to proceed for the West-Indies, not doubting to find a Remedy for all these Evils, and to retreive their Loss.

In the Latitude of Deseada, one of the Islands, they took two Sloops, which supply'd them with Provisions and other Necessaries; and a few Days afterwards, took a Brigantine belonging to Rhode Island, and then proceeded to Barbadoes, off of which Island, they fell in with a Bristol Ship of 10 Guns, in her Voyage out, from whom they took abundance of Cloaths, some Money, twenty five Bales of Goods, five Barrels of Powder, a Cable, Hawser, 10 Casks of Oatmeal, six Casks of Beef, and several other Goods, besides five of their Men; and after they had detained her three Days, let her go; who being bound for the abovesaid Island, she acquainted the Governor with what had happened, as soon as she arrived.

Whereupon a Bristol Galley that lay in the Harbour, was ordered to be fitted out with all imaginable Expedition, of 20 Guns, and 80 Men, there being then no Man of War upon that Station, and also a Sloop with 10 Guns, and 40 Men: The Galley was commanded by one Captain Rogers, of Bristol, and the Sloop by Captain Graves, of that Island, and Captain Rogers by a Commission from the Governor, was appointed Commadore.

The second Day after Rogers sailed out of the Harbour, he was discovered by Roberts, who knowing nothing of their Design, gave them Chase: The Barbadoes Ships kept an easy sail till the Pyrates came up with them, and then Roberts gave them a Gun, expecting they would have immediately struck to his pyratical Flag, but instead thereof, he was forced to receive the Fire of a Broadside, with three Huzzas at the same Time; so that an Engagement ensued, but Roberts being hardly put to it, was obliged to crowd all the Sail the Sloop would bear, to get off: The Galley sailing pretty well, kept Company for a long while, keeping a constant Fire, which gail'd the Pyrate; however, at length by throwing over their Guns, and other heavy Goods, and thereby light'ning the Vessel, they, with much ado, got clear; but Roberts could never endure a Barbadoes Man afterwards, and when any Ships belonging to that Island fell in his Way, he was more particularly severe to them than others.

Captain Roberts sailed in the Sloop to the Island of Dominico, where he watered, and got Provisions of the Inhabitants, to whom he gave Goods in Exchange. At this Place he met with 13 Englishmen, who had been set ashore by a French Guard de la Coste, belonging to Martinico, taken out of two New-England Ships, that had been seiz'd, as Prize, by the said French Sloop: The Men willingly entered with the Pyrates, and it proved a seasonable Recruit.

They staid not long here, tho' they had immediate Occasion for cleaning their Sloop, but did not think this a proper Place, and herein they judg'd right; for the touching at this Island, had like to have been their Destruction, because they having resolved to go away to the Granada Islands, for the aforesaid Purpose, by some Accident it came to be known to the French Colony, who sending Word to the Governor of Martinico, he equipped and manned two Sloops to go in Quest of them. The Pyrates sailed directly for the Granadilloes, and hall'd into a Lagoon, at Corvocoo, where they cleaned with unusual Dispatch, staying but a little above a Week, by which Expedition they missed of the Martinico Sloops, only a few Hours; Roberts sailing over Night, that the French arrived the next Morning. This was a fortunate Escape, especially considering, that it was not from any Fears of their being discovered, that they made so much hast from the Island; but, as they had the Impudence themselves to own, for the want of Wine and Women.

Thus narrowly escaped, they sailed for Newfoundland, and arrived upon the Banks the latter end of June, 1720. They entered the Harbour of Trepassi, with their black Colours flying, Drums beating, and Trumpets sounding. There were two and twenty Vessels in the Harbour, which the Men all quitted upon the Sight of the Pyrate, and fled ashore. It is impossible particularly to recount the Destruction and Havock they made here, burning and sinking all the shipping, except a Bristol Galley, and destroying the Fisheries, and Stages of the poor Planters, without Remorse or Compunction; for nothing is so deplorable as Power in mean and ignorant Hands, it makes Men wanton and giddy, unconcerned at the Misfortunes they are imposing on their Fellow Creatures, and keeps them smiling at the Mischiefs, that bring themselves no Advantage. They are like mad Men, that cast Fire-Brands, Arrows, and Death, and say, are not we in Sport?

Roberts mann'd the Bristol Galley he took in the Harbour, and mounted 16 Guns on Board her, and cruising out upon the Banks, he met with nine or ten Sail of French Ships, all which he destroyed except one of 26 Guns, which they seiz'd, and carried off for their own Use. This Ship they christ'ned the Fortune, and leaving the Bristol Galley to the French Men, they sailed away in Company with the Sloop, on another Cruise, and took several Prizes, viz. the Richard of Biddiford, Jonathan Whitfield Master; the Willing Mind of Pool; the Expectation of Topsham; and the Samuel, Captain Cary, of London; out of these Ships they encreased their Company, by entring all the Men they could well spare, in their own Service. The Samuel was a rich Ship, and had several Passengers on Board, who were used very roughly, in order to make them discover their Money, threatning them every Moment with Death, if they did not resign every Thing up to them. They tore up the Hatches and entered the Hold like a parcel of Furies, and with Axes and Cutlashes, cut and broke open all the Bales, Cases, and Boxes, they could lay their Hands on; and when any Goods came upon Deck, that they did not like to carry aboard, instead of tossing them into the Hold again, threw them over-board into the Sea; all this was done with incessant cursing and swearing, more like Fiends than Men. They carried with them, Sails, Guns, Powder, Cordage, and 8 or 9000 l. worth of the choicest Goods; and told Captain Cary, That they should accept of no Act of Grace; that the K— and P—t might be damned with their Acts of G— for them; neither would they go to Hope-Point, to be hang'd up a Sun drying, as Kidd's, and Braddish's Company were; but that if they should ever be overpower'd, they would set Fire to the Powder, with a Pistol, and go all merrily to Hell together.

After they had brought all the Booty aboard, a Consultation was held whether they should sink or burn the Ship, but whilst they were debating the Matter, they spyed a Sail, and so left the Samuel, to give her Chace; at Midnight they came up with the same, which proved to be a Snow from Bristol, bound for Boston, Captain Bowles Master: They us'd him barbarously, because of his Country, Captain Rogers, who attack'd them off Barbadoes, being of the City of Bristol.

July the 16th, which was two Days afterwards, they took a Virginia Man called the Little York, James Philips Master, and the Love, of Leverpool, which they plundered and let go; the next Day a Snow from Bristol, call'd the Phoenix, John Richards Master, met with the same Fate from them; as also a Brigantine, Captain Thomas, and a Sloop called the Sadbury; they took all the Men out of the Brigantine, and sunk the Vessel.

When they left the Banks of Newfoundland, they sailed for the West-Indies, and the Provisions growing short, they went for the Latitude of the Island Deseada, to cruise, it being esteemed the likeliest Place to meet with such Ships as (they used in their Mirth to say) were consigned to them, with Supplies. And it has been very much suspected that Ships have loaded with Provisions at the English Colonies, on pretence of Trading on the Coast of Africa, when they have in reality been consigned to them; and tho' a shew of Violence is offered to them when they meet, yet they are pretty sure of bringing their Cargo to a good Market.

However, at this Time they missed with their usual Luck, and Provisions and Necessaries becoming more scarce every Day, they retired towards St. Christophers, where being deny'd all Succour or Assistance from the Government, they fir'd in Revenge on the Town, and burnt two Ships in the Road, one of them commanded by Captain Cox, of Bristol; and then retreated farther to the Island of St. Bartholomew, where they met with much handsomer Treatment. The Governor not only supplying them with Refreshments, but he and the Chiefs carressing them in the most friendly Manner: And the Women, from so good an Example, endeavoured to outvie each other in Dress, and Behaviour, to attract the good Graces of such generous Lovers, that paid well for their Favours.

Sated at length with these Pleasures, and having taken on Board a good supply of fresh Provisions, they voted unanimously for the Coast of Guiney, and in the Latitude of 22 N. in their Voyage thither, met with a French Ship from Martinico, richly laden, and, which was unlucky for the Master, had a property of being fitter for their Purpose, than the Banker. Exchange was no Robbery they said, and so after a little mock Complaisance to Monsieur, for the Favour he had done them, they shifted their Men, and took leave: This was their first Royal Fortune.

In this Ship Roberts proceeded on his designed Voyage; but before they reached Guiney, he proposed to touch at Brava, the Southermost of Cape Verd Islands and clean. But here again by an intolerable Stupidity and want of Judgment, they got so far to Leeward of their Port, that despairing to regain it, or any of the Windward Parts of Africa, they were obliged to go back again with the Trade-Wind, for the West-Indies; which had very near been the Destruction of them all. Surinam was the Place now designed for, which was at no less than 700 Leagues Distance, and they had but one Hogshead of Water left to supply 124 Souls for that Passage; a sad Circumstance that eminently exposes the Folly and Madness among Pyrates, and he must be an inconsiderate Wretch indeed, who, if he could separate the Wickedness and Punishment from the Fact, would yet hazard his Life amidst such Dangers, as their want of Skill and Forecast made them liable to.

Their Sins, we may presume were never so troublesome to their Memories, as now, that inevitable Destruction seem'd to threaten them, without the least Glympse of Comfort or Alleviation to their Misery; for, with what Face could Wretches who had ravaged and made so many Necessitous, look up for Relief; they had to that Moment lived in Defiance of the Power that now alone they must trust for their Preservation, and indeed without the miraculous Intervention of Providence, there appeared only this miserable Choice, viz. a present Death by their own Hands, or a ling'ring one by Famine.

They continued their Course, and came to an Allowance of one single Mouthful of Water for 24 Hours; many of them drank their Urine, or Sea Water, which, instead of allaying, gave them an inextinguishable Thirst, that killed them: Others pined and wasted a little more Time in Fluxes and Apyrexies, so that they dropped away daily. Those that sustain'd the Misery best, were such as almost starved themselves, forbearing all sorts of Food, unless a Mouthful or two of Bread the whole Day, so that those who survived were as weak as it was possible for Men to be and alive.

But if the dismal Prospect they set out with, gave them Anxiety, Trouble, or Pain, what must their Fears and Apprehensions be, when they had not one Drop of Water left, or any other Liquor to moisten or animate. This was their Case, when (by the working of Divine Providence, no doubt,) they were brought into Soundings, and at Night anchored in seven Fathom Water: This was an inexpressible Joy to them, and, as it were, fed the expiring Lamp of Life with fresh Spirits; but this could not hold long. When the Morning came, they saw Land from the Mast-Head, but it was at so great a Distance, that it afforded but an indifferent Prospect to Men who had drank nothing for the two last Days; however, they dispatch'd their Boat away, and late the same Night it return'd, to their no small Comfort, with a load of Water, informing them, that they had got off the Mouth of Meriwinga River on the Coast of Surinam.

One would have thought so miraculous an Escape should have wrought some Reformation, but alass, they had no sooner quenched their Thirst, but they had forgot the Miracle, till Scarcity of Provisions awakened their Senses, and bid them guard against starving; their allowance was very small, and yet they would profanely say, That Providence which had gave them Drink, would, no doubt, bring them Meat also, if they would use but an honest Endeavour.

In pursuance of these honest Endeavours, they were steering for the Latitude of Barbadoes, with what little they had left, to look out for more, or Starve; and, in their Way, met a Ship that answered their Necessities, and after that a Brigantine; the former was called the Greyhound, belonging to St. Christophers, and bound to Philadelphia, the Mate of which signed the Pyrate's Articles, and was afterwards Captain of the Ranger, Consort to the Royal Fortune.

Out of the Ship and Brigantine, the Pyrates got a good supply of Provisions and Liquor, so that they gave over the designed Cruise, and watered at Tobago, and hearing of the two Sloops that had been fitted out and sent after them at Corvocoo, they sailed to the Island of Martinico, to make the Governor some sort of an Equivalent, for the Care and Expedition he had shewn in that Affair.

It is the Custom at Martinico, for the Dutch Interlopers that have a Mind to Trade with the People of the Island, to hoist their Jacks when they come before the Town: Roberts knew the Signal, and being an utter Enemy to them, he bent his Thoughts upon Mischief; and accordingly came in with his Jack flying, which, as he expected, they mistook for a good Market, and thought themselves happiest that could soonest dispatch off their Sloops and Vessels for Trade. When Roberts had got them within his Power, (one after another,) he told them, he would not have it said that they came off for nothing, and therefore ordered them to leave their Money behind, for that they were a Parcel of Rogues, and hoped they would always meet with such a Dutch Trade as this was; he reserved one Vessel to set the Passengers on Shore again, and fired the rest, to the Number of twenty.

Roberts was so enraged at the Attempts that had been made for taking of him, by the Governors of Barbados and Martinico, that he ordered a new Jack to be made, which they ever after hoisted, with his own Figure pourtray'd, standing upon two Skulls, and under them the Letters A B H and A M H, signifying a Barbadian's and a Martinican's Head, as may be seen in the Plate of Captain Roberts.

At Dominico, the next Island they touched at, they took a Dutch Interloper of 22 Guns and 75 Men, and a Brigantine belonging to Rhode-Island, one Norton Master. The former made some Defence, till some of his Men being killed, the rest were discouraged and struck their Colours. With these two Prizes they went down to Guadalupe, and brought out a Sloop, and a French Fly-Boat laden with Sugar; the Sloop they burnt, and went on to Moonay, another Island, thinking to clean, but finding the Sea ran too high there to undertake it with Safety, they bent their Course for the North Part of Hispaniola, where, at Bennet's Key, in the Gulf of Saminah, they cleaned both the Ship and the Brigantine. For tho' Hispaniola be settled by the Spaniards and French, and is the Residence of a President from Spain, who receives, and finally determines Appeals from all the other Spanish West-India Islands; yet is its People by no Means proportioned to its Magnitude, so that there are many Harbours in it, to which Pyrates may securely resort without Fear of Discovery from the Inhabitants.

Whilst they were here, two Sloops came in, as they pretended, to pay Roberts a Visit, the Masters, whose Names were Porter and Tuckerman, addressed the Pyrate, as the Queen of Sheba did Solomon, to wit, That having heard of his Fame and Atchievements, they had put in there to learn his Art and Wisdom in the Business of pyrating, being Vessels on the same honourable Design with himself; and hoped with the Communication of his Knowledge, they should also receive his Charity, being in want of Necessaries for such Adventures. Roberts was won upon by the Peculiarity and Bluntness of these two Men, and gave them Powder, Arms, and what ever else they had Occasion for, spent two or three merry Nights with them, and at parting, said, he hoped the L— would Prosper their handy Works.

They passed some Time here, after they had got their Vessel ready, in their usual Debaucheries; they had taken a considerable Quanty of Rum and Sugar, so that Liquor was as plenty as Water, and few there were, who denied themselves the immoderate Use of it; nay, Sobriety brought a Man under a Suspicion of being in a Plot against the Commonwealth, and in their Sense, he was looked upon to be a Villain that would not be drunk. This was evident in the Affair of Harry Glasby, chosen Master of the Royal Fortune, who, with two others, laid hold of the Opportunity at the last Island they were at, to move off without bidding Farewel to his Friends. Glasby was a reserved sober Man, and therefore gave Occasion to be suspected, so that he was soon missed after he went away; and a Detachment being sent in quest of the Deserters, they were all three brought back again the next Day. This was a capital Offence, and for which they were ordered to be brought to an immediate Tryal.

Here was the Form of Justice kept up, which is as much as can be said of several other Courts, that have more lawful Commissions for what they do.—Here was no feeing of Council, and bribing of Witnesses was a Custom not known among them; no packing of Juries, no torturing and wresting the Sense of the Law, for bye Ends and Purposes, no puzzling or perplexing the Cause with unintelligible canting Terms, and useless Distinctions; nor was their Sessions burthened with numberless Officers, the Ministers of Rapine and Extortion, with ill boding Aspects, enough to fright Astræa from the Court. The Place appointed for their Tryals, was the Steerage of the Ship; in order to which, a large Bowl of Rum Punch was made, and placed upon the Table, the Pipes and Tobacco being ready, the judicial Proceedings began; the Prisoners were brought forth, and Articles of Indictment against them read; they were arraigned upon a Statute of their own making, and the Letter of the Law being strong against them, and the Fact plainly proved, they were about to pronounce Sentence, when one of the Judges mov'd, that they should first Smoak t'other Pipe; which was accordingly done.

All the Prisoners pleaded for Arrest of Judgment very movingly, but the Court had such an Abhorrence of their Crime, that they could not be prevailed upon to shew Mercy, till one of the Judges, whose Name was Valentine Ashplant, stood up, and taking his Pipe out of his Mouth, said, he had something to offer to the Court in behalf of one of the Prisoners; and spoke to this Effect.— By G—, Glasby shall not dye; d—n me if he shall. After this learned Speech, he sat down in his Place, and resumed his Pipe. This Motion was loudly opposed by all the rest of the Judges, in equivalent Terms; but Ashplant, who was resolute in his Opinion, made another pathetical Speech in the following Manner. G— d—n ye Gentlemen, I am as good a Man as the best of you; d—m my S—l if ever I turned my Back to any Man in my Life, or ever will, by G—; Glasby is an honest Fellow, notwithstanding this Misfortune, and I love him, D—l d—n me if I don't: I hope he'll live and repent of what he has done; but d—n me if he must dye, I will dye along with him. And thereupon, he pulled out a pair of Pistols, and presented them to some of the learned Judges upon the Bench; who, perceiving his Argument so well supported, thought it reasonable that Glasby should be acquitted; and so they all came over to his Opinion, and allowed it to be Law.

But all the Mitigation that could be obtained for the other Prisoners, was, that they should have the Liberty of choosing any four of the whole Company to be their Executioners. The poor Wretches were ty'd immediately to the Mast, and there shot dead, pursuant to their villainous Sentence.

When they put to Sea again, the Prizes which had been detained only for fear of spreading any Rumour concerning them, which had like to have been so fatal at Corvocoo, were thus disposed of: They burnt their own Sloop, and mann'd Norton's Brigantine, sending the Master away in the Dutch Interloper, not dissatisfied.

With the Royal Fortune, and the Brigantine, which they christened the Good Fortune, they pushed towards the Latitude of Deseada, to look out for Provisions, being very short again, and just to their Wish, Captain Hingstone's ill Fortune brought him in their Way, richly laden for Jamaica; him they carried to Berbudas and plundered; and stretching back again to the West-Indies, they continually met with some Consignment or other, (chiefly French,) which stored them with Plenty of Provisions, and recruited their starving Condition; so that stocked with this sort of Ammunition, they began to think of something worthier their Aim, for these Robberies that only supplied what was in constant Expenditure, by no Means answered their Intentions; and accordingly they proceeded again for the Coast of Guiney, where they thought to buy Gold-Dust very cheap. In their Passage thither, they took Numbers of Ships of all Nations, some of which they burnt or sunk, as the Carriage or Characters of the Masters displeased them.

Notwithstanding the successful Adventures of this Crew, yet it was with great Difficulty they could be kept together, under any kind of Regulation; for being almost always mad or drunk, their Behaviour produced infinite Disorders, every Man being in his own Imagination a Captain, a Prince, or a King. When Roberts saw there was no managing of such a Company of wild ungovernable Brutes, by gentle means, nor to keep them from drinking to excess, the Cause of all their Disturbances, he put on a rougher Deportment, and a more magesterial Carriage towards them, correcting whom he thought fit; and if any seemed to resent his Usage, he told them, they might go ashore and take Satisfaction of him, if they thought fit, at Sword and Pistol, for he neither valu'd or fear'd any of them.

About 400 Leagues from the Coast of Africa, the Brigantine who had hitherto lived with them, in all amicable Correspondence, thought fit to take the Opportunity of a dark Night, and leave the Commadore, which leads me back to the Relation of an Accident that happened at one of the Islands of the West-Indies, where they water'd before they undertook this Voyage, which had like to have thrown their Government (such as it was) off the Hinges, and was partly the Occasion of the Separation: The Story is as follows.

Captain Roberts having been insulted by one of the drunken Crew, (whose Name I have forgot,) he, in the Heat of his Passion killed the Fellow on the Spot, which was resented by a great many others, put particularly one Jones, a brisk active young Man, who died lately in the Marshalsea, and was his Mess-Mate. This Jones was at that Time ashore a watering the Ship, but as soon as he came on Board, was told that Captain Roberts had killed his Comrade; upon which he cursed Roberts, and said, he ought to be served so himself. Roberts hearing Jones's Invective, ran to him with a Sword, and ran him into the Body; who, notwithstanding his Wound, seized the Captain, threw him over a Gun, and beat him handsomely. This Adventure put the whole Company in an Uproar, and some taking Part with the Captain, and others against him, there had like to have ensued a general Battle with one another, like my Lord Thomont's Cocks; however, the Tumult was at length appeas'd by the Mediation of the Quarter-Master; and as the Majority of the Company were of Opinion that the Dignity of the Captain, ought to be supported on Board; that it was a Post of Honour, and therefore the Person whom they thought fit to confer it on, should not be violated by any single Member; wherefore they sentenced Jones to undergo two Lashes from every one of the Company, for his Misdemeanour, which was executed upon him as soon as he was well of his Wound.

This severe Punishment did not at all convince Jones that he was in the wrong, but rather animated him to some sort of a Revenge; but not being able to do it upon Roberts's Person, on Board the Ship, he and several of his Comrades, correspond with Anstis, Captain of the Brigantine, and conspire with him and some of the principal Pyrates on Board that Vessel, to go off from the Company. What made Anstis a Malecontent, was, the Inferiority he stood in, with Respect to Roberts, who carried himself with a haughty and magisterial Air, to him and his Crew, he regarding the Brigantine only as a Tender, and, as such, left them no more than the Refuse of their Plunder. In short, Jones and his Consort go on Board of Captain Anstis, on Pretence of a Visit, and there consulting with their Brethren, they find a Majority for leaving of Roberts, and so came to a Resolution to bid a soft Farewel, as they call it, that Night, and to throw over-board whosoever should stick out; but they proved to be unanimous, and effected their Design as above-mentioned.

I shall have no more to say of Captain Anstis, till the Story of Roberts is concluded, therefore I return to him, in the pursuit of his Voyage to Guiney. The loss of the Brigantine was a sensible Shock to the Crew, she being an excellent Sailor, and had 70 Hands aboard; however, Roberts who was the Occasion of it, put on a Face of Unconcern at this his ill Conduct and Mismanagement, and resolved not to alter his Purposes upon that Account.

Roberts fell in to Windward nigh the Senegal, a River of great Trade for Gum, on this Part of the Coast, monopolized by the French, who constantly keep Cruisers, to hinder the interloping Trade: At this Time they had two small Ships on that Service, one of 10 Guns and 65 Men, and the other of 16 Guns and 75 Men; who having got a Sight of Mr. Roberts, and supposing him to be one of these prohibited Traders, chased with all the Sail they could make, to come up with him; but their Hopes which had brought them very nigh, too late deceived them, for on the hoisting of Jolly Roger, (the Name they give their black Flag,) their French Hearts failed, and they both surrendred without any, or at least very little Resistance. With these Prizes they went into Sierraleon, and made one of them their Consort, by the Name of the Ranger, and the other a Store-Ship, to clean by.

Sierraleon River disgorges with a large Mouth, the Starboard-Side of which, draughts into little Bays, safe and convenient for cleaning and watering; what still made it preferable to the Pyrates, is, that the Traders settled here, are naturally their Friends. There are about 30 English Men in all, Men who in some Part of their Lives, have been either privateering, buccaneering, or pyrating, and still retain and love the Riots, and Humours, common to that sort of Life. They live very friendly with the Natives, and have many of them of both Sexes, to be their Grometta's, or Servants: The Men are faithful, and the Women so obedient, that they are very ready to prostitute themselves to whomsoever their Masters shall command them. The Royal African Company has a Fort on a small Island call'd Bence Island, but 'tis of little Use, besides keeping their Slaves; the Distance making it incapable of giving any Molestation to their Starboard Shore. Here lives at this Place an old Fellow, who goes by the Name of Crackers, who was formerly a noted Buccaneer, and while he followed the Calling, robb'd and plundered many a Man; he keeps the best House in the Place, has two or three Guns before his Door, with which he Salutes his Friends, (the Pyrates, when they put in) and lives a jovial Life with him, all the while they are there.

Here follows a List, of the rest of those lawless Merchants, and their Servants, who carry on a private Trade with the Interlopers, to the great Prejudice of the Royal African Company, who with extraordinary Industry and Expence, have made, and maintain, Settlements without any Consideration from those, who, without such Settlements and Forts, would soon be under an Incapacity of pursuing any such private Trade. Wherefore, 'tis to be hop'd, proper Means will be taken, to root out a pernicious set of People, who have all their Lives, supported themselves by the Labours of other Men.

Two of these Fellows enter'd with Robert's Crew, and continued with them, till the Destruction of the Company.

A List of the White-Men, now living on the high Land of Sierraleon, and the Craft they occupy.

JOHN Leadstone, three Boats and Periagoe.

His Man Tom,

His Man John Brown.

Alexander Middleton, one Long-Boat,

His Man Charles Hawkins.

John Pierce, Partners, one Long-Boat.

William Mead, Partners, one Long-Boat.

Their Man John Vernon.

David Chatmers, one Long-Boat.

John Chatmers, one Long-Boat.

Richard Richardson, one Long-Boat.

Norton, Partners, two Long-Boats, and two small Boats.

Richard Warren, Partners, two Long-Boats, and two small Boats.

Roberts Glynn, Partners, two Long-Boats, and two small Boats.

His Man John Franks.

William Waits, and one young Man.

John Bonnerman.

John England, one Long-Boat.

Robert Samples, one Long-Boat.

William Presgrove, one Sloop, two Long-Boats, a small Boat, and Periagoe.

Harry, one Sloop, two Long-Boats, a small Boat, and Periagoe.

Davis, one Sloop, two Long-Boats, a small Boat, and Periagoe.

Mitchel, one Sloop, two Long-Boats, a small Boat, and Periagoe.

Richard Lamb,

With Roquis Rodrigus, a Portuguese.

George Bishop.

Peter Brown.

John Jones, one Long-Boat,

His Irish young Man.

At Rio Pungo, Benjamen Gun.

At Kidham, George Yeats.

At Gallyneas, Richard Lemmons.

The Harbour is so convenient for Wooding and Watering, that it occasions many of our trading Ships, especially those of Bristol, to call in there, with large Cargoes of Beer, Syder, and strong Liquors, which they Exchange with these private Traders, for Slaves and Teeth, purchased by them at the Rio Nune's, and other Places to the Northward, so that here was what they call good Living.

Hither Roberts came the End of June, 1721, and had Intelligence that the Swallow, and Weymouth, two Men of War, of 50 Guns each, had left that River about a Month before, and designed to return about Christmas; so that the Pyrates could indulge themselves with all the Satisfaction in the World, in that they knew they were not only secure whilst there, but that in going down the Coast, after the Men of War, they should always be able to get such Intelligence of their Rendezvous, as would serve to make their Expedition safe. So after six Weeks stay, the Ships being cleaned and fitted, and the Men weary of whoring and drinking, they bethought themselves of Business, and went to Sea the Beginning of August, taking their Progress down the whole Coast, as low as Jaquin, plundering every Ship they met, of what was valuable in her, and sometimes to be more mischieviously wicked, would throw what they did not want, overboard, accumulating Cruelty to Theft.

In this Range, they exchanged their old French Ship, for a fine Frigate built Ship, call'd the Onslow, belonging to the Royal African Company, Captain Gee Commander, which happened to lye at Sestos, to get Water and Necessaries for the Company. A great many of Captain Gee's Men were ashore, when Robert's bore down, and so the Ship consequently surpriz'd into his Hands, tho' had they been all on Board, it was not likely the Case would have been otherwise, the Sailors, most of them, voluntarily joyning the Pyrates, and encouraging the same Disposition in the Soldiers, (who were going Passengers with them to Cape-Corso-Castle) whose Ears being constantly tickled with the Feats and Gallantry of those Fellows, made them fancy, that to go, was only being bound on a Voyage of Knight Errantry (to relieve the Distress'd, and gather up Fame) and so they likewise offer'd themselves; but here the Pyrates were at a Stand, they entertain'd so contemptible a Notion of Landmen, that they put 'em off with Refusals for some time, till at length, being weary'd with Solicitations, and pittying a Parcel of stout Fellows, which they said, were going to starve upon a little Canky and Plantane, they accepted of them, and allow'd them ¼ Share, as it was then term'd out of Charity.

There was a Clergyman on Board the Onslow, sent from England, to be Chaplain of Cape-Corso-Castle, some of the Pyrates were for keeping him, alledging merrily, that their Ship wanted a Chaplain; accordingly they offered him a Share, to take on with them, promising, he should do nothing for his Money, but make Punch, and say Prayers; yet, however brutish they might be in other Things, they bore so great a Respect to his Order, that they resolved not to force him against his Inclinations; and the Parson having no Relish for this sort of Life, excused himself from accepting the Honour they designed him; they were satisfied, and generous enough to deliver him back every Thing he owned to be his: The Parson laid hold of this favourable Disposition of the Pyrates, and laid Claim to several Things belonging to others, which were also given up, to his great Satisfaction; in fine, they kept nothing which belonged to the Church, except three Prayer-Books, and a Bottle-Screw.

The Pyrates kept the Onslow for their own Use, and gave Captain Gee the French Ship, and then fell to making such Alterations as might fit her for a Sea-Rover, pulling down her Bulk-Heads, and making her flush, so that she became, in all Respects, as compleat a Ship for their Purpose, as any they could have found; they continued to her the Name of the Royal Fortune, and mounted her with 40 Guns.

She and the Ranger proceeded (as I said before,) to Jaquin, and from thence to Old Calabar, where they arrived about October, in order to clean their Ships, a Place the most suitable along the whole Coast, for there is a Bar with not above 15 Foot Water upon it, and the Channel intricate, so that had the Men of War been sure of their being harbour'd here, they might still have bid Defiance to their Strength, for the Depth of Water at the Bar, as well as the want of a Pilot, was a sufficient Security to the Rovers, and invincible Impediments to them. Here therefore they sat easy, and divided the Fruits of their dishonest Instustry, and drank and drove Care away. The Pilot who brought them into this Harbour, was Captain L—e, who for this, and other Services, was extreamly well paid, according to the Journal of their own Accounts, which do not run in the ordinary and common way, of Debtor, contra Creditor, but much more concise, lumping it to their Friends, and so carrying the Debt in their Heads, against the next honest Trader they meet. They took at Calabar, Captain Loane, and two or three Bristol Ships, the Particulars of all which would be an unnecessary Prolixity, therefore I come now to give an Account of the Usage they received from the Natives of this Place. The Calabar Negroes did not prove so civil as they expected, for they refused to have any Commerce or Trade with them, when they understood they were Pyrates: An Indication that these poor Creatures, in the narrow Circumstances they were in, and without the Light of the Gospel, or the Advantage of an Education, have, notwithstanding, such a moral innate Honesty, as would upbraid and shame the most knowing Christian: But this did but exasperate these lawless Fellows, and so a Party of 40 Men were detach'd to force a Correspondence, or drive the Negroes to Extremities; and they accordingly landed under the Fire of their own Cannon. The Negroes drew up in a Body of 2000 Men, as if they intended to dispute the Matter with them, and staid till the Pyrates advanced within Pistol-shot; but finding the Loss of two or three, made no Impression on the rest, the Negroes thought fit to retreat, which they did, with some Loss: The Pyrates set Fire to the Town, and then return'd to their Ships. This terrified the Natives, and put an entire stop to all the Intercourse between them; so that they could get no Supplies, which obliged them, as soon as they had finished the cleaning and triming of their Ships, to lose no Time, but went for Cape Lopez, and watered, and at Anna-Bona took aboard a Stock of fresh Provisions, and then sailed for the Coast again.

This was their last and fatal Expedition, which we shall be more particular in, because, it cannot be imagined that they could have had Assurance to have undertaken it, but upon a Presumption, that the Men of War, (whom they knew were upon the Coast,) were unable to attack them, or else pursuant to the Rumour that had indiscretionally obtained at Sierraleon, were gone thither again.

It is impossible at this Time, to think they could know of the weak and sickly Condition they were in, and therefore founded the Success of this second Attempt upon the Coast, on the latter Presumption, and this seems to be confirmed by their falling in with the Coast as low as Cape Lahou, (and even that was higher than they designed,) in the beginning of January, and took the Ship called the King Solomon, with 20 Men in their Boat, and a trading Vessel, both belonging to the Company. The Pyrate Ship happened to fall about a League to Leeward of the King Solomon, at Cape Appollonia, and the Current and Wind opposing their working up with the Ship, they agreed to send the Long-Boat, with a sufficient Number of Men to take her: The Pyrates are all Voluntiers on these Occasions, the Word being always given, who will go? And presently the stanch and firm Men offer themselves; because, by such Readiness, they recommend their Courage, and have an Allowance also of a Shift of Cloaths, from Head to Foot, out of the Prize.

They rowed towards the King Solomon with a great deal of Alacrity, and being hailed by the Commander of her, answered, Defiance; Captain Trahern, before this, observing a great Number of Men in the Boat, began not to like his Visitors, and prepared to receive them, firing a Musket as they come under his Stern, which they returned with a Volley, and made greater Speed to get on Board: Upon this, he applied to his Men, and ask'd them, whether they would stand by him, to defend the Ship, it being a Shame they should be taken by half their Number, without any Repulse? But his Boatswain, Philips, took upon him to be the Mouth of the People, and put an End to the Dispute; he said plainly, he would not, laid down his Arms in the King's Name, as he was pleased to term it, and called out to the Boat for Quarters, so that the rest, by his Example, were mislead to the losing of the Ship.

When they came on Board, they brought her under Sail, by an expeditious Method, of cutting the Cable; Walden, one of the Pyrates, telling the Master, this yo hope of heaving up the Anchor was a needless trouble, when they designed to burn the Ship. They brought her under Commadore Roberts's Stern, and not only rifled her of what Sails, Cordage, &c. they wanted for themselves, but wantonly throw'd the Goods of the Company overboard, like Spend-thrifts, that neither expected or designed any Account.

On the same Day also, they took the Flushing, a Dutch Ship, robbed her of Masts, Yards and Stores, and then cut down her Fore-Mast; but what sat as heavily as any thing with the Skipper, was, their taking some fine Sausages he had on Board, of his Wife's making, and stringing them in a ludicrous Manner, round their Necks, till they had sufficiently shew'd their Contempt of them, and then threw them into the Sea. Others chopp'd the Heads of his Fowls off, to be dressed for their Supper, and courteously invited the Landlord, provided he would find Liquor. It was a melancholly Request to the Man, but it must be comply'd with, and he was obliged, as they grew drunk, to sit quietly, and hear them sing French and Spanish Songs out of his Dutch Prayer-Books, with other Prophaness, that he (tho' a Dutch Man) stood amazed at.

In chasing too near in, they alarmed the Coast, and Expresses were sent to the English and Dutch Factories, giving an Account of it: They were sensible of this Error immediately, and because they would make the best of a bad Market, resolved to keep out of sight of Land, and lose the Prizes they might expect between that and Whydah, to make the more sure of that Port, where commonly is the best Booty; all Nations trading thither, especially Portuguese, who purchase chiefly with Gold, the Idol their Hearts were bent upon. And notwithstanding this unlikely Course, they met and took several Ships between Axim and that Place; the circumstantial Stories of which, and the pannick Terrors they struck into his Majesty's Subjects, being tedious and unnecessary to relate, I shall pass by, and come to their Arrival in that Road.

They came to Whydah with a St. George's Ensign, a black Silk Flag flying at their Mizen-Peek, and a Jack and Pendant of the same: The Flag had a Death in it, with an Hour-Glass in one Hand, and cross Bones in the other, a Dart by it, and underneath a Heart dropping three Drops of Blood.—The Jack had a Man pourtray'd in it, with a flaming Sword in his Hand, and standing on two Skulls, subscribed A B H and A M H i. e. a Barbadian's and a Martinican's Head, as has been before taken Notice of. Here they found eleven Sail in the Road, English, French and Portuguese; the French were three stout Ships of 30 Guns, and upwards of 100 Men each, yet when Roberts came to Fire, they, with the other Ships, immediately struck their Colours and surrendred to his Mercy. One Reason, it must be confess'd, of his easy Victory, was, the Commanders and a good Part of the Men being ashore, according to the Custom of the Place, to receive the Cargoes, and return the Slaves, they being obliged to watch the Seasons for it, which otherwise, in so dangerous a Sea as here, would be impracticable. These all, except the Porcupine, ransomed with him for eight Pound of Gold-Dust, a Ship, not without the trouble of some Letters passing and repassing from the Shore, before they could settle it; and notwithstanding the Agreement and Payment, they took away one of the French Ships, tho' with a Promise to return her, if they found she did not sail well, taking with them several of her Men for that End.

Some of the Foreigners, who never had Dealing this Way before, desired for Satisfaction to their Owners, that they might have Receipts for their Money, which were accordingly given, a Copy of one of them, I have here subjoined, viz.

THIS is to certify whom it may or doth concern, that we GENTLEMEN OF FORTUNE, have received eight Pounds of Gold-Dust, for the Ransom of the Hardey, Captain Dittwitt Commander, so that we Discharge the said Ship,

Witness our Hands, this

13th of Jan. 1721-2.

Batt. Roberts,

Harry Glasby.

Others were given to the Portuguese Captains, which were in the same Form, but being sign'd by two waggish Fellows, viz. Sutton, and Sympson, they subscribed by the Names of,

Aaron Whifflingpin,

Sim. Tugmutton.

But there was something so singularly cruel and barbarous done here to the Porcupine, Captain Fletcher, as must not be passed over without special Remark.

This Ship lay in the Road, almost slaved, when the Pyrates came in, and the Commander being on Shore, settling his Accounts, was sent to for the Ransom, but he excused it, as having no Orders from the Owners; though the true Reason might be, that he thought it dishonourable to treat with Robbers; and that the Ship, separate from the Slaves, towards whom he could mistrust no Cruelty, was not worth the Sum demanded; hereupon, Roberts sends the Boat to transport the Negroes, in order to set her on Fire; but being in hast, and finding that unshackling them cost much Time and Labour, they actually set her on Fire, with eighty of those poor Wretches on Board, chained two and two together, under the miserable Choice of perishing by Fire or Water: Those who jumped overboard from the Flames, were seized by Sharks, a voracious Fish, in Plenty in this Road, and, in their Sight, tore Limb from Limb alive. A Cruelty unparalell'd! And for which had every Individual been hanged, few I imagine would think that Justice had been rigorous.

The Pyrates, indeed, were obliged to dispatch their Business here in hast, because they had intercepted a Letter from General Phips to Mr. Baldwin, the Royal African Company's Agent at Whydah, (giving an Account, that Roberts had been seen to Windward of Cape Three Points,) that he might the better guard against the Damages to the Company's Ships, if he should arrive at that Road before the Swallow Man of War, which he assured him, (at the Time of that Letter,) was pursuing them to that Place. Roberts call'd up his Company, and desired they would hear Phip's Speech, (for so he was pleased to call the Letter,) and notwithstanding their vapouring, perswaded them of the Necessity of moving; for, says he, such brave Fellows cannot be supposed to be frightned at this News, yet that it were better to avoid dry Blows, which is the best that can be expected, if overtaken.

This Advice weigh'd with them, and they got under Sail, having stay'd only from Thursday to Saturday Night, and at Sea voted for the Island of Anna Bona; but the Winds hanging out of the Way, crossed their Purpose, and brought them to Cape Lopez, where I shall leave them for their approaching Fate, and relate some further Particulars of his Majesty's Ship the Swallow, viz. where it was she had spent her Time, during the Mischief that was done, and by what Means unable to prevent it; what also was the Intelligence she received, and the Measures thereon formed, that at last brought two such Strangers as Mr Roberts and Capt. Ogle, to meet in so remote a Corner of the World.

The Swallow and Weymouth left Sierraleon, May 28, where, I have already taken Notice, Roberts arrived about a Month after, and doubtless learn'd the Intent of their Voyage, and cleaning on the Coast; which made him set down with more Security to his Diversion, and furnish him with such Intimations, as made his first Range down the Coast in August following, more prosperous; the Swallow and Weymouth being then at the Port of Princes a cleaning.

Their Stay at Princes was from July 28 to Sept. 20, 1721, where, by a Fatality, common to the Irregularities of Seamen, (who cannot in such Cases be kept under due Restraints,) they buried 100 Men in three Weeks time, and reduced the Remainder of the Ships Companies into so sickly a State, that it was with Difficulty they brought them to sail; and this Misfortune was probably the Ruin of Roberts, for it prevented the Men of War's going back to Sierraleon, as it was intended, there being a Necessity of leaving his Majesty's Ship Weymouth (in much the worse Condition of the two) under the Guns of Cape Corso, to impress Men, being unable at this Time, either to hand the Sails, or weigh her Anchor; and Roberts being ignorant of the Occasion or Alteration of the first Design, fell into the Mouth of Danger, when he thought himself the farthest from it; for the Men of War not endeavouring to attain further to Windward (when they came from Princes) then to secure Cape Corso Road under their Lee, they luckily hovered in the Track he had took.

The Swallow and Weymouth fell in with the Continent at Cape Appollonia, Octo. 20th, and there received the ungrateful News from one Captain Bird; a Notice that awaken'd and put them on their Guard; but they were far from expecting any Temerity should ever bring him a second Time on the Coast, while they were there; therefore the Swallow having seen the Weymouth into Cape Corso Road Nov. 10th, she ply'd to Windward as far as Bassam, rather as an Airing to recover a sickly Ship's Company, and shew herself to the Trade, which was found every where undisturb'd, and were, for that Reason, returning to her Consort, when accidently meeting a Portuguese Ship, she told her, that the Day before she saw two Ships Chace into Junk, an English Vessel, which she believed must have fallen into their Hands. On this Story, the Swallow clung her Wind, and endeavoured to gain that Place, but receiving soon after (Octo. the 14th) a contrary Report from Captain Plummer, an intelligent Man, in the Jason of Bristol, who had come further to Windward, and neither saw or heard any Thing of this; she turned her Head down the second Time, anchored at Cape Appollonia the 23d, at Cape Tres Puntas the 27th, and in Corso Road January the 7th, 1721-2.

They learned that their Consort the Weymouth, was, by the Assistance of some Soldiers from the Castle, gone to Windward, to demand Restitution of some Goods or Men belonging to the African Company, that were illegally detained by the Dutch at Des Minas; and while they were regretting so long a Separation, an Express came to General Phips, from Axim, the 9th, and followed by another from Dixcove, (an English Factory,) with Information that three Ships had chased and taken a Galley nigh Axim Castle, and a trading Boat belonging to the Company: No doubt was made, concerning what they were, it being taken for granted they were Pyrates, and supposed to be the same that had the August before infested the Coast. The natural Result therefore, from these two Advices, was, to hasten for Whydah; for it was conclued the Prizes they had taken, had informed them how nigh the Swallow was, and withal, how much better in Health than she had been for some Months past; so that unless they were very mad indeed, they would (after being discovered) make the best of their Way for Whydah, and secure the Booty there, without which, their Time and Industry had been entirely lost; most of the Gold lying in that Corner.

The Swallow weighed from Cape-Corso, January the 10th, but was retarded by waiting some Hours on the Margaret, a Company's Ship, at Accra, again on the Portugal, and a whole Day at Apong, on a Person they used to stile Miss Betty: A Conduct that Mr. Phips blamed, when he heard the Pyrates were miss'd at Whydah, altho' he had given it as his Opinion, they could not be passed by, and intimated, that to stay a few Hours would prove no Prejudice.

This, however, hinder'd the Swallow's catching them at Whydah, for the Pyrates came into that Road, with a fresh Gale of Wind, the same Day the Swallow was at Apong, and sail'd the 13th of January from thence, that she arrived the 17th. She gained Notice of them by a French Shallop from Grand Papa, the 14th at Night, and from Little Papa next Morning by a Dutch Ship; so that the Man of War was on all Sides, as she thought, sure of her Purchase, particularly when she made the Ships, and discovered three of them to get under Sail immediately at Sight of her, making Signals to one another, as tho' they designed a Defence; but they were found to be three French Ships; and those at Anchor, Portuguese and English, all honest Traders, who had been ransack'd and ransom'd.

This Disappointment chagreen'd the Ship's Company, who were very intent upon their Market; which was reported to be an Arm-Chest full of Gold, and kept with three Keys; tho' in all liklyhood, had they met with them in that open Road, one or both would have made their Escapes; or if they had thought sit to have fought, an Emulation in their Defence would probably have made it desperate.

While they were contemplating on the Matter, a Letter was received from Mr. Baldwin, (Governor here for the Company,) signifying, that the Pyrates were at Jaquin, seven Leagues lower. The Swallow weighed at two next Morning, January the 16th, and got to Jaquin by Day-

Light, but to no other End, than frightening the Crews of two Portuguese Ships on Shore, who took her for the Pyrate that had struck such Terror at Whydah: She returned therefore that Night, and having been strengthened with thirty Voluntiers, English and French, the discarded Crews of the Porcupine, and the French Ship they had carried from hence, she put to Sea again January the 19th, conjecturing, that either Calabar, Princes, the River Gabone, Cape Lopez, or Annabona, must be touched at for Water and Refreshment, tho' they should resolve to leave the Coast. As to the former of those Places, I have before observed, it was hazardous to think of, or rather impracticable; Princes had been a sower Grape to them, but being the first in the Way, she came before the Harbour the 29th, where learning no News, without loosing Time, steered for the River Gabone, and anchored at the Mouth of it February the 1st.

This River is navigable by two Channels, and has an Island about five Leagues up, called Popaguays or Parrots, where the Dutch Cruisers, for this Coast, generally Clean, and where sometimes Pyrates come in to look for Prey, or to Refit, it being very convenient, by Reason of a soft Mud about it, that admits a Ship's lying on Shore, with all her Guns and Stores in, without Damage. Hither Captain Ogle sent his Boat and a Lieutenant, who spoke with a Dutch Ship, above the Island, from whom he had this Account, viz. That he had been four Days from Cape Lopez, and had left no Ship there. However, they beat up for the Cape, without regard to this Story, and on the 5th, at Dawning, was surprized with the Noise of a Gun, which, as the Day brightened, they found was from Cape Lopez Bay, where they discovered three Ships at Anchor, the largest with the King's Colours and Pendant flying, which was soon after concluded to be Mr. Roberts and his Consorts; but the Swallow being to Windward, and unexpectedly deep in the Bay, was obliged to Steer off, for avoiding a Sand, called the French Man's Bank, which the Pyrates observed for some Time, and rashly interpreting it to be Fear in her, righted the French Ranger, which was then on the Heel, and ordered her to chase out in all hast, bending several of their Sails in the Pursuit. The Man of War finding they had foolishly mistaken her Design, humoured the Deceit, and kept off to Sea, as if she had been really afraid, and managed her Steerage so, under the Direction of Lieutenant Sun, an experienced Officer, as to let the Ranger come up with her, when they thought they had got so far as not to have their Guns heard by her Consort at the Cape. The Pyrates had such an Opinion of their own Courage, that they could never dream any Body would use a Stratagem to speak with them, and so was the more easily drawn into the Snare.

The Pyrates now drew nigh enough to fire their Chase Guns; they hoisted the black Flag that was worn in Whydah Road, and got their Spritsail Yard along-ships, with Intent to board; no one having ever asked, all this while, what Country Ship they took the Chase to be; they would have her to be a Portuguese, (Sugar being then a Commodity among them,) and were swearing every Minute at the Wind or Sails to expedite so sweet a Chase; but, alass, all turned sour in an Instant: It was with the utmost Consternation they saw her suddenly bring to, and hawl up her lower Ports, now within Pistol-shot, and struck their black Flag upon it directly. After the first Surprize was over, they kept firing at a Distance, hoisted it again, and vapoured with their Cutlashes on the Poop; tho' wisely endeavouring at the same Time to get away. Being now at their Wits end, boarding was proposed by the Heads of them, and so to make one desperate Push; but the Motion not being well seconded, and their Main-Top-Mast coming down by a Shot, after two Hours firing, it was declin'd; they grew Sick, struck their Colours, and called out for Quarters; having had 10 Men killed out right, and 20 wounded, without the loss or hurt of one of the King's Men. She had 32 Guns, mann'd with 16 French Men, 20 Negroes, and 77 English. The Colours were thrown over board, that they might not rise in Judgment, nor be display'd in Tryumph over them.

While the Swallow was sending their Boat to fetch the Prisoners, a Blast and Smoak was seen to pour out of the great Cabin, and they thought they were blowing up; but upon enquiry afterwards, found that half a dozen of the most Desperate, when they saw all Hopes fled, had drawn themselves round what Powder they had left in the Steerage, and fired a Pistol into it, but it was too small a Quantity to effect any Thing more, than burning them in a frightful Manner.

This Ship was commanded by one Skyrme, a Welch Man, who, tho' he had lost his Leg in the Action, would not suffer himself to be dressed, or carried off the Deck; but, like Widrington, fought upon his Stump. The rest appeared gay and brisk, most of them with white Shirts, Watches, and a deal of Silk Vests, but the Gold-Dust belonging to them, was most of it left in the Little Ranger in the Bay, (this Company's proper Ship,) with the Royal Fortune.

I cannot but take Notice of two among the Crowd, of those disfigured from the Blast of Powder just before mentioned, viz. William Main and Roger Ball. An Officer of the Ship seeing a Silver Call hang at the Wast of the former, said to him, I presume you are Boatswain of this Ship. Then you presume wrong, answered he, for I am Boatswain of the Royal Fortune, Captain Roberts Commander. Then Mr. Boatswain you will be hanged I believe, replies the Officer. That is as your Honour pleases, answered he again, and was for turning away: But the Officer desired to know of him, how the Powder, which had made them in that Condition, came to take Fire.—By G— says he, they are all mad and bewitch'd, for I have lost a good Hat by it. (the Hat and he being both blown out of the Cabin Gallery, into the Sea.) But what signifies a Hat Friend, says the Officer.-Not much answer'd he, the Men being busy in stripping him of his Shoes and Stockings.—The Officer then enquired of him, whether Roberts's Company were as likely Fellows as these.— There are 120 of them, (answered he) as clever Fellows as ever trod Shoe Leather: Would I were with them!—No doubt on't, says the Officer.—By G— it is naked Truth, answered he, looking down and seeing himself, by this Time, quite striped.

The Officer then approached Roger Ball, who was seated in a private Corner, with a Look as sullen as Winter, and asked him, how he came blown up in that frightful Manner.—Why, says he, John Morris fired a Pistol into the Powder, and if he had not done it, I would, (bearing his Pain without the least Complaint.) The Officer gave him to understand he was Surgeon, and if he desired it, he would dress him; but he swore it should not be done, and that if any Thing was applied to him, he would tear it off.—Nevertheless the Surgeon had good Nature enough to dress him, tho' with much trouble: At Night he was in a kind of Delirium, and raved on the Bravery of Roberts, saying, he should shortly be released, as soon as they should meet him, which procured him a lashing down upon the Forecastle, which he resisting with all his Force, caused him to be used with the more Violence, so that he was tied down with so much Severity, that his Flesh being sore and tender with the blowing up, he died next Day of a Mortification.

They secured the Prisoners with Pinions, and Shackles, but the Ship was so much disabled in the Engagement, that they had once Thoughts to set her on Fire; but this would have given them the Trouble of taking the Pyrates wounded Men on Board themselves, and that they were certain the Royal Fortune would wait for their Consort's Return, they lay by her two Days, repaired her Rigging and other Damages, and sent her into Princes, with the French Men, and four of their own Hands.

On the 9th in the Evening, the Swallow gained the Cape again, and saw the Royal Fortune standing into the Bay with the Neptune, Captain Hill, of London: A good Presage of the next Day's Success, for they did not doubt but the Temptation of Liquor, and Plunder, they might find in this their new Prize, would make the Pyrates very confused; and so it happened.

On the 10th, in the Morning, the Man of War bore away to round the Cape. Roberts's Crew discerning their Masts over the Land, went down into the Cabin, to acquaint him of it, he being then at Breakfast with his new Guest, Captain Hill, on a savory Dish of Solomongundy, and some of his own Beer. He took no Notice of it, and his Men almost as little, some saying she was a Portuguese Ship, others a French Slave Ship, but the major Part swore it was the French Ranger returning, and were merrily debating for some Time, on the Manner of Reception, whether they should salute, or not; but as the Swallow approached nigher, Things appeared plainer, and though they were stigmatiz'd with the Name of Cowards, who shewed any Apprehension of Danger, yet some of them, now undeceived, declared it to Roberts, especially one Armstrong, who had deserted from that Ship, and knew her well: Those Roberts swore at as Cowards, who meant to dishearten the Men, asking them if it were so, whether they were afraid to fight, or no? And hardly refrained from Blows. What his own Apprehensions were, till she hawled up her Ports, and hoisted their proper Colours, is uncertain; but then being perfectly convinced, he slipped his Cable, got under Sail, and ordered his Men to Arms, without any shew of Timidity, dropping a first Rate Oath, that it was a Bite, but, at the same Time, resolved, like a gallant Rogue, to get clear, or die.

There was one Armstrong, as I just mention'd, a Deserter from the Swallow, whom they enquired of concerning the Trim and Sailing of that Ship; he told them she sail'd best upon a Wind, and therefore, if they designed to leave her, they should go before it.

The Danger was imminent, and Time very short, to consult of Means to extricate himself; his Resolution in this Streight, was as follows: To pass close to the Swallow, with all their Sails, and receive her Broadside, before they returned a Shot; if disabled by this, or that they could not depend on sailing, then to run on Shore at the Point, (which is steep to) and every one to shift for himself among the Negroes; or failing in these, to board, and blow up together, for he saw that the greatest Part of his Men were drunk, passively Couragious, unfit for Service.

Roberts himself made a gallant Figure, at the Time of the Engagement, being dressed in a rich crimson Damask Wastcoat and Breeches, a red Feather in his Hat, a Gold Chain round his Neck, with a Diamond Cross hanging to it, a Sword in his Hand, and two Pair of Pistols hanging at the End of a Silk Sling, flung over his Shoulders (according to the Fashion of the Pyrates;) and is said to have given his Orders with Boldness, and Spirit; coming, according to what he had purposed, close to the Man of War, received her Fire, and then hoisted his Black Flag, and returned it, shooting away from her, with all the Sail he could pack; and had he took Armstrong's Advice, to have gone before the Wind, he had probably escaped; but keeping his Tacks down, either by the Winds shifting, or ill Steerage, or both, he was taken a-back with his Sails, and the Swallow came a second Time very nigh to him: He had now perhaps finished the Fight very desperately, if Death, who took a swift Passage in a Grape-Shot, had not interposed, and struck him directly on the Throat. He settled himself on the Tackles of a Gun, which one Stephenson, from the Helm, observing, ran to his Assistance, and not perceiving him wounded, swore at him, and bid him stand up, and fight like a Man; but when he found his Mistake, and that his Captain was certainly dead, he gushed into Tears, and wished the next Shot might be his Lot. They presently threw him over-board, with his Arms and Ornaments on, according to the repeated Request he made in his Life-time.

Roberts was a tall black Man, near forty Years of Age, born at Newey-bagh, nigh Haverford-West, in Pembrokshire, of good natural Parts, and personal Bravery, tho' he applied them to such wicked Purposes, as made them of no Commendation, frequently drinking D—n to him who ever lived to wear a Halter. He was forc'd himself at first among this Company out of the Prince, Captain Plumb at Anamaboe, about three Years before, where he served as second Mate, and shed, as he us'd to tell the fresh Men, as many Crocodile Tears then as they did now, but Time and good Company had wore it off. He could not plead Want of Employment, nor Incapacity of getting his Bread in an honest way, to favour so vile a Change, nor was he so much a Coward as to pretend it; but frankly own'd, it was to get rid of the disagreeable Superiority of some Masters he was acquainted with, and the Love of Novelty and Change, Maritime Peregrinations had accustom'd him to. In an honest Service, says he, there is thin Commons, low Wages, and hard Labour; in this, Plenty and Satiety, Pleasure and Ease, Liberty and Power; and who would not ballance Creditor on this Side, when all the Hazard that is run for it, at worst, is only a sour Look or two at choaking. No, A merry Life and a short one, shall be my Motto. Thus he preach'd himself into an Approbation of what he at first abhorr'd; and being daily regal'd with Musick, Drinking, and the Gaiety and Diversions of his Companions, these deprav'd Propensities were quickly edg'd and strengthen'd, to the extinguishing of Fear and Conscience. Yet among all the vile and ignominious Acts he had perpetrated, he is said to have had an Aversion towards forcing Men into that Service, and had procured some their Discharge, notwithstanding so many made it their Plea.

When Roberts was gone, as tho' he had been the Life and Soul of the Gang, their Spirits sunk; many deserted their Quarters, and all stupidly neglected any Means for Defence, or Escape; and their Main-mast soon after being shot by the Board, they had no Way left, but to surrender and call for Quarters. The Swallow kept aloof, while her Boat passed, and repassed for the Prisoners; because they understood they were under an Oath to blow up; and some of the Desperadoes shewed a Willingness that Way, Matches being lighted, and Scuffles happening between those who would, and those who opposed it: But I cannot easily account for this Humour, which can be term'd no more than a false Courage, since any of them had Power to destroy his own Life, either by Pistol, or Drowning, without involving others in the same Fate, who are in no Temper of Mind for it: And at best, it had been only dying, for fear of Death.

She had 40 Guns, and 157 Men, 45 whereof were Negroes; three only were killed in the Action, without any Loss to the Swallow. There was found upwards of 2000 l. in Gold-Dust in her. The Flag could not be got easily from under the fallen Mast, and was therefore recover'd by the Swallow; it had the Figure of a Skeleton in it, and a Man pourtray'd with a flaming Sword in his Hand, intimating a Defyance of Death it self.

The Swallow returned back into Cape Lopez Bay, and found the little Ranger, whom the Pyrates had deserted in hast, for the better Defence of the Ship: She had been plunder'd, according to what I could learn, of 2000 l. in Gold-Dust, (the Shares of those Pyrates who belonged to her;) and Captain Hill, in the Neptune, not unjustly suspected, for he would not wait the Man of War's returning into the Bay again, but sail'd away immediately, making no Scruple afterwards to own the Seizure of other Goods out of her, and surrender'd, as a Confirmation of all, 50 Ounces at Barbadoes, for which, see the Article at the End of this Book.

All Persons who after the 29th of Septem. 1690, &c.

To sum up the whole, if it be considered, first, that the sickly State of the Men of War, when they sail'd from Princes, was the Misfortune that hindered their being as far as Sierraleon, and consequently out of the Track the Pyrates then took. That those Pyrates, directly contrary to their Design, in the second Expedition, should get above Cape Corso, and that nigh Axim, a Chace should offer, that inevitably must discover them, and be soon communicated to the Men of War. That the satiating their evil and malicious Tempers at Whydah, in burning the Porcupine, and running off with the French Ship, had strengthened the Swallow with 30 Men. That the Swallow should miss them in that Road, where probably she had not, or at least so effectually obtained her End. That they should be so far infatuated at Cape Lopez, as to divide their Strength, which when collected, might have been so formidable. And lastly, that the Conquest should be without Bloodshed: I say, considering all these Circumstances, it shews that the Hand of Providence was concerned in their Destruction. As to their Behaviour after they were taken, it was found that they had great Inclinations to rebel, if they could have laid hold of any Opportunity. For they were very uneasy under Restraint, having been lately all Commanders themselves; nor could they brook their Diet, or Quarters, without cursing and swearing, and upbraiding each other, with the Folly that had brought them to it.

So that to secure themselves against any mad desperate Undertaking of theirs, they strongly barricado'd the Gun-Room, and made another Prison before it; an Officer, with Pistols and Cutlashes, doing Duty, Night and Day, and the Prisoners within, manacled and shackled.

They would yet in these Circumstances be impudently merry, saying, when they viewed their Nakedness, that they had not left them a halfpenny, to give old Charon, to ferry them over Stix: And at their thin Commons, they would observe, that they fell away so fast, that they should not have Weight left to hang them. Sutton used to be very prophane; he happening to be in the same Irons with another Prisoner, who was more serious than ordinary, and read and pray'd often, as became his Condition; this Man Sutton used to swear at, and ask him, what he proposed by so much Noise and Devotion? Heaven, says the other, I hope. Heaven, you Fool, says Sutton, did you ever hear of any Pyrates going thither? Give me H—ll, it's a merrier Place; I'll give Roberts a Salute of 13 Guns at Entrance. And when he found such ludicrous Expressions had no Effect on him, he made a formal Complaint, and requested that the Officer would either remove this Man, or take his Prayer-Book away, as a common Disturber.

A Combination and Conspiracy was formed, betwixt Moody, Ashplant, Magnes, Mare, and others, to rise, and kill the Officers, and run away with the Ship. This they had carried on by Means of a Mulatto Boy, who was allow'd to attend them, and proved very trusty in his Messages, between the Principals; but the Evening of that Night they were to have made this Struggle, two of the Prisoners that sat next to Ashplant, heard the Boy whisper them upon the Project, and naming to him the Hour they should be ready, presently gave Notice of it to the Captain, which put the Ship in an Alarm, for a little Time; and, on Examination, several of them had made shift to break off, or lose, their Shackles, (no doubt for such Purpose;) but it tended only to procure to themselves worse Usage and Confinement.

In the same Passage to Cape Corso, the Prize, Royal Fortune, was in the same Danger. She was left at the Island of St. Thomas's, in the Possession of an Officer, and a few Men, to take in some fresh Provisions, (which were scarce at Cape Corso) with Orders to follow the Ship. There were only some of the Pyrates Negroes, three or four wounded Prisoners, and Scudamore, their Surgeon; from whom they seemed to be under no Apprehension, especially from the last, who might have hoped for Favour, on Account of his Employ; and had stood so much indebted for his Liberty, eating and drinking constantly with the Officer; yet this Fellow, regardless of the Favour, and lost to all Sense of Reformation, endeavoured to bring over the Negroes to his Design of murdering the People, and running away with the Ship. He easily prevailed with the Negroes to come into the Design; but when he came to communicate it to his Fellow Prisoners, and would have drawn them into the same Measures, by telling them, he understood Navigation, that the Negroes were stout Fellows, and by a Smattering he had in the Angolan Language, he had found willing to undertake such an Enterprize; and that it was better venturing to do this, run down the Coast, and raise a new Company, than to proceed to Cape Corso, and be hanged like a Dog, and Sun dry'd. One of them abhorring the Cruelty, or fearing the Success, discovered it to the Officer, who made him immediately a Prisoner, and brought the Ship safe.

When they came to be lodg'd in Cape Corso-Castle, their Hopes of this kind all cut off, and that they were assured they must there soon receive a final Sentence; the Note was changed among most of them, and from vain insolent jesting, they became serious and devout, begging for good Books, and joyning in publick Prayers, and singing of Psalms, twice at least every Day.

As to their Tryals, if we should give them at length, it may appear tedious to the Reader, for which Reason, I have, for the avoiding Tautology and Repetition, put as many of them together as were try'd for the same Fact, reserving the Circumstances which are most material, with Observations on the dying Behaviour of such of them, as came to my Knowledge.

And first, it may be observed from the List, that a great Part of these Pyrate Ships Crews, were Men entered on the Coast of Africa, not many Months before they were taken; from whence, it may be concluded, that the pretended Constraint of Roberts, on them, was very often a Complotment between Parties equally willing: And this Roberts several Times openly declared, particularly to the Onslow's People, whom he called aft, and ask'd of them, who was willing to go, for he would force no Body? As was deposed, by some of his best Hands, after Acquittal; nor is it reasonable to think, he should reject Irish Voluntiers, only from a Pique against Kennedy, and force others, that might hazard, and, in Time, destroy his Government: But their Behaviour soon put him out of this Fear, and convinc'd him, that the Plea of Force was only the best Artifice they had to shelter themselves under, in Case they should be taken; and that they were less Rogues than others, only in Point of Time.

It may likewise be taken Notice of, that the Country, wherein they happened to be tried, is among other Happinesses, exempted from Lawyers, and Law-Books, so that the Office of Register, of necessity fell on one, not versed in those Affairs, which might justify the Court in want of Form, more essentially supply'd with Integrity and Impartiality.

But, perhaps, if there was less Law, there might be more Justice, than in some other Courts; for, if the civil Law be a Law of universal Reason, judging of the Rectitude, or Obliquity of Mens Actions, every Man of common Sense is endued with a Portion of it, at least sufficient to make him distinguish Right from Wrong, or what the Civilians call, Malum in se.

Therefore, here, if two Persons were equally Guilty of the same Fact, there was no convicting one, and bringing the other off, by any Quirk, or turn of Law; for they form'd their Judgments upon the Constraint, or Willingness, the Aim, and Intention of the Parties, and all other Circumstances, which make a material Difference. Besides, in Crimes of this Nature, Men bred up to the Sea, must be more knowing, and much abler, than others more learned in the Law; for, before a Man can have a right Idea of a Thing, he must know the Terms standing for that Thing: The Sea-Terms being a Language by it self, which no Lawyer can be supposed to understand, he must of Consequence want that discriminating Faculty, which should direct him to judge right of the Facts meant by those Terms.

The Court well knew, it was not possible to get the Evidence of every Sufferer by this Crew, and therefore, first of all, considered how that Deficiency should be supplied; whether, or no, they could pardon one Jo. Dennis, who had early offered himself, as King's Evidence, and was the best read in their Lives and Conversations: Here indeed, they were at a Loss for Law, and concluded in the Negative, because it look'd like compounding with a Man to swear falsly, losing by it, those great Helps he could have afforded.

Another great Difficulty in their Proceedings, was, how to understand those Words in the Act of Parliament, of, particularly specifying in the Charge, the Circumstances of Time, Place, &c. i. e. so to understand them, as to be able to hold a Court; for if they had been indicted on particular Robberies, the Evidence had happened mostly from the Royal African Company's Ships, on which these Gentlemen of Cape-Corso-Castle, were not qualify'd to sit, their Oath running, That they have no Interest directly, or indirectly, in the Ship, or Goods, for the Robbery of which, the Party stands accused: And this they thought they had, Commissions being paid them, on such Goods: And on the other Side, if they were incapacitated, no Court could be formed, the Commission absolutely requiring three of them by Name.

To reconcile all Things, therefore, the Court resolved, to bottom the whole of their Proceedings on the Swallow's Depositions, which were clear and plain, and had the Circumstance of Time when, Place where, Manner how, and the like, particularly specified according to the Statute in that Case made, and provided. But this admitted only a general Intimation of Robbery in the Indictment, therefore to approve their Clemency, it looking Arbitrary on the Lives of Men, to lump them to the Gallows, in such a summary Way as must have been done, had they solely adhered to the Swallow's Charge, they resolved to come to particular Tryals.

Secondly, That the Prisoners might not be ignorant whereon to answer, and so have all fair Advantages, to excuse and defend themselves; the Court farther agreed with Justice and Equanimity, to hear any Evidence that could be brought, to weaken or corroborate the three Circumstances that compleat a Pyrate; first, being a Voluntier amongst them at the Beginning; secondly, being a Voluntier at the taking or robbing of any Ship; or lastly, voluntarily accepting a Share in the Booty of those that did; for by a Parity of Reason, where these Actions were of their own disposing, and yet committed by them, it must be believed their Hearts and Hands joyned together, in what they acted against his Majesty's Ship the Swallow.

Calico Jack, Anne Bonny and Mary Read's Entries in A General History of the Pyrates

THIS John Rackam, as has been mentioned in the last Chapter, was Quarter-Master to Vane's Company, till they were divided, and Vane turned out for refusing to board and fight the French Man of War; then Rackam was voted Captain of that Division that remained in the Brigantine. The 24th of November 1718, was the first Day of his Command, and his first Cruize was among the Caribbee Islands, where he took and plunder'd several Vessels.

We have already taken Notice, that when Captain Woodes Rogers went to the Island of Providence, with the King's Pardon to such as should surrender, this Brigantine, which Rackam now commanded, made its Escape, thro' another Passage, bidding Defiance to Mercy.

To Windward of Jamaica, a Madera Man fell into the Pyrates Way, which they detained two or three Days, till they had made their Market out of her, and then gave her back to the Master, and permitted one Hosea Tisdell, a Tavern-Keeper at Jamaica, who had been pick'd up in one of their Prizes, to depart in her, she being then bound for that Island.

After this Cruize, they went into a small Island and cleaned, and spent their Christmas ashore, drinking and carousing as long as they had any Liquor left, and then went to Sea again for more, where they succeeded but too well, though they took no extraordinary Prize, for above two Months, except a Ship laden with Thieves from Newgate, bound for the Plantations, which, in a few Days, was retaken with all her Cargo, by an English Man of War.

Rackam stood off towards the Island of Burmudas, and took a Ship bound to England from Carolina, and a small Pink from New-England, and brought them to the Bahama Islands, where with the Pitch, Tar, and Stores, they clean'd again, and refitted their own Vessel; but staying too long in that Neighbourhood, Captain Rogers, who was Governor of Providence, hearing of these Ships being taken, sent out a Sloop well mann'd and arm'd, which retook both the Prizes, and in the mean while the Pyrate had the good Fortune to escape.

From hence they sailed to the Back of Cuba, where Rackam kept a little kind of a Family, at which Place, they staid a considerable Time, living ashore with their Dalilahs, till their Money and Provision were expended, and then they concluded it Time to look out: They repaired to their Vessel, and was making ready to put Sea, when a Guarda del Costa came in with a small English Sloop, which she had taken as an Interloper on the Coast. The Spanish Guardship attack'd the Pyrate, but Rackam being close in behind a little Island, she could do but little Execution where she lay, therefore the Spaniard warps into the Channel that Evening, in order to make sure of her the next Morning. Rackam finding his Case desperate, and hardly any Possibility of escaping, resolved to attempt the following Enterprize: The Spanish Prize lying for better Security close into the Land, between the little Island and the Main; Rackam takes his

Crew into the Boat, with their Pistols and Cutlashes, rounds the little Island, and falls aboard their Prize silently in the dead of the Night, without being discovered, telling the Spaniards that were aboard of her, that if they spoke a Word, or made the least Noise, they were dead Men, and so became Master of her; when this was done, he slipt her Cable, and drove out to Sea: The Spanish Man of War, was so intent upon their expected Prize, that they minded nothing else, and assoon as Day broke, made a furious Fire upon the empty Sloop, but it was not long before they were rightly apprized of the Matter, and cursed themselves for Fools, to be bit out of a good rich Prize, as she prov'd to be, and to have nothing but an old crazy Hull in the room of her.

Rackam and his Crew had no Occasion to be displeased at the Exchange, that enabled them to continue some Time longer in a Way of Life that suited their depraved Tempers: In August 1720, we find him at Sea again, scouring the Harbours and Inlets of the North and West Parts of Jamaica, where he took several small Craft, which proved no great Booty to the Rovers, but they had but few Men, and therefore they were obliged to run at low Game, till they could encrease their Company.

In the Beginning of September, they took seven or eight Fishing-Boats in Harbour Island, stole their Nets and other Tackle, and then went off the French Part of Hispaniola, and landed, and took Cattle away, with two or three French Men they found near the Water-Side, hunting of wild Hogs in the Evening: The French Men came on Board, whether by Consent or Compulsion, I can't say. They afterwards plundered two Sloops, and returned to Jamaica, on the North Coast of which Island, near Porto Maria Bay, they took a Scooner, Thomas Spenlow Master; it was then the 19th of October. The next Day, Rackam seeing a Sloop in Dry Harbour Bay, he stood in and fired a Gun; the Men all run ashore, and he took the Sloop and Lading, but when those ashore found them to be Pyrates, they hailed the Sloop, and let them know they were all willing to come aboard of them.

Rackam's coasting the Island in this Manner, proved fatal to him, for Intelligence came to the Governor, of his Expedition, by a Canoa which he had surprized ashore, in Ocho Bay; upon which a Sloop was immediately fitted out, and sent round the Island in quest of him, commanded by Captain Barnet, with a good Number of Hands. Rackam rounding the Island, and drawing near the Westermost Point, called Point Negril, saw a small Pettiauger, which at sight of the Sloop, run ashore and landed her Men; when one of them hailed her, Answer was made, They were English Men, and desired the Pettiauger's Men to come on Board, and drink a Bowl of Punch, which they were prevailed upon to do; accordingly the Company came all aboard of the Pyrate, consisting of nine Persons, in an ill Hour; they were armed with Muskets and Cutlashes, but, what was their real Design by so doing, I shall not take upon me to say; but they had no sooner laid down their Arms, and taken up their Pipes, but Barnet's Sloop, which was in Pursuit of Rackam's, came in Sight.

The Pyrates finding she stood directly towards her, fear'd the Event, and weighed their Anchor, which they but lately let go, and stood off: Captain Barnet gave them Chace, and having the Advantage of little Breezes of Wind, which blew off the Land, came up with her, and, after a very small Dispute, took her, and brought her into Port Royal, in Jamaica.

In about a Fortnight after the Prisoners were brought ashore, viz. November 16, 1720, a Court of Admiralty was held at St. Jago de la Vega, before which the following Persons were convicted, and Sentence of Death passed upon them, by the President, Sir Nicholas Laws, viz. John Rackam Captain, George Fetherston Master, Richard Corner Quarter-Master, John Davis, John Howell, Patrick Carty, Thomas Earl, James Dobbin and Noah Harwood. The five first were executed the next Day at Gallows Point, at the Town of Port Royal, and the rest, the Day after, at Kingston; Rackam, Feverston and Corner, were afterwards taken down and hang'd up in Chains, one at Plumb Point, one at Bush Key, and the other at Gun Key.

But what was very surprizing, was, the Conviction of the nine Men that came aboard the Sloop the same Day she was taken. They were try'd at an Adjournment of the Court, on the 24th of January, waiting all that Time, it is supposed, for Evidence, to prove the pyratical Intention of going aboard the said Sloop; for it seems there was no Act of Pyracy committed by them, after their coming on Board, as appeared by the Witnesses against them, who were two French Men taken by Rackam, off from the Island of Hispaniola, and deposed in the following Manner.

'That the Prisoners at the Bar, viz. John Eaton, Edward Warner, Thomas Baker, Thomas Quick, John Cole, Benjamin Palmer, Walter Rouse, John Hanson, and John Howard, came aboard the Pyrate's Sloop at Negril Point, Rackam sending his Canoe ashore for that Purpose: That they brought Guns and Cutlashes on Board with them: That when Captain Barnet chased them, some were drinking, and others walking the Deck: That there was a great Gun and a small Arm fired by the Pyrate Sloop, at Captain Barnet's Sloop, when he chased her; and that when Captain Barnet's Sloop fired at Rackam's Sloop, the Prisoners at the Bar went down under Deck. That during the Time Captain Barnet chased them, some of the Prisoners at the Bar (but which of them he could not tell) helped to row the Sloop, in order to escape from Barnet: That they all seemed to be consorted together.

This was the Substance of all that was evidenced against them, the Prisoners answered in their Defence,

'That they had no Witnesses: That they had bought a Pettiauger in order to go a Turtleing; and being at Negril Point, and just got ashore, they saw a Sloop with a white Pendant coming towards them, upon which they took their Arms, and hid themselves in the Bushes: That one of them hail'd the Sloop, who answer'd, They were English Men, and desired them to come aboard and drink a Bowl of Punch; which they at first refused, but afterwards with much perswasion, they went on Board, in the Sloop's Canoe, and left their own Pettiauger at Anchor: That they had been but a short Time on Board, when Captain Barnet's Sloop heaved in Sight: That Rackam ordered them to help to weigh the Sloop's Anchor immediately, which they all refused: That

Rackam used violent Means to oblige them; and that when Captain Barnet came up with them, they all readily and willingly submitted.

When the Prisoners were taken from the Bar, and the Persons present being withdrawn, the Court considered the Prisoners Cases, and the Majority of the Commissioners being of Opinion, that they were all Guilty of the Pyracy and Felony they were charged with, which was, the going over with a pyratical and felonious Intent to John Rackam, &c. then notorious Pyrates, and by them known to be so, they all received Sentence of Death; which every Body must allow proved somewhat unlucky to the poor Fellows.

On the 17th of February, John Eaton, Thomas Quick and Thomas Baker, were executed at Gallows Point, at Port Royal, and the next Day John Cole, John Howard and Benjamin Palmer, were executed at Kingston; whether the other three were executed afterwards, or not, I never heard.

Two other Pyrates were try'd that belonged to Rackam's Crew, and being convicted, were brought up, and asked if either of them had any Thing to say why Sentence of Death should not pass upon them, in like Manner as had been done to all the rest; and both of them pleaded their Bellies, being quick with Child, and pray'd that Execution might be stay'd, whereupon the Court passed Sentence, as in Cases of Pyracy, but ordered them back, till a proper Jury should be appointed to enquire into the Matter.

NOW we are to begin a History full of surprizing Turns and Adventures; I mean, that of Mary Read and Anne Bonny, alias Bonn, which were the true Names of these two Pyrates; the odd Incidents of their rambling Lives are such, that some may be tempted to think the whole Story no better than a Novel or Romance; but since it is supported by many thousand Witnesses, I mean the People of Jamaica, who were present at their Tryals, and heard the Story of their Lives, upon the first discovery of their Sex; the Truth of it can be no more contested, than that there were such Men in the World, as Roberts and Black-beard, who were Pyrates.

Mary Read was born in England, her Mother was married young, to a Man who used the Sea, who going a Voyage soon after their Marriage, left her with Child, which Child proved to be a Boy. As to the Husband, whether he was cast away, or died in the Voyage, Mary Read could not tell; but however, he never returned more; nevertheless, the Mother, who was young and airy, met with an Accident, which has often happened to Women who are young, and do not take a great deal of Care; which was, she soon proved with Child again, without a Husband to Father it, but how, or by whom, none but her self could tell, for she carried a pretty good Reputation among her Neighbours. Finding her Burthen grow, in order to conceal her Shame, she takes a formal Leave of her Husband's Relations, giving out, that she went to live with some Friends of her own, in the Country: Accordingly she went away, and carried with her her young Son, at this Time, not a Year old: Soon after her Departure her Son died, but Providence in Return, was pleased to give her a Girl in his Room, of which she was safely delivered, in her Retreat, and this was our Mary Read.

Here the Mother liv'd three or four Years, till what Money she had was almost gone; then she thought of returning to London, and considering that her Husband's Mother was in some Circumstances, she did not doubt but to prevail upon her, to provide for the Child, if she could but pass it upon her for the same, but the changing a Girl into a Boy, seem'd a difficult Piece of Work, and how to deceive an experienced old Woman, in such a Point, was altogether as impossible; however, she ventured to dress it up as a Boy, brought it to Town, and presented it to her Mother in Law, as her Husband's Son; the old Woman would have taken it, to have bred it up, but the Mother pretended it would break her Heart, to part with it; so it was agreed betwixt them, that the Child should live with the Mother, and the supposed Grandmother should allow a Crown a Week for it's Maintainance.

Thus the Mother gained her Point, she bred up her Daughter as a Boy, and when she grew up to some Sense, she thought proper to let her into the Secret of her Birth, to induce her to conceal her Sex. It happen'd that the Grandmother died, by which Means the Subsistance that came from that Quarter, ceased, and they were more and more reduced in their Circumstances; wherefore she was obliged to put her Daughter out, to wait on a French Lady, as a Foot-boy, being now thirteen Years of Age: Here she did not live long, for growing bold and strong, and having also a roving Mind, she entered her self on Board a Man of War, where she served some Time, then quitted it, went over into Flanders, and carried Arms in a Regiment of Foot, as a Cadet; and tho' upon all Actions, she behaved herself with a great deal of Bravery, yet she could not get a Commission, they being generally bought and sold; therefore she quitted the Service, and took on in a Regiment of Horse; she behaved so well in several Engagements, that she got the Esteem of all her Officers; but her Comrade who was a Fleming, happening to be a handsome young Fellow, she falls in Love with him, and from that Time, grew a little more negligent in her Duty, so that, it seems, Mars and Venus could not be served at the same Time; her Arms and Accoutrements which were always kept in the best Order, were quite neglected: 'tis true, when her Comrade was ordered out upon a Party, she used to go without being commanded, and frequently run herself into Danger, where she had no Business, only to be near him; the rest of the Troopers little suspecting the secret Cause which moved her to this Behaviour, fancied her to be mad, and her Comrade himself could not account for this strange Alteration in her, but Love is ingenious, and as they lay in the same Tent, and were constantly together, she found a Way of letting him discover her Sex, without appearing that it was done with Design.

He was much surprized at what he found out, and not a little pleased, taking it for granted, that he should have a Mistress solely to himself, which is an unusual Thing in a Camp, since there is scarce one of those Campaign Ladies, that is ever true to a Troop or Company; so that he thought of nothing but gratifying his Passions with very little Ceremony; but he found himself strangely mistaken, for she proved very reserved and modest, and resisted all his Temptations, and at the same Time was so obliging and insinuating in her Carriage, that she quite changed his Purpose, so far from thinking of making her his Mistress, he now courted her for a Wife.

This was the utmost Wish of her Heart, in short, they exchanged Promises, and when the Campaign was over, and the Regiment marched into Winter Quarters, they bought Woman's Apparel for her, with such Money as they could make up betwixt them, and were publickly married.

The Story of two Troopers marrying each other, made a great Noise, so that several Officers were drawn by Curiosity to assist at the Ceremony, and they agreed among themselves that every one of them should make a small Present to the Bride, towards House-keeping, in Consideration of her having been their fellow Soldier. Thus being set up, they seemed to have a Desire of quitting the Service, and settling in the World; the Adventure of their Love and Marriage had gained them so much Favour, that they easily obtained their Discharge, and they immediately set up an Eating House or Ordinary, which was the Sign of the Three Horse-Shoes, near the Castle of Breda, where they soon run into a good Trade, a great many Officers eating with them constantly.

But this Happiness lasted not long, for the Husband soon died, and the Peace of Reswick being concluded, there was no Resort of Officers to Breda, as usual; so that the Widow having little or no Trade, was forced to give up House-keeping, and her Substance being by Degrees quite spent, she again assumes her Man's Apparel, and going into Holland, there takes on in a Regiment of Foot, quarter'd in one of the Frontier Towns: Here she did not remain long, there was no likelihood of Preferment in Time of Peace, therefore she took a Resolution of seeking her Fortune another Way; and withdrawing from the Regiment, ships herself on Board of a Vessel bound for the West-Indies.

It happen'd this Ship was taken by English Pyrates, and Mary Read was the only English Person on Board, they kept her amongst them, and having plundered the Ship, let it go again; after following this Trade for some Time, the King's Proclamation came out, and was publish'd in all Parts of the West-Indies, for pardoning such Pyrates, who should voluntarily surrender themselves by a certain Day therein mentioned. The Crew of Mary Read took the Benefit of this Proclamation, and having surrender'd, liv'd quietly on Shore; but Money beginning to grow short, and hearing that Captain Woods Rogers, Governor of the Island of Providence, was fitting out some Privateers to cruise against the Spaniards, she with several others embark'd for that Island, in order to go upon the privateering Account, being resolved to make her Fortune one way or other.

These Privateers were no sooner sail'd out, but the Crews of some of them, who had been pardoned, rose against their Commanders, and turned themselves to their old Trade: In this Number was Mary Read. It is true, she often declared, that the Life of a Pyrate was what she always abhor'd, and went into it only upon Compulsion, both this Time, and before, intending to quit it, whenever a fair Opportunity should offer it self; yet some of the Evidence against her, upon her Tryal, who were forced Men, and had sailed with her, deposed upon Oath, that in Times of Action, no Person amongst them were more resolute, or ready to Board or undertake any Thing that was hazardous, as she and Anne Bonny; and particularly at the Time they were attack'd and taken, when they came to close Quarters, none kept the Deck except Mary Read and Anne Bonny, and one more; upon which, she, Mary Read, called to those under Deck, to come up and fight like Men, and finding they did not stir, fired her Arms down the Hold amongst them, killing one, and wounding others.

This was part of the Evidence against her, which she denied; which, whether true or no, thus much is certain, that she did not want Bravery, nor indeed was she less remarkable for her Modesty, according to her Notions of Virtue: Her Sex was not so much as suspected by any Person on Board, till Anne Bonny, who was not altogether so reserved in point of Chastity, took a particular liking to her; in short, Anne Bonny took her for a handsome young Fellow, and for some Reasons best known to herself, first discovered her Sex to Mary Read; Mary Read knowing what she would be at, and being very sensible of her own Incapacity that Way, was forced to come to a right Understanding with her, and so to the great Disappointment of Anne Bonny, she let her know she was a Woman also; but this Intimacy so disturb'd Captain Rackam, who was the Lover and Gallant of Anne Bonny, that he grew furiously jealous, so that he told Anne Bonny, he would cut her new Lover's Throat, therefore, to quiet him, she let him into the Secret also.

Captain Rackam, (as he was enjoined,) kept the Thing a Secret from all the Ship's Company, yet, notwithstanding all her Cunning and Reserve, Love found her out in this Disguise, and hinder'd her from forgetting her Sex. In their Cruize they took a great Number of Ships belonging to Jamaica, and other Parts of the West-Indies, bound to and from England; and when ever they meet any good Artist, or other Person that might be of any great Use to their Company, if he was not willing to enter, it was their Custom to keep him by Force. Among these was a young Fellow of a most engageing Behaviour, or, at least, he was so in the Eyes of Mary Read, who became so smitten with his Person and Address, that she could neither rest, Night or Day; but as there is nothing more ingenious than Love, it was no hard Matter for her, who had before been practiced in these Wiles, to find a Way to let him discover her Sex: She first insinuated her self into his liking, by talking against the Life of a Pyrate, which he was altogether averse to, so they became Mess-Mates and strict Companions: When she found he had a Friendship for her, as a Man, she suffered the Discovery to be made, by carelesly shewing her Breasts, which were very White.

The young Fellow, who was made of Flesh and Blood, had his Curiosity and Desire so rais'd by this Sight, that he never ceased importuning her, till she confessed what she was. Now begins the Scene of Love; as he had a Liking and Esteem for her, under her supposed Character, it was now turn'd into Fondness and Desire; her Passion was no less violent than his, and perhaps she express'd it, by one of the most generous Actions that ever Love inspired. It happened this young

Fellow had a Quarrel with one of the Pyrates, and their Ship then lying at an Anchor, near one of the Islands, they had appointed to go ashore and fight, according to the Custom of the Pyrates: Mary Read, was to the last Degree uneasy and anxious, for the Fate of her Lover; she would not have had him refuse the Challenge, because, she could not bear the Thoughts of his being branded with Cowardise; on the other Side, she dreaded the Event, and apprehended the Fellow might be too hard for him: When Love once enters into the Breast of one who has any Sparks of Generosity, it stirs the Heart up to the most noble Actions; in this Dilemma, she shew'd, that she fear'd more for his Life than she did for her own; for she took a Resolution of quarreling with this Fellow her self, and having challenged him ashore, she appointed the Time two Hours sooner than that when he was to meet her Lover, where she fought him at Sword and Pistol, and killed him upon the Spot.

It is true, she had fought before, when she had been insulted by some of those Fellows, but now it was altogether in her Lover's Cause, she stood as it were betwixt him and Death, as if she could not live without him. If he had no regard for her before, this Action would have bound him to her for ever; but there was no Occasion for Ties or Obligations, his Inclination towards her was sufficient; in fine, they applied their Troth to each other, which Mary Read said, she look'd upon to be as good a Marriage, in Conscience, as if it had been done by a Minister in Church; and to this was owing her great Belly, which she pleaded to save her Life.

She declared she had never committed Adultery or Fornication with any Man, she commended the Justice of the Court, before which she was tried, for distinguishing the Nature of their Crimes; her Husband, as she call'd him, with several others, being acquitted; and being ask'd, who he was? she would not tell, but, said he was an honest Man, and had no Inclination to such Practices, and that they had both resolved to leave the Pyrates the first Opportunity, and apply themselves to some honest Livelyhood.

It is no doubt, but many had Compassion for her, yet the Court could not avoid finding her Guilty; for among other Things, one of the Evidences against her, deposed, that being taken by Rackam, and detain'd some Time on Board, he fell accidentally into Discourse with Mary Read, whom he taking for a young Man, ask'd her, what Pleasure she could have in being concerned in such Enterprizes, where her Life was continually in Danger, by Fire or Sword; and not only so, but she must be sure of dying an ignominious Death, if she should be taken alive?—She answer'd, that as to hanging, she thought it no great Hardship, for, were it not for that, every cowardly Fellow would turn Pyrate, and so infest the Seas, that Men of Courage must starve:— That if it was put to the Choice of the Pyrates, they would not have the punishment less than Death, the Fear of which, kept some dastardly Rogues honest; that many of those who are now cheating the Widows and Orphans, and oppressing their poor Neighbours, who have no Money to obtain Justice, would then rob at Sea, and the Ocean would be crowded with Rogues, like the Land, and no Merchant would venture out; so that the Trade, in a little Time, would not be worth following.

Being found quick with Child, as has been observed, her Execution was respited, and it is possible she would have found Favour, but she was seiz'd with a violent Fever, soon after her Tryal, of which she died in Prison."

The LIFE of ANNE BONNY,

AS we have been more particular in the Lives of these two Women, than those of other Pyrates, it is incumbent on us, as a faithful Historian, to begin with their Birth. Anne Bonny was born at a Town near Cork, in the Kingdom of Ireland, her Father an Attorney at Law, but Anne was not one of his legitimate Issue, which seems to cross an old Proverb, which says, that Bastards have the best Luck. Her Father was a Married Man, and his Wife having been brought to Bed, contracted an Illness in her lying in, and in order to recover her Health, she was advised to remove for Change of Air; the Place she chose, was a few Miles distance from her Dwelling, where her Husband's Mother liv'd. Here she sojourn'd some Time, her Husband staying at Home, to follow his Affairs. The Servant-Maid, whom she left to look after the House, and attend the Family, being a handsome young Woman, was courted by a young Man of the same Town, who was a Tanner; this Tanner used to take his Opportunities, when the Family was out of the Way, of coming to pursue his Courtship; and being with the Maid one Day as she was employ'd in the Houshold Business, not having the Fear of God before his Eyes, he takes his Opportunity, when her Back was turned, of whipping three Silver Spoons into his Pocket. The Maid soon miss'd the Spoons, and knowing that no Body had been in the Room, but herself and the young Man, since she saw them last, she charged him with taking them; he very stifly denied it, upon which she grew outragious, and threatned to go to a Constable, in order to carry him before a Justice of Peace: These Menaces frighten'd him out of his Wits, well knowing he could not stand Search; wherefore he endeavoured to pacify her, by desiring her to examine the Drawers and other Places, and perhaps she might find them; in this Time he slips into another Room, where the Maid usually lay, and puts the Spoons betwixt the Sheets, and then makes his Escape by a back Door, concluding she must find them, when she went to Bed, and so next Day he might pretend he did it only to frighten her, and the Thing might be laugh'd off for a Jest.

As soon as she miss'd him, she gave over her Search, concluding he had carried them off, and went directly to the Constable, in order to have him apprehended: The young Man was informed, that a Constable had been in Search of him, but he regarded it but little, not doubting but all would be well next Day. Three or four Days passed, and still he was told, the Constable was upon the Hunt for him, this made him lye concealed, he could not comprehend the Meaning of it, he imagined no less, than that the Maid had a Mind to convert the Spoons to her own Use, and put the Robbery upon him.

It happened, at this Time, that the Mistress being perfectly recovered of her late Indisposition, was return'd Home, in Company with her Mother-in-Law; the first News she heard, was of the Loss of the Spoons, with the Manner how; the Maid telling her, at the same Time, that the young

Man was run away. The young Fellow had Intelligence of the Mistress's Arrival, and considering with himself, that he could never appear again in his Business, unless this Matter was got over, and she being a good natured Woman, he took a Resolution of going directly to her, and of telling her the whole Story, only with this Difference, that he did it for a Jest.

The Mistress could scarce believe it, however, she went directly to the Maid's Room, and turning down the Bed Cloaths, there, to her great Surprize, found the three Spoons; upon this she desired the young Man to go Home and mind his Business, for he should have no Trouble about it.

The Mistress could not imagine the Meaning of this, she never had found the Maid guilty of any pilfering, and therefore it could not enter her Head, that she designed to steal the Spoons her self; upon the whole, she concluded the Maid had not been in her Bed, from the Time the Spoons were miss'd, she grew immediately jealous upon it, and suspected, that the Maid supplied her Place with her Husband, during her Absence, and this was the Reason why the Spoons were no sooner found.

She call'd to Mind several Actions of Kindness, her Husband had shewed the Maid, Things that pass'd unheeded by, when they happened, but now she had got that Tormentor, Jealousy, in her Head, amounted to Proofs of their Intimacy; another Circumstance which strengthen'd the whole, was, that tho' her Husband knew she was to come Home that Day, and had had no Communication with her in four Months, which was before her last Lying in, yet he took an Opportunity of going out of Town that Morning, upon some slight Pretence: —All these Things put together, confirm'd her in her Jealousy.

As Women seldom forgive Injuries of this Kind, she thought of discharging her Revenge upon the Maid: In order to this, she leaves the Spoons where she found them, and orders the Maid to put clean Sheets upon the Bed, telling her, she intended to lye there herself that Night, because her Mother in Law was to lye in her Bed, and that she (the Maid) must lye in another Part of the House; the Maid in making the Bed, was surprized with the Sight of the Spoons, but there were very good Reasons, why it was not proper for her to tell where she found them, therefore she takes them up, puts them in her Trunk, intending to leave them in some Place, where they might be found by chance.

The Mistress, that every Thing might look to be done without Design, lies that Night in the Maid's Bed, little dreaming of what an Adventure it would produce: After she had been a Bed some Time, thinking on what had pass'd, for Jealousy kept her awake, she heard some Body enter the Room; at first she apprehended it to be Thieves, and was so fright'ned, she had not Courage enough to call out; but when she heard these Words, Mary, are you awake? She knew it to be her Husband's Voice; then her Fright was over, yet she made no Answer, least he should find her out, if she spoke, therefore she resolved to counterfeit Sleep, and take what followed.

The Husband came to Bed, and that Night play'd the vigorous Lover; but one Thing spoil'd the Diversion on the Wife's Side, which was, the Reflection that it was not design'd for her; however she was very passive, and bore it like a Christian. Early before Day, she stole out of Bed, leaving him asleep, and went to her Mother in Law, telling her what had passed, not forgetting how he had used her, as taking her for the Maid; the Husband also stole out, not thinking it convenient to be catch'd in that Room; in the mean Time, the Revenge of the Mistress was strongly against the Maid, and without considering, that to her she ow'd the Diversion of the Night before, and that one good Turn should deserve another; she sent for a Constable, and charged her with stealing the Spoons: The Maid's Trunk was broke open, and the Spoons found, upon which she was carried before a Justice of Peace, and by him committed to Goal.

The Husband loiter'd about till twelve a Clock at Noon, then comes Home, pretended he was just come to Town; as soon as he heard what had passed, in Relation to the Maid, he fell into a great Passion with his Wife; this set the Thing into a greater Flame, the Mother takes the Wife's Part against her own Son, insomuch that the Quarrel increasing, the Mother and Wife took Horse immediately, and went back to the Mother's House, and the Husband and Wife never bedded together after.

The Maid lay a long Time in the Prison, it being near half a Year to the Assizes; but before it happened, it was discovered she was with Child; when she was arraign'd at the Bar, she was discharged for want of Evidence; the Wife's Conscience touch'd her, and as she did not believe the Maid Guilty of any Theft, except that of Love, she did not appear against her; soon after her Acquittal, she was delivered of a Girl.

But what alarm'd the Husband most, was, that it was discovered the Wife was with Child also, he taking it for granted, he had had no Intimacy with her, since her last lying in, grew jealous of her, in his Turn, and made this a Handle to justify himself, for his Usage of her, pretending now he had suspected her long, but that here was Proof; she was delivered of Twins, a Boy and a Girl.

The Mother fell ill, sent to her Son to reconcile him to his Wife, but he would not hearken to it; therefore she made a Will, leaving all she had in the Hands of certain Trustees, for the Use of the Wife and two Children lately born, and died a few Days after.

This was an ugly Turn upon him, his greatest Dependence being upon his Mother; however, his Wife was kinder to him than he deserved, for she made him a yearly Allowance out of what was left, tho' they continued to live separate: It lasted near five Years; at this Time having a great Affection for the Girl he had by his Maid, he had a Mind to take it Home, to live with him; but as all the Town knew it to be a Girl, the better to disguise the Matter from them, as well as from his Wife, he had it put into Breeches, as a Boy, pretending it was a Relation's Child he was to breed up to be his Clerk.

The Wife heard he had a little Boy at Home he was very fond of, but as she did not know any

Relation of his that had such a Child, she employ'd a Friend to enquire further into it; this Person by talking with the Child, found it to be a Girl, discovered that the Servant-Maid was its Mother, and that the Husband still kept up his Correspondence with her.

Upon this Intelligence, the Wife being unwilling that her Children's Money should go towards the Maintenance of Bastards, stopped the Allowance: The Husband enraged, in a kind of Revenge, takes the Maid home, and lives with her publickly, to the great Scandal of his Neighbours; but he soon found the bad Effect of it, for by Degrees lost his Practice, so that he saw plainly he could not live there, therefore he thought of removing, and turning what Effects he had into ready Money; he goes to Cork, and there with his Maid and Daughter embarques for Carolina.

At first he followed the Practice of the Law in that Province, but afterwards fell into Merchandize, which proved more successful to him, for he gained by it sufficient to purchase a considerable Plantation: His Maid, who passed for his Wife, happened to dye, after which his Daughter, our Anne Bonny, now grown up, kept his House.

She was of a fierce and couragious Temper, wherefore, when she lay under Condemnation, several Stories were reported of her, much to her Disadvantage, as that she had kill'd an English Servant-Maid once in her Passion with a Case-Knife, while she look'd after her Father's House; but upon further Enquiry, I found this Story to be groundless: It was certain she was so robust, that once, when a young Fellow would have lain with her, against her Will, she beat him so, that he lay ill of it a considerable Time.

While she lived with her Father, she was look'd upon as one that would be a good Fortune, wherefore it was thought her Father expected a good Match for her; but she spoilt all, for without his Consent, she marries a young Fellow, who belonged to the Sea, and was not worth a Groat; which provoked her Father to such a Degree, that he turned her out of Doors, upon which the young Fellow, who married her, finding himself disappointed in his Expectation, shipped himself and Wife, for the Island of Providence, expecting Employment there.

Here she became acquainted with Rackam the Pyrate, who making Courtship to her, soon found Means of withdrawing her Affections from her Husband, so that she consented to elope from him, and go to Sea with Rackam in Men's Cloaths: She was as good as her Word, and after she had been at Sea some Time, she proved with Child, and beginning to grow big, Rackam landed her on the Island of Cuba; and recommending her there to some Friends of his, they took Care of her, till she was brought to Bed: When she was up and well again, he sent for her to bear him Company.

The King's Proclamation being out, for pardoning of Pyrates, he took the Benefit of it, and surrendered; afterwards being sent upon the privateering Account, he returned to his old Trade, as has been already hinted in the Story of Mary Read. In all these Expeditions, Anne Bonny bore him Company, and when any Business was to be done in their Way, no Body was more forward or couragious than she, and particularly when they were taken; she and Mary Read, with one more, were all the Persons that durst keep the Deck, as has been before hinted.

Her Father was known to a great many Gentlemen, Planters of Jamaica, who had dealt with him, and among whom he had a good Reputation; and some of them, who had been in Carolina, remember'd to have seen her in his House; wherefore they were inclined to shew her Favour, but the Action of leaving her Husband was an ugly Circumstance against her. The Day that Rackam was executed, by special Favour, he was admitted to see her; but all the Comfort she gave him, was, that she was sorry to see him there, but if he had fought like a Man, he need not have been hang'd like a Dog.

She was continued in Prison, to the Time of her lying in, and afterwards reprieved from Time to Time; but what is become of her since, we cannot tell; only this we know, that she was not executed."

Made in the USA
Las Vegas, NV
13 April 2021